READING RICHARD DAWKINS

READING RICHARD DAWKINS

A THEOLOGICAL DIALOGUE WITH NEW ATHEISM

GARY KEOGH

Fortress Press
Minneapolis

READING RICHARD DAWKINS

A Theological Dialogue with New Atheism

Email correspondence with Daniel Dennett conducted in May 2012 is reproduced here by permission of Daniel Dennett.

Cover design: Tory Herman

Library of Congress Cataloging-in-Publication Data

Print ISBN: 978-1-4514-7204-2

eBook ISBN: 978-1-4514-7978-2

The paper used in this publication meets the minimum requirements of American National Standard for Information Sciences — Permanence of Paper for Printed Library Materials, ANSI Z329.48-1984.

Manufactured in the U.S.A.

This book was produced using PressBooks.com, and PDF rendering was done by PrinceXML.

CONTENTS

Acknowledgements

There are many people, without whom the writing of this book would not have been possible.

I would like to extend my gratitude to those at Trinity College, Dublin, who supported this project: Stanford Kingston and John Scally. I must also graciously acknowledge the support of my colleagues and students at All Hallows College, Dublin City University, particularly Patrick McDevitt, Tom Dalzell, Jim Doyle, Siobhán Larkin, Colm Kilgallon, Jean Berry, and Ronan Tobin, among many others! I would also like to thank Siobhán Cahillane-McGovern of Hibernia College, Dublin.

Mostly, I would like to thank those closest to me; Edel, my brother Eric, and particularly my parents for their unconditional love and support. I could not have completed this book without you.

> *I can no other answer make, but thanks and*
> *thanks and ever thanks.*
>
> ——William Shakespeare, *The*
> *Twelfth Night*

Abbreviations

TSG
Richard Dawkins, *The Selfish Gene* (Oxford: Oxford University Press, 1976)

ROOE
Richard Dawkins, *River Out of Eden: A Darwinian View of Life* (London: Orion, 1996)

TGD
Richard Dawkins, *The God Delusion* (Kent: Bantam, 2006)

TGSOE
Richard Dawkins, *The Greatest Show on Earth: The Evidence for Evolution* (London: Bantam, 2009)

DDI
Daniel C. Dennett, *Darwin's Dangerous Idea: Evolutions and the Meaning of Life* (London: Penguin, 1995)

BTS
Daniel C. Dennett, *Breaking the Spell: Religion as Natural Phenomenon* (London: Penguin, 2006)

Introduction

In modern times, contemporary academia is acquiring an increasingly public character. Technological advancements over the last number of years have led to an unprecedented accessibility of knowledge. As such, we can no longer be content with conceptual partisans that keep academic disciplines separate. Similarly, the distance between ideologies and value systems is being contracted more and more as time passes, with steady advancements in global communications. This is the context in which this work rests. Consequently, this book will espouse the view that theology must open itself further to the prospects of dialogue with multifarious areas of academia and diverse ideologies. It will advance current efforts in this task not just by engaging in dialogue with worldviews that are easily amenable to theology, but to inherently antithetical perspectives. "Philosophy is dead", proclaims Stephen Hawking on the first page of his 2010 international bestseller *The Grand Design* co-authored with Leonard Mlodinow.[1] The public character of such sentiments, it will be argued, must be engaged with if theology is to progress, and not fall into a perpetual regression of inward analysis. Theology needs to look outward and engage with the intellectual mosaic of diverse disciplines and philosophies that the modern world has made increasingly accessible.

This book will demonstrate how a dialogical approach to theology can be beneficial, even when dialogue partners advocate a strident hostility toward religious belief. To achieve this aim, we will explore the possibilities of a dialogue with British evolutionary biologist Richard Dawkins. Dawkins [b. 1942] was trained and has taught at Oxford University, where he held the position of Charles Simonyi Professor for the Public Understanding of Science from 1995 to 2008. In 2007 *Time* magazine included Dawkins in its rankings of the top 100 most influential people in the world, while *Prospect* magazine voted him third in a list of the top 100 public intellectuals, behind novelist Umberto Eco and Noam Chomsky. He achieved such prominence principally for two reasons. Firstly, he has been an ardent defender of a gene-centered perspective of Darwinian evolution, and promotes the use of this perspective as an explanatory framework in which we can understand human behavior. Secondly, he has been a militant advocate of atheism and virulent critic of religion. Throughout his published work and lectures, he has always denounced religious belief peripherally, and he eventually devoted a full book to the topic—his 2006 *The God Delusion*. It is for these two reasons that Dawkins should be taken as a dialogue partner. He represents a view from a distant outskirt of the academic realm, which can be identified as atheistic materialism/naturalism advocated from a scientific standpoint. It is exactly because Dawkins is so disagreeable to theology that he is a good choice as a dialogue partner. This will allow us to illustrate how engaging with a contrary worldview can be beneficial. For the purposes of this academic work, this dialogue has been delineated into chapters and subsections. However, it must be noted that these delineations are for practical purposes only; the true dialogue is more holistic and is less amenable to such compartmentalizing. Therefore, throughout this thesis, we will find overlaps between the themes explored in the various chapters and sections. This will unfortunately require that we reiterate/repeat particular aspects of the thesis as we progress.

The first chapter will outline the methodological premises for the dialogue. It will present the motives, method, and limitations of this work. This chapter will justify this dialogue with Dawkins by reference to theological method—the emphasis on interfaith and interdisciplinary dialogue as seen in the work of leading theologians such as Hans Küng, David Tracy, and Pope John Paul II. It will show how engaging in dialogue with Dawkins contributes to both the pressing need for pluralistic dialogue between ideologies and the need for dialogue with other disciplines such as science. This chapter will also explore the approaches we will adopt toward the relationship between science and religion and the philosophy of science. Moreover, we will seek a fresh approach to Dawkins himself, an earnest dialogical relationship as opposed to a confrontational model—which has predominantly been the case. However, given Dawkins' hostility toward theology and the thrust of his position, there are significant caveats in attempting to open a mutual conversation and therefore, these caveats will also be explored in this opening chapter.

As Dawkins seeks to ground his worldview in his interpretation of evolutionary science, Chapter Two will then establish an understanding of this science. This is a necessary task, as an appreciation of evolutionary theory will be indispensible if we are to open a dialogical relationship with his worldview. As Dawkins is chosen as the central dialogue partner for the thesis, we will predominantly explore his interpretation of evolution. However, we will indicate where Dawkins has significant support for his view. Conversely, we will also show that while there is a consensus view on evolution among the scientific community, there are also significant areas of disagreement between authoritative voices. As such, we will also outline a critique of Dawkins' perspective. Moreover, this chapter will show that these areas of dissonance are particularly significant in the context of this thesis, as they point towards philosophical differences that may drastically influence how the science is interpreted. In addition, although we decided to develop a dialogue with an atheistic portrayal of science, there are significant interpretations of evolution that are more easily amenable to a theological position. Three examples of such views will thus be presented and critiqued to further strengthen our reasons for engaging with Dawkins' interpretation.

The philosophical view implicit in the work of Dawkins will then be explored in Chapter Three. We will encounter four specific aspects of Dawkins' materialist worldview that have decidedly theological implications: the evolution of consciousness, memetics (cultural evolution), a purposeless world and the evolution of altruism. These aspects of Dawkins' philosophy will provide direct opportunities for dialogue with theology, given their theological connotations. The American philosopher Daniel C. Dennett, whom Dawkins once labeled as his "intellectual older brother", will feature prominently in this chapter for several reasons, but most significantly, because Dawkins explicitly points to Dennett's thinking on the issue of the evolution of consciousness. Dawkins does not delve into this area himself, but he does note its significance. Moreover, Dennett supports Dawkins on the issues of cultural evolution, purposelessness, and the evolution of altruism. In this sense, Dennett can be seen as an important figure in a dialogue with Dawkins. We will also present arguments against the materialism of Dawkins with regard to these philosophical issues.

Chapter Four will then analyze the concept of religious belief in the context of a dialogue with an evolutionary worldview. Although it is debatable whether religious belief is definable, we will examine the cross-cultural elements of theism, providing a panoramic approach to religion in general. This approach can be problematic, and as such, we will outline limitations to viewing religion in this way. However, within the context of a dialogue with Dawkins, an evolutionary perspective on religion must be considered. Dawkins attempts to use evolution to explain human societal behavior, and religious practices are a prevalent feature across human civilizations. Therefore, if Dawkins' view is maintained, then religious belief must be explicable by referral to evolutionary theory. Moreover, theology itself can be understood as the analysis of religious beliefs. Therefore, an evolutionary analysis of religion such as the one Dawkins promotes could be considered consistent with the aims of the theologian. In this sense, Dawkins' evolutionary view on religion may provide new material for theological consideration, thus contributing to the overall aim: to demonstrate how a dialogue with Dawkins may be beneficial for theology.

In Chapter Five, we reach the culmination of the book, which will open a direct dialogue between Dawkins and theology. This chapter will largely be based upon two of Dawkins' cardinal critiques of theism: namely, what we can call his theodicy challenge, and how God can be relevant in a world that science understands as governed by strict laws (though the strict cause-and-effect interpretation of the world has been significantly challenged, as we will note, particularly in Chapter Two). This chapter will first contextualize Dawkins' version of the problem of evil by looking at its previous incarnations and the rich history of theological responses. It will then ask how dialoguing with Dawkins' interpretation of the problem of evil (which stems from the scientific understanding of evolution) may provide a new dimension to theological discourse in this area. We will also examine how dialogue with Dawkins' materialist worldview may offer new considerations in ongoing theological discourse regarding God's relationship with creation. We will ask how God can be considered relevant when the phenomena of the world can largely be explained naturalistically: Where does God fit into the causal world?

It is ultimately the contention of this project that perpetuating theological discourse by focusing on scholarly material that is inherently agreeable to theology will not suffice in the current context of modern academia. Therefore, theology needs to test its boundaries and venture into dialogue with those from antithetical positions. We have chosen Dawkins as the embodiment of such a position to illustrate how such dialogue may offer new perspectives on classical theological problems. Therefore, we will show how this dialogical paradigm may take shape, as opposed to merely discussing it as a theoretical framework. Moreover, such a dialogue will send a message to the intellectual marketplace that theology has the confidence to earnestly consider even its most vehement critics, and attempt to learn from them. Of course, the dialogue with Dawkins proposed in this thesis has significant caveats, particularly given that the two dialogue partners may disagree on a fundamental question regarding the existence of God. However, a dialogue between such opposing hermeneutics may provide a method for a new paradigm of theological scholarship—one that is up to the task of facing its critics in the unprecedentedly public and pluralistic context of modern academia.

Notes

1. Stephen Hawking and Leonard Mlodinow, *The Grand Design: New Answers to the Ultimate Questions of Life* (London: Bantam, 2010), 8.

1

A Distinct Methodological Framework

INTRODUCTION

This chapter will present the methodological foundation of this book. The aim of this book is to demonstrate how engaging in a dialogical relationship with a contrary ideology can be beneficial to theology. It will argue that such a dialogue has become a theological necessity in twenty-first-century academia, by exploring the emphasis on pluralism in contemporary theology. The Oxford biologist and prominent religious antagonist Richard Dawkins will thus be taken as the embodiment of a contrary ideology. Dawkins' worldview exemplifies a particular school of thought on evolutionary science, which he presents as materialist and atheistic. Dawkins also represents the view that theology is an intellectually weak discipline, failing to engage in an honest philosophical analysis of its own themes. By entering into a dialogue with Dawkins, we can contribute to combating this public perception which undermines theological endeavours. We can show how theology is prepared to directly take on its most vehement critics, thereby demonstrating how theology can be a self-critiquing discipline.

The questioning of the legitimacy of theology by figures such as Dawkins cannot be ignored. Therefore, this work will show how a dialogical approach to theology and those of Dawkins' 'anti-theology' persuasion may be played out. In doing so, it will advocate a framework for future theological projects to consider a wider range of intellectual sources, as opposed to focusing on perspectives more obviously amenable to a theological position. It will show that acknowledging the merits and weaknesses of an alternative worldview, even one that is overtly atheistic and anti-religious, may offer a new dimension to theological debate. Therefore, the interest of this work lies not with Dawkins *per se*, but with how theology is approached in a pluralistic world. To clarify, by 'pluralism', I mean simply a plurality or variety of worldviews in constant dialogue with one another sharing but not necessarily adopting each other's beliefs (though this may occur). We will consider what influence a dialogue with a hostile worldview may have for a religious philosophy, and we have taken Dawkins as an example to illustrate such a dialogue. In order to embark on this theological venture, a firm foundation of the motives, method, and limitations of the study must be presented. This will be the task of this chapter.

MOTIVES AND PRESUPPOSITIONS

The setting of the modern intellectual marketplace in which this book is situated brings with it particular considerations pertaining to how one does theology. The technological advances in information sharing have led to the realization that there is an ever-pressing need for an open, dialogical theology. This section will focus on the recognition of this point in contemporary theology. It will place emphasis on the need for theological dialogue with diverse ideologies, and then show how Dawkins will be taken as a representative of such an ideology. The focus will then shift to the emphasis placed on interdisciplinary dialogue in modern theology, and subsequently elaborate on why Dawkins is a suitable candidate for an interdisciplinary dialogue.

DAWKINS AS AN IDEOLOGICAL 'OTHER'

The post-globalization academic realm can be characterized by the significant dissolution of barriers between academic disciplines and spiritual traditions. The technological advancements over the last several decades have allowed an unprecedented flow of information among the world's diverse population. The Latin American theologian Leonardo Boff considers the implications of this realization, as he suggests that a diverse intercultural dialogue can now take place:

> The process of globalization signifies more than just an economic-financial-media phenomenon . . . it is the time when all the tribes can meet each other and exchange knowledge, values, and ethical and spiritual traditions and usher in a dialogue among the most diverse cultures and religions.[1]

In the passage quoted here, Boff is referring to the emergence of a post-globalization scenario in which theology and religion are exposed to other disciplines and value systems.

Similarly, in 1983, a symposium was held to address the development of a new theological paradigm that sought to meet the requirements of this scenario.[2] At this symposium, the prominent Swiss theologian Hans Küng[3] stressed that theology should strive to develop a pluralistic model, transforming from particularist to universal thinking: "Our goal is a plural theology, open to learn and ready to discuss; one which—rooted in the Christian tradition—can provide an answer to the challenges of our time".[4] This approach potentially represents a decisive shift away from the outlook of classical theological scholars such as St. Augustine, who contested that the pursuit of knowledge was an irresistible evil.[5] A pluralistic, dialogical model of theology had also previously been posited by Karl Rahner, who insightfully proposed that ". . . given that every 'world-view' wants to pass off its very nature from an actually particular view to being also an actually universal one, there remains no other means open to it apart from the mission by talk and the attempt to convince, in short, . . . dialogue".[6] Rahner, furthermore, contested that the appropriate way to engage with such pluralism ". . . can only consist in an attitude which carefully and critically examines, holds itself open to further knowledge and modifications of previous knowledge, is modest, tries to discover the transcendental experience in all the 'systems' put forward, and yet has the courage to make decisions . . . ".[7] Rahner can be interpreted here as espousing a model of dialogue that is modestly open to the "careful and critical" examination of other viewpoints. Comparably, the influential Canadian theologian Bernard Lonergan also highlights the need for a pluralistic approach, given the diversity of humanity.[8]

As we have seen above, through the writings of several important theological figures, there is an incontrovertible significance attributed to pluralistic dialogue in modern theology. However, as the Irish theologian Dermot Lane explains, the issue of the relationship between Christianity and other cultures has always been prominent:

> The question about the relationship between faith and culture is in one sense as old as Christianity itself. It arose in a particularly acute form in the first century when the early Church was faced with difficult questions about the admission of Gentiles into the Christian community without circumcision. It continued to exercise the early Church towards the end of the first century and well into the second century as the Church made her pilgrim way from a largely Jewish matrix into a Hellenistic culture.[9]

Notwithstanding the history of Christianity's relationship with the non-Christian world, Lane also suggests that the character of the modern world brings anew the necessity of a multicultural dialogue:

Another reason why inculturation is a relatively recent issue is that cultural differences in this century have created a new challenge to the meaning of the gospel in the twentieth century. These cultural changes have included a movement from the classical culture to a historical one, the shift from a pre-scientific culture to a scientific one and the emergence of a second enlightenment which now focuses not simply on the age of reason but on the question of practical reason. . . . To ignore these cultural changes is to end up giving answers to questions people no longer ask.[10]

Lane's reference to a scientific culture is particularly pertinent to our current task of engaging with Dawkins, because as we shall see in the next section, he is also taken as a representative of the discipline of evolutionary science. At this point, however, we are seeking to establish that modern cultural shifts create a more pressing need for a pluralistic theology.

Further support for this pluralistic approach can be found from the theologian David Ford. Writing in 1996, Ford envisioned that the future of theology would be pluralistic and hospitable to others: "A theology under the sign of hospitality is formed through its generous welcome to others—theologies, traditions, disciplines, and spheres of life . . . ".[11] Harvard theological scholar Francis Schüssler Fiorenza also insists that theology must "take pluralism seriously",[12] while Oxford theologian Alister McGrath signifies radical global migration as a catalyst for Christian theologians to provide a "theological account of the relation of Christianity to other religions".[13] Similarly, Irish biblical scholar Máire Byrne highlights how the international experience of religious and secular pluralism is having a marked influence on how theology and religious studies are approached.[14]

It can be discerned then, that there is a powerful emphasis on a dialogical and pluralistic theology, which is particularly relevant in light of the transformational advances in information sharing in modern society. The Irish theologian Enda McDonagh goes as far as to say that "at its best, theology has been a truly dialogical discipline".[15] Theology needs to be pluralist, and again, by pluralist I mean that theology must be open to others' beliefs, not necessarily adopting them, but at least willing to investigate whether they can provide insight. Consistent with the theological motif of pluralism, this work will open a dialogical relationship with Dawkins. Dawkins is taken in this project to represent an example of an ideological system that, according to Rahner, theology must examine and open itself to. The ideology Dawkins is taken to represent can be discerned as atheistic naturalism or materialism[16]—he has been identified as such by authoritative scholars such as Keith Ward,[17] John Haught,[18] Ian S. Markham,[19] and others. Consequently, we are showing how the dialogical model advocated by Rahner and others mentioned above may operate in the concrete, as opposed to in the abstract. We are not just *discussing* a methodology that engages with ideologies inimical to theology, but *employing* such a methodology.

In a dialogue with naturalism a caveat immediately presents itself, as 'naturalism' is not a definitive term and we should be aware of the ambiguity in its use. Cambridge philosopher Simon Blackburn, in *The Oxford Dictionary of Philosophy*, defines 'naturalism' as "the view that ultimately nothing resists explanation by the methods characteristic of the natural sciences".[20] However, scientists Karl Giberson and Mariano Artigas make the important clarification between 'methodological naturalism' and 'ontological naturalism'.[21] They perceptively note that methodological naturalism is the commitment to seek natural explanations. Ontological naturalism, though, denies the existence of anything that cannot be studied by scientific method. Ontological naturalism is then ultimately a *philosophical* position—predominantly an atheistic position, if one accepts that God cannot be studied through science.[22] The eminent philosopher of religion David Ray Griffin also argues that what is usually understood by the term 'naturalism' is the claim that "nature is all there is".[23] Comparable to Giberson and Artigas, Griffin distinguishes between naturalism in this sense (ontological) and naturalism "properly supposed", which involves the "rejection of supernatural interruptions of the normal causal processes of the world".[24] As it pertains to our current study, the salient point from these clarifications is that naturalism is not synonymous with atheism—although for Dawkins, as we shall see in Chapter Three, the naturalistic explanation of life excludes God. We will encounter critiques of Dawkins in this regard in more detail in Chapter Five. At this point, however, we can establish that Dawkins is to be taken as the embodiment of a naturalistic standpoint (in both senses of naturalism), an ideology with which theology can engage dialogically. The need for such dialogue with a naturalistic worldview can be further substantiated by acknowledging along with Keith Ward that naturalism/materialism has become a fashionable position in academia.[25]

In addition, atheism itself could be considered a model of 'faith'. As the highly influential French philosopher Paul Ricoeur posited, atheism can be considered ". . . a type of faith that might be called . . . a postreligious faith or a faith for a postreligious age".[26] The Irish theologian James Mackey similarly suggests that atheism, if it has been arrived at through philosophical reasoning, can be considered a theology.[27] If we accept Ricoeur and Mackey's views in this regard, then Dawkins' atheistic ideology could be considered a 'faith' or perhaps even a theology. If this were the case, than it would add further weight to our motives for engaging with him, as the eminent American theologian David Tracy and others insist that interfaith dialogue is no longer a luxury but a theological necessity.[28] However, even if the premise that atheism can be equated to a faith/theology is not accepted, we can still hold Dawkins as an ideological 'other'; a representative of atheistic materialism, as outlined above. We can also find precedent support from the Catholic Church for the need for a dialogue with atheism as a part of the ideologically pluralistic world. The theologian Michael Paul Gallagher gives a brief synopsis of how in 1965, Pope Paul VI established a Secretariat for Non-Believers with the intention of forming a dialogue with secularization.[29] In 1988 the Secretariat then became the Pontifical Council for Dialogue with Non-Believers. However, most pertinently, in 1993 Pope John Paul II amalgamated this council with the Pontifical Council for Culture, which sought a dialogue between the Church and other faiths and cultures.[30] In this sense, it could be argued that Pope John Paul II identified a dialogue with atheism or nonbelief as an element of a dialogue with other faiths/ideologies. Therefore, in opening a dialogical relationship with Dawkins as a part of the current pluralistic setting of modern academia, this work may be considered to echo the goals of the Pontifical Council for Culture.

DAWKINS AS AN INTERDISCIPLINARY 'OTHER'

For the purposes of this project, Dawkins is also taken as a representative of the discipline of evolutionary science. David Tracy has asserted his belief in the importance of theology's engagement with other disciplines, particularly within contemporary academia. He proposes that theology should not be a stand-alone field in the university setting in which it finds itself: "Indeed the university setting of theology, by forcing theology to engage itself with other disciplines, also forces to the centre of theological attention the public character of any theological statement".[31] Pope John Paul II also expressed corresponding views. In addressing an international congress for university cooperation,[32] he proclaimed that humans are by nature interdisciplinary, and therefore, due to the rapid fragmentation of knowledge, there is an urgent need to cultivate a counterbalancing integrative approach to study and research.[33] The distinguished theologian John B. Cobb and others have also professed that through correlations with secular disciplines, theology itself finds deeper justification as an academic field.[34] This need for an interdisciplinary approach to theology is also a motive for engaging with Dawkins as a representative of another discipline, namely science, or more specifically, evolutionary biology. The importance of mutual discussion between science and theology, despite its tumultuous history,[35] has been stressed by seminal scholars such as continental theologians Jürgen Moltmann[36] and Hans Küng,[37] among others.[38]

Furthermore, the eminent British theologian Tina Beattie has stressed the dissolution of boundaries between science, theology, and philosophy in modern times.[39] In this context, Dawkins also becomes a conspicuous choice for dialogue with theology as he, intentionally or not, attempts to intellectually pass freely between these disciplines. For example, the prominent theologian Alister McGrath[40] explains that Dawkins champions his own scientific field of evolutionary biology as an atheistic worldview.[41] McGrath illustrates that Dawkins has presented Darwinism (which, as we shall see, is itself an indefinite term and thus requires a caveat of the language often employed in discourse on the issue), as transcending the confines of science, morphing into a philosophical outlook.[42] To strengthen this interpretation, Dawkins has been identified as an honorary philosopher of sorts by his intellectual ally, authoritative philosopher Daniel C. Dennett (Dennett's own philosophical views on evolution as they pertain to our project will be considered in more detail in Chapter Three): "Dawkins' contribution on this conceptual front is philosophy at its best, informed by a wealth of empirical work and alert to the way subtle differences in expression can either trap a thinker in an artificial cul-de-sac or open up new vistas of implications heretofore only dimly imagined".[43]

Whether or not using Darwinism as a worldview is a positive step is the subject of disagreement among scientists and philosophers.[44] In the current context, however, we are establishing that Dawkins is amenable to interdisciplinary dialogue because of the fact that his work is not strictly confined to biology. Dawkins' forays into the topics of religion and theology are also of particular significance in the context of a theological project. His hostility toward theology makes him a credible, albeit unlikely, figure for theological consideration.[45] Though he will be criticized for his misunderstandings and lack of theological substance later in this chapter, the public character of his hostility toward religious ideas has accentuated public interest in theological questions; as Tina Beattie suggests, Dawkins has reawakened public interest in God "more effectively than any preacher could have done".[46] Paradoxically, Dawkins' hostility toward theology can be seen to have enlivened theological debate in the public sphere. Dawkins' focus on religion therefore offers a common ground to engage with—even if from an apologetic standpoint. Moreover, Dawkins presents his scientific/pseudo-philosophical worldview to the nonscientist.[47] This makes the scientific elements of his worldview accessible to the theologian, and thus allows for a less restricted dialogue. This also aids the overall aim of this book, which is to exhibit how theology can broaden its horizons to include sources from other areas in the intellectual marketplace.

METHOD

In the previous section, we have outlined the motives for concentrating on Dawkins as a dialogue partner for theology—in a sense, the 'why' of the book. This current section will now present the 'how'. We will look at how this book serves a niche of theological dialogue that rests within a wider context of dialogues. As we seek to present a dialogue with external sources, we must also be aware that theology has a broad scheme of internal dialogues that contextualise an engagement with Dawkins. This section will introduce the conceptual approach to science and religion/theology that will be adopted for this work, and then indicate the aspects of Dawkins' approach to theology/ religion that we will not specifically engage with given that a) they have already been dealt with by several scholars, and b) they do not pertain to the task of this project. It should be disclaimed, however, that although we will not specifically engage with certain aspects of Dawkins' views on religion given that they have already received significant attention, there may be overlapping themes. We will then outline our approach to the philosophy of science and truth as it pertains to a dialogue with Dawkins.

A DIALOGICAL NICHE

The proposed dialogical framework, exemplified in the context of this book as a theological dialogue with Dawkins, must be understood as one string in the much wider bow of theology; we are focusing on one part of the mosaic of theology. The style of dialogue proposed, which seeks to incorporate antithetical perspectives, is not a methodology that theology should solely focus on. However, it is argued that it will significantly contribute to the wider tapestry of theological projects. While the dialogue we seek could be described as an 'external dialogue', given that we seek to engage with a nontheologian (perhaps even an anti-theologian), there are also important 'internal dialogues'. Aside from a dialogue with its 'others', theology also has its own rich scholarly history.[48] Theology must therefore continually explore its own past, from classical theological scholars such as Tertullian, Pelagius, Augustine, and Aquinas, to more modern scholars such as Hans Urs von Balthasar, Karl Barth, and Edward Schillebeeckx. We can see evidence of how this exploration of classical theologians continues to lead to insightful discourse in Fergus Kerr and Brian Davies' recent studies of Aquinas,[49] or Carly Daniel-Hughes' recent analysis of Tertullian.[50] Correspondingly, theology continues to gain from ongoing studies of twentieth-century theologians, such as Karen Kilby's fascinating work on Rahner,[51] or Aberdeen theologian John Webster's study of Karl Barth.[52]

Moreover, there is also the need for commitment to the renewal of past theological figures as dialogue partners for present theology. For example, the Archbishop of Canterbury Rowan Williams published a fascinating study of Teresa of Avila, which demonstrates how her writings can be a potent source for consideration when faced with our contemporary social issues. Harvard divinity professor Beverly Mayne-Kienzle also contributes to the task of renewing historical theological figures with her examination of Hildegard of Bingen,[53] as does Irish theologian John Scally in his discussion of the legacy of Catherine of Siena.[54] Another interesting work in this area is James Bremner's *The Power of Then*, which explores a variety of scholars from the past and applies their teachings to modern problems, such as Hildegard of Bingen's emphasis on an environmental ethic.[55] For the purposes of this book, we are focusing on a very particular element of theological dialogue, namely, engaging with external sources, even those who appear to be inimical to theology. However, this task should be placed in the context of wider theological endeavours. It is not the sole future of theology, and indeed, cannot be truly appreciated unless placed in this context. For example, we will see in Chapter Five how a dialogue with Dawkins can be placed against the backdrop of theology's rich history of contemplating issues such as the problem of evil in the works of Augustine and Irenaeus. This theological approach based on dialogue is not actually new. It has a rich and honorable tradition.

The mode of dialogue proposed in this book is therefore one element of theology's multifaceted pilgrimage toward the understanding of God; it is one contributory facet of the Anselmian endeavour, "faith seeking understanding". As Dublin-based theologian Maureen Junker-Kenny suggests, "faith seeking understanding" no longer has a "singular defined counterpart to connect with".[56] In fact, even the classical Anselmian approach of *fides quaerens intellectum* cannot be viewed as the sole option for theology. For example, Saint Ephrem of Syria's theology has been described as *fides adorans mysterium* (faith adoring the mystery), providing an alternative to Anselm. However, the Eurocentric account of church history tends to favor Anselm while Ephrem's theology has, to an extent, been lost in the West.[57] As has been suggested, it is the multicultural context of information sharing in the modern world that exposes theology to new avenues that must be explored. Bishop of Durham David Jenkins suggests that with the challenges and opportunities of this modern setting, the image of the pilgrimage surfaces; we are on a pilgrimage of exploration, seeking to deepen our understanding.[58] If we take this image of a theological pilgrimage seriously, then we must acknowledge that on this pilgrimage we leave our comfort zone and expose ourselves to our opposition. This element of the pilgrimage is manifest in this book by an exploration of one of theology's most adverse critics. However, it is through this pilgrimage, becoming exposed to our opposition, that theology can find new ways forward and gain new insights. As John Scally explains, "Yet it is only as the pilgrim faces these temptations and leaves behind the security of the known that the way itself becomes clear".[59] Although dialogues with perspectives that appear antagonistic toward theology are in their early stages, we can see evidence of rich theological dividend in works such as Neil Messer's *Selfish Genes and Christian Ethics*, as he explores the possibility of dialogue with an evolutionary perspective on our moral experience.[60] Consequently, engaging with external, even hostile worldviews can be discerned as the dialogical niche of this book, which fits into the wider web of theological dialogue by cautiously advancing into these rarely explored areas—though this is not to understate previous studies of atheism from theologians such as Henri de Lubac,[61] Alister McGrath,[62] and Michael Paul Gallagher.[63]

APPROACHES TO RELIGION AND SCIENCE

Religion and science have had a complex and fractious historical relationship. As such, there has been a variety of relational models adopted toward the interplay between the two disciplines. This section will outline three major positions: conflict, independence, and dialogue. One popular relational model between science and religion is that of conflict, even described by some as "warfare".[64] Scientists such as Dawkins himself hold this interpretation.[65] Correspondingly, certain religious scientists have viewed evolution as hostile toward their own belief systems, and thus emphatically rejected them, as geologist Kurt Wise (who studied under the late Stephen Jay Gould, to be introduced below) states: "[I]f all the evidence in the universe turns against creationism [a literal belief in the Genesis cosmogony], I would be the first to admit it, but I would still be a creationist because that is what the word of God seems to indicate".[66] However, it is also clear that highly respected scholars from both scientific and theological disciplines disregard the conflict model in favor of a mutually communicative approach; besides the theologians already mentioned

(Moltmann and Küng), scientists such as physicist Paul Davies,[67] geneticist Francis Collins,[68] and biologist Kenneth Miller[69] are prominent examples.

An alternative to the 'conflict' model was proposed by the renowned Harvard paleontologist Stephen Jay Gould. In Gould's model, science and religion are two distinct 'nonoverlapping magisteria' or 'NOMA'. Gould (whom we will include as a prominent adversary of Dawkins on issues in evolutionary science) developed the approach upon reflection subsequent to Pope John Paul's 1996 address to the Pontifical Academy of Sciences.[70] Gould argues that science and religion are concerned with distinctly separate topics, and thus cannot be in conflict:

> [E]ach subject has a legitimate magisterium, or domain of teaching authority—and these magisteria do not overlap (the principle that I would like to designate as NOMA, or "nonoverlapping magisteria"). The net of science covers the empirical universe: what it is made of (fact) and why does it work this way (theory). The net of religion extends over questions of moral meaning and value.[71]

For Gould, science does not impose itself on the religious domain, or vice versa, as both have decidedly separate arenas of inquiry. Elaborating upon the concept, Gould prudently states two distinguishing features of his NOMA approach. The first, he explains, is that both science and religion have equal status as magisteria. He defends the legitimacy and importance of religion in moral discourse, which he suggests is nonabsolute, and therefore, beyond the scope of science.[72] He highlights morality as a religious subject of equitable importance to scientific interests. In developing the concept of NOMA, Gould does concede that such questions of morality need not appeal directly to religion in its formal incarnations: "I will . . . construe as fundamentally religious . . . . all moral discourse on principles that might activate the ideal of universal fellowship among people".[73] The second distinguishing feature pertains to the central premise of NOMA itself: that both magisteria are independent. "I hold that this non-overlapping runs to completion only in the important logical sense that standards for legitimate questions, and criteria for resolution, force the magisteria apart on the model of immiscibility".[74] Gould is not the sole protagonist of this view. The eminent biologist Francisco J. Ayala, a significant authority on science and religion, adopts a similar perspective: "[P]roperly understood, they [science and religion] *cannot* be in contradiction because science and religion concern different matters".[75] He echoes Gould by pointing out distinct matters dealt with independently by science and religion:

Science concerns the processes that account for the natural world: how the planets move, the composition of matter and space, the origin and function of organisms. Religion concerns the meaning and purpose of the world and of human life, the proper relation of people to their Creator and to each other, the moral values that inspire and govern people's life.[76]

Gould further defends the outlook by insisting that its reasoning does not lie with diplomacy. He portrays NOMA as an authentic intellectual option with solid premises—those outlined above:

NOMA is no whimpish, wallpapering, superficial device, acting as a mere diplomatic fiction and smoke screen to make life more convenient by compromise in a world of diverse and contradictory passions. NOMA is a proper and principled solution—based on sound philosophy—to an issue of great historical and emotional weight.[77]

NOMA is marketed as a 'taskmaster' that seeks to establish the boundaries between science and religion. NOMA then, at least in part, has an active role in determining which niches of the intellectual marketplace science and religion individually encompass.[78] However, despite Gould's promotion of this relational model of science and religion, he admits that categorizing these boundaries may be an onerous task. "Many of our deepest questions call upon aspects of both for different parts of a full answer—and the sorting of legitimate domains can become quite complex and difficult".[79] It is this aspect of the relational model of NOMA that will persuade us toward an alternative approach to the science-religion dialogue. Moreover, the explicit division of science and religion in the NOMA approach may be interpreted as conflicting with the emphasis on interdisciplinary dialogue in contemporary theology, which requires less compartmentalizing and a more integrated dialogue.

Gould himself admits that confining scientific and religious investigations to separate areas of inquiry can become highly intricate. It is predominantly for this reason that the model is rejected in the context of this project in favor of a more integrative approach. There are inherent problems with the NOMA model, which can be exemplified by reference to Gould's own thought on humanity's perceived place in the animal kingdom. He suggests that the Catholic concept of the human soul stems from the classical view of human superiority.[80] This theme is prevalent in classical theology and philosophy, as in Gen. 1:26: "Then God said, 'Let Us make man in Our image, according to

Our likeness; let them have dominion over the fish of the sea, over the birds of the air, and over the cattle, over all the earth and over every creeping thing that creeps on earth'". The image of God (*imago Dei*) has been understood by classical theologians such as Augustine to be humanity's faculty for reason, which distinguishes humanity from the animal kingdom: "We ought therefore to cultivate in ourselves the faculty through which we are superior to the beasts . . .".[81] A hierarchical vision of living creatures is also evident in classical thinkers such as Plato and Aristotle, who proposed images of a 'Great Chain of Being' in which humanity was above all living things on earth in a hierarchical model.[82]

However, this image, Gould acknowledges, is in contradiction with the view of evolutionary science, which we will encounter in more detail in Chapter Two. Evolution sees every living thing as descended from the same source (save to the extent of synthetically created life, which will be noted in Chapter Two), and thus none can be held to be superior:

> I may for example, privately suspect that papal insistence on divine infusion of the soul represents a sop to our fears, a device for maintaining belief in human superiority within an evolutionary world offering no privileged position to any creature.[83]

Here, Gould hints at an issue within the bounds of religious thought (the human soul/human superiority) for which evolutionary science has profound implications. He deflects the issue by placing the soul outside of the magisteria of science, despite the fact that he had acknowledged an overlap of interests between religion and science on the subject.[84] Ayala, who also seeks conceptual divisions between science and theology, goes slightly further than Gould, to explain that evolutionary science has dispelled the concept of a nonmaterial force in life; that the phenomena of life are not the result of "orthogenetic activity of any immanent nonmaterial force, be it called 'élan vital,' 'radial energy' or 'vital force'". (Such nonmaterial forces could be interpreted as a 'soul', which Gould maintained was beyond the realm of science.)[85] Based on their scientific interpretations, Gould and Ayala's thoughts on the soul or nonmaterial forces demonstrate inconsistency in attempting to maintain divisions between science and religion. Gould and Ayala propose that evolution has precluded the concepts of human superiority and the soul respectively, despite claiming that science and religion do not overlap.

Furthermore, Gould has been strident in his portrayal of randomness in the evolutionary process. He proffered the analogy in his acclaimed work *A Wonderful Life*, that if we rewound the history of evolution and let it play again, there is such a massive degree of randomness that the results would be very different.[86] In this view, biological evolution is not teleological; it does not have directionality. This premise is also a key theme in the evolutionary view of Dawkins, as we shall see. Although evolution has resulted in self-reflecting humans, there is no *a priori* reason that this was inevitable. As such, Gould is congruent with the philosophical position of Dawkins, which only acknowledges purpose as a human construct; the idea of purpose only exists subsequent to the recent evolutionary development of human consciousness (which we will explore in Chapter Three). Consequently, though perhaps unwittingly, Gould has made a subtle transition between the scientific and religious realms, as the insistence on a happenstance view of the evolution of human beings carries implications for the theological issue of whether the world is inherently random or runs according to a divine plan. Although we will deliberate on this issue in Chapter Five, it is the aim at this point to demonstrate how Gould's NOMA model turns out to be inconsistent when the implications of science for theology become fully thought out. Ayala is also unequivocal in denouncing teleology in evolution:

> The over-all process of evolution cannot be said to be teleological in the sense of proceeding towards certain specified goals, preconceived or not. The only non-random process in evolution is natural selection understood as differential re-production. Natural selection is a purely mechanistic process . . .[87]

He reiterates this sentiment in a more recent publication. "The scientific account of these events does not necessitate recourse to a preordained plan, whether imprinted from the beginning or through successive interventions by an omniscient and almighty Designer".[88] These statements reflect a philosophical position, deeply rooted in science, that has profound implications for theological reflection on the nature of creation.

A further example that substantiates the argument that the NOMA approach is wrought with inconsistencies can be found in Ayala's work, which delves into the realm of theodicy (the theological problem of evil)—another important theological issue that we will be considering in Chapter Five. Although Ayala claims to support a nonrelational view of science and religion, he conversely maintains that evolution provides an account for the existence of evil/suffering in the living world. As such, evolution partly provides a response to the theodicy problem (this will be discussed in more detail in Chapter Five).[89] Therefore, we can acknowledge that the three overlapping issues between evolution and religion outlined above (the soul/immaterial life force, purpose or plan in nature, and the problem of evil) constitute considerable challenges for the NOMA approach. It is due to these challenges that we can validate our choice for using an alternative methodology, namely, establishing a dialogical relationship.

It has already been ascertained that highly influential theological figures such as John Paul II and David Tracy, among others, have stressed the need for theology to have an interdisciplinary dimension. Tracy has also proposed that theology must acknowledge any movement that brings with it religious implications: "Practical theologies are related principally to the social reality of some particular social, political, cultural or pastoral movement or problematic which is argued to possess major religious import . . . ".[90] In the context of this work, we can propose that evolutionary science be taken to represent a scientific movement with "major religious import". In our critique of NOMA, we have indicated areas in which evolution may have religious implications, and Chapters Four and Five will provide further examples. Moreover, the concept that evolution carries theological import has been acknowledged since Charles Darwin himself first publicized evolution by natural selection as an account for the existence of living organisms, as he wrote:

> I see no good reason why the views given in this volume should shock the religious feelings of anyone. . . . A celebrated author and divine has written to me that he has gradually learnt to see that it is just as noble a conception of the Deity to believe that He created a few original forms capable of self development into other needful forms. . . .[91]

In the 1950s, the highly influential Swiss theologian Hans Urs von Balthasar also believed evolution to be of theological significance, as he felt it was indispensable for a universal conception of man, life, and nature.[92] Consequently, this project will adopt an integrative approach to science and religion. This approach can be summarized by referral to Alister McGrath, who draws from Gould and proposes that science and religion are ". . . 'partially overlapping magisteria' (a POMA so to speak), reflecting a realization that science and religion offer possibilities of cross-fertilization on account of the interpretation of their subjects and methods".[93] While we will proceed with this methodology toward science and theology, there are elements of Dawkins' work that we will not specifically set out to engage with, though there may be partial overlaps. These elements of Dawkins will now be discussed.

DAWKINS, ATHEISM, AND RELIGION

Although Dawkins' atheistic and religiously antagonistic stance is evident throughout his work,[94] his most explicit pronouncement of atheism and his views on religion are found in *The God Delusion*, a book dedicated to the topic. In *The God Delusion*, we can discern two elements of Dawkins' worldview that we will not directly engage with: his arguments against the existence of God, and his critique of religion. In *The God Delusion*, Dawkins attempts to deconstruct and demonstrate fallacies in arguments for the existence of God that are commonly proposed by religious apologists.[95] Correspondingly, he also offers arguments that seek to demonstrate the improbability of the existence of God from a scientific perspective.[96] In addition to his arguments for atheism, Dawkins also critiques the premise of religion and faith, which he believes can be morally dubious: "Faith can be very very dangerous, and deliberately to implant it into the vulnerable mind of an innocent child is a grievous wrong".[97] This work will not seek to refute Dawkins' arguments with regard to these two premises (atheism and the evil of religion) given that a significant amount of publications have already provided substantial rebuttals to Dawkins on these points. Particularly notable are publications by Keith Ward[98] and Alister McGrath.[99] However, other authoritative rebuttals come from Ian S. Markham,[100] Karl Giberson and Mariano Artigas,[101] John Haught,[102] Kathleen Jones,[103] Mike Starkey,[104] Rob Slane,[105] R. J. Fallon,[106] David Robertson,[107] John Blanchard,[108] John Cornwall,[109] Richard Grigg,[110] and Thomas Crean.[111] Dawkins' arguments for atheism and the evils of religion have been persuasively shown to be philosophically weak and often inconsistent by the scholars mentioned here. While noting these rebuttals, we will alternatively seek to engage specifically with Dawkins' scientific/pseudo-philosophical worldview, which will be explored in Chapters Two and Three.

With regard to Dawkins' stance on atheism and religion, we will however, acknowledge the thesis put forth by British theologian Gerard J. Hughes, who suggested that even though Dawkins ultimately fails in his task to repudiate religion, Christians may have something to learn from him.[112] Thus in the context of this work, Dawkins' criticisms of theism/religion will be taken into consideration as a part of the dialogue we hope to establish. This is opposed to aiming toward a refutation of such criticisms, given that such attempts have already been made by several scholars, and that such direct argumentation is not conducive of advancing theological dialogue. An analogous outlook is put forth by influential German theologian Wolfhart Pannenberg, who insisted on the importance of articulating a convincing response to atheist critiques.[113] Dawkins' atheism can also be considered beneficial to a theological dialogue with science for reasons outlined by the Irish theologian James Mackey. Mackey proposed that opening dialogue with atheist scientists can mitigate potential criticisms of subjectivity; that scientists who profess religiosity "might be suspect of tinting the picture painted in order to bring out some recognisable religious colouring".[114] Mackey, therefore, felt it safer to engage with confirmed atheists such as physicist David Deutsch and philosopher Bertrand Russell.[115] By engaging with Dawkins, we cannot be accused of choosing a scientific model that is easily amenable to a theological worldview, which may perhaps hinder a balanced approach. In the next section, we will outline the philosophical approach to scientific truth that will be adopted in the context of a dialogue with Dawkins.

SCIENCE AND TRUTH

Another interesting dimension of a possible dialogue with Dawkins that should be acknowledged is the spectrum of philosophical/theological attitudes toward scientific truth. Pertaining to this topic, Küng's theology provides an example of where an approach to scientific truth becomes consequential for a science-religion dialogue.[116] Küng directly cites two key twentieth-century philosophers as influences on his thought in this regard: Karl Popper and Thomas Kuhn.[117] The Austrian-born philosopher Karl Popper postulated that legitimate assertions on what is scientifically empirical or not, rests not with the verifiability of a hypothesis, but with falsifiability: "not the verifiability but the falsifiability of a system is to be taken as a criterion of demarcation".[118] A statement cannot be considered scientifically demonstrable unless it is falsifiable. Küng offers the following example:

> [W]ere a statement such as "All copper conducts electricity" to be verified in experience, all the copper in the universe would have to be examined for this property, and of course, that is impossible. So no theory can be as reliable as the experiment on which it bases itself in generalization.[119]

Therefore Küng, following from Popper, asserts that scientific statements based upon verifiability cannot be held to be fundamentally true. "Thus science appears to be a continually ongoing process of trial and error, which does not lead to the secure possession of truth but rather to a progressive approximation of truth, a process in other words of continual alteration and evolution".[120] In the context of this work, this premise could be used as a critique/limitation of Dawkins, by holding that his scientific views cannot be considered fundamentally true; they can only be described as a "progressive approximation to truth".[121] The potential for this critique, however, is not a route that this work will explore, though it is worth acknowledging.

From the distinguished philosopher/historian of science Thomas Kuhn, Küng adopts the thesis that science can be dogmatic, working within the framework of a system of beliefs and values (a paradigm). Therefore, scientific claims to legitimate objectivity are suspect. Kuhn articulates his perspective: "Scientific knowledge, like language, is intrinsically the common property of a group or else nothing at all. To understand it we shall need to know the special characteristics of the groups that create and use it".[122] In this view, scientific statements may be vulnerable to subjectivity, given that they necessarily arise from within a context of an ideology. Küng insightfully explains, "Natural Science is by no means merely ideologically neutral, simply ascertaining the data, the facts, in an entirely objective fashion without making value judgments".[123] A similar outlook is defended by Paul Ricoeur, who felt that knowledge is only obtained through a detour of analysis.[124] The physicist/ theologian John Polkinghorne also portrayed this view metaphorically, by suggesting that scientists wear spectacles behind their eyes.[125] Science can be understood thus, at least in part, as hermeneutical. The hermeneutical nature of science may be held as a caveat in studying Dawkins, as it could be suggested that his scientific outlook is predicated upon an ideological position and consequently, nonempirical. Notwithstanding, while the claim will be made that Dawkins' philosophical worldview influences his elucidation of natural selection (see Chapter Two), it will not be suggested that science is *wholly* reducible to hermeneutical factors. Moreover, it is the fact that Dawkins represents an ideological view that partly makes him an appropriate dialogue partner for this book. In this sense, we will align ourselves with the contemporary theologian Nancey Murphy and scientist George F. R. Ellis, who propose the following interpretation of science:

> While we recognize the thoroughly human character of scientific knowledge and culturally specific factors in the origin of the scientific enterprise itself, we reject the various sociological critiques that reduce science to culture—or gender-specific factors. We claim that objective, cross-cultural criteria exist for rational justification of scientific research programmes.[126]

For the purposes of dialogue, we will adopt the view that science is a practical method of reasoning that seeks to ascertain a 'technical truth'. This truth may not be absolute given Popper's philosophical reflections on falsifiability, though it may be utilized for practical purposes. Such a view is outlined by Bertrand Russell, who offers the following insight:

> Science thus encourages abandonment of the search for absolute truth, and the substitution of what may be called "technical" truth, which belongs to any theory that can be successfully employed in inventions or in predicting the future. "Technical" truth is a matter of degree: a theory from which more successful inventions and predictions spring is truer than one which gives rise to fewer.[127]

Dawkins himself outlines a similar position with regard to the abandonment of the search for an absolute truth:

> It is forever true that DNA is a double helix, true that if you and a chimpanzee (or an octopus or kangaroo) trace your ancestors back far enough you will eventually hit a shared ancestor. To a pedant, these are still hypotheses which might be falsified tomorrow. But they never will be. . . . Even if they are nominally hypotheses on probation, these statements are true in exactly the same sense as the ordinary truths of everyday life; true in the same sense that you have a head, and that my desk is wooden.[128]

Certain scientific premises, such as the general edifice of evolutionary theory, can be taken as 'true' in the 'practical' or 'ordinary' sense as outlined by Russell and Dawkins (this can be substantiated by the convergence of conflicting schools of thought such as Dawkins and Gould on key points in evolutionary theory). Scientific statements are interpreted in this view, not as elements of a paradigm or ideology but as a reflection of the world in common mental experience.

LIMITATIONS

Heretofore in this chapter, we have mapped out our motives for engaging dialogically with Dawkins and the methodological approach we will adopt for such a dialogue. We will now acknowledge the limitations of considering Dawkins as a conversation partner for theology. Firstly, we will exhibit Dawkins' contempt for religion and theology as a legitimate discipline in the intellectual marketplace. Secondly, we will suggest that Dawkins' lack of theological background, evident in the absence of theological substance in his work, may pose a challenge to establishing an intellectual relationship. Lastly, we will discuss criticisms aimed at Dawkins on the basis of his intolerance toward contrary worldviews; that his perspective is overtly monist, and thus difficult to engage with dialogically.

DAWKINS' CONTEMPT FOR RELIGION AND THEOLOGY

Dawkins is unabashed in proclaiming his contempt for the subject of theology. In a letter to the UK *Independent* newspaper in 2007, Dawkins addresses a criticism put forth by John Cornwall[129]—that he is not proficiently versed in the subject of theology to provide a convincing argument against God. He responds to this criticism as follows: "It assumes there is a serious subject called theology, which one must study in depth before one can disbelieve in God. . . . Would you need to read learned volumes on leprechology before disbelieving in leprechauns?"[130] Here, Dawkins equates theology to the hypothetical study of leprechauns to convey his contempt toward the discipline. His disregard for the legitimacy of theology is also salient as he writes that theology "lacks even the smallest hint of a connection with the real world. As Thomas Jefferson said, when founding his University of Virginia, 'A professorship of Theology should have no place in our institution'".[131] Dawkins also challenges the intellectual productivity of theology, as he states:

> What has theology ever said that is of the smallest use to anybody? When has theology ever said anything that is demonstrably true and not obvious? I have listened to theologians, read them, debated against them. I have never heard any of them ever say anything of the smallest use, anything that was not either platitudinously obvious or downright false.[132]

Dawkins' clear distain for theology is an obvious barrier in attempting to foster an intellectual relationship with him. His repudiation of the subject might influence his appraisal of theological ideas to the point where it may be difficult to appreciate his arguments as objective or balanced. The theologian Nicholas Lash articulates a similar criticism:

> Now it is a fundamental feature of good academic work in *any* field that it is undertaken with a passion for accurate description and disinterested respect for the materials with which one is working. Dawkins, the biologist, seems not to have acquired the mental discipline necessary for work in the humanities and social sciences.

> One cannot imagine a physicist holding an atomic particle, or a zoologist a yak, with the same sustained contempt and loathing, the same cavalier disregard for accurate description, the same ignorance of the literature, with which Dawkins treats all religious beliefs, ideas and practices.[133]

It is bad academic practice to treat subjects with such contempt, as opposed to making an accurate and balanced evaluation. This can be treated as a limitation of engaging in a theological dialogue with Dawkins, as such a dialogue will not be mutually respectful. Literary theorist Terry Eagleton offers a comparable critique, by inferring that Dawkins' discarding of theology makes him particularly ill-positioned to provide a persuasive argument against theological ideas:

> Card-carrying rationalists like Dawkins, who is the nearest thing to a professional atheist we have had since Bertrand Russell, are in one sense the least well-equipped to understand what they castigate, since they don't believe there is anything there to be understood, or at least anything worth understanding. This is why they invariably come up with vulgar caricatures of religious faith that would make a first-year theology student wince. The more they detest religion, the more ill-informed their criticisms of it tend to be. . . . When it comes to theology . . . any shoddy old travesty will pass muster.[134]

Dawkins' repudiation of theology may, by proxy, prevent him from finding solid academic footing from which to provide a solid criticism against it. This point leads us on to our next limitation of dialogue with Dawkins: his lack of theological understanding.

ABSENCE OF THEOLOGICAL SUBSTANCE IN DAWKINS

John Haught, whose work on the implications of evolutionary theory for theology will be a significant resource in this book (particularly in Chapter Five), suggests that Dawkins avoids a serious engagement with critically reflective theological scholarship. "Clearly the new atheists[135] are not familiar with any of these religious thinkers,[136] and the hostility to what they call theology has almost nothing to do with theology as I use the term".[137] Consequently, the intellectual quality of his atheism is unnecessarily diminished.[138] Keith Ward has also claimed that Dawkins "knows nothing about theology",[139] and moreover, misunderstands the concept of God and the nature of belief.[140] Ward, furthermore, also criticizes Dawkins for his lack of philosophical prowess in espousing an atheistic materialism.[141] Consistent criticisms are also produced by Terry Eagleton[142] and theologian Owen C. Thomas, who writes of Dawkins, "His understanding of Christianity and religion in general is massively uninformed and amounts to a caricature consisting of its most fundamentalist and obscurantist forms".[143] Dawkins' ignorance of theology may signify a limitation of a theological project such as this one, as Nicholas Lash perceptively illustrates by quoting Dawkins: "There are some weird things (such as the Trinity, transubstantiation, incarnation) that we are not *meant* to understand. Don't even *try* to understand one of these, for the attempt might destroy it".[144] Lash's response is enlightening, as he explains: "That sentence gives me a strange feeling, as I sit reading it in my study—the walls of which are filled, from top to bottom, with volumes dedicated to attempts at just such understanding".[145] Lash thus insists that Dawkins is ". . . polemically ignorant of the extent to which faith's quest for understanding has, for century after century, been central to the practice and identity of those educational enterprises which we call the great religious traditions of the world . . .".[146]

In a similar vein, Gerard J. Hughes also illustrates Dawkins' lack of understanding about the nature of theological studies. He points to another of Dawkins' critiques of Christianity, which, similar to Lash's point, suggests that Christianity avoids self-criticism:

> His [Dawkins'] . . . point is that Christians hold a view of faith which places religious faith completely beyond reasonable discussion or scientific counter-argument. In our modern world, such unsupported prejudices deserve no credence, and can be positively damaging. Any beliefs worthy of respect must stand up to scientific criticism.[147]

However, contrary to Dawkins' criticism, Hughes explains how Christianity has never sought to promote anything that conflicts with rational thinking:

> Very few Christians, and certainly very few Catholics, have seriously maintained that anyone has to believe, in faith, something which is contrary to what can be rationally established. Even the classical American Fundamentalists in the late nineteenth and twentieth centuries in their various ways held that science could indeed support what they believed to be the truths taught by the bible. They thought there was, or could be found, archaeological evidence for the age of

the earth which could match calculations made from biblical data on the ages of the patriarchs, or would demonstrate the universality of the Flood, or the existence of leviathans capable of giving hospitality to Jonah. Whatever one might think about the reasonableness of such expectations, they were part of an overall view that faith and human reason could not end in conflict.[148]

Hughes points out that even believers in a literal interpretation of the Bible have often sought to harmonize their beliefs with reason by searching for supporting evidence. Hughes therefore, echoing Lash, exposes Dawkins' ignorance of Christianity's commitment to reason.

Furthermore, Dawkins' representation of religion in history is strongly biased toward portraying its negative impact on the world, attributing several human-made catastrophes to religion:

Imagine . . . a world with no religion. Imagine no suicide bombers, no 9/11, no 7/7, no Crusades, no witch-hunts, no Gunpowder plot, no Indian partition, no Israeli/Palestinian wars, no Serb/Croat/ Muslim massacres, no persecution of the Jews as 'Christ-killers', no Northern Ireland troubles, no 'honour killings'. . . no Taliban to blow up ancient statues, no public beheadings of blasphemers . . .[149]

However, here Dawkins fails to discuss the complex political and sociological circumstances that had a far greater influence in many of these atrocities. For example, he attributes the troubles in Northern Ireland to religion, as opposed to the centuries of political instability on the island of Ireland. Similarly, he proclaims that without religion, the 9/11 terrorist attacks would not have taken place, yet he again makes no reference to the intricate political history between the United States and the Middle East.

Moreover, Dawkins conveniently ignores or downplays the positive impact that religion has had on the world to suit his own purposes. For example, he notes that "[i]t is surely true that black slaves in America were consoled by promises of another life, which blunted their dissatisfaction with this one and thereby benefited their owners".[150] Yet Dawkins understates the role that religious belief had in the African American civil rights movement, particularly with regard to Martin Luther King, one the movement's most influential proponents:

In America, the ideals of racial equality were fostered by political leaders of the calibre of Martin Luther King. . . . The emancipations of slaves and of women owed much to charismatic leaders. Some of these leaders were religious; some were not. . . . Although Martin Luther King was a Christian, he derived his philosophy of non-violent civil disobedience directly from Gandhi, who was not.[151]

King, himself holding a Ph.D. in theology, may have been influenced by Gandhi, a non-Christian. However, he explicitly referred to a faithfulness in his 'I Have a Dream' speech in 1963:

> I have a dream that one day every valley shall be exalted, every hill and mountain shall be made low, the rough places will be made plain, and the crooked places will be made straight, and the glory of the Lord shall be revealed, and all flesh shall see it together. This is our hope. This is the faith that I go back to the South with. With this faith we will be able to hew out of the mountain of despair a stone of hope. With this faith we will be able to transform the jangling discords of our nation into a beautiful symphony of brotherhood. With this faith we will be able to work together, to pray together, to struggle together, to go to jail together, to stand up for freedom together, knowing that we will be free one day.[152]

The sentiment of King was also a major influence on James Cone, considered the founder of the Black Liberation Theology movement. Cone used the Christian message of the Bible to empower and liberate African Americans from previous generations' oppression, which demonstrates how religion can, contrary to Dawkins' statements, be used to encourage equality over slavery.[153] Thus Dawkins suffers from a form of at best academic 'looseness', at worst academic malpractice in his selective reading of history.

Lash and Ward also both single out Dawkins' attempt to invalidate Aquinas' 'five proofs' for the existence of God as an example of his lack of theological comprehension. Lash reviews Dawkins' arguments against Aquinas' five proofs by stating, "What, in fact, we are given is a shoddy misrepresentation of Aquinas' arguments, with no indication of where they might be found, what others have made of them, or what purpose they were constructed to serve".[154] Ward echoes this criticism, as he responds to Dawkins' alleged intellectual victory:

> Dawkins claims that they [Aquinas' five ways] are easily exposed as vacuous, and he does so in just three pages. This would be a very impressive achievement, except that he does not in fact deal with

Aquinas' Five Ways at all. What he does is to consider instead five arguments of his own, which bear a vague resemblance to those of Aquinas—in some cases, a resemblance so vague that it can no longer be recognized.[155]

We will not, at this point, analyze Dawkins' opposition to Aquinas' five ways, as this would take us into the arguments for/against atheism, which have already been given significant attention. We seek to ascertain here that Dawkins has been criticized for the weakness of his theological scholarship, which we can distinguish as a legitimate limitation in opening a dialogical relationship with his work. In addition to Dawkins' lack of theological substance, criticisms of his lack of atheistic substance have also been proffered by authorities such as Haught, who deems Dawkins' atheism to be "soft".[156] Haught criticizes the substance of Dawkins' atheism in comparison to highly influential thinkers such as Ludwig Feuerbach, Karl Marx, and Sigmund Freud, who "provide interesting theoretical frameworks for their theories".[157] Moreover, he argues that Dawkins et al. do not think out the implications of their rejection of theism as thoroughly as thinkers such as Friedrich Nietzsche, Bertrand Russell, Albert Camus, and Jean-Paul Sartre.[158] Similarly, Tina Beattie and Ian S. Markham (who are critical of Dawkins) profess their appreciation for the arguments of atheists such as Nietzsche, of whom Beattie admiringly writes:

> Theologians as well as philosophers and cultural theorists recognise in his critiques of religion and in his challenging of established truths, values and meanings a profound unmasking of the deceptions which allow power and ideology to masquerade as truth, often in the name of God.[159]

Markham is more abrupt; as he compares Dawkins and Nietzsche, he concludes ". . . Nietzsche has better arguments".[160] Again, it is not necessary in the context of this work to provide a comparison between the atheism of Dawkins and Nietzsche and other "hard core atheists" as classified by Haught. We are highlighting that Dawkins' deficiency in theological and atheistic argumentation is an obstacle to considering him as a potential dialogue partner for theology.

DAWKINS' INTOLERANCE

One further limitation that should be acknowledged is the criticism put forth that Dawkins is dogmatic in his beliefs, leaving him intolerant of others.

Theologian and former pupil of Dawkins, Timothy Jenkins, writes of the biologist that "he simply believes the books he agrees with are true, and the books he disagrees with are false".[161] Jenkins here criticizes Dawkins for a lack of openness toward alternative views. Alister McGrath provides further criticism in this regard. He perceives Dawkins as purposefully excluding the history of the perennial revision of scientific theories from his espousal of science:

> How can Dawkins be so sure that his current beliefs are true, when history shows a persistent pattern of the abandonment of scientific theories as better approaches emerge? What historian of science can fail to note that what was once regarded as secure knowledge was eroded through the passage of time? Conveniently enough, Dawkins turns a blind eye to history.[162]

Thus Dawkins may be overly confident in his promotion of science. He neglects to express that science is constantly open to revision, consequently showing an intolerance toward those who do not share his scientific outlook. Ward echoes McGrath's criticism, as he insists that Dawkins holds a perspective intolerant of others.[163] Hughes poses a similar critique, as he highlights Dawkins' strident promotion of "science as the gold standard for all truth".[164] Hughes distinguishes this as a significant problem with Dawkins' view, as he explains how science is not capable of explaining certain phenomena—this is a similar point to Stephen Jay Gould's NOMA, although Hughes does not, as Gould does, imply that religion and science are completely separate disciplines:

> Where I think Dawkins is at his weakest is in what I would term his 'scientism'. This is disguised by the fact that he at every turn insists upon the importance of evidence, as indeed he should (though it must be said that he does not in this respect always practise what he preaches). The claim that every question about ourselves and our world can in principle be settled by methods which can ultimately be reduced to those of physics is a highly disputable claim, disputable for reasons which have nothing to do with religion . . .[165]

In essence, Hughes criticizes Dawkins for elevating scientific reason to the highest order of importance. He gives scientific knowledge primacy. Yet this elevation of scientific knowledge may diminish other legitimate paths to truth such as emotions and intuition. David Hume, for example, makes this point in his *Treatise of Human Nature*, which became a widely influential sentiment in philosophy: "Reason is, and ought only to be the slave of the passions, and can never pretend to any other office than to serve and obey them".[166] Dawkins' commitment to the primacy of scientific knowledge will thus prevent him, as Hughes states, from acknowledging subjects that are beyond the realm of scientific inquiry, yet equally valid: "Whether there are good reasons for holding that God exists is indeed a controversial question; but it is not, nor ✶ is it reducible to, a scientific question".[167] Dawkins can therefore be seen as intolerant of nonscientific modes of inquiry.

With regard to Dawkins' intolerance, we can also discern his atheism as a related limitation. As we have already noted, Dawkins was chosen as a dialogue partner for theology in part due to the fact that his view was significantly distant from a theologically sympathetic stance. However, such conceptual distance may prove hindering in seeking to establish an intellectual relationship, particularly if as the critics above suggest, he is uncompromising in his position. However, despite these important limitations, we can suggest that they are outweighed by the motives presented earlier. Moreover, it is precisely because of the hostility between Dawkins and his theological critics that we should seek to engage with him, thereby demonstrating how theology can gain insight from views unsympathetic to theology. Dawkins' uncompromising atheism and ignorance of theology highlights his 'otherness', which as we have discussed, can be an obstacle to dialogue. However, paradoxically, it is also his otherness that makes him a good candidate for theology to consider, as it broadens the scope of theology to seek insight in less obvious areas of the intellectual marketplace.

CONCLUSION

We have now established the methodological background for this project. We noted that this book will proceed in the context of the post-globalization intellectual world. In recent decades, several authoritative theologians have placed emphasis on the necessity for pluralistic and interdisciplinary theological investigations in this post-globalization context, which is arguably becoming more and more prominent as the years pass. Therefore, we can follow theologians such as Leonardo Boff and insist that in this context, theology must espouse a pluralistic character. With this appreciation of the current situation, we have opted to open a dialogical relationship with a worldview that is presented as contrary to theology—the view of Dawkins who could be considered as an ideological and interdisciplinary other, making him a good choice as a conversation partner. By engaging with Dawkins, we are advocating for a theological paradigm that seeks to expand the scope of traditional theological resources; we are seeking new areas to explore.

We then outlined the approach that will be taken toward a dialogue with Dawkins. We noted that while others have promoted a confrontational model for the relationship between science and religion (for example Dawkins himself), or a view that sees science and religion as completely separate domains of inquiry (such as Gould), we will prefer an integrative approach—similar to McGrath's 'POMA'. Moreover, pertaining to Dawkins' views on atheism and religion, we acknowledged that a significant deal of attention has been given to refuting his arguments from a variety of scholars. Therefore, we will not seek to add to this body of critical work. Rather, we will examine Dawkins' scientific/philosophical perspective, and demonstrate how engaging with this perspective may be beneficial to the theologian. The approach toward science and truth was also outlined. We noted that we will not challenge Dawkins on the basis of whether science can claim absolute truth. We will proceed acknowledging, with Russell, Dawkins, and others, that science can lead us to a 'practical truth'.

We also acknowledged the limitations of opening a dialogue with Dawkins. Dawkins' unabashed contempt for theology as a subject can be considered a serious hindrance, as it will undoubtedly compromise his objectivity when considering theological arguments. Moreover, his lack of theological and atheistic substance was discussed. This may also be a significant caveat in attempting to intellectually converse with his work. Similarly, his single-minded intolerance of other viewpoints can be interpreted as a substantial weakness in his work, which may also hinder dialogue. Notwithstanding these limitations, however, we can give greater weight to our motives for engaging with Dawkins. As such, we will begin this intellectual conversation by considering the scientific foundations of his worldview in the next chapter.

Notes

1. Leonardo Boff, 'Is Cosmic Christ Greater Than Jesus of Nazareth?', *Concilium* 1 (2007): 1: 57

2. The symposium was held at the University of Tübingen. The lectures were eventually published in Hans Küng and David Tracy, eds., *Paradigm Change in Theology: A Symposium for the Future* (Worcester: Billings & Sons, 1989).

3. Küng was stripped of his license to teach Catholic theology on December 18, 1979 by the Congregation of the Doctrine of the Faith, largely due to his critique of the doctrine of papal infallibity in his *Infallible? An Inquiry* (New York: Doubleday, 1983). See John Kiwiet, *Hans Küng* (Waco, TX: Word, 1985), 88–89. However, Küng remained engaged in scholarship, and his interest in the field of science and theology make him a noteworthy theologian for this book. He acknowledged the significance of science in theological reasoning in *Does God Exist?* (London:

Collins, 1978) and also devoted one publication completely to the issue, *The Beginning of All Things: Science and Religion* (Grand Rapids: Eerdmans, 2007).

4. Hans Küng 'A New Basic Model for Theology: Divergencies and Convergencies', in Küng and Tracy, eds., *Paradigm Change in Theology*, 440.

5. Hans Küng, *Does God Exist?*, 87. Küng explains that Augustine held the pursuit of knowledge with the desire for pleasures of the flesh, and desire for power as three irresistible evils.

6. Karl Rahner, *Theological Investigations, Vol. VI: Concerning Vatican Council II*, trans. Karl H. and Boniface Kruger (London: Darton, Longman & Todd, 1969), 33.

7. Ibid., 50.

8. Bernard Lonergan, *Method in Theology* (London: Darton, Longman & Todd, 1972), 276. Lonergan, however, discussed pluralism in the context of evangelisation: that socio-cultural plurality requires a pluralistic approach to preaching the gospel.

9. Dermot A. Lane, 'Faith and Culture: The Challenge of Inculturation', in Dermot A. Lane, ed., *Religion and Culture in Dialogue: A Challenge for the Next Millennium* (Dublin: Columba, 1993), 11.

10. Ibid., 19.

11. David F. Ford, 'Epilogue: Christian Theology at the Turn of the Millennium', in David F. Ford, ed., *The Modern Theologians: An Introduction to Christian Theology in the Twentieth Century* (Malden, MA: Blackwell, 1997), 72.

12. Francis Schüssler Fiorenza, 'Systematic Theology: Tasks and Methods', in Francis Schüssler Fiorenza and John Galvin, eds., *Systematic Theology: Roman Catholic Perspectives* (Dublin: Gill & Macmillan, 1992), 68.

13. Alister McGrath, *Christian Theology: An Introduction*, 3rd ed. (Oxford: Blackwell, 2003), 535.

14. Máire Byrne, *The Names of God in Judaism, Christianity and Islam: A Basis for Interfaith Dialogue* (Dublin: Continuum, 2011), 3.

15. Enda McDonagh, 'Beyond 'Pure' Theology', *The Furrow* 50, no. 11 (Nov. 2009): 581.

16. Though naturalism and materialism are not strictly synonymous, we can understand, along with the renowned Australian philosopher David M. Armstrong, materialism (or physicalism) as a subset of naturalism; see David M. Armstrong, 'Naturalism, Materialism and First Philosophy', *Philosophia* 8, no. 2–3 (1978): 261.

17. Keith Ward, *Is Religion Dangerous?* (Oxford: Lion, 2006), 90.

18. John Haught, *God After Darwin* (Oxford: Westview, 2000), 26.

19. Ian S. Markham, *Against Atheism: Why Dawkins, Hitchens, and Harris Are Fundamentally Wrong* (Chichester: Wiley-Blackwell, 2010), 15–16.

20. Simon Blackburn, 'Naturalism', in Simon Blackburn, ed., *The Oxford Dictionary of Philosophy* (Oxford: Oxford University Press, 2008).

21. Karl Giberson and Mariano Artigas, *Oracles of Science: Celebrity Scientists Versus God and Religion* (Oxford: Oxford University Press, 2007), 234.

22. Ibid., 234.

23. David Ray Griffin, *Reenchantment Without Supernaturalism: A Process Philosophy of Religion* (Ithaca, NY: Cornell University Press, 2001), 18.

24. Ibid., 18.

25. Keith Ward, *God, Chance and Necessity* (Oxford: Oneworld, 1996), 11; also, *Why There Almost Certainly Is a God: Doubting Dawkins* (Oxford: Lion, 2008), 20. However, Ward also suggests that this position has serious philosophical weaknesses and is not held in high esteem among his academic peers, *Is Religion Evil?* 87–90; also, *Why There Almost Certainly Is a God*, 14–15. This is particularly due to ongoing scientific debate on the nature of matter itself.

26. Paul Ricoeur, *The Conflict of Interpretations*, ed. Don Hide (Evanston, IL: Northwestern University Press, 1974), 440.

27. James Mackey, *Christianity and Creation: The Essence of Christian Faith and Its Future among Religions* (New York: Continuum, 2006), 64.

28. David Tracy, *Dialogue with the Other: The Inter-Religious Dialogue* (Leuven: Peeters, 1990), 95. Jesuit theologian Francis X. Clooney makes a congruent point, as he suggests that an interfaith methodology is necessary given that the distance between faith traditions is ever diminishing; see 'Comparative Theology', John Webster et al., eds., *The Oxford Handbook of Systematic Theology* (New York: Oxford University Press, 2007), 654.

29. Michael Paul Gallagher, *What Are They Saying about Unbelief?* (Mahwah, NJ: Paulist, 1995), 2.

30. Ibid., 2.

31. David Tracy and John B. Cobb, *Talking About God: Doing Theology in the Context of Modern Pluralism* (New York: Seabury, 1983), 2.

32. Held in Rome on April 1, 1980. The international congress, titled 'Univ '80', addressed six thousand students from forty-three countries.

33. Don O'Leary, *Roman Catholicism and Modern Science: A History* (New York: Continuum, 2007), 193. For the full address, see Pope John Paul II, 'The Moral Dimension of Study and Research', available online.

34. John Cobb, 'Response to Johann Baptist Metz and Langdon Gilkey', in Küng and Tracy, eds., *Paradigm Change in Theology*, 386. Theologians Erik Borgman and Wilfred Felix have made similar statements, as they co-wrote that interdisciplinary research "can be a way to rediscover theology as a discipline", 'Introduction', *Concilium* 2 (2006): 9.

35. I refer here to the church's history of condemnation of scientific hypotheses such as Copernicanism and the censuring of Galileo, encapsulated in the introduction to Don O'Leary's *Roman Catholicism and Modern Science: A History*, xi-xx.

36. Jürgen Moltmann, *Science and Wisdom*, trans. Margaret Kohl (London: SCM, 2003), 7.

37. Hans Küng, *The Beginning of All Things*, xii.

38. For example, Professor of Religion Robert Crawford, *Is God a Scientist: A Dialogue Between Science and Religion* (New York: Palgrave Macmillan, 2004), 1; also, Alister McGrath, *The Foundations of Dialogue in Science and Religion* (Oxford: Blackwell, 1998), 1.

39. Tina Beattie, *The New Atheists: The Twilight of Reason and the War on Religion* (London: Darton, Longman & Todd, 2007), 15.

40. Alister McGrath has written extensively on Dawkins, publishing two books, *Dawkins' God: Genes, Memes and the Meaning of Life* (Oxford: Blackwell, 2005) and *The Dawkins Delusion: Atheist Fundamentalism and Denial of the Divine* (London: SPCK, 2007) among other publications on the topics of Dawkins, science, and religion, for example, 'Has Science Eliminated God?—Richard Dawkins and the Meaning of Life', *Science and Christian Belief* 17, no. 2 (Oct. 2005): 115–35. McGrath was also interviewed by Dawkins for his television series *The Root of all Evil*. Though the particular interview with McGrath did not make the edited version aired on UK television station Channel 4, the full interview is available online.

41. Alister McGrath, 'Evolutionary Biology in Recent Atheist Apologetics', in Denis R. Alexander and Ronald L. Numbers, eds., *Biology and Ideology: From Descartes to Dawkins* (Chicago: University of Chicago Press, 2010), 331.

42. Ibid., 331.

43. Daniel C. Dennett, 'The Selfish Gene as a Philosophical Essay', in Alan Grafen and Mark Ridley, eds., *Richard Dawkins: How a Scientist Changed the Way We Think* (Oxford: Oxford University Press, 2006), 101.

44. Alister McGrath, 'Evolutionary Biology in Recent Atheist Apologetics', Denis R. Alexander and Ronald L. Numbers. eds., *Biology and Ideology: From Descartes to Dawkins*, 331.

45. Atheistic undertones and explicit denunciation of religious concepts are ubiquitous in Dawkins' work, in particular, *The God Delusion*. Dawkins also has a prominent public profile as a champion of atheism.

46. Beattie, *The New Atheists: The Twilight of Reason and the War on Religion*, vii.

47. This feature of Dawkins' work has been discerned and articulated by reviewers of his publications, for example, David Hull, 'A Quartet of Volumes on Genetics and Evolution' *The Quarterly Review of Biology* 62, no. 3 (Sept. 1987): 290; also, Janet L. Leonard, 'Review: Untitled', *The Quarterly Review of Biology* 70, no. 3 (Sept. 1995): 331; also, Laura Betzig, 'Review: Untitled', *The Quarterly Review of Biology* 72, no. 4 (Dec. 1997): 467; also, Kim Sterelny, 'Never Apologise, Always Explain', *Bioscience* 54, no. 5 (May 2004): 460; also, Ursula Goodenough, 'Walking Back Through Evolutionary Time', *BioScience*, 55, no. 10 (Sept. 2005): 798.

48. In tandem with such scholarly dialogues is the constant need for continuing dialogue and reform within the church. For discussion on this issue, see Gary Keogh, 'How Can the Church Survive? Reflections of a Celtic Tiger Cub', The Furrow 62, no. 4 (Apr. 2011); also, 'A New Generation of Family Values', The Furrow 63, no. 3 (Mar. 2012); also, 'An Irish Church Reform Movement?', The Furrow 63, no. 7/8 (July/Aug. 2012).

49. For examples, see Fergus Kerr, ed., *Contemplating Aquinas: On the Varieties of Interpretation* (London: SCM, 2003); also, Fergus Kerr, *After Aquinas: Versions of Thomism* (Oxford: Blackwell, 2002), and Brian Davies, *Thomas Aquinas on God and Evil* (Oxford: Oxford University Press, 2011); also, Brian Davies, ed., *Aquinas' Summa Theologiae: Critical Essays* (Oxford: Rowman & Littlefield, 2006).

50. Carly Daniel-Hughes, *The Salvation of the Flesh in Tertullian of Carthage: Dressing for the Resurrection* (New York: Palgrave Macmillan, 2011)

51. Karen Kilby, *Karl Rahner: Theology and Philosophy* (London: Routledge, 2004); also, Karen Kilby, 'Karl Rahner's Ecclesiology', *New Blackfriars* 90, no. 1026 (Mar. 2009): 188–200.

52. John Webster, *Barth* (London: Continuum, 2004).

53. Beverly Mayne-Kienzle, *Hildegard of Bingen and Her Gospel Homilies: Speaking New Mysteries* (Turnhout, Belgium: Brepols, 2009).

54. John Scally, 'A Woman for Our Time: The Enduring legacy of Catherine of Siena', *Religious Life Review 50, no. 267 (Mar.–Apr. 2011).*

55. James Bremner, *The Power of Then: How the Sages of the Past Can Help Us in Our Everyday Lives* (London: Hay House, 2012).

56. Maureen Junker-Kenny, *Habermas and Theology* (London: T. & T. Clark, 2011), 1.

57. Sebastian Brock, *The Luminous Eye: The Spiritual World Vision of Saint Ephrem the Syrian* (Kalamazoo, MI: Cistercian Publications, 1992), 21.

58. David E. Jenkins, *God, Jesus and Life in the Spirit* (London: SCM, 1988), 37.

59. John Scally, *To Speed on Angel's Wings: The Story of the Sisters of St. John of God* (Dublin: Columba, 1995), 117.

60. Neil Messer, *Selfish Genes and Christian Ethics: Theological and Ethical Reflections on Evolutionary Biology* (London: SCM, 2007), 246.

61. Henri de Lubac, *The Drama of Atheistic Humanism* (London: Sheed & Ward, 1949).

62. Alister McGrath, *The Twilight of Atheism: The Rise and Fall of Disbelief in the Modern World* (London: Rider, 2004).

63. Gallagher, *What Are They Saying about Unbelief?*

64. McGrath, *The Foundations of Dialogue in Science and Religion*, 20.

65. TGD, particularly pp. 54–61 and 282–86; also, Richard Dawkins, 'Obscurantism to the Rescue', *The Quarterly Review of Biology* 72, no. 4 (Dec. 1997): 397–99.

66. Kurt Wise in John F. Ashton, ed., *In Six Days: Why 50 Scientists Choose to Believe in Creation* (London: New Holland, 1999), 332.

67. Paul Davies, *The Mind of God: Science and the Search for Ultimate Meaning* (London: Penguin, 1992), 16.

68. Francis Collins, *The Language of God: A Scientist Presents Evidence for Belief* (New York: Basic Books, 2006), 6.

69. Kenneth Miller, *Finding Darwin's God, A Scientist's Search for the Common Ground Between God and Evolution* (New York: HarperCollins, 1999), 17.

70. The address was made on October 22, 1996, titled 'Truth Cannot Contradict Truth'. In this address, Pope John Paul II updated the Catholic position on evolution from Pope Pius XII's encyclical *Humani Generis*, who advocated for scepticism in approaching evolution, though did not explicitly reject it: Some however, rashly transgress this liberty of discussion, when they act as if the origin of the human body from pre-existing and living matter were already completely certain and proved by the facts which have been discovered up to now and by reasoning on those facts, and as if there were nothing in the sources of divine revelation which demands the greatest moderation and caution in this question. (*HG*: 37) John Paul recognised the scepticism in *Humani Generis*, though acknowledged that advancements in science verified the hypothesis of evolution, "Today, almost half a century after the publication of the encyclical, new knowledge has led to the recognition of the theory of evolution as more than a hypothesis". Therefore, John Paul's address signified a substantial shift in the pontifical attitude with respect to evolution.

71. Stephen Jay Gould, 'Nonoverlapping Magisteria', *Natural History* 106, no. 2 (Mar. 1997), 16–22, reprinted in *Leonardo's Mountain of Claims and the Diet of Worms: Essays on Natural History* (New York: Random House, 1998), 269–84.

72. Stephen Jay Gould, *Rocks of Ages: Science and Religion in the Fullness of Life* (London: Jonathan Cape, 1999), 59–63.

73. Ibid., 62.

74. Ibid., 65.

75. Francisco J. Ayala, *Darwin's Gift to Science and Religion* (Washington, DC: Joseph Henry, 2007), ix. Italics in original.

76. Francisco J. Ayala, Statement at Templeton Prize News Conference (25 March 2010). Full text available online. It was for the strident opposition to the entanglement of science and religion that Ayala was awarded the Templeton Prize in 2010.

77. Stephen Jay Gould, *Rocks of Ages: Science and Religion in the Fullness of Life*, 92.

78. Ibid., 94.

79. Stephen Jay Gould, *Leonardo's Mountain of Claims and the Diet of Worms: Essays on Natural History*, 274.

80. Ibid., 282.

81. St. Augustine, quoted in Alister McGrath, *Christian Theology: An Introduction*, 441.

82. For an in-depth study of this idea, see Arthur O. Lovejoy, *The Great Chain of Being: A Study in the History of an Idea* (Cambridge, MA: Harvard University Press, 1998), originally published in 1936.

83. Stephen Jay Gould, *Leonardo's Mountain of Claims and the Diet of Worms: Essays on Natural History*, 282.

84. Ibid., 282.

85. Francisco J. Ayala, 'Teleological Explanations in Evolutionary Biology', *Philosophy of Science* 37, no. 1 (Mar. 1970): 8.

86. Stephen Jay Gould, *A Wonderful Life: The Burgess Shale and the Nature of History* (London: Vintage, 1990), 51.

87. Francisco J. Ayala, 'Teleological Explanations in Evolutionary Biology', *Philosophy of Science* 37, no. 1 (Mar. 1970): 10.

88. Francisco J. Ayala, 'Darwin's Greatest Discovery: Design Without Designer', *Proceedings of the National Academy of Science of the United States of America* 104 (May 2007): 8573.

89. Francisco J. Ayala, *Darwin's Gift to Science and Religion*, 3 and 5; also, see Cornelia Dean, 'Scientist at Work: Francisco J. Ayala', *New York Times*, 29 Apr. 2008; also, Chris Doran, 'From Atheism to Theodicy to Intelligent Design: Responding to the Work of Francisco J. Ayala', *Theology and Science* 7, no. 4 (Nov. 2009): 337–44.

90. Tracy and Cobb, *Talking About God*, 3.

91. Charles Darwin, *On the Origin of Species* (New York: Prometheus, 1991), 401, originally published in 1859.

92. Hans Urs von Balthasar, *Science, Religion and Christianity* (London: Burns & Oates, 1958), 9.

93. McGrath, *The Dawkins Delusion: Atheist Fundamentalism and Denial of the Divine*, 19.

94. For example, see *ROOE*, 111–55.

95. Dawkins attempts to refute eight arguments; Aquinas' proofs, the ontological and *a priori* arguments, the argument from beauty, the argument from personal experience, the argument from scripture, the argument from admired religious scientists, Pascal's wager, and Bayesian arguments.

96. Ibid., 113–59.

97. Ibid., 308. Original text reads "very very". Dawkins also attributes a variety of atrocities to religious belief, such as the terrorist attacks on New York and London in 2011 and 2005 respectively, the Crusades, the Israeli/Palestinian conflicts, and the troubles in Northern Ireland. Ibid., 1.

98. Ward, *Why There Almost Certainly Is a God.*

99. McGrath. *Dawkins' God: Genes, Memes and the Meaning of Life*; also, *The Dawkins Delusion: Atheist Fundamentalism and Denial of the Divine*; also, *Why God Won't Go Away: Engaging with the New Atheism* (London: SPCK, 2011).

100. Markham, *Against Atheism: Why Dawkins, Hitchens, and Harris Are Fundamentally Wrong.*

101. Giberson and Artigas, *Oracles of Science: Celebrity Scientists Versus God and Religion.*

102. John Haught, *God and the New Atheism: A Critical Response to Dawkins, Harris and Hitchens* (Louisville: Westminster John Knox, 2008).

103. Kathleen Jones, *Challenging Richard Dawkins: Why Richard Dawkins Is Wrong about God* (London: Canterbury, 2007).

104. Mike Starkey, *Whose Delusion? Responding to The God Delusion by Richard Dawkins* (Kent: Church Army, 2007).

105. Rob Slane, *The God Reality: A Critique of Richard Dawkins' The God Delusion* (Eastnor Castle, Herefordshire: Day One, 2008).

106. R. J. Fallon, *Is Richard Dawkins the New Messiah? A Layman's Critique of The God Delusion* (Hull: Eka Books, 2008).

107. David Robertson, *The Dawkins Letters: Challenging Atheist Myths* (Fearn, Ross-shire: Christian Focus, 2007).

108. John Blanchard, *Dealing with Dawkins* (Darlington: E.Books, 2010).

109. John Cornwall, *Darwin's Angel: A Seraphic Response to The God Delusion* (London: Profile Books, 2007).

110. Richard Grigg, *Beyond the God Delusion: How Radical Theology Harmonizes Science and Religion* (Minneapolis: Fortress Press, 2008).

111. Thomas Crean O.P., *A Catholic Replies to Professor Dawkins* (Oxford: Family Publications, 2008).

112. Gerard J. Hughes, 'Dawkins: What He, and We, Need to Learn', *Thinking Faith—The Online Journal of the British Jesuits* (18 Jan. 2008), Web, 20 Dec., 2011.

113. Wolfhart Pannenberg, *Basic Questions in Theology Vol. II* (London: SCM, 1971), 195.

114. James Mackey, *The Scientist and the Theologian: On the Origins and Ends of Creation* (Dublin: Columba, 2007), 52.

115. Ibid., 46–63.

116. Although we can take Küng as an example, there is much discourse on approaches to truth in the context of the science-religion dialogue. For example, see two articles by Andreas Losch, 'On the Origins of Critical Realism', *Theology and Science* 7, no. 1 (Feb. 2009): 85–106, and

'Critical Realism—A Sustainable Bridge Between Science and Religion?', *Theology and Science* 8, no. 4 (Nov. 2010): 393–416.

117. Hans Küng, 'Paradigm Change in Theology: A Proposal for Discussion', in Küng and Tracy, eds., *Paradigm Change in Theology*, 3–33; also, Hans Küng, *Theology for the Third Millennium: An Ecumenical View* (London: HarperCollins, 1991), 123–69, and *The Beginning of All Things*, 28–29 and 52.

118. Karl Popper, *The Logic of Scientific Discovery* (New York: Routledge, 1959), 18.

119. Küng, *The Beginning of All Things*, 28.

120. Küng, *Theology for the Third Millennium: An Ecumenical View*, 130.

121. Ibid., 130.

122. Thomas Kuhn, *The Structure of Scientific Revolutions*, 3rd ed. (Chicago: University of Chicago Press, 1962), 210.

123. Hans Küng, *Does God Exist?*, 110.

124. Paul Ricoeur, *Oneself as Another*, trans. Kathleen Blamey (Chicago: University of Chicago Press, 1992), 297.

125. John Polkinghorne, *Quarks, Chaos and Christianity: Questions to Science and Religion* (London: Triangle, 1994), 5.

126. Nancey Murphy and George F. R. Ellis, *On the Moral Nature of the Universe: Theology, Cosmology and Ethics* (Minneapolis: Fortress Press, 1996), 5.

127. Bertrand Russell, *Religion and Science* (New York: Oxford University Press, 1935), 15.

128. Richard Dawkins, *A Devil's Chaplain: Selected Essays* (London: Phoenix, 2003), 21. Dawkins, in this passage, is addressing philosophies such as Popper's and Kuhn's. Though he names both Popper and Kuhn, he does not make explicit reference to their texts, but rather offers an approximation of their views.

129. Cornwall, *Darwin's Angel: A Seraphic Response to The God Delusion.*

130. Richard Dawkins, 'Do You Have to Read Up on Leprechology before Disbelieving in Them?', *The Independent* (UK), 17 Sept. 2007.

131. Richard Dawkins, 'Afterword' to Lawrence Krauss, *A Universe from Nothing* (New York: Free Press, 2012), 190. Dawkins also begins chapter 3 of *TGD* with this Thomas Jefferson quotation.

132. Richard Dawkins, 'The Emptiness of Theology', *Free Inquiry* 18, no. 2 (Spring 1998). See also, 'Reply to Michael Pool', *Science and Christian Belief* 7, no. 1 (Apr. 1995): 45–50.

133. Nicholas Lash, 'Where Does the God Delusion Come From?', *New Blackfriars* 88, no. 1017 (Sept. 2007): 508.

134. Terry Eagleton, 'Lunging, Flailing, Mispunching', *The London Review of Books*, 19 Oct. 2006.

135. Haught uses the term 'new atheists' to refer to Dawkins, philosopher Sam Harris, and writer Christopher Hitchens. Harris and Hitchens also published books critical of religion between 2004 and 2007, *The End of Faith: Religion, Terror and the Future of Reason* (London: W. W. Norton, 2004) and *God Is Not Great: How Religion Poisons Everything* (London: Atlantic, 2007) respectively.

136. Haught refers here to theological thinkers such as Paul Tillich, Alfred North Whitehead, Paul Ricoeur, Rudolf Bultmann, Edward Schillibeeckx, Bernard Lonergan, Karl Barth, John Bowker, Elizabeth Johnson, Karl Rahner, Jürgen Moltmann, Wolfhart Pannenberg, Ian Barbour, David Tracy, Dorothee Soelle, Sallie McFague, Henri de Lubac, Hans Jonas, Emil Fackenheim, and Seyyed Hossein Nasr, among others.

137. Haught, *God and the New Atheism: A Critical Response to Dawkins, Harris and Hitchens*, xii.

138. Ibid., xii–xiii.

139. Ward, *Why There Almost Certainly Is a God*, 8.

140. Ward, *God, Chance and Necessity*, 96

141. Ward, *Is Religion Evil?* 90.

142. Terry Eagleton, *Reason, Faith and Revolution: Reflections on the God Debate* (London: Yale University Press, 2007), 2.

143. Owen C. Thomas, 'The Atheist Surge: Faith in Science, Secularism, and Atheism', *Theology and Science* 8, no. 2 (May 2010): 196.

144. *TGD*, 200, quoted in Lash, 'Where Does the God Delusion Come From?', 512.

145. Ibid., 512.

146. Ibid., 512.

147. Hughes, 'Dawkins: What He, and We, Need to Learn'.

148. Ibid.

149. *TGD*, 1–2.

150. Ibid., 169.

151. Ibid., 271.

152. Martin Luther King, 'I Have a Dream Speech', 28 Aug. 1963, Web, 10 Aug. 2012.

153. James Cone, 'Jesus Christ in Black Theology', in Curt Cadorette et al., eds., *Liberation Theology; An Introductory Reader* (New York: Orbis, 1997), 142.

154. Ibid., 509.

155. Ward, *Why There Almost Certainly Is a God*, 102. Capitalisation of 'five ways' in original.

156. Haught, *God and the New Atheism: A Critical Response to Dawkins, Harris and Hitchens*, 15–27.

157. Ibid., 18.

158. Ibid., 20–24.

159. Beattie, *The New Atheists: The Twilight of Reason and the War on Religion*, 149–50.

160. Markham, *Against Atheism: Why Dawkins, Harris and Hitchens Are Fundamentally Wrong*, 27.

161. Quoted in Lash, 'Where Does the God Delusion Come From?', 508.

162. McGrath, *The Twilight of Atheism: The Rise and Fall of Disbelief in the Modern World*, 95.

163. Ward, *Is Religion Dangerous?*, 150.

164. Hughes, 'Dawkins: What He, and We, Need to Learn'.

165. Ibid.

166. David Hume, *A Treatise on Human Nature* (New York: Dover, 2003), 295, originally published in 1739.

167. Hughes, 'Dawkins: What He, and We, Need to Learn'.

2

Encountering Evolution
Dawkins' Perspective

INTRODUCTION

In order to pursue the objectives of this project (a dialogue with Dawkins) we must, as an essential prerequisite, understand the scientific foundation from which Dawkins develops his worldview. As stated in the previous chapter, Dawkins is being held as a representative of an interpretation of evolutionary science in order to pursue an interdisciplinary dialogue. This dialogue, we noted, was seen as an imperative by theologians such as David Tracy and John Paul II, among others. However, it would be highly limiting to attempt to enter into a dialogical relationship with Dawkins without ascertaining the edifice of the scientific picture as he presents it. This endeavour is also necessary for two further reasons. Firstly, possessing a comprehension of the scientific theory of evolution is needed, as it is inevitable that scientific aspects of the evolutionary process will be encountered throughout this work. Therefore, we will develop a rudimentary grasp of the science in order to keep our study within the parameters of what we would call 'informed discussion'. Secondly, by looking at Dawkins' view of evolution, we are allowing a degree of objectivity into our work. This point relates to the motives of the project outlined in the previous chapter, where it was suggested that encompassing the views of nontheological scholars, or in Dawkins' case, anti-theological, we may limit potential criticisms of religious subjectivity. This chapter therefore relates to the theological paradigm of broadening the ambit of traditional subject matter.

We presented in the previous chapter how Dawkins' otherness makes him a suitable candidate for a project seeking to pursue the pluralistic/interdisciplinary paradigm pronounced in the writings of thinkers such as Rahner and Küng, among others. Therefore, Dawkins will be our guide through the complex field of evolutionary theory. However, Dawkins' ideology, identified as atheistic naturalism/materialism, will shape his illustration of evolution. Consequently, focusing solely on Dawkins' depiction will have its limitations (particularly, given that Dawkins has been criticized significantly for his explanatory monism or intolerance of other views). To alleviate this problem, while keeping Dawkins to the forefront of our exploration we will incorporate other authorities in the field. This will help to alleviate potential criticism of giving Dawkins' position too much weight, which would be particularly limiting given the criticisms of Dawkins' monistic stance. Moreover, as we progress, we will indicate specific aspects of Dawkins' view on evolution with theological ramifications that will be addressed throughout the following three chapters.

Biological Evolution: An Overview

In order to present an overview of Dawkins' perspective on evolution, we must firstly obtain a preliminary understanding of genes, given their centrality in his approach. Dawkins regards genes as information, which contain the blueprint of an organism.[1] In conjunction with this, he postulates that the genetic code is analogous to a computer program, "a better analogy for a gene than a word or a sentence is a toolbox subroutine in a computer".[2] Dawkins can obtain support for this interpretation from scholars such as Nobel laureate James Watson,[3] co-discoverer of the double helix structure of DNA with Francis Crick in 1953 (we will discuss DNA below), among others.[4] Genes transmit the information that 'instructs' organisms to develop according to a particular plan/blueprint. They are manifest as an organism's characteristics, that is, genes that allow for a lion to run faster, or a human to be taller, and so forth (though this is somewhat of an oversimplification, it does not bear weight upon a rudimentary understanding of evolution, such as we are seeking to establish).[5]

This initial understanding of genes equips us to embark on our overview of Dawkins' position on evolution. He encapsulates the premise of his view of Darwinism as follows (though the term 'Darwinism' can be problematic):

> Since all organisms inherit their genes from their ancestors, rather than from their ancestors' unsuccessful contemporaries, all organisms tend to possess successful genes. They have what it takes to become ancestors—and that means to survive and reproduce. This is why organisms tend to inherit genes with a propensity to build a well-designed machine—a body that actively works as if is striving to become an ancestor . . . we all, without a single exception, inherit

genes from an unbroken line of successful ancestors. The world becomes full of organisms that have what it takes to become ancestors. That in a sentence is Darwinism.[6]

From this definition, two significant premises can be discerned. The first concerns the survival longevity of our ancestors; it holds that all of our ancestors succeeded in surviving for a sufficient amount of time in order to copulate. The logic of this point is obvious: if an individual did not have the survivability to procreate, they would have no descendants to contemplate the issue. The second arresting point we obtain relates to, but progresses from the first: if all organisms come from an unbroken line of parental predecessors, then consequently, we are faced with the truth that we are all derivatives of a seamless, unbroken ancestral line that leads back indefinitely. Advancing his summary of evolution above, Dawkins employs the metaphor of rivers to represent these unbroken ancestral lines. He illustrates that these rivers converge at varying locations if we are to follow them backwards through time, and ultimately, all convene at one point in the distant past.[7] In other words, all living things are descended from the same source. This statement is substantiated by the recognition that all observable life shares the chemical composition of DNA, consisting of four chemical bases—adenine, thymine, cytosine, and guanine—commonly referred to as A, T, C, and G.[8] The homogeneous nature of all living organisms evident in their shared DNA make-up, is for Dawkins, the most compelling evidence that all life has evolved from a single origin:[9] ". . . DNA code is invariant across all living creatures. . . . This is a truly astounding fact, which shows more clearly than anything else that all living creatures are descended from a single ancestor".[10] On this point, prominent zoologist Matt Ridley offers a comparable perspective: "The universality of the (DNA) code is easy to understand if every species is descended from a common ancestor".[11]

The interconnectedness of all life stemming from one focal point in history is the central thesis established from Dawkins' definition of evolution. Another definition that Dawkins posits will offer two supplementary characteristics that will aid our understanding. He presents this definition as follows: "Modern biologists use the word 'evolution' to mean a rather carefully defined process of systematic shifts in gene frequencies in populations, together with the resulting changes in what animals and plants actually look like as the generations go by".[12] The first characteristic we are introduced to in this quotation is the concept of 'gene frequencies'. Amid the hereditary transferring of genes through ancestral lines, the genes that have greater survival longevity will inevitably become more frequent in the gene pool. The important element of this definition is the word 'frequencies', which was absent from the first definition cited. The term's notability becomes apparent when we consider the influence its inclusion has on our understanding of the evolutionary process. The inclusion of the concept of 'gene frequencies' subdues the rigidness one might have perceived in the first definition. Evolution is therefore presented in a more permissive fashion, which is closer to the concurrent view in modern science, as we shall see. The second point we can take from the second definition is that the fluctuations in gene frequencies result in variance in the biosphere. Subsequently, if we amalgamate the points discussed so far, we begin to understand the edifice of Dawkins' view of evolution; genes are transmitted hereditarily through a seamless ancestral line, during which certain genes become more or less frequent resulting in variance in the biosphere.

To view evolution as ongoing shifts in gene frequencies is, however, an idiosyncrasy of a particular school of evolutionary thought, for which Dawkins is a proud proponent: 'neo-Darwinian synthesis'.[13] Here, Dawkins' thought can be traced to his neo-Darwinian predecessors, such as the highly influential scientist R. A. Fisher. Dawkins' pronounced admiration of Fisher is evident in introductory notes to an extract of Fisher's included in Dawkins' *Oxford Book of Modern Science Writing*. Dawkins labels Fisher as a founder of evolutionary genetics and neo-Darwinian synthesis, and Darwin's great twentieth-century successor.[14] If we consider Fisher's stance on the variance among plants and animals, we can identify palpable similarities between his view and that of Dawkins: ". . . any changes in variability which may be in progress must be ascribed to changes in frequency, including origination and extinction, of the different kinds of genes".[15] The parallels between Dawkins and Fisher in this regard are unsurprising, given their mutual advocacy of neo-Darwinian synthesis. In both Dawkins' and Fisher's respective opinions, the predominant theme is that fluctuating gene frequencies result in the diversity of life.

Another authority on neo-Darwinism is the eminent geneticist Theodosius Dobzhanksy, who is also a significant influence on Dawkins' thought.[16] In the context of this work, Dobzhansky is an interesting figure given that he has been identified as a "religious man" who grounded his religiosity in his belief that there is meaning in the universe.[17] As such, contrary to Dawkins, Dobzhansky's portrayal of evolution is less likely to be intentionally presented as atheistic. However, with regard to the influence gene frequencies have on evolutionary changes, Dawkins' view is reminiscent of Dobzhansky, who posits that "[t]he elementary components of evolutionary changes are alterations of the frequencies of gene alleles or chromosomal variants in the gene pool of a population".[18]

Two further features of Dawkins' perspective on evolution that have decidedly theological implications arise from the following passage in his *The Blind Watchmaker*:

> How, then, did they (living creatures) come into existence? The answer, Darwin's answer, is by gradual, step by step transformations from simple beginnings, from primordial entities sufficiently simple to have come into existence by chance. Each successful change in the gradual evolutionary process was simple enough, relative to its predecessor, to have arisen by chance. But the whole sequence of cumulative steps constitutes anything but a chance process.[19]

The first feature, which we had briefly mentioned above, is that all living things are the result of the natural process of evolution (save to the extent of synthetically created life). Moreover, Dawkins stresses the gradualness of the evolutionary process. This is an important feature of Dawkins' perspective, which will also be a source of contention when we review his position. The second notable feature prevalent in this passage is the role of chance or randomness in evolution. He reiterates a similar sentiment in a later publication by stating, "Core Darwinism, I shall suggest, is the minimal theory that evolution is guided in adaptively non-random directions by the non-random survival of small random hereditary changes . . . ".[20] Throughout the hereditary process, and the transmission of genes along the ancestral lines, changes will occur at the genetic level. This concept will be discussed with greater depth later. At this point, however, we will continue our introductory overview, and discuss the function of chance in the evolutionary process. Dawkins illustrates that changes within the hereditary transferring of genes are governed by randomness, although the survival efficiency of these changes is contingent on nonrandom factors. These nonrandom factors can be identified as natural selection.

Given that Dawkins views genetic changes (mutations) as random, it could be suggested that at bottom, evolution is a random process. Here, Dawkins' atheism becomes apparent. If as he suggests, the mutations that guide evolution are inherently random, then evolution has no teleology (directionality). This is consequential for theology, given that it brings to the fore the question of how purposeful or random the world is. This question will be a significant theological problem for this book, and will be addressed in Chapter Five. It will also be discussed further in terms of how it shapes Dawkins' worldview in Chapter Three. Dawkins' atheism may in part stem from this interpretation, or conversely, his atheism may influence his interpretation. This is an interesting philosophical question that may not have a definitive answer (although we will propose that his philosophical worldview does influence his scientific stance). Theologian Alister McGrath, whom we encountered in Chapter One as a notable critic of Dawkins, is particularly well placed to comment on Dawkins' stance on the issue of chance given that he has a background in the study of biochemistry, obtaining a doctorate from Oxford University. Moreover, Dawkins himself acknowledges that McGrath presents an "admirably fair summary" of his scientific works.[21] McGrath points out that although Dawkins views mutations as random, he is insistent that whether or not these mutations survive is decidedly nonrandom; Dawkins stresses the nonrandom factor of natural selection over the happenstance of mutations.[22]

To clarify Dawkins' interpretation of the role of chance in evolution, we can consult Ernst Mayr, an influential evolutionary biologist whom Dawkins identified as a "giant of the neo-Darwinian synthesis".[23] Mayr explains that evolution is a two-fold process: "The first factor, genetic variability, is entirely a matter of chance, whether it is produced by mutation, recombination, or by whatever other mechanism. Precisely the opposite is true of the second factor, natural selection, which is decidedly an "anti-chance" factor".[24] The striking similarity between Dawkins' and Mayr's interpretations is that evolution is understood as a two-tiered process, one governed by randomness, and one bound by nonrandom processes of natural selection. Mayr encapsulates, "Mutation-Selection is . . . a tandem dualism",[25] and reiterates the two steps of natural selection in a later publication: "step one: the production of variation . . . step two: non-random aspects of survival and reproduction".[26] However, Dawkins also accepts that there may be instances in which genetic mutations are not random. "Even mutations are, as a matter of fact, non-random in various senses . . . ".[27] This again reinforces the theme that evolution is not a stringent process.

To conclude this section then, we have been introduced to the field of evolutionary science by following Dawkins' depiction of the process. The important features of our overview, such as the interconnectedness of all life, shifts in genetic frequencies, and the role of chance in evolution, will play an important role in the dialogue between theology and evolution throughout this work. However, several issues must now be explored in order to ensure we have a sufficient understanding of the topic. We will now elaborate on genes and natural selection respectively.

GENES

Advancing our exploration of evolutionary science, we must now engage with Dawkins' explanation of the workings of genes. This endeavour serves two purposes; firstly, this will augment our overview, broadening our understanding of the evolutionary process. Secondly, a sufficient apprehension of genetics will be required to investigate Dawkins' stance on natural selection. To briefly recapitulate, in our overview of evolution, a preliminary definition of genes was presented—that genes can be regarded as information, analogous to a computer program containing the blueprint of an organism. Permitting Dawkins' use of analogy in his explanation of biology, we understand that the 'language' in which genetic information is bequeathed is DNA, the four chemical bases found in all living organisms. However, in practical operation, what Dawkins equates to bequeathed information is in fact a complex chemical process.

An arresting feature of Dawkins' view is that bodies that subjectively appear to be single units are in fact temporary amalgams of genes: "Genetically speaking, individuals and groups are like clouds in the sky or dust storms in the desert. They are temporary aggregations or federations".[28] The apparent unity, Dawkins explains, is unsurprising as natural selection has favored genes that cooperate proficiently:

> Colonies of genes they may be but, in their behaviour, bodies have undeniably acquired an individuality of their own. An animal moves as a coordinated whole, as a unit. Subjectively I feel like a unit, not a colony. This is to be expected. Selection has favoured genes which cooperate with others. . . . Nowadays, the intricate mutual co-evolution of genes has proceeded to such an extent that the communal nature of an individual survival machine is virtually unrecognizable.[29]

Dawkins then, views bodies as assemblies of genes. McGrath offers some clarification on this point: "This distinction could be formalized in terms of the *replicators* and *vehicles*—that is, between small genetic units ("genes") themselves, and the higher level entities (typically organisms . . .) which transmit those genes onward in the evolutionary process".[30] Dawkins essentially understands organisms as "gene survival machines" that "reproduce their genes, and die; it is the genes that survive not the vehicles, in the form of information copies of themselves".[31] This interpretation, however, is an example of where Dawkins crosses the boundaries between science and philosophy. McGrath perceptively illustrates this point, by noting that Dawkins takes empirical observations, such as the fact that "genes are in you and me" and continues to make metaphysical judgments on the nature of individual organisms.[32] He views organisms as colonies of genes and writes off the subjective experience of oneness to how well genes operate together. On this point, we will critique Dawkins in two distinct ways: firstly, on his failure to clarify between what is empirical and what is scientific, and secondly, on the scientific basis for this gene-centred approach. Both of these points will form elements of our critique later in this chapter.

Dawkins further explains that almost every cell in an organism contains all of the organism's genes, but in each individual cell, only a few genes will be 'turned on' at any one time. "Every cell, with very few exceptions . . . contains the genes for making all the enzymes. But in any one cell, only a few genes will be turned on at any one time".[33] This quotation presents two interesting problems. The first is the question of how particular genes 'turn on', while counterpart genes do not. In addressing this problem, Dawkins demonstrates that whether a gene is 'on' or 'off' is contingent on a process known as 'bootstrapping'. He acknowledges that at the beginning of an organism's development, the fertilized egg (an embryo) develops by multiplying itself firstly into two, then into four, and so on. Furthermore, the fertilized egg has "polarity in its internal chemistry".[34] Consequently, throughout the process of exponential multiplication, the polarity is amplified and the cells become varied, as opposed to replicating identically. The 'on' or 'off' status of the genes, then, is determined by the variations in the polarity of the genes. A subissue will inevitably arise at this point, in the form of questioning how the process of exponential multiplication initiates. There is a degree of ambiguity in Dawkins' explanation of this issue. He articulates, "If he (God) made anything (he didn't in my view, but let it pass, that's not what I'm about here), what he made was an embryological *recipe* . . . ".[35] Dawkins also observes that embryological development is a planless process with no instructions, choreographer, or blueprint. It can appropriately be equated to the building of a termite mound or ant's nest; it self-assembles. The cardinal point that we should acknowledge now, however, is that the 'on/off' status of genes is contingent on cellular polarity:

> What then determines which genes are switched on in a particular cell? . . . When the egg has divided into, say thirty-two cells—that is, after five divisions—some of those thirty-two cells will have more than their fair share of topside chemicals, others may have more than their fair share of bottomside chemicals. These differences are

enough to cause different combinations of genes to be turned on in different cells.[36]

The second issue that demands our attention is the introduction of 'enzymes' into Dawkins' explanation of genes. The creation of enzymes is the result of the 'on' or 'off' status of genes. Enzymes, Dawkins explains, can essentially be considered as catalysts that allow various chemical reactions to occur in the cell. These chemical reactions influence how the cell is shaped, how it behaves, and how it interacts with other cells, which Dawkins describes as 'origami-like': "Finally, the chemical reactions that go on in a cell determine the way that cell is shaped and the way it behaves, and the way it participates in origami-style interactions with other cells".[37] Therefore, it is the genes that ultimately determine how the organism forms: "So the differences in genes can, at the originating end of the complex chain of events, cause differences in the way embryos develop, and hence differences in the form and behavior of adults".[38] This is the chief point that we can extrapolate from our analysis of genes, viewed through the lens of Dawkins' work; genes are the origin of a complex chain of chemical events that result in the development of organisms. We must now examine how genes are transmitted though the ancestral lines.

Genes, in a given organism, are inherited proportionately from their parents; 50 percent are acquired maternally, and 50 percent are acquired paternally. They are replicated and transmitted through the process of reproduction. The inherited genes do not blend in forming an embryo, and consequently, it is only 50 percent of a person's genes that are passed on to their offspring. There is a 50 percent chance, therefore, that a gene came from an individual's father, a 25 percent chance that the gene came from the paternal grandfather, a 12.5 percent chance that the gene came from the father's paternal grandfather, and so on:

> In every one of your cells, half of your mother's genes rub shoulders with half your father's genes. Your maternal genes and your parental genes conspire with one another most intimately to make you the subtle and indivisible amalgam you are. . . . A given gene in you either came from your mother or your father. It also came from one, and only one of your four grandparents; and so on back.[39]

Following from this, the genes that contribute to an organism capable of reproducing will be inherited by the organism's offspring. Correspondingly, genes that reside within an organism or phenotype[40] that does not possess the survival efficacy to reproduce will not be transmitted to the next generation.

Consequently, whether or not genes multiply and populate the gene pool is contingent upon whether or not the genes reside in organisms capable of procreation. Therefore, as Dawkins articulates, each generational transmission of genes becomes a sieve:

> Bad genes may pass through the sieve for a generation or two, perhaps because they have the luck to share a body with good genes. But you need more than luck to navigate successfully through a thousand sieves in succession, one sieve under the other. After a thousand successive generations, the genes that have made it through are likely to be the good ones.[41]

In this outline of the functionality of the generational sieve, Dawkins acknowledges that bad genes may avoid their abstraction from the gene pool for several generations if they share a body with good genes. As a result, the generational sieve lacks exhaustive precision, as bad genes may pass through it in the company of good genes. This highlights the significance of the collaborative nature of genes mentioned earlier in this section, which gives rise to the subjective feeling of unity. It is clear from Dawkins' summary that over great amounts of time it is only the good genes that consistently pass through the generational sieve. It is, nevertheless, the likelihood of the elimination of bad genes in favor of their positive counterparts that becomes a prominent feature, as it conveys that the generational sieve is at least to some extent, a permissive process.

This understanding of genes and their transmission is crucial to our appreciation of Dawkins' thought, as we are taking Dawkins as a representative of both an ideological and interdisciplinary other with whom we will open a dialogical relationship. Therefore, it is crucial that we develop an understanding of genes in the context of a theological dialogue with him. We have already indicated that his view on the role of chance in evolution has decidedly theological consequences pertaining to the nature of the world. Dawkins' understanding of genes will also be theologically consequential as it forms the basis for his perspective on morality and on religious belief itself.

Natural Selection

The central premise of natural selection for Dawkins is explicit in the following definition: "Natural Selection is the differential survival of successful genes rather than the alternative, less successful genes in the gene pools".[42] The process of natural selection is akin, therefore, to the generational sieve. How this process operates, however, requires our immediate attention. Dawkins explains that the genetic replication process, which we encountered in our previous two sections, is highly efficacious.[43] He observes, "Genes . . . can self-copy for ten million generations and scarcely degrade at all. Darwinism works only because—apart from discrete mutations, which natural selection either weeds out or preserves—the copying process is perfect".[44] The degree of efficiency in the copying process is emphasized in this particular reference. If the genetic replication process is perfect, it would be expected that the gene pool be made up of identical genes. Alister McGrath also points out this problem: "Surely the fidelity of transmission points to a static, not dynamic, situation".[45]

However, the other conspicuous element in Dawkins' description of the replication process is the concept of discrete mutations. He also draws attention to this in an earlier publication. "[N]ow we must mention an important property of any copying process: it is not perfect. Mistakes will happen".[46] These discrepancies in the replication process (random mutations) result in variance in the gene pool, and furthermore, may result in tangible phenotypic differences. Such differences then have either a positive, negative, or—as most often—an indifferent consequence for the organism's ability to copulate. The positive and negative effects of genetic mutations are what designates genes as either 'good' or 'bad' when they are subjected to the generational sieve discussed above.[47] This is the central thesis of natural selection. The esteemed British evolutionary biologist John Maynard Smith also puts forth a similar perspective, by suggesting that the mistakes made in the hereditary transfer of genes are then subject to natural selection.[48] This reminds us of the two-tier nature of evolution; random changes subject to nonrandom selection. Moreover, consistent with the concept of 'gene frequencies' and the generational sieve, Dawkins summarizes natural selection as follows:

> Natural selection doesn't choose genes directly. Instead it chooses their proxies, individual bodies; and those individuals are chosen—obviously and automatically and without deliberative intervention—by whether they survive to reproduce copies of the very same genes. . . . Statistically, therefore, a gene that tends, on average, to have a good effect on the survival prospects of the bodies in which it finds itself will tend to increase in frequency in the gene pool.[49]

Statistically, the genes that are of greater benefit to their organisms will be passed on to the next generation, and those that are deleterious to their organisms' ability to survive, will not. Overall, then, certain genes become more or less frequent. Dawkins, therefore, describes the process of natural selection as 'narrowing down' the gene pool. "Natural selection itself, when you think about it, is a narrowing down from a wide initial field of possible alternatives, to the narrower field of alternatives actually chosen".[50] As observed earlier, both Dawkins and Ernst Mayr maintained that selection was nonrandom. Therefore, this 'narrowing down' is provisioned on whether a gene resides in/contributes to an organism successful at copulating. "The narrowing is non-random, in the direction of improvement, where improvement is defined, in the Darwinian way, as improvement in fitness to survive and reproduce".[51]

Continuing our exposition of Dawkins' stance on natural selection, we can identify another important feature: he considers genes as the 'units of selection'. The following passage will clarify this point and encapsulate Dawkins' interpretation of natural selection:

> It is its potential immortality that makes a gene a good candidate as the basic unit of natural selection. But the time has come to stress the word 'potential'. A gene *can* live for a million years, but many new genes do not even make it past their first generation. The few new ones that succeed do so partly because they are lucky, but mainly because they have what it takes, and that means they are good at making survival machines. They have an effect on the embryonic development of each successive body in which they find themselves, such that that body is a little bit more likely to live and reproduce than it would have been under the influence of the rival gene . . .[52]

It is evident from this passage that Dawkins feels selection is based on the gene's propensity to either positively or negatively influence the development of organisms. Moreover, in the introductory chapter to *The Selfish Gene*, he also explicitly states, "I shall argue that the fundamental unit of selection . . . is not the species, nor the group, nor even, strictly, the individual. It is the gene, the unit of heredity."[53] McGrath also emphasizes this feature of Dawkins' view:

> For Dawkins, the most satisfying rationale of the evolutionary process is framed in terms of gene lineages. The changes required for evolution to develop take place very slowly. The life of an individual organism, is small in comparison with the time required for these changes to come about. This demands a stable and very long-term

unit of genetic transmission—and only gene lineages can satisfy this condition.[54]

This important aspect of Dawkins' work is another point of contention that we will look at later. This gene-centred approach also leads Dawkins to characterize genes as 'selfish' in order to portray how they behave. Permitting Dawkins' anthropomorphism, he describes the behavior of genes as ⚹ fundamentally selfish; the only 'concern' of genes is to become more numerous in the gene pool:

> If we allow ourselves the license of talking about genes as if they had conscious aims, always reassuring ourselves that we could translate our sloppy language back into respectable terms if we wanted to, we could ask the question, what is a single selfish gene trying to do? It is trying to get more numerous in the gene pool.[55]

On the issue of describing genes as selfish, Dawkins has received criticism, notably by the philosopher Mary Midgley, who contested Dawkins' views on the premise that genes are not conscious agents, capable of acting selfish. "Genes cannot be selfish or unselfish, any more than atoms jealous, elephants abstract or biscuits teleological".[56] However, Alister McGrath, who again is recognized as a prominent critic of Dawkins, notes that this criticism was ". . . lost in the noise of a scientifically confused piece of polemic which managed to misrepresent Dawkins' views on the gene".[57] Dawkins himself addresses this criticism by explaining, "We do not even mean the words in a *metaphorical* sense. We *define* altruism and selfishness in a purely behaviouristic way". Dawkins advocates that genes have selfish behaviouristic traits, but are not consciously selfish.[58]

This understanding of Dawkins' thought is essential to our project, because as we have already stated, it forms the basis for his views on issues with decidedly theological implications such as morality and religious belief. Dawkins presents his views on these theologically important matters as atheist and materialist, a worldview contrary to a theological understanding. Yet, it is not in spite of, but because of the conflict between Dawkins and theology, that we are engaging with him. This is to demonstrate how theology can find insight in diverse areas of academia, such as an understanding of Dawkins' view of evolution. However, this understanding is not quite complete. There are two outstanding issues that demand our attention, namely how the ancestral lines discussed diverge to form different species, and how the process of evolution began.

SPECIATION

It has been demonstrated in this chapter how Dawkins explains variance among organisms—through the natural selection of mutating genes, bequeathed through ancestral lines. When such a degree of variance is introduced to these ancestral lines, the lines diverge. When this happens, the diverging ancestral lines can no longer be considered the same species. This process is known as speciation. By Dawkins' own admission, the precise elements of the process of speciation are equivocal. Dawkins does explain, however, that it is unanimously agreed upon that the most significant determinant in speciation is accidental geographical separation.[59] To suggest that an idea is unanimously agreed upon requires validation. As such, we can turn to prominent biologists Jerry A. Coyne and H. Allen Orr, who are highly critical of Dawkins' arguments against religion and theism.[60] Coyne and Orr, among others,[61] substantiate Dawkins' assertion—that geographical separation is the central point of our understanding of speciation (although there are other factors).[62] Dawkins outlines the natural mechanisms that lead to segregation in the gene pool, and subsequently, to new species:

> We start with the ancestral species, a large population of rather uniform, mutually interbreeding animals, spread over a large land mass. . . . The landmass is cut in two by a mountain range. . . . Now the two populations breed and breed separately, mixing their genes . . . any changes in the genetic composition of one population are spread by breeding throughout that population but not across to the other population. . . . So the populations diverge genetically.[63]

Dawkins reiterates this premise in a later publication:

> The standard neo-Darwinian view of the evolution of diversity is that a species splits in two when populations become sufficiently unalike that they can no longer interbreed. Often the populations begin diverging when they chance to be geographically separated. The separation means that they no longer mix their genes sexually and this permits them to evolve in different directions . . . when they have evolved sufficiently far apart that they could no longer interbreed even if they were geographically united again, they are defined as belonging to separate species.[64]

Accidental geographical separation results in two distinct gene pools being subjected to the processes of natural selection. Consequently, due to inconsistencies in the randomness of genetic mutations, both gene pools will continue to evolve distinctly. After vast amounts of time, there will be such variation between the two gene pools that if they were reintroduced to one another, they could not successfully interbreed. At this point, they are considered separate species. Dawkins selects the grey and red squirrel to exemplify this:

> They cannot interbreed . . . they cannot mate to produce fertile offspring. Their genetic rivers have drifted too far apart, which is to say that their genes are no longer well suited to cooperate with one another in bodies. Many generations ago, ancestors of gray squirrels and red squirrels were one in the same individuals. But they became geographically separated . . . and their genetic ensembles grew apart. Geographical separation bred a lack of compatibility.[65]

Dawkins therefore defines a species as separate when they can no longer interbreed with the species from which they became separated geographically. "The biological definition of a species is a group of individuals that interbreed with each other and not others".[66] Although Dawkins adopts this definition, there is a sense of uncertainty among certain scholars on this issue, as Ernst Mayr among others,[67] suggests:

> An evolutionary definition of species has not been widely accepted because it is only applicable to monotypic species. . . . The main objective of the evolutionary species definition was to permit a clear delimitation of a species in the time dimension, but this hope has turned out to be illusory in all cases of gradual species transformation.[68]

While acknowledging that there is some contention on the definition of a species, Dawkins' opinion is supported by notable evolutionists such as Stephen Jay Gould. Gould offers a consistent perspective on what constitutes a separate species:

> Species branch off from ancestral stocks, usually as small, discrete populations inhabiting a definite geographical area. They establish their uniqueness by evolving a genetic program sufficiently distinct

that the members of the species breed with each other, but not with members of other species.[69]

Further corroboration of the validity of this position can be found with John Maynard Smith, who insightfully notes:

> Species exist because organisms reproduce sexually. Blue tits are genetically similar to one another (and different from great tits) because they are descendant from a common set of interbreeding ancestors (and great tits are descendant from a different set). The two species will remain distinct in the future because they do not interbreed.[70]

To summarize at this point, in Dawkins' view, which as we noted is not deviant from the consensus of the scientific community, gene lineages become separated predominantly because of geographical isolation. When the gene lineage becomes separate to the extent that the two gene pools can no longer interbreed, they are considered a separate species. This is another aspect of Dawkins' perspective on evolution that arguably carries significant theological implications. Dawkins' view emphasizes here that humanity is the result of the separation of gene pools that were once one. Consequently, this stresses again the connectedness of all life, and the relationship of humans to the animal kingdom. We have already encountered this issue as an example of the entanglement between science and theology. This point will also be of importance when we consider the traditional anthropocentric explanations of the encounter with evil in Chapter Five. There is, however, one further aspect of Dawkins' portrayal of evolution that needs to be considered: the origin of the evolutionary process.

The Origin of Evolution

As we have ascertained throughout this chapter, evolution relies on the replication of genes in order for them to be transmitted to the next generation. We established that genes are replicated and transmitted through procreation, thus begetting the ancestral lineage that binds all life. We now need to provide an account of how this process began. Although Dawkins admits there is an absence of empirical evidence of this primordial event, he insists that it must have happened. "We have no direct evidence of the replication event that initiated the proceedings on this planet. We can only infer that it must have happened because of the gathering explosion of which we are a part".[71]

Dawkins notes that there is no direct evidence of the origin of life, but still 'believes' it happened. This may indicate an inconsistency in Dawkins' insistence on the necessity of evidence for belief. Dawkins postulates further, that the origin of the 'phenomenon of heredity' must have been a chemical event given the chemical composition of DNA.[72] Conventionally, molecules do not possess the unusual replication prowess of DNA. Notwithstanding this, scientists have been able to produce experimental results in which molecules show traits of self-replication, given emulated natural conditions. Dawkins presents an account of one such experiment carried out by chemist Julius Rebek and his colleagues at the Massachusetts Institute of Technology. Rebek and his team of chemists produced molecules that were seen to exhibit self-replicating behavior.[73] In addition, Dawkins informs us that chemists have also carried out experiments that emulate the conditions of what it would have been like on early earth (no oxygen, no ozone layer, plenty of hydrogen, water and carbon dioxide, and other simple organic gases), and passed through electricity to simulate ultraviolet light and lightning. On these experiments, he comments, "The results . . . have been exciting. Organic molecules, some of them of the same general types as are normally only found in living things, have spontaneously assembled themselves in these flasks".[74] Although experimentation did not result in the formation of legitimate self-replicating molecules such as DNA, constituents of these molecules were formed. Therefore, Dawkins concedes, "the missing link for this class of theories is still the origin of replication".[75] Dawkins, though, maintains his conviction that this original replication was under the sole influence of natural processes: "[B]efore the coming of life on earth, some rudimentary evolution of molecules could have occurred by ordinary processes of physics and chemistry".[76] Dawkins is led to this conclusion by consideration of probability.

The spontaneous origination of self-replicating molecules may seem an improbable event; however, there is a three-fold proposition that, for Dawkins, explains how this seemingly improbable event is in fact, quite probable. Firstly, humans are unaccustomed to contemplating the vast time-scale over which this process took place. "This may seem a very unlikely sort of accident to happen. So it was. It was exceedingly improbable. . . . But in our human estimates of what is probable and what is not, we are not used to dealing with hundreds of millions of years".[77] Secondly, this event only needed to happen on one occasion.[78] Thirdly, the experiments discussed above show that pseudo-self-replicating molecules or their constituents can originate under natural conditions. These points amalgamate to solidify Dawkins' belief that the natural origin of self-replicating molecules is not, *de facto*, improbable. With regard to this issue, Dawkins has strong support even from his formidable academic opponent, Stephen Jay Gould, who postulates that life's origin was not only probable, but a necessity:

> Life arose at least 3.5 billion years ago, about as soon as the earth became cool enough for the stability of the chief chemical components. I do not, by the way, view the origin of life as a chancy or unpredictable event. I suspect that given the composition of the early atmospheres and oceans, life's origin was a chemical necessity.[79]

Theodosius Dobzhansky, who we recall was identified as a religious man, suggesting that his views on evolution are not intentionally swayed toward an atheistic portrayal, is also in agreement with the probability (or inevitability) of life's natural origin: "Since life has in fact appeared, its origin was indeed inevitable".[80]

Fundamentally, it must be maintained that Dawkins et al.'s conclusion on the natural origin of life is speculative as there is no direct evidence. Dawkins himself acknowledges this. "The account of the origin of life which I shall give is necessarily speculative; by definition, nobody was around to see what happened".[81] Moreover, "We can hope for nothing more than speculation when the events we are talking about took place four billion years ago and took place, moreover, in a world that must have been radically different from that which we know today".[82] Nevertheless, Dawkins' conclusion is credible speculation, grounded in the laws of chemistry:

> Though the chemistry of the world may have changed, the laws of chemistry have not changed (that's why they are called laws), and modern chemists know enough about those laws to make some well-informed speculations, speculations that have to pass rigorous tests of plausibility imposed by the laws . . . of all possible speculations about the origin of life, most run foul of the laws of chemistry and can be ruled out . . .[83]

Again, Dawkins can find support for this. John Maynard Smith is also insistent that the lack of direct evidence does not preclude an evolutionary understanding of life's origin. "One does not need a detailed history of pre-biotic conditions and events in order to discover the evolutionary laws that led to the first life on earth".[84] With this contention, Dawkins' ontological naturalism becomes apparent. Dawkins is resolute that life's origin was a natural event, highlighting the naturalistic worldview that he is taken to represent as a conversation partner for this theological project.

CRITIQUE OF DAWKINS' PERSPECTIVE ON EVOLUTION

To ensure that our dialogue with Dawkins' model of evolution is balanced, we must now place it in the context of his critics. As we have opted to select Dawkins as a representative of the discipline of evolutionary science, we must be aware of the limitations in focusing an analysis on his point of view. Contextualising Dawkins' position among his scientific critics will demonstrate that there are particular elements of his perspective on evolution that are not universally held. The two main protagonists in this section will be philosopher of evolution Fern Elsdon-Baker and Stephen Jay Gould. Elsdon-Baker was chosen as she provides a recent, scientific critique of Dawkins' position, described by a reviewer as the first legitimate challenge to Dawkins' science since Gould.[85] Gould is then introduced as Dawkins' most significant opposition on the topic of evolution, with commentaries citing the prominence of their scientific debate.

Elsdon-Baker critiques Dawkins' portrayal of evolution as excessively monist or oversimplified. "While Dawkins' contribution is indisputable, his strong advocacy of a narrow focus view of evolution is rightly being called into question. It paints an inflexible picture not only of the evolutionary sciences, but also of how science works".[86] Moreover, she explains, ". . . I started to see that Dawkins' version of history wasn't altogether accurate—I found it so oversimplified, indeed that I made it the subject of my Ph.D. in order to explore what really happened".[87] This particular criticism echoes those of Dawkins we discussed earlier. It pertains to a lack of openness toward alternative viewpoints in Dawkins' work. If we recall Dawkins' portrayal of evolution, he asserts that the process operates through the natural selection of genes which are passed on hereditarily. Elsdon-Baker notes, however, that "things are a lot more complicated and subtle".[88] This aspect of Dawkins' work becomes, for Elsdon-Baker, a caveat for how science is conducted, as such a monist perspective can threaten to hinder progress:

> This in turn closes off dialogue in both public and academic spheres. It can, at worst, constrain future research. . . . We must think about moving on from communicating evolutionary science with the kind of rhetoric and sweeping advocacy Dawkins' metaphors have encouraged towards a more nuanced exploration of the complexity involved.[89]

What has been identified as intolerance on Dawkins' part pertaining to his castigation of religion/theism is, according to Elsdon-Baker, also prevalent in his scientific work. She identifies Dawkins' inflexible outlook as a potential limitation for scientific advancement, similar to our identification of his inflexibility as a potential limitation for a dialogue with theology.

This criticism of Dawkins can be ameliorated by acknowledging that his portrayal of evolution lacks sufficient depth, failing to incorporate key research in biology that may drastically influence how the evolutionary process is perceived. Elsdon-Baker maintains that Dawkins' depiction of the evolutionary process is 'Dawkinsian' as opposed to 'Darwinian'; it is too narrowly focused on his own opinions.[90] In Dawkins' account, evolution is characterized by its exclusive emphasis on hereditary gene lineages. However, Elsdon-Baker cites significant research that indicates traits may be transmitted epigenetically (outside of genetics), articulating that external forces may influence whether genes are turned on or off.[91] This concept is not fundamentally opposed with Dawkins' depiction, in which the on/off status of genes is contingent on internal factors (the bootstrapping process). However, it may offer corroboration to Elsdon-Baker's critique that Dawkins' portrayal of evolution is incomplete.

A further point absent from Dawkins' strict gene-line perspective of evolution is apparent in the concept of 'Horizontal Gene Transfer' or 'HGT'. Elsdon-Baker explains that new research indicates that genetic information can be transmitted through individuals irrespective of reproductive processes.[92] She refers to an article by Graham Lawton of *New Scientist* which considers the issue of HGT. Lawton interestingly notes, ". . . patterns of relatedness could only be explained if bacteria and archaea were routinely swapping genetic material with other species—often across huge taxonomic distances—in a process called horizontal gene transfer (HGT)".[93] Although debate on the issue remains, evidence suggests HGT is a significant factor in evolution, particularly among bacteria, archaea, and unicellular eukaryotes (which even today represent 90 percent of all known species).[94] Therefore, it becomes apparent that Dawkins' unilateral view of vertical genetic transmission (from parent to offspring) is incomplete. In Elsdon-Baker's account then, we perceive evolution as a more permissive process, in which there are tendencies as opposed to stringent 'rules'. This can be substantiated by acknowledging that the absence of stringent laws in evolution has been deliberated upon by established philosophers of biology such as Elliott Sober[95] and John H. Beatty.[96] Sober explains that although he and Beatty disagree on aspects of the contingency of evolution, they both agree that there are no empirical laws of evolution.

THE DAWKINS-GOULD POLEMIC

In order for us to take Dawkins as a conversation partner for theology, it is vital that we consider not just his view on evolution, but also his critics. This puts us in a better position to get a mature and balanced view of the merits or otherwise of his view. The most substantial criticism Dawkins has been subject to is manifest in the work of the influential paleontologist Stephen Jay Gould. As we have already stated, Dawkins and Gould hold diverging approaches to the science-religion dialogue. Dawkins criticizes Gould for being unrealistic in advocating his NOMA approach, and suggests that, in reference to Gould, "A cowardly flabbiness of the intellect afflicts otherwise rational people confronted with long-established religions".[97] Pertaining to Dawkins' science, however, Elsdon-Baker also notes the significance of Dawkins and Gould's polemical debate on evolution:

> Dawkins has always had his scientific as well as religious, opponents. The most famous was the American paleontologist Stephen Jay Gould, who died in 2002. For decades, a battle royal was waged between Dawkins and Gould, with intellectual heavyweight supporters joining in on both sides. So prolonged and so polemical were the exchanges . . . that it has created a major chasm in the intellectual community.[98]

The Australian philosopher Kim Sterelny also contributes a full publication to the Dawkins-Gould debate, in which he notes that "Richard Dawkins and Stephen Jay Gould have different views on evolution, and they and their allies have engaged in a public and polemical exchange . . . ".[99] The prominence of this dispute in academia therefore requires our consideration at this point, given that we are seeking to contextualize Dawkins among his critics.

Commentaries consistently cite Dawkins' emphasis on 'gene selectionism' as the fundamental point of contention between Dawkins and other biologists.[100] Ed Sexton, who has a background in the study of biology and philosophy, articulates this point:

> The disagreement between evolutionary biologists usually focuses on the second of these questions [that natural selection only operates at the level of the gene]. Many feel that Dawkins is asking selection to act exclusively on genes. While almost everyone agrees that much selection happens at the gene level, some argue that selective forces act on organisms, and possibly on groups as well. Some deny that

genes can possibly have the causal power that Dawkins demands of them.[101]

This issue is the foci of disagreement between Dawkins and Gould; however, there is also disagreement on the rate of evolution, that is, whether it is gradual (Dawkins) or punctuated (Gould). We will now identify five distinct points of dispute between Dawkins and Gould. The first four pertain to gene selectionism: the interconnectedness of genes, the sufficient stability (longevity) of bodies, the role of genes in heredity and selection, and emergence. The fifth point of dispute pertains to the rate of evolution. This is not an exhaustive critique, nor should we offer to favor one approach to evolution over another. Our task at this point is to make evident that Dawkins' depiction of evolution is not unanimously accepted and has authoritative critics. We will then show that this scientific dispute may be founded upon philosophical differences, and it is precisely because Dawkins can be seen to hold an ideological view that makes him a good candidate for a theological dialogue.

THE RELATIONSHIP BETWEEN GENES AND THE ENVIRONMENT

The first aspect of disputation we will look at is based upon the premise that the interconnectedness of genes prevents their direct interaction with the environment. Therefore, they cannot be individually subject to natural selection, as Gould explains:

> Still I find a fatal flaw in Dawkins' attack from below. No matter how much power Dawkins wishes to assign to genes, there is one thing that he cannot give them—direct visibility to natural selection. Selection simply cannot see genes and pick among them directly. It must use bodies as an intermediary. A gene is a bit of DNA hidden within a cell. Selection views bodies. It favors some bodies because they are stronger, better insulated, earlier in their sexual maturation, fiercer in combat, or more beautiful to behold. If, in favoring a stronger body, selection acted directly upon a gene for strength, then Dawkins might be vindicated. If bodies were unambiguous maps of their genes, then battling bits of DNA would display their colors externally and selection might act upon them directly. But bodies are no such things.[102]

The intricate amalgamation of genes within bodies precludes the possibility of selection of genes, and therein lies Gould's issue with Dawkins' gene selectionism. To illustrate this point, it can be noted that the human genome, for example, contains approximately 23,000 genes. Consequently, Gould seeks 'interactors' as the units of selection—something that has direct interaction with the environment, as he explains with biologist Elisabeth A. Loyd:

> The logic of the theory of natural selection . . . assigns the status of causal agency in selection to *interactors*, defining them as individuals that: (i) interact with the environment . . . in such a way that (ii) one or more of their traits imparts differential reproductive success through the interaction, so that (iii) relatively more or less (compared with other individuals at their level) of their hereditary material (however packaged) passes to the next generation.[103]

Genes do not meet these criteria to be deemed interactors. Therefore, the crux of Gould's criticism holds that genes cannot be the units of selection as they do not interact with the environment. Consequently, he opts to consider bodies or phenotypes as the units of selection. On this matter, Ernst Mayr is in agreement with Gould, as he notes, "Selection does not deal with single genes because its target is the phenotype of the entire individual".[104] Dawkins himself acknowledges the apparent problem:

> Now at this point many biologists will get carried away and say that natural selection must work at the level of the whole crew as a unit [a reference to an analogy he used previously, the image of genes as a rowing crew as working together], the whole suite of genes, or the whole individual organism. They are right that the individual organism is a very important unit in the hierarchy of life. And it really does display unitary qualities. . . . But, however unitary and discrete an individual wolf or buffalo, say, may be, the package is temporary and it is unique. Successful buffaloes don't duplicate themselves around the world in the form of multiple copies, they duplicate their genes. The true unit of natural selection has to be a unit of which you can say it has frequency. It has a frequency which goes up when it is successful and goes down when it fails. This is exactly what you can say of genes in gene pools.[105]

Dawkins contests that genes must be the unit of selection, as organisms are too ephemeral. Genes possess greater longevity than organisms in their replication and transmission, and subsequently, Dawkins insists they must be the target of selection: "It is its potential immortality that makes a gene a good candidate as the basic unit of natural selection".[106] Dawkins is also not the sole proponent of this view. Influential evolutionary biologist George C. Williams illustrates that bodies are too ephemeral to be the units of selection, and thus opts to consider the gene as selection's true target.[107] Moreover, R. A. Fisher and Dobzhansky were seen to hold similar views. Although Dawkins has support on this point, it is important to acknowledge in the current context that he does not hold a monopoly on interpretations of evolution, which may be considered a limitation in holding him as a representative of an interdisciplinary other.

SUFFICIENT STABILITY

The second point of conflict we can discern between Gould and Dawkins is the issue of 'sufficient stability'. As we have noted above, Dawkins suggests that bodies as amalgamations of genes are too ephemeral to be subject to natural selection. On this matter, Gould diverges. Gould maintains that bodies/organisms do indeed possess the longevity for natural selection to act upon them:

> 'Sufficient Stability' surely ranks as an important criterion for the 'evolutionary individuality' required of a 'unit of selection.' But, in the Darwinian theory and the search for units of selection, 'sufficient stability' can only be defined as enough coherence to participate as an unchanged individual in the causal process of struggle for differential reproductive success. To be causal units under this criterion, organisms need only persist for the single generation of their lifetimes—as they do.[108]

Gould postulates that units of selection need only exist for one generation to qualify as units of selection, a criterion that organisms/bodies meet. Moreover, Gould suggested that the consensus among evolutionists is congruent with holding organisms as the predominant object of selection, ". . . evolutionists have generally held fast to the overwhelming predominance, if not exclusivity, of organisms as the objects of selection—Dawkins' attempt at further reduction to the gene notwithstanding".[109] Mayr posits a similar interpretation of the consensus, suggesting that the individual has generally been perceived to be the object of selection since the 1940s.[110]

These assertions from Gould and Mayr are interesting given that they suggest Dawkins' perspective on gene selection is actually deviant from the consensus position of the scientific community. However, as we have already noted, Dawkins has authoritative support from figures such as Dobzhansky and

Williams cited above. The zoologist Matt Ridley also conforms to Dawkins' stance.[111] In the context of this project, we need not opt to favor one approach over another. It can be demonstrated, however, that on the issue of gene selection, disputation exists; we can assert that this is not a conclusive issue.

GENES AND CAUSALITY

The third of Gould's criticisms concerns the role of genes in the hereditary transfer of traits. On this point, Gould suggests that Dawkins makes a conceptual error regarding causality in evolution. Dawkins views genes as the units of selection, and therefore, genes are causal factors in the evolutionary process. Gould disagrees on this point: "The misidentification of replicators as causal agents—the foundation of the gene-centred approach—rests upon a logical error best characterized as a confusion of bookkeeping with causality".[112] This, Gould maintains, is the fundamental error of gene selectionism.[113] Gould agrees with Dawkins that variation is introduced into the gene pool through random mutations on the genetic level: "Mutation is the ultimate source of variation, and genes are the unit of variation".[114] He uses the term 'bookkeeping' to refer to how genes keep records of these mutations. However, while this 'bookkeeping' is an important element of the evolutionary process, Gould insists that it is not causal:

> [C]hanges at the genetic level do play a fundamental part in characterizing evolution, and records of these changes (bookkeeping) do maintain an important role in evolutionary theory. But the error remains: bookkeeping is not causality; natural selection is a causal process, and units or agents of selection must be defined as overt actors in the mechanism, not merely as preferred items for tabulating results.[115]

Moreover, Gould then advocates again for interactors (bodies/organisms) to be considered as the causal agents of selection: "Only interactors can be deemed *causal* agents in any customary or reasonable use of this central term. Replicators are important in evolution, but in a different role as items for bookkeeping. Replicators are not causal agents".[116] Therefore, Gould maintains Dawkins has confused causality with 'bookkeeping', and consequently, holds the view that bodies (what he sometimes refers to as 'interactors') must be the true units of selection.

EMERGENCE

The fourth point of conflict we can identify between Gould and Dawkins is the concept of 'emergence'. As noted earlier, Dawkins considers bodies to be temporary amalgams of genes, "Genetically speaking, individuals and groups are like clouds in the sky or dust storms in the desert. They are temporary aggregations or federations".[117] Furthermore, he explains:

> Colonies of genes they may be but, in their behaviour, bodies have undeniably acquired an individuality of their own. An animal moves as a coordinated whole, as a unit. Subjectively I feel like a unit, not a colony. This is to be expected. Selection has favoured genes which cooperate with others. . . . Nowadays the intricate mutual co-evolution of genes has proceeded to such an extent that the communal nature of an individual survival machine is virtually unrecognizable.[118]

We have already noted that on this point, Dawkins is making a philosophical proposition—that the subjective oneness of everyday experience is illusory and explicable due to the cooperativeness of genes. Such a statement, we noted along with Alister McGrath, blurs the boundaries of empirical science and metaphysics. The theological implications of this perspective are striking, as it may also further emphasize the interconnectedness of all living things; if all living systems are different amalgams of genes, humanity is a fleeting glimpse in an ongoing process of changing gene frequencies. This will be an important issue in Chapter Five, when we address theological problems such as evil and humanity's relationship with God, which have classically been understood anthropocentrically.

However, Gould offers a contrary perspective to Dawkins. In assessing Dawkins' argument, he insists that Dawkins has mistakenly suggested that bodies are reducible to their constituents:

> Dawkins' argument collapses for many reasons, most notably the issue of emergence. A higher unit may form historically by aggregation of lower units. But so long as the higher unit develops emergent properties by nonadditive interaction among parts (lower units), the higher unit becomes, by definition, an independent agent in its own right, and not the passive "slave" of controlling constituents.[119]

Furthermore, Gould maintains that the fact genes precede organisms in
historical origin does not prevent organisms from having an independent
nature:

> Dawkins then commits one of the classical errors in historical
> reasoning by arguing that because genes preceded organisms in
> time, and then aggregated to form cells and organisms, genes must
> therefore control organisms—a confusion of historical priority with
> current domination.[120]

In contrast to Dawkins, Gould lambasts the notion that organisms are mere
amalgams of genes and insists that they are higher units that have emerged
as independent agents. Consequently, Dawkins' view of nature's causality is
reversed. Gould views organisms as individual units, and hence the objects
of selection (as seen above): ". . . Dawkins has reversed nature's causality:
organisms are active units of selection; genes, while lending a helping hand as
architects, remain stuck within these genuine units".[121] In substantiating this
criticism, Gould then suggests that if Dawkins views organisms as temporary
amalgams of genes, subsequent selection upon the organism is selection of all
individual genes residing within that body. "If this view could be defended,
then bodies would become passive aggregates of genes—mere packaging—and
selection on a body could then be read as a convenient shorthand summary for
selection on all resident genes, considered individually".[122]

In recapitulating Dawkins' view, however, this particular critique may
be problematic. As Dawkins explained, the functionality of the generational
sieve may permit bad genes to pass through several sieves in certain instances
(when they share bodies with good genes). However, after vast numbers of
generations, bad genes will most likely fail to circumvent selection.[123]
Conversely, we can logically suggest that good genes may fail to pass through
a generational sieve as they share a body with bad genes. Nonetheless, in the
gene pool, the good gene will still maintain a statistically higher frequency than
its negative counterpart. Dawkins stressed the fluctuation of gene frequencies
in the gene pool, not the selection of individual genes in individual bodies.[124]
Therefore, on this point, Gould's critique could be contested. In Dawkins' view,
selection upon an organism does not equate to selection of that organism's
constituent genes. Rather, it is suggested that selection results in statistically
fluctuating gene frequencies, averaged out over the gene pool.
Notwithstanding this weakness in Gould's criticism, his point can still be
somewhat vindicated. He insightfully notes:

Any nonlinearity precludes the causal decomposition of a body into genes considered individually—for bodies become, in the old adage, "more than the sum of their parts." In technical parlance, nonlinearity leads to "emergent" properties and fitness at the organismic level—and when selection acts upon such emergent features, then causal reduction to individual genes and their independent summations becomes logically impossible.[125]

As we have demonstrated, it is not necessary to reduce bodies to individually considered genes in order to maintain a gene selectionist view, as selection can be viewed in terms of gene frequencies. Genes that have a deleterious effect on organisms will statistically become less frequent in the gene pool. This again reminds us of the lack of empiricism in evolution, as discussed by Elliott Sober and others. Consequently, it is not 'logically impossible' to hold a gene selectionist view, as Gould suggests. However, adhering to an emergent view of evolution, selection at the level of the organism may be contested to hold greater logical coherence, and subsequently, Dawkins' gene selection would still be incongruous with nature's causality. Support for this perspective can be found from Ernst Mayr, who as we have seen, supports Gould's view—that evolution cannot be adequately represented by reducing bodies to their genes:

> [M]ost treatments of evolution are written in a reductionist manner in which all evolutionary phenomena are reduced to the level of the gene. . . . This approach inevitably fails. Evolution deals with phenotypes of individuals, with populations, with species; it is not "a change in gene frequencies".[126]

Again, we need not favor one perspective over another in this theological work, as this is a matter for science. We can note, however, that there are important theological consequences for how evolution is portrayed. Viewing bodies as colonies of genes may dissolve the individuality of humanity in the grand scheme of evolution, which can have important implications for the anthropocentric nature of aspects of traditional theologies. However, as we noted, Gould himself advocates that humanity cannot be considered as superior to other life in light of evolution (a topic that we suggested highlighted an overlap between science and theology—something Gould sought to avoid). Notwithstanding, Gould's view on emergence may mitigate the interconnectedness to some extent when compared with Dawkins' perspective. Moreover, it is the primary task at this point to highlight the fact that Dawkins' scientific account of evolution is not universally held.

THE RATE OF EVOLUTIONARY CHANGE

The fifth point of disagreement between Dawkins and Gould we will consider is the rate of evolutionary change. As indicated earlier, Dawkins places emphasis on the gradualness of the evolutionary process. However, Gould, along with fellow American paleontologist Niles Eldridge, proposed that "punctuational change dominates the history of life: evolution is concentrated in very rapid events of speciation . . . ".[127] Evolution, in their view, was periodically stable with sudden and great changes, as opposed to the consistently gradual change in Dawkins' view. This theory is labeled 'punctuated equilibrium'. The seminal paleontologist Robert T. Bakker who supports the theory, suggests that this concept was one of the most significant proposals in paleontology of the twentieth century.[128] On this issue, however, Dawkins denies that punctuated equilibrium is especially revolutionary. He also asserts that it does not represent a great divergence between himself and Gould.[129] Moreover, Gould proposes that he is in favor of a pluralistic approach to the rates of evolution, although he himself believes in a punctuational view: ". . . I confess to a personal belief that a punctuational view may prove to map tempos of biological and geologic change more accurately and more often than any of its competitors . . . ".[130] The rate of evolutionary change (punctuational or gradual) can have significant theological implications. We will encounter, in Chapter Five, how punctuated equilibrium may provide support for theologies that consider a sharp distinction between humanity and other animals. Presently, however, we can further point out that Dawkins' perception of evolution is not ubiquitous among evolutionary theorists.

PHILOSOPHICAL BASIS OF THE DAWKINS-GOULD POLEMIC

In addition to critiquing Dawkins from a scientific standpoint, Gould also deliberates on the philosophical undertones of Dawkins' gene selectionist view, which has "inspired both fervent following of a quasi-religious nature and strong opposition from many evolutionists, who tend to regard the uncompromising version as a form of Darwinian fundamentalism".[131] In considering the theoretical background of gene selectionism, Gould suggests that it is underpinned by a reductionist system that has historically permeated much Western scientific thought:

> I think, in short, that the fascination generated by Dawkins' theory arises from some bad habits of Western scientific thought—from attitudes (pardon the jargon) that we call atomism, reductionism, and determinism. The idea that wholes should be understood by

decomposition into "basic" units; that properties of microscopic units can generate and explain the behavior of macroscopic results; that all events and objects have definite predictable, determined causes. These ideas have been successful in our study of simple objects.[132]

The reductionist mode of thought, which views objects as the interactions between their constituent parts, has been so successful in Western science that Dawkins has persisted with this methodology when it comes to biology. This is indicative of the suggestion made in the previous chapter, that science can be hermeneutical; that it is subject to ideological influences, in Dawkins' case, reductionism. Dawkins himself is explicit in his espousal of reductionism:

> For those that like '-ism' sorts of names, the aptest name for my approach to understanding how things work is probably 'hierarchical reductionism'. . . . The hierarchical reductionist . . . explains a complex entity at any particular level in the hierarchy of organization, in terms of entities only one level down the hierarchy; entities which, themselves, are likely to be complex enough to need further reducing to their own component parts; and so on.[133]

The foundational premise from which Dawkins' view develops, is that entities can be explained in terms of their constituents one level down the hierarchy. Dawkins' reductionism does not maintain that entities can be explained directly in terms of their smallest parts, which is an important distinction. Gould nonetheless proceeds within a different theoretical framework when it comes to biology:

> But organisms are much more than amalgamations of genes. They have a history that matters; their parts interact in complex ways. Organisms are built by genes acting in concert; influenced by environments, translated into parts that selection sees and parts invisible to selection. Molecules that determine the properties of water are poor analogies for genes and bodies. I may not be the master of my fate, but my intuition of wholeness probably reflects a biological truth.[134]

Gould dispraises a reductionist interpretation of biology, as there is a subjective sense of wholeness in an organism. Corroborating opinions are apparent in the writing of Dobzhansky, who quotes another esteemed evolutionist, George Gaylord Simpson:

In biology then a second kind of explanation must be added to the first or reductionist explanation made in terms of physical, chemical, and mechanical principles. This second form of explanation, which can be called compositionist in contrast to reductionist, is in terms of adaptive structures and processes to the whole organism and to the species of which it is part . . .[135]

This profound philosophical disparity between Gould and Dawkins may then set the precedent for their differences in opinion on matters of evolution and natural selection.

A scathing critique of Gould's opposition to reductionism is offered by Daniel C. Dennett. Dennett describes the reductionist mode of thought as the central premise of Darwinism: "Gould's ultimate target is Darwin's Dangerous Idea itself; that evolution is, in the end, just an algorithmic process".[136] Here is where the term 'Darwinism' becomes problematic; despite the fact Gould is a prominent Darwinist (Dawkins labels him a 'Darwinian Heavyweight'[137]), Dennett suggests that he is opposed to the core premise of Darwinism. Therefore, the term becomes stretched to the point where it encompasses polarized perspectives (Gould and Dennett/Dawkins). Dawkins also endorsed Dennett's critique of Gould's outlook in his *Unweaving the Rainbow*.[138] Gould, however, also hints that Dawkins' view of gene selectionism may stem from humanity's primitive fascination with immortality, as he attributes pseudo-immortality to the gene:

Dawkins's extended defense of genes as *the* unit of selection invokes a set of related criteria bearing unmistakable concordance with primal virtues of our culture, another extrascientific reason for the argument's appeal—namely, faithfulness, (near) immortality, and ancestral priority.[139]

Consequently, the salient philosophical disparities in Gould's and Dawkins' respective outlooks may set a precedent for their subsequent scientific views. The Dawkins–Gould polemic therefore is eventuated by profound epistemic diversity. This realization will assist us in our transition into the next chapter, which will shift our focus from this preliminary understanding of evolutionary science, toward analyzing features of a particular evolutionary ideology, namely, atheistic materialism, which is represented by Dawkins in the context of this project.

Although our incursion into criticisms of Dawkins was both enlightening and a vital undertaking, the edifice of evolution theory was never questioned. Differing opinions on the precise mechanisms of natural selection raise interesting problems with theological implications, but the general theory remains steadfast within the scientific community. To illustrate this we can note collaboration between Dawkins and Gould. Although they maintained an academic rivalry, they had planned to co-publish a letter defending the general outline of evolution theory against assaults from creationism. Correspondence between Dawkins and Gould, and the letter suggesting that to engage in debate with creationism was a futile endeavour, only contributing to creationist propaganda, was published by Dawkins in his *A Devil's Chaplain*.[140] Gould, however, never had the opportunity to revise the letter, as he fell ill and subsequently passed away.

The task of this critique of Dawkins' perspective on evolution was to acknowledge that Dawkins does not hold a monopoly on interpretations on evolutionary theory; he has his share of scientific critics. However, his particular view on evolution, which is presented as hostile toward religion, makes him a good candidate as a primary dialogue partner for the aims of this project—to exhibit how a dialogical relationship with contrary worldviews may be of benefit to theology. It is not in spite of, but because of the fact that Dawkins' worldview is atheistic that makes him a good conversation partner. However, at this point, it should also be acknowledged that alternative interpretations of evolution exist that would be more amenable to a theological position. We will now briefly consider three theistic interpretations of evolution. We will also exhibit critiques of these theistic views, which will ultimately further substantiate our decision to focus primarily on Dawkins.

THEISTIC INTERPRETATIONS OF EVOLUTION

QUANTUM INDETERMINACY

As we have outlined, Dawkins emphasizes the essential randomness in genetic mutations. Moreover, he holds a reductionist view of how the physical world interacts with itself. "The hierarchical reductionist . . . explains a complex entity at any particular level in the hierarchy of organization, in terms of entities only one level down the hierarchy".[141] However, it has been suggested that the reductionist approach is not tenable in light of quantum indeterminacy (a concept introduced by physicists in the early twentieth century). Briefly put, quantum indeterminacy has been interpreted by some to imply that the world at the subatomic level is inherently unpredictable.[142] There is an uncertainty in the behavior of subatomic particles that is not present in the mechanistic operations of macroscopic objects. Therefore, Keith Ward suggests that extreme reductionism is not just wrong, but is in complete contradiction of the best scientific evidence.[143] Higher levels cannot be explained by lower levels if the lower levels are unpredictable. The theological implications of an inherent unpredictability in the mechanisms of the world is a lively topic in the ongoing dialogue between physics and theology that runs parallel to our current focus on evolutionary science.[144]

However, there have been notable authorities who postulate that the unpredictability of quantum mechanics allows God room to act in the world, and thus perhaps influence the evolutionary process. Addressing this matter, it is apt that we should turn our attention toward the Christian medical doctor Francis Collins, a world-leading geneticist who also wrote on quantum mechanics for his Ph.D.[145] Collins' theism in part leans on the pliability of the physical order, which he considers to allow God room to influence the physical realm:

> [W]ithin the crannies of this orderly world, tiny bits of freedom lurk. It is thus perfectly possible that God might influence the creation in subtle ways that are unrecognizable to scientific observation. In this way, modern science opens the door to divine action without the need for law-breaking miracles. Given the impossibility of absolute prediction or explanation, the laws of nature no longer preclude God's action in the world. Our perception of the world opens once again to the possibility of divine interaction.[146]

In Collins' (and Karl Giberson's) conception of our current scientific understanding, God may act in the world without the interruption of the physical laws that govern it. Consequently, it is contested that there is a subtle but deeply significant relationship between God and creation.

In the context of evolution, prominent scientists such as Paul Davies and Irish-born geneticist Johnjoe McFadden have proposed that quantum indeterminacy may be a causal factor in genetic mutations, which in turn account for variety in the biosphere. Davies explains the proposal as follows: "Mutations are the driver of evolution, so in this limited sense, quantum mechanics is certainly a contributory factor to evolutionary change".[147] McFadden offers a similar argument as he suggests that the source of genetic mutations is "quantum-mechanical".[148] Consequently, if as it has been suggested, God may influence the indeterminacy in quantum physics, and if these quantum events may influence the course of evolution, then it could be postulated that God may guide the evolutionary process. Such a conclusion is adopted by Catholic biochemist Kenneth Miller; as he explains, ". . . events with quantum unpredictability . . . exert direct influences on the sequences of bases in DNA. . . . In other words, evolutionary history can turn on a very, very small dime—the quantum state of a single subatomic particle".[149] Subsequently, similar to Francis Collins and others, Miller considers the idea that quantum events may be reflective of divine action. He explains that the scientific worldview, inclusive of quantum mechanics, ". . . ought to allow even the most critical scientist to admit that the breaks in causality at the atomic level make it fundamentally impossible to exclude the idea that what we have really caught a glimpse of might indeed reflect the mind of God".[150] Miller, therefore, informed by science, interprets evolution theistically. This demonstrates that Dawkins' atheistic portrayal of evolution is not the only interpretation available in the intellectual marketplace.

CRITIQUE OF INDETERMINACY

The suggestion of divine involvement in the evolutionary process is predicated upon causal lapses apparent in quantum indeterminacy. In this subsection, we will firstly criticize this view as too reliant on a particular understanding of physics, which is still shrouded in debate and uncertainty. Secondly, from a theological perspective, founding a particular view of God upon such uncertain scientific theories becomes an intellectually precarious stance, as it is left open to refutation at any point. Within science, the acclaimed physicist Stephen Hawking has recently championed a class of theories known as 'M-theory'.[151] According to Hawking, M-theory precludes divine involvement in the physical universe, even at its origin—or at least, allows for the universe's origin without recourse to a mindful creator. "It is not necessary to invoke God to light the blue torch paper and set the universe going".[152] M-theory (which is itself an amalgamation of various other concepts in physics) holds that the apparent lapses in causality can be explained by the postulation of multiple dimensions and multiple universes.[153] We will not digress into a full investigation of M-theory or its implications for theology or indeterminacy, as this would lead us into the dialogue between physics and theology. Notwithstanding, Hawking's pronounced defense of M-theory makes evident that there is continuing debate over the fundamental principles of physics—whereas the founding principles of evolutionary science are steadfast, as we have seen. Hawking himself concedes that the matter is far from resolved.[154] This echoes the sentiment of mathematician Ian Stewart's acclaimed work *Does God Play Dice? The New Mathematics of Chaos*.[155]

Consequently, this work maintains that it is unwise to seek vindication for a theological conception of God from scientific theories that are still uncertain. A consistent opinion is expressed by eminent theologian Ian G. Barbour, a prolific figure in the science-religion dialogue as both a theologian and physicist. Barbour exhibits a deep scepticism in building religious belief upon the foundation of specific scientific theories.[156] A similar sentiment has also been expressed by Catholic astronomers George Coyne and Allessandro Omizzolo, who write:

> Yet we must resist the ever-recurring temptation to drag in the so-called "God of the Gaps" to attempt to supply our own ignorance in the natural sciences by some theological or philosophical construct which we have no rational grounds to supply.[157]

Therefore, it can be contested that considering God's intervention through quantum events can be problematic from both a scientific and theological perspective.

EVOLUTIONARY CONVERGENCE

The prominent Christian biochemist Simon Conway Morris rejects the view of divine influence in the evolutionary process through quantum indeterminacy: "[T]he various attempts to reconcile physics, quantum mechanics and God fail to convince me". Yet Morris does produce a theistic interpretation of evolutionary science that can be considered to be teleological; the notion of 'evolutionary convergence'.[158] Morris defines evolutionary convergence as "the phenomenon that animals and other organisms often resemble each other despite having evolved from very difference ancestors".[159] He offers the concept of evolutionary convergence as an alternative to the perspective of Dawkins and Gould, who both view evolution as governed by inherently random genetic mutations. This is a perspective that, Morris suggests, is underpinned by atheistic motivations:

> [A]ll these [Gould's and Dawkins' views on randomness] are consistent with the notion that both the process and, more importantly, the end result are random and accidental. These, and similar, tags reflect also a variety of agendas, including those of atheism . . .[160]

Morris insists that such atheistic interpretations of evolution become paradoxical as they fail to account for the subjective feelings of meaning and awe prevalent in human experience.[161] He asserts that evolution has *a priori* metaphysical implications.[162]

Morris derives the concept of evolutionary convergence from the "recurrent and independent emergence of given features".[163] The fact that certain biological features are recurrent suggests for Morris that evolution is inherently nonrandom. Certain biological features, the eye being a salient example, have evolved independently many times.[164] This implies, for Morris, that there are particular tendencies in the evolutionary process, and therefore, the process itself is not random.[165] Although he does not offer an intensive deliberation on the metaphysical implications of nonrandom evolution, he does allude to the fact that the prospect engages in "some of the oldest and deepest philosophical and theological debates".[166] He vaguely refers to a "controlling hand of convergence", which is easily construed as a conscious agent, consistent with a theistic creator. However, Morris does not offer evolutionary convergence as an argument for the existence of God. He ends his *Life's Solution* with the concession that evolutionary convergence does not prove the existence of a deity, although he does acknowledge that the two hypotheses (God and convergence) would be consistent. "None of it presupposes, let alone proves the existence of God, but all is congruent".[167]

CRITIQUE OF EVOLUTIONARY CONVERGENCE

The case for evolutionary convergence and its subsequent metaphysical implications have been seriously considered to ameliorate a theology of evolution. For example, the influential theologian/physicist John Polkinghorne commends Morris for his "detailed professional investigations into the phenomenon of widespread evolutionary convergence", which is offered as a corrective to the "false view of evolution as being 'meaninglessly' open ended".[168] Notwithstanding this support, there is, as we have established, a consensus between several of the most influential biologists of the last century on randomness in the evolutionary process. Moreover, theologians such as Ian G. Barbour believe that randomness is not in contradiction with a theological worldview.[169] Francisco J. Ayala also continues to explicitly profess Christian belief, while simultaneously insisting that the evolutionary process is inherently random. So the apparent randomness in evolution should not be seen as counter-Christian, or indeed counter-theistic. Moreover, the 'randomness interpretation' certainly appears to be far more prominent in the writings of most biologists. Therefore, we will not seek to challenge the apparent randomness in the evolutionary process—though that may be a legitimate theological or scientific approach.

INTELLIGENT DESIGN

The American philosopher Michael Ruse and leading proponent of 'intelligent design' (I.D.) William Dembski briefly define I.D. as "the hypothesis that in order to explain life it is necessary to suppose the action of an unevolved intelligence".[170] The two theistic interpretations of evolution that have been discussed above allow for subtle yet significant divine influence in nature either through quantum uncertainty or guided convergence. However, we will now discuss alleged scientific understandings of biology that insist on more direct involvement from a creator. There have been a significant number of works published on the rejection of evolutionary science *en masse*, which favor a literalist interpretation of the Genesis cosmogony in the First Testament.[171] As these accounts hold no scientific or theological credibility, they need not be considered here.[172] However, other attempts to scientifically demonstrate direct divine action in the evolutionary process are worth considering, and although they will be ultimately shown as fallacious, they demonstrate the extent to which evolutionary biology is scrutinized by peer-reviews and intellectual challengers. Such perennial scrutiny ultimately substantiates the edifice of evolution theory if such scrutiny is shown to fail. Moreover, the theological implications of considering God's direct interjection in the origin of life require attention.

IRREDUCIBLE COMPLEXITY

Catholic biochemistry professor Michael J. Behe champions I.D. by using the apparent complexity in nature as evidence for a divine creator.[173]

He explains that his stance on intelligent design is predicated on the indefinite nature of accounts of the origins of the evolutionary process (the general premises of which Behe accepts) and the complex nature of biochemical systems:

> Perusing the technical literature myself for detailed, meaty answers to the question of how the fantastically intricate mechanisms of the cell could develop step by step without guidance, as Darwinian theory said they must, yielded only sparse, hand waving conjectures. My skepticism about Darwinism quickly led me further; I later became convinced, based on the interactive complexity of biochemical

systems, that they were deliberately designed by an intelligent agent.[174]

Certain biochemical systems, Behe maintains, are 'irreducibly complex', which he defines as ". . . a single system composed of several well-matched, interacting parts that contribute to the basic function, wherein the removal of any one of the parts causes the system to effectively cease functioning".[175] A biological system akin to, but exponentially more complex than a mousetrap (Behe's analogy), could not have arisen through evolution, as the system would not function without all constituent parts existing and originating simultaneously. "For example, a spring by itself, or a platform by itself, would not catch mice, and adding a piece to the first non-functioning piece wouldn't make a trap either".[176] Charles Darwin himself recognized that such a biological system, if it were to be found, would exemplify a detrimental case against the theory of evolution by natural selection, "if it could be demonstrated that any complex organ existed which could not possibly have been formed by numerous, successive, slight modifications, my theory would absolutely break down".[177]

Behe is adamant that examples of irreducibly complex biological systems are omnipresent in nature.[178] He presents a technical elucidation on several such systems in *Darwin's Black Box*,[179] such as the cilium and the bacterial flagellum, which Kenneth Miller describes as the "poster child" of the modern anti-evolution movement.[180] Behe insists that these biological mechanisms that reside in the living cell are complex beyond the explanatory prowess of gradual evolution; they are 'irreducibly complex'. "As the number of systems that are resistant to gradualist explanation mounts, the need for the new kind of explanation grows more apparent. Cilia and flagella are far from the only problems for Darwinism".[181] In a more recent publication, despite severe scrutiny in the intervening years, Behe reiterates this sentiment:

> The structural elegance of systems such as the cilium, the functional sophistication of the pathways that construct them, and the total lack of serious Darwinian explanations all point insistently to the same conclusion: They are far past the edge of evolution. Such coherent, complex, cellular systems did not arise by random mutation and natural selection, any more than the Hoover Dam was built by the random accumulation of twigs, leaves, and mud.[182]

AN INTELLIGENT DESIGNER

Behe subsequently concludes that if gradual processes such as Darwinian evolution cannot account for the irreducible complexity of certain biological systems, then such biological systems must have arisen "quickly or even suddenly".[183] Furthermore, and most significantly from a theological perspective, it is implied that with such abrupt origin, these systems were purposefully designed:

> [T]he straightforward conclusion is that many biochemical systems were designed. They were designed not by the laws of nature, not by chance and necessity; rather, they were *planned*. . . . Life on Earth at its most fundamental level, in its most critical components, is the product of intelligent activity.[184]

The cardinal implication of irreducible complexity, then, is that such biological systems cannot have come into being without influence from a "directing intelligence".[185] A virtually synonymous interpretation is put forth by Dembski, who proclaims that "our best evidence points to the specified complexity (and therefore design) of the bacterial flagellum".[186] Behe's conceptual outlook of intelligent design has also gained support from significant figures such as philosopher Alvin Plantinga.[187]

The postulation of an intelligent designer bears striking parallels with the classic theological argument from design of William Paley, and thus has protruding theological overtones.[188]

Moreover, those who resort to intelligent design, as Dembski and Ruse highlight, are generally of a theistic persuasion (usually Christian).[189] Despite these points, and the fact the Behe himself unequivocally professes Catholicism,[190] Behe does not delve into the realm of theology, preferring to make evident the conceptual leap one must make from the inference of design to the identification of the designer. "The inference to design can be held with all the firmness that is possible in this world, without knowing anything about the designer".[191] Again, he insists that noting design in nature is devoid of theological connotations. "[I]f one wishes to be academically rigorous, one can't leap directly from design to a transcendent God. To reach a transcendent God, other, non-scientific arguments have to be made".[192]

CRITIQUE OF INTELLIGENT DESIGN

I.D. has been severely criticized by biologists such as Kenneth Miller. Miller asserts that certain complex biological systems such as those Behe highlighted are not irreducibly complex. He explains that although certain systems will not function unless all of its constituent parts operate in tandem, this does not necessarily imply irreducible complexity. Miller challenges Behe's conclusion that complexity infers abrupt origin, and consequently, design. He demonstrates his point by adopting Behe's mousetrap analogy:

> [A]re subsets of the five-part mouse trap useful (selectable) in different contexts? Considering the following examples from my personal use, I sometimes wear a tie clip consisting on just three parts (platform, spring and hammer) and use a key chain consisting of just two (platform and hammer). It is possible, in fact, to imagine a host of uses for the parts of the "irreducibly complex" mousetrap . . .[193]

Miller insightfully deconstructs the logic of Behe's mousetrap analogy, by explaining that although a complex system may not function without all of its working components, the individual components may have evolved to serve another, more primal purpose. Thus, the logic in inferring design from irreducible complexity is erroneous. The logical underpinning of Behe's argument for intelligent design is also vigorously criticized by Dawkins, who suggests that if a hypothesis (A) is insufficient at providing an explanation for a given phenomenon, it is illogical to then contend that another theory (B) is correct purely on the merit of the failings of hypothesis A. He labels this intellectual trapping 'arguing by default':

> It commits the logical error of arguing by default. Two rival theories, A and B, are set up. Theory A explains loads of facts and is supported by mountains of evidence. Theory B has no supporting evidence, nor is any attempt made to find any. Now a single little fact is discovered, which A allegedly can't explain. Without even asking whether B can explain it, the default conclusion is fallaciously drawn: B must be correct.[194]

To support the criticisms of Behe's logic, Dawkins then refers to Kenneth Miller's scientific refutation of Behe's intelligent design. "Incidentally, further research usually reveals that A can explain the phenomenon after all: thus the biologist Kenneth R. Miller beautifully showed how the bacterial flagellar motor could evolve via known functional intermediates".[195] Miller indicates that the perennial advancement of scientific knowledge has offered insight into explanations of alleged irreducible complexity, such as the flagellum:

The most powerful rebuttals to the flagellum story, however, have not come from direct attempts to answer the critics of evolution. Rather, they have emerged from the steady progress of scientific work on the genes and proteins associated with the flagellum and other cellular structures. Such studies have now established that the entire premise by which this molecular machine has been advanced as an argument against evolution is wrong—**the bacterial flagellum is not irreducibly complex.**[196]

Studies have established how alleged irreducibly complex biochemical systems are within the boundaries of the explanatory prowess of evolution—they have come about through the gradual, incremental process of natural selection.[197] Francisco Ayala presents a similar summary of the current scientific consensus:

> But evolutionists have pointed out, again and again, with supporting evidence, that organs and other components of living beings are not irreducibly complex—they do not come about suddenly, or in one fell swoop. Evolutionists have shown that the organs and systems claimed by intelligent design theorists to be irreducibly complex—such as . . . the bacterial flagellum—are not irreducible at all; rather, less complex variations of the same systems can be found in today's organisms.[198]

A significant, demonstrative indication of the failings of intelligent design can be derived from the ruling of the 2005 *Kitzmiller v. Dover* court case, at which both Miller and Behe gave testimonies.[199] The case sought the establishment of the legitimacy of intelligent design as a science to be taught in U.S. schools. In the case, the presiding judge unequivocally favored Miller's testimony. "Contrary to Professor Behe's assertions with respect to these few biochemical systems among the myriad existing in nature, Dr. Miller presented evidence, based upon peer-reviewed studies, that they are not in fact irreducibly complex".[200] In addition, Judge E. Jones III commented on the dismissive attitude of Behe, with regard to the evidence he was presented:

> Professor Behe was questioned concerning his 1996 claim that science would never find an evolutionary explanation for the immune system. He was presented with fifty-eight peer-reviewed publications, nine books and several immunology textbook chapters about the evolution of the immune system; however, he simply

insisted that this was still not sufficient evidence of evolution, and that it was not "good enough" . . .[201]

In addition to this court ruling, Behe's absence from academia despite the revolutionary character of his ideas is indicative that he is not held in high esteem among the scientific community, as Miller insinuates:

> You might think, given the revolutionary character of science, that people like . . . Behe would be peppering the scientific press with well-considered papers against evolution, that they'd be speaking at scientific meetings, and challenging the dominance of evolution on its own turf. They aren't, and neither are their colleagues. To many scientists, this alone speaks volumes.[202]

Both Dawkins and philosopher Daniel C. Dennett have also separately acknowledged Behe's unfavorable status among the scientific community. Dawkins strongly criticizes Behe's absence from the peer-review process to which scientific theories are usually subjected, by exclaiming that he "has bypassed the peer-review procedure altogether, gone over the heads of the scientists he once aspired to number among his peers, and appealed directly to a public that—as he and his publisher know—is not qualified to rumble him".[203] Dennett, similarly, insists that Behe's work has been exhaustively considered and subsequently denounced by the scientific community. "Behe's so-called scientific work has been carefully judged by the scientific community and thoroughly rejected".[204]

Conclusion

The overall goal of this project is to demonstrate how an ideological other, even one as hostile to theology as Dawkins, can in fact be a useful conversation partner in theology today. It will show how considering a worldview such as the scientific materialism Dawkins represents may offer a new point of view on theological discourse. To achieve this aim we have to explore Dawkins' own position, which is deeply grounded in his field of evolutionary science. In the dialogical setting of this book, which has an interdisciplinary dimension, we had to establish a rudimentary grasp of key aspects of Dawkins' science. This will equip us to appreciate where Dawkins comes from intellectually. Developing an appreciation of Dawkins' scientific background will thus allow a more fluid dialogue, and one that we can call 'informed'. Consequently, this chapter explored Dawkins' stance on evolution. Along with this exploration, we also indicated particular elements of his approach that have pertinent theological connotations.

However, consistent with the caveats of opening a dialogue with Dawkins, we also noted that Dawkins is a representative of a particular strain of evolutionary thought, and by no means speaks for the entirety of evolutionary scientists. While we noted Dawkins has authoritative supporters for his mode of Darwinian evolution, he also has his share of equally authoritative critics—Stephen Jay Gould being the most prominent example. Therefore, we incorporated particular criticisms of Dawkins' stance on evolution. Moreover, we also encountered three examples of theistic interpretations of evolution that run contrary to Dawkins' atheistic interpretation. However, we also put forth scientific and/or theological arguments against these theistic interpretations. This demonstrates that the decision to take Dawkins as the subject for a theological dialogue was carefully considered. To progress now into Chapter Three, we can recall that the scientific polemic between Dawkins and Gould may in fact be the result of philosophical differences. Therefore, Chapter Three will explore how Dawkins stretches his scientific understanding into an ideology—one that enters into realms in which theology has traditionally had vested interests. It will present Dawkins' evolutionary *weltanschauung*.

Notes

1. *ROOE*, 14.

2. Richard Dawkins, *The Ancestor's Tale: A Pilgrimage to the Dawn of Life* (London: Weidenfeld & Nicolson, 2004), 156.

3. James Watson, *DNA: The Secret of Life* (London: Heinemann, 2003), 35 and 53–54. Watson traces the idea of genes being regarded of as information to the Austrian physicist Erwin Schrödinger's influential work *What Is Life?*, which, at the risk of being parochial, was based upon a series of lectures at Trinity College, Dublin, in 1940.

4. For examples, see geneticists Kenneth M. Weiss and Anne V. Buchanan, *Genetics and the Logic of Evolution* (Hoboken, NJ: John Wiley & Sons, 2004), ix, zoologist Mark Ridley, *Genome: The Autobiography of a Species in 23 Chapters* (London: Fourth Estate, 1999), 11, and acclaimed palaeontologist Richard Fortey, *Life: An Unauthorised Biography, A Natural History of the First Four Thousand Million Years of Life on Earth* (London: HarperCollins, 1997), 39.

5. Kenneth Weiss and Anne V. Buchanan recognise this oversimplification, though suggest that it is an appropriate way to understand genes, *Genetics and the Logic of Evolution*, 69.

6. *ROOE*, 2.

7. Ibid., 5–9.

8. Ibid., 166–68.

9. However, the conviction that life is a unique phenomenon is not an inexorable belief safeguarded within the stronghold of scientific certainty. Renowned physicist Paul Davies has suggested that life may be polyphyletic, that it originated more than once. Davies does note that there is no evidence to support such a claim, but he explores the possibility of what he labels 'Strange Life', i.e., life that perhaps does not function with the same chemical components. Paul

Davies, *The Eerie Silence: Are We Alone in the Universe?* (London: Penguin, 2010). Moreover, molecular biologist Craig J. Venter and his team in 2010, created a synthetic living cell, which can be seen as a living thing of a different genetic lineage than all other life, as it was created in a laboratory. Results of this experiment were published in Daniel G. Gibson et al., 'Creation of a Bacterial Cell Controlled by a Chemically Synthesized Genome', *Science* 329, no. 5987 (July 2010): 52–56.

10. *TGSOE*, 315.

11. Matt Ridley, *The Problems of Evolution* (Oxford: Oxford University Press, 1985), 10.

12. Richard Dawkins, *Unweaving the Rainbow: Science, Delusion and the Appetite for Wonder* (London: Penguin, 1998), 193.

13. 'Neo-Darwinian synthesis' can be described as the amalgamation of genetics with Darwin's theory of evolution by natural selection. Distinguished philosopher of biology Michael Ruse comprises a summary of neo-Darwinism in *Charles Darwin* (Oxford: Blackwell, 2008), 75–98.

14. Richard Dawkins, ed., *The Oxford Book of Modern Science Writing* (Oxford: Oxford University Press, 2008), 18.

15. R. A. Fisher, *The Genetical Theory of Natural Selection* (Oxford: Oxford University Press, 1958), 70.

16. Dawkins, ed., *The Oxford Book of Modern Science Writing*, 22.

17. Franciso J. Ayala, 'Theodosius Dobzhansky: The Man and the Scientist', *Annual Review of Genetics* 10 (1976): 6.

18. Theodosius Dobzhansky, *Genetics of the Evolutionary Process* (New York: Columbia University Press, 1970), 230.

19. Richard Dawkins, *The Blind Watchmaker: Why the Evidence of Evolution Reveals a Universe Without Design* (London: Penguin, 1986), 43.

20. Richard Dawkins, *A Devil's Chaplain: Selected Essays* (London: Weidenfeld & Nicolson, 2003), 95.

21. *TGD*, 54.

22. Ibid., 37.

23. Dawkins, ed., *The Oxford Book of Modern Science Writing*, 259.

24. Ernst Mayr, *Evolution and the Diversity of Life: Selected Essays* (Cambridge, MA: Harvard University Press, 1976), 9–10.

25. Ibid., 10.

26. Ernst Mayr, *What Evolution Is* (London: Phoenix, 2001), 132.

27. Richard Dawkins, *Climbing Mount Improbable* (London: Penguin, 1996), 71. To ensure that this quote is not taken out of context, the text continues, ". . . although these senses aren't relevant to our discussion". It does not weaken the point we wish to make: that evolution is not a strict rule-abiding process.

28. *TSG*, 34.

29. *ROOE*, 27–29.

30. Alister McGrath, *Dawkins' God: Genes, Memes and the Meaning of Life* (Oxford: Blackwell, 2005), 37.

31. Ibid., 37.

32. Alister McGrath, *A Fine-Tuned Universe: The Quest for God in Science and Theology* (Louisville: Westminster John Knox, 2009), 169.

33. *TGSOE*, 242.

34. *ROOE*, 25.

35. *TGSOE*, 213.

36. *ROOE*, 27–29.

37. *TGSOE*, 242.

38. Ibid., 242.

39. *ROOE*, 5.

40. The phenotype is the object influenced by genes, most commonly the organism. Dawkins also considers that the phenotype may also include external subjects that genes indirectly influence. He gives the example of an area flooded by a beaver's dam, in which case the lake and dam can be considered as phenotypic effects of the beaver's genes. Richard Dawkins, *The Extended Phenotype: The Long Reach of the Gene* (New York: Oxford University Press, 1982), 200.

41. *ROOE*, 3. It should be noted that the use of 'bad' and 'good' in this context relates to the positive or negative influence genes have on contributing to the production of organisms capable of producing offspring.

42. *TGSOE*, 248.

43. *TSG*, 17.

44. *ROOE*, 23

45. McGrath, *Dawkins' God: Genes, Memes and the Meaning of Life*, 36.

46. *TSG*, 17.

47. Dawkins suggests that in the instances where a mutation has an indifferent effect on the organism's ability to copulate, it may be hidden from natural selection. Dawkins, *A Devil's Chaplain: Selected Essays*, 95.

48. John Maynard Smith, *On Evolution* (Edinburgh: Edinburgh University Press, 1972), 83–84.

49. *TGSOE*, 248–49.

50. Dawkins, *A Devil's Chaplain: Selected Essays*, 120.

51. Ibid., 120.

52. *TSG*, 36.

53. Ibid., 11.

54. McGrath, *Dawkins' God: Genes, Memes and the Meaning of Life*, 35.

55. *TSG*, 88.

56. Mary Midgley, 'Gene-Juggling', *Philosophy* 54, no. 210 (Oct. 1979): 439–58.

57. McGrath, *Dawkins' God: Genes, Memes and the Meaning of Life*, 42.

58. Richard Dawkins, 'In Defence of Selfish Genes', *Philosophy* 56, no. 218 (Oct. 1981): 557.

59. *ROOE*, 7.

60. H. Allen Orr, 'A Mission to Convert', *The New York Review of Books* 54, no. 1 (Jan. 2007).

61. For examples, see Ernst Mayr, *Systematics and the Origin of Species from the Vewpoint of a Zoologist* (Cambridge, MA: Harvard University Press, 1999), xiv–xxii; also Ulf Dieckmann et al., eds., *Adaptive Selection* (Cambridge: Cambridge University Press, 2004), 380–81; also Jan Klien and Naoyuki Takahata, *Where Do We Come From? The Molecular Evidence for Human Descent* (Berlin: Springer, 2002), 74.

62. Jerry Coyne and H. Allen Orr, *Speciation* (Sunderland, MA: Sinauer Associates, 2004), 1–3.

63. Dawkins, *The Blind Watchmaker: Why the Evidence of Evolution Reveals a Universe Without Design*, 238. Dawkins uses shrews as an example here. A group of shrews migrate to one side of the mountain range, where they flourish and give rise to an outlying population.

64. Dawkins, *Unweaving the Rainbow: Science, Delusion and the Appetite for Wonder*, 200.

65. *ROOE*, 7. Dawkins spells 'gray' in text.

66. Richard Dawkins, *The Ancestor's Tale: A Pilgrimage to the Dawn of Life*, 354.

67. For example, French biologist Jean-Baptiste de Panafieu, *Evolution [In Action]* (London: Thames & Hudson, 2007), 70.

68. Ernst Mayr, *One Long Argument: Charles Darwin and the Genesis of Modern Evolutionary Thought* (London: Penguin, 1992), 28.

69. Stephen Jay Gould, *The Panda's Thumb* (New York: Penguin, 1980), 172.

70. John Maynard Smith, *Evolutionary Genetics* (Oxford: Oxford University Press, 1989), 274.

71. *ROOE*, 160. 'The gathering explosion' refers to the ongoing evolution of life.

72. Ibid., 161.

73. Ibid., 166.

74. Dawkins, *The Blind Watchmaker: Why the Evidence of Evolution Reveals a Universe Without Design*, 148.

75. Ibid.

76. *TSG*, 13.

77. Ibid., 15.

78. *ROOE*, 159–60.

79. Stephen Jay Gould, *Wonderful Life: The Burgess Shale and the Nature of History*, 309. From Gould's statement here, we are also informed of an approximate timeline; life began approximately 3.5 billion years ago.

80. Dobzhansky, *Genetics of the Evolutionary Process*, 8.

81. *TSG*, 14.

82. Dawkins, *The Blind Watchmaker: Why the Evidence of Evolution Reveals a Universe Without Design*, 147.

83. Ibid., 147.

84. John Maynard Smith, *Evolution Now: A Century After Darwin* (London: Macmillan, 1982), 10.

85. Keith Muscott, 'The Selfish Genius: How Richard Dawkins Rewrote Darwin's Legacy', *Biologist* 57, no. 1 (Feb. 2010): 59.

86. Fern Elsdon-Baker, 'The Dawkins Dogma,' *New Scientist* 203, no. 2717 (July 2009): 25.

87. Fern Elsdon-Baker, *The Selfish Genius: How Richard Dawkins Rewrote Darwin's Legacy* (London: Icon Books, 2009), 20.

88. Elsdon-Baker, 'The Dawkins Dogma', 25.

89. Ibid., 25.

90. Elsdon-Baker, *The Selfish Genius: How Richard Dawkins Rewrote Darwin's Legacy*, 103.

91. Ibid., 119–21.

92. Ibid., 133–35.

93. Graham Lawton, 'Axing Darwin's Tree', *New Scientist* 201, no. 2692 (Jan. 2009): 34–39.

94. Ibid., 34.

95. Elliott Sober, 'Two Outbreaks of Lawlessness in Recent Philosophy of Biology', in Elliott Sober, ed., *Conceptual Issues in Evolutionary Biology*, 3rd ed. (Cambridge, MA: MIT Press, 2006), 250.

96. John H. Beatty, 'The Evolutionary Contingency Thesis', in Sober, ed., *Conceptual Issues in Evolutionary Biology*, 217–47

97. Richard Dawkins, 'Obscurantism to the Rescue', *The Quarterly Review of Biology* 72, no. 4 (Dec. 1997): 397–99.

98. Elsdon-Baker, *The Selfish Genius: How Richard Dawkins Rewrote Darwin's Legacy*, 8.

99. Kim Sterelny, *Dawkins vs. Gould: Survival of the Fittest* (Cambridge: Icon Books, 2007), 3.

100. For examples, see Ed Sexton, 'Dawkins and the Selfish Gene', in Richard Appignanesi, ed., *Postmodernism and Big Science: Einstein Dawkins Kuhn Hawking Darwin* (Cambridge: Icon Books, 2002), 170; also, Kim Sterelny, *Dawkins vs. Gould: Survival of the Fittest*, 7–14; also, Elsdon-Baker, *The Selfish Genius: How Richard Dawkins Rewrote Darwin's Legacy*, 128–29.

101. Sexton, 'Dawkins and the Selfish Gene', 170.

102. Gould, *The Panda's Thumb*, 76.

103. Stephen Jay Gould and Elisabeth A. Lloyd, 'Individuality and Adaptation across Levels of Selection: How Shall We Name and Generalize the Unit of Darwinism?', *Proceedings of the Natural Academy of Sciences of the United States of America* 96, no. 21 (Oct. 1999): 11904.

104. Mayr, *Evolution and the Diversity of Life: Selected Essays*, 13.

105. Dawkins, *Unweaving the Rainbow: Science, Delusion and the Appetite for Wonder*, 216–17.

106. *TSG*, 136.

107. George C. Williams, *Adaption and Natural Selection: A Critique of Some Current Evolutionary Thought* (Princeton: Princeton University Press, 1966), 23.

108. Stephen Jay Gould, *The Structure of Evolutionary Theory* (Cambridge, MA: Harvard University Press, 2002), 620–21.

109. Stephen Jay Gould, 'Darwinism and the Expansion of Evolutionary Theory', *Science* 216, no. 4544 (Apr. 1982).

110. Mayr, *One Long Argument: Charles Darwin and the Genesis of Modern Evolutionary Thought*, 144.

111. Ridley, *The Problems of Evolution*, 45.

112. Gould, *The Structure of Evolutionary Theory*, 614.

113. Ibid., 632.

114. Gould, *The Panda's Thumb*, 72.

115. Gould, *The Structure of Evolutionary Theory*, 632.

116. Ibid., 616.

117. *TSG*, 36.

118. Ibid., 50.

119. Gould, *The Structure of Evolutionary Theory*, 618.

120. Ibid.

121. Ibid., 620.

122. Ibid., 627.

123. *ROOE*, 3.

124. Dawkins, *Unweaving the Rainbow*, 192.

125. Gould, *The Structure of Evolutionary Theory*, 627.

126. Mayr, *What Evolution Is*, xiv.

127. Stephen Jay Gould and Niles Eldredge, 'Punctuated Equilibria: The Tempo and Mode of Evolution Reconsidered', *Paleobiology* 3, no. 2 (Spring 1977), 115.

128. Robert T. Bakker, *The Dinosaur Heresies: A Revolutionary View of Dinosaurs* (Harlow, Essex: Longman, 1986), 397.

129. Dawkins, *The Blind Watchmaker: Why the Evidence of Evolution Reveals a Universe Without Design*, 250.

130. Stephen Jay Gould, *The Richness of Life: The Essential Stephen Jay Gould*, in Paul McGarr and Steven Rose, eds. (London: Jonathan Cape, 2006), 266.

131. Gould, *The Structure of Evolutionary Theory*, 613.

132. Gould, *The Panda's Thumb*, 77.

133. Dawkins, *The Blind Watchmaker: Why the Evidence of Evolution Reveals a Universe Without Design*, 13.

134. Gould, *The Panda's Thumb*, 77–78.

135. Dobzhansky, *Genetics of the Evolutionary Process*, 4.

136. *DDI*, 266.

137. Dawkins, *A Devil's Chaplain: Selected Essays*, 256.

138. Dawkins, *Unweaving the Rainbow: Science, Delusion and the Appetite for Wonder*, 207–8.

139. Gould, *The Structure of Evolutionary Theory*, 617.

140. Dawkins, *A Devil's Chaplain: Selected Essays*, 256–61.

141. Dawkins, *The Blind Watchmaker: Why the Evidence of Evolution Reveals a Universe Without Design*, 13.

142. This refers to the 'uncertainty principle', developed by seminal physicist Werner Heisenberg. For examples of discussion, see physicist/theologian John Polkinghorne, *The Quantum World* (London: Longman, 1984), 2–3; also, physicist Alastair Rae, *Quantum Physics: Illusion or Reality?* (Cambridge: Cambridge University Press, 1986), 11–13.

143. Keith Ward, *The Big Questions in Science and Religion* (Philadelphia: Templeton Foundation, 2008), 267.

144. For example, many theologians have suggested that the chasms in the causal chain of the physical world may allow God to intervene in the physical world. For examples of such discourse, see John Polkinghorne, *One World: The Interaction of Science and Theology* (London: Templeton Foundation, 1986), 84; Murphy and Ellis, *On the Moral Nature of the Universe*, 246; Ward, *The Big Questions in Science and Religion*, 244–71; and Ian G. Barbour, *When Science Meets Religion: Enemies, Strangers or Partners?* (New York: HarperCollins, 2000), 65–89, among others.

145. Francis Collins was the director of the Human Genome Project, which successfully mapped the 20–25,000 (approx.) genes in the human genome. He has also been an outspoken proponent of seeking harmony between religion and science. See David Van Brema, 'Reconciling God and Science', *Time*, 10 July 2006; also interview with *Newsweek*, 27 Dec. 2010 .

146. Karl W. Giberson and Francis S. Collins, *The Language of Science and Faith: Straight Answers to Genuine Questions* (Downers Grove, IL: IVP, 2011), 119.

147. Paul Davies, 'The Quantum Life', *Physicsworld* 22, no. 7 (July 2009): 26.

148. Johnjoe McFadden, *Quantum Evolution* (London: HarperCollins, 2000): 66.

149. Kenneth R. Miller, *Finding Darwin's God: A Scientist's Search for the Common Ground Between God and Evolution* (New York: HarperCollins, 1999), 207.

150. Ibid., 214.

151. Stephen Hawking and Leonard Mlodinow, *The Grand Design: New Answers to the Ultimate Questions of Life* (New York: Bantam, 2010), 8.

152. Ibid., 180. These statements by Hawking provoked substantial reaction from the media; for example, the UK *Times* published a front-page piece by Hannah Devlin, titled 'Hawking: God Did Not Create the Universe', *The Times* (UK), 2 Sept. 2010. Hawking has also been criticised for the atheistic sentiment of his book by Paul Davies, 'Stephen Hawking's Big Bang Gaps', *The Guardian*, 4 Sept. 2010.

153. Hawking and Mlodinow, *The Grand Design: New Answers to the Ultimate Questions of Life*, 116–19.

154. Ibid., 181.

155. Ian Stewart, *Does God Play Dice? The New Mathematics of Chaos* (London: Penguin, 1989), 329–30.

156. Barbour, *When Science Meets Religion: Enemies, Strangers, or Partners?*, 64.

157. George V. Coyne S.J. and Alessandro Omizzolo, *Wayfarers in the Cosmos: The Human Quest for Meaning* (New York: Crossroad, 2002), 158.

158. Simon Conway Morris, 'A Response to Richard Sturch', *Science and Christian Belief* 19, no. 7 (Apr. 2007): 85–86.

159. Simon Conway Morris, *The Crucible of Creation: The Burgess Shale and the Rise of Animals* (Oxford: Oxford University Press, 1998), 202.

160. Simon Conway Morris, 'Evolution and Convergence', in Simon Conway Morris, ed., *The Deep Structure of Biology: Is Convergence Sufficiently Ubiquitous to Give a Directional Signal?* (Philadelphia: Templeton Foundation, 2008), 46.

161. Ibid., 46.

162. Simon Conway Morris, *Life's Solution: Inevitable Humans in a Lonely Universe* (Cambridge: Cambridge University Press, 2003), xv.

163. Conway Morris, 'Evolution and Convergence', 46.

164. Conway Morris, *Life's Solution: Inevitable Humans in a Lonely Universe*, 151–70.

165. Ibid., xii.

166. Conway Morris, 'Evolution and Convergence', 60.

167. Conway Morris, *Life's Solution: Inevitable Humans in a Lonely Universe*, 330.

168. John Polkinghorne, 'Rich Reality: A Response to the Boyle Lecture by Simon Conway Morris', *Science and Christian Belief* 18, no. 1 (Apr. 2006): 32.

169. Barbour, *When Science Meets Religion: Enemies, Strangers, or Partners?*, 63.

170. William A. Dembski and Michael Ruse, 'General Introduction', in William A. Dembski and Michael Ruse, eds., *Debating Design: From Darwin to DNA* (Cambridge: Cambridge University Press, 2004), 3.

171. For example, Henry Morris, *The Remarkable Birth of Planet Earth* (San Diego: Creation Life, 1972) and *Scientific Creationism* (San Diego: Creation Life, 1972).

172. The wealth of scientific evidence for evolution is so voluminous that we need not digress into an attempt to establish its legitimacy. For such an attempt, in the context of this book, see Dawkins' *The Greatest Show on Earth: The Evidence for Evolution*. Theologically, a literal reading of the Genesis cosmogony has been eschewed since Augustine, who feared that a literal reading of Genesis would severely damage the credibility of Christianity: "Now it is a disgraceful and dangerous thing for an infidel to hear a Christian, presumably giving the meaning of Holy Scripture, talking nonsense on these topics; and we should take all means to prevent such an embarrassing situation, in which people show up vast ignorance in a Christian and laugh it to scorn". St. Augustine, *On the Literal Meaning of Genesis Vol. 1*, trans. John Hammond Taylor S.J. (Mahwah, NJ: Paulist, 1982), 43.

173. The Department of Biological Sciences at Leigh University, Pennsylvania, where Behe is a faculty member, states that: "The department faculty . . . are unequivocal in their support of evolutionary theory, which has its roots in the seminal work of Charles Darwin and has been supported by findings accumulated over 140 years. The sole dissenter from this position, Prof. Michael Behe, is a well-known proponent of 'intelligent design.' While we respect Prof. Behe's right to express his views, they are his alone and are in no way endorsed by the department. It is our collective position that intelligent design has no basis in science, has not been tested experimentally, and should not be regarded as scientific." Taken from homepage of the Department of Biological Sciences, at the website of Leigh University. http://www.lehigh.edu/~inbios/news/evolution.htm (19 July 2011). Behe is also considered one of the leading proponents of intelligent design by several authors, for example, Francisco J. Ayala, *Darwin and Intelligent Design* (Minneapolis: Fortress Press, 2006), 71; and Miller, *Finding Darwin's God: A Scientist's Search for the Common Ground Between God and Evolution*, 130.

174. Michael J. Behe, 'A Catholic Scientist Looks at Darwinism', in William A. Dembski, ed., *Uncommon Dissent: Intellectuals Who Find Darwinism Unconvincing* (Wilmington, DE: ISI Books, 2004), 135.

175. Michael J. Behe, *Darwin's Black Box: The Biochemical Challenge to Evolution* (New York: Free Press, 1996), 39.

176. Michael J. Behe, 'Irreducible Complexity: Obstacle to Darwinian Evolution', in Dembski and Ruse, eds., *Debating Design: From Darwin to DNA*, 353.

177. Charles Darwin, *On the Origin of Species*, 158 (also quoted in ibid., 353).

178. Behe, *Darwin's Black Box: The Biochemical Challenge to Evolution*, 160.

179. Specifically, 'Part II: Examining the Contents of the Box', 51–161.

180. Kenneth Miller, 'The Flagellum Unspun: The Collapse of "Irreducible Complexity"', in Dembski and Ruse, eds., *Debating Design: From Darwin to DNA*, 81.

181. Behe, *Darwin's Black Box: The Biochemical Challenge to Evolution*, 73.

182. Michael J. Behe, *The Edge of Evolution: The Search for the Limits of Darwinism* (New York: Free Press, 2007), 102.

183. Behe, *Darwin's Black Box: The Biochemical Challenge to Evolution*, 187.

184. Ibid., 193.

185. Behe, *The Edge of Evolution: The Search for the Limits of Darwinism*, 217.

186. William A. Dembski, 'The Logical Underpinnings of Intelligent Design', in Dembski and Ruse, eds., *Debating Design: From Darwin to DNA*, 326.

187. Daniel C. Dennett and Alvin Plantinga, *Science and Religion: Are They Compatible?* (Oxford: Oxford University Press, 2011), 42.

188. In his *Natural Theology*, originally published in 1802, Paley was attempting to prove beyond a reasonable doubt that the world must have had a designer. Consequently, he would make religion more rational. His infamous analogy reads as follows: "In crossing a heath, suppose I pitched my foot against a *stone* and were asked how the stone came to be there, I might possibly answer that for anything I knew to the contrary it had lain there forever; nor would it, perhaps, be very easy to show the absurdity of this answer. But suppose I had found a *watch* upon the ground, and it should be inquired how the watch happened to be in that place, I should hardly think of the answer which I had before given, that for anything I knew the watch might have always been there." Essentially, Paley uses the analogy of a watch to postulate that, given the remarkable degree of complexity found in many things in the natural world, including humans, it would be irrational to consider that they had not been designed. William Paley, *Natural Theology* (Oxford: Oxford University Press, 2006), 7.

189. William A. Dembski and Michael Ruse, 'General Introduction', in Dembski and Ruse, eds., *Debating Design: From Darwin to DNA*, 3.

190. Michael J. Behe, *The Edge of Evolution: The Search for the Limits of Darwinism*, 228.

191. Michael J. Behe, *Darwin's Black Box: The Biochemical Challenge to Evolution*, 197.

192. Michael J. Behe, *The Edge of Evolution: The Search for the Limits of Darwinism*, 229.

193. Kenneth Miller, 'Answering the Biochemical Argument from Design', in Mary Kathleen Cunningham, ed., *God and Evolution: A Reader* (London: Routledge, 2007), 170–71. A further substantial critique of Behe can be found in Miller's *Finding Darwin's God: A Scientist's Search for the Common Ground Between God and Evolution*, 130–64. Further unfavourable reviews of Behe's *The Edge of Evolution: The Search for the Limits of Darwinism* can be found in Miller's 'Falling over the Edge', *Nature* 447, no. 28 (June 2007), and 'Faulty Design', *Commonweal* 134, no. 17 (Oct. 2007). Behe replies to the latter of these reviews, although focused solely on the theological aspects of Miller's review. Miller in turn replied, "My substantive criticisms, however, which he does not challenge, center on the scientific errors and misstatements in his book. These mistakes would render the work hopeless, even if it had theological merit (which it does not)". 'Letting God Off the Hook? Reviewer Replies', *Commonweal* 134, no. 20 (Nov. 2007).

194. Richard Dawkins, 'Inferior Design', *The New York Times*, 1 July 2007.

195. Ibid.; Dawkins also labeled Kenneth Miller a 'godsend' for his critique of intelligent design. Richard Dawkins, 'An Atheist's Call to Arms', TED lecture (Feb. 2002).

196. Kenneth Miller, 'The Flagellum Unspun: The Collapse of "Irreducible Complexity"', in Dembski and Ruse, eds., *Debating Design: From Darwin to DNA*, 81. Bold in original.

197. See ibid. for examples of such technical studies.

198. Ayala, *Darwin and Intelligent Design*, 78.

199. In December 2004, eleven parents in the Dover school district, Pennsylvania, USA, filed a lawsuit claiming that the Dover Board of Education had used government power to seek the teaching of intelligent design in public schools. The case was called to order on September 25, 2005, presided over by Judge E. Jones III. Kenneth Miller, 'Darwin, God and Dover', in Harold W. Attridge, ed., *The Religion and Science Debate: Why Does It Continue?* (New Haven: Yale University Press, 2009), 60–61. See also, Kenneth Miller, 'Of Darwin, Dover and (un)intelligent design, *Church and State* 62, no. 2 (Feb. 2009). This was a highly significant case in that it involved the U.S. Federal Court, although there have been many others in the United States. The teaching of intelligent design was such a contentious topic that George W. Bush (then U.S. President) felt the need to publicly address the situation; see Kenneth Miller, *Only a Theory: Evolution and the Battle for America's Soul* (New York: Penguin, 2008), 7; also Claudia Wallis, 'The Evolution Wars', *Time*, 2 Aug. 2005.

200. Quoted in Kenneth Miller, 'Darwin, God and Dover', in Attridge, ed., *The Religion and Science Debate: Why Does It Continue?*, 74.

201. Ibid., 76.

202. Miller, *Finding Darwin's God: A Scientist's Search for the Common Ground Between God and Evolution*, 163.

203. Dawkins, 'Inferior Design'.

204. Dennett and Plantinga, *Science and Religion: Are They Compatible?*, 32–33.

3

Beyond Biology
An Evolutionary Weltanschauung

INTRODUCTION

The German term '*weltanschauung*', meaning a conceptual understanding of the world from a particular perspective, aptly describes what this chapter will establish: a philosophy extrapolated from the evolutionary science presented in Chapter Two. In our review of Dawkins' scientific position, we discovered that his view on evolution was significantly hermeneutical. Polemical divergences between Dawkins and Gould on aspects of evolution had profoundly philosophical connotations. This realization adds weight to the view asserted by Ricoeur, Küng, and others, that science can be influenced by ideology. As Ricoeur suggested, the world is accessed through a detour of interpretation.[1] This chapter will therefore explore the philosophical dimension of Dawkins' interpretation of evolutionary science. The theological implications for this philosophical approach will open direct passages for interdisciplinary engagement between theology and evolutionary science as it is presented by Dawkins.

In researching this work, correspondence was sought and received from the American philosopher Daniel C. Dennett (see appendix), who has been identified as a 'staunch ally' of Dawkins (I have as of yet been unable to contact Prof. Dawkins himself).[2] There is very little that separates the two thinkers in terms of their conceptual approach to philosophy, science, and theology. When I put the question to Dennett whether he disagrees with any aspects of Dawkins' perspective on evolution, he responded as follows: "On some technical details I don't feel qualified to disagree publicly even when I have my doubts. We discuss these issues, as yet unresolved. I haven't seen anything beyond a few rash overstatements to disavow in his work".[3] Moreover, Dawkins and Dennett have publicly endorsed each other on several occasions.[4] As such, Dennett can also be taken as a representative of the school of thought Dawkins espouses. Consequently, given the similarities between Dawkins and Dennett, this work will also feature Dennett's philosophy of evolution prominently throughout, while maintaining its primary focus on Dawkins.

Given that this work is advocating a theological paradigm that seeks to engage with antagonistic worldviews, I thought that the nature of theology itself should be an element of this dialogue. To illustrate, I questioned Dennett on his views on the illegitimacy of theology (a view he shares with Dawkins). I suggested that given the importance of religion in human history, theological ideas need to be studied and understood, therefore highlighting one element of the importance of theology that may be acknowledged even from an atheist perspective. Dennett responded as follows:

> I am sure that theology can be studied objectively as a complex and fascinating set of intellectual systems, but I don't think that inquiry would count as theology, since it would be 100% uncommitted to any of the doctrines. It would be a kind of anthropology, or like the sociology of science (an intermittently useful field plagued by lots of silly misunderstanding), or like literary criticism, I suppose. Dickens experts have a scholarly love of all his fictional characters, and a Christianity expert should have the same informed (and respectful) acquaintance with the many characters, saints, stories, liturgies . . . of the denominations. That is not theology, methinks, but it is what theology could become, if divorced from apologetics and sectarian loyalties.[5]

Therefore, Dennett accepts that theology could be an objective discipline, though he feels that this would not count as theology—however, we should not leave him as the arbiter of what constitutes theology. If one were to adopt a theology that is, as Dennett says, divorced from specific religious doctrines, then it would seem from this correspondence, that Dennett would be open to the possibility of a dialogue with such a theology. I do not necessarily seek to propose such a theology. However, it will be suggested in Chapter Five that certain aspects of the ongoing dialogue between theology and evolutionary science may be too narrowly Christian in the context of a dialogue with Dawkins. A similar point was stressed by Karl Rahner in *Theological Investigations*, as he noted that an engagement with atheism ". . . would have to be addressed to human beings in all their dimensions and in the way that they are today . . . a shift of emphasis in our proclamation is absolutely indispensable".[6] This cautionary approach to Christian themes may be substantiated by referral to the above correspondence with Dennett. However, there could be objections to this approach, following the thought of Émile Durkheim, who suggested that "[h]e who does not bring to the study of religion a sort of religious sentiment cannot speak about it. He is like a blind man trying to talk about color".[7] More immediately, Dennett will feature prominently in this chapter; for him, Darwinism is as relevant for philosophy as it is for science. He proposes that evolution has "far-reaching implications for our vision of what the meaning of life is or could be".[8] His emphasis on the pertinence of evolution for philosophy, coupled with his intellectual allegiance with Dawkins, makes him a conspicuous choice for inclusion within this study. In addition, Dawkins' own forays into philosophy and theology, intentional or not, allow us to consider his own philosophical perspectives.

THE EVOLUTION OF CONSCIOUSNESS

In Chapter Two, we followed Dawkins through his evolutionary explanation of all life, from its primordial origins through to its current manifestations, presented in terms of his interpretation of evolutionary science. However, his methodical quest for a holistic picture of the evolution of life runs into difficulty when the issue of consciousness arises. Dawkins articulates that the issue of how consciousness evolved is, in his view, the most profound mystery in modern biology.[9] Although Dawkins suggests that the ability to simulate events in the brain is explicable given that it would undoubtedly offer an evolutionary advantage over those who can only learn through trial and error, it is difficult to envisage how subjective consciousness itself offers selective advantage.[10] He admits his deficiency in the philosophical prowess necessary to engage in the study of consciousness, and consequently, we must move from Dawkins' biology and enter the philosophical domain.[11] Dennett, as a philosopher, has held the issue of consciousness to the forefront of his academic endeavours for the majority of his career, since his first book *Content and Consciousness*, published in 1969. This section will offer an appraisal of the materialist view of consciousness, and rely significantly on Dennett, who presents a Darwinian explanation of the phenomenon—though as we have noted in Chapter Two, the term 'Darwinism' is problematic, as there are different interpretations evident in the Dawkins-Gould polemic. Dennett agrees with Dawkins' approach, though he is highly critical of Gould's.[12] For Dennett, examining the issue of consciousness necessitates an inherently interdisciplinary methodology, consisting of several scientific fields in addition to advances in the philosophy of mind.[13] Seeking to disavow the apparent partisanship in academia, Dennett's theory of consciousness is an attempt to juxtapose common mental observations and feelings onto the modern discoveries of cybernetics, neurophysiology, biology, and other scientific arenas.[14]

AN EVOLUTIONARY PHILOSOPHY OF CONSCIOUSNESS

As an advocate of materialism, Dawkins interprets consciousness as another aspect of biological evolution. He sees no reason to demarcate between the physical and the mental, which is the basis for philosophical dualism. Philosophical dualism, such as is attributed to René Descartes, supposes the self or the mind to be separate from the body; there is a distinction between the mental and the physical. Dawkins is explicit in his disapproval of dualism: ". . . I am not a dualist".[15] Dennett similarly challenges the logical basis for distinguishing between the mental and the physical, which underpins the dualist approach. This philosophy has, according to Dennett, become entrenched in our ways of speaking, and hence, thinking, pervading much discourse on subjects relating to consciousness and mind.[16] For dualists, there exists what Dennett labels 'mind stuff', separate from the brain, where imagined subjects are manifest.[17] In essence, dualism proposes that thoughts are immaterial. Descartes postulated a specific area as the foci of brain activity where immaterial consciousness exists: the pineal gland of the physical brain.[18] Dennett labels this the 'Cartesian Theatre', though he categorically rejects the concept: "[I]t is not the 'place where it all comes together' for consciousness, nor does any other place fit this description. . . . There is no Cartesian theatre in the brain. This is a fact".[19]

The fatal flaw of dualism, in Dennett's view, is the concept of nonphysical 'mind stuff' maintaining an influence on the physical body—which the nonphysical 'mind-stuff' must do in order to influence the movement of the body. "This confrontation between quite standard physics and dualism has been endlessly discussed since Descartes' own day, and is widely regarded as the inescapable and fatal flaw of dualism".[20] If thoughts are in fact immaterial, then they could not influence the material body. Here, Dennett's repudiation of dualism is indicative of his position that nothing exists beyond the physical. He espouses a materialistic model, akin to one that Dawkins is taken to represent in the context of this book. In Dennett's view, there is no nonphysical element of which mind is comprised; it is intrinsically physical: "The prevailing wisdom, variously expressed and argued for, is materialism: there is only one sort of stuff, namely matter—the physical stuff of physics, chemistry, and physiology—and the mind is somehow nothing but a physical phenomenon. In short, the mind is the brain".[21] Dennett's materialist perspective can also be confirmed from personal correspondence (see appendix).

Consistent with Dawkins' materialism, Dennett asserts that mental events are in essence physiological; to distinguish between physical events and mental events is fallacious, even though it has been ingrained in our psyche to make such distinctions. Dennett speculates then, that if conscious events are inherently physiological, they are locatable physical events in the brain. "Conscious experiences are real events occurring in the real time and space of the brain, and hence they are clockable and locatable within the appropriate limits of precision for real phenomena of their type".[22] Conscious thought can, in principle, be located and studied, in the same way kidney functions can be. The materialistic perspective of consciousness then, takes 'mind' and 'brain' as synonymous terms; mind is how we experience physical operations within the brain. If true, then in principle, a physical object could be produced to emulate the physical process of the brain in the same way dialysis machines can be produced to emulate the physical processes of a human kidney. This realization leads Dennett to the conviction that artificial intelligence (A.I.) is a legitimate possibility.[23]

Dawkins' renunciation of dualism, shared by others[24], leads him to suggest an alternative model of consciousness. The model of consciousness he proposes is analogous to parallel computer processing, yet he points to Dennett for a more detailed discussion.[25] Dennett defines this alternative model of consciousness as a 'multiple drafts model'. In this model, various brain operations function simultaneously in parallel; multiple inputs are registered and interpreted by the conscious brain:

> According to the multiple drafts model, all varieties of perception—indeed, all varieties of thought or mental activity—are accomplished in the brain by parallel, multitrack processes of interpretation and elaboration of sensory inputs. Information entering the nervous system is under continuous "editorial revision".[26]

In Dennett's view, the brain does not function through a simple input-interpretation model. He proposes a more complex system of multiple sensory inputs (vision, smell, taste, touch, and hearing) and constant parallel interpretation. Our experience of sights, sounds, and feelings are thus a product of many processes of interpretation in the brain.[27] Dennett thus concludes that if consciousness is the result of purely physical elements, and its functionality is consistent with the multiple drafts model, then an artificially intelligent machine is plausible. However, the important point in the context of this project is that the alleged possibility of artificial consciousness serves to strengthen Dennett's view—that consciousness is purely physical. He posits the title for this hypothetical A.I. instrument, a 'Joycean Machine', named after Irish novelist James Joyce's portrayal of conscious thought in his novels, which depict thought processes as meandering sequences—consistent with the multiple drafts model.[28]

HOW CONSCIOUSNESS EVOLVES

Heretofore, we have outlined Dennett's materialist model of consciousness, which Dawkins signifies as consistent with his approach. From this point, we must now attend to the central issue in the context of this project, which is how the phenomenon of consciousness evolved. The evolutionary system we are engaged with, championed by Dawkins, maintains that evolution is a series of accumulating steps, each enabling the next in a linear fashion. Change exists in the biosphere due to genetic mutations; the change comes from within the process itself, and not from an external source. To represent this linear, mechanical process of evolution, Dennett adopts 'cranes' as an analogy.[29] A crane, in this context, is defined as

> [a] subprocess or special feature of a design process that can be demonstrated to permit the local speeding up of the basic, slow process of natural selection, *and* that can be demonstrated to be itself the predictable (or retrospectively explicable) product of the basic process.[30]

Cranes, then, help advance evolution, but are themselves products of the same process they propel. The evolution of the conscious mind then, Dennett articulates, cannot be exempt from this linear progression. "A mind is a crane, made of cranes, made of cranes, a mechanism of not quite unimaginable complexity . . . ".[31] Fundamentally, the nonmiraculous, mechanical progression of evolution produced the human mind from less complex systems.[32] The language Dennett employs here, however, has been criticized by Gould as overly simplistic.[33] This is a similar criticism to Fern Elsdon-Baker's critique on Dawkins, which suggests that both Dawkins and Dennett's portrayal of evolution may be too narrow—which may be a limitation of dialogue.

A theory of how consciousness evolved within this system is conjectured by Dennett, which suggests that the simple organisms of early life, after subjection to evolution by natural selection, evolved a primitive way of avoiding 'bad things' and seeking out 'good things'. This description is of course explained anthropomorphically to convey the substance of the argument,[34] although again it could be questioned whether or not this anthropomorphic language is a help or a hindrance to our understanding of the process. Notwithstanding such potential criticism, in Dennett's view, entities that prolong their life span by discovering 'good' in the environment will be favored by natural selection. Through a long series of intermediates, biological systems will become aware to such a degree that they can avoid predators or other subjects detrimental to their own survival, or pursue other subjects that will prolong their life. This degree of awareness results in what we would label 'self-awareness' or 'consciousness'. Consciousness evolves then, in essence, from less complex variants.[35] One example of evidence to support this view comes from the correlation between human and chimpanzee brains (as seen above, Dawkins and Dennett see no distinction between brain and mind). The fact that human and chimpanzee brains are identical in structure is interpreted by Dennett to suggest that both brains are products of the same evolutionary lineage.[36] Moreover, this suggests that there is no other element that makes human brains unique, other than the fact that they are four times larger. [37]

CONSCIOUSNESS AND FREE WILL

In Dennett's suppositions of consciousness, which this section has examined, he encounters a dilemma that is synopsised by author Robert Wright, a prominent journalist and author of several books on science and religion. Wright formalises his critique as follows: "Of course the problem here is with the claim that consciousness is 'identical' to brain states. The more Dennett et al. try to explain to me what they mean by this, the more convinced I become that what they really mean is that consciousness doesn't exist".[38] Dennett uses Wright's words here as a starting point in addressing the problem. As we have seen in Dennett's model, there is nothing more than physical, algorithmic brain process in consciousness. This raises an interesting and relevant philosophical problem: Does consciousness or free will really exist, or is it an illusory by-product of unconscious events? This enigma is attended to in Dennett's *Freedom Evolves*. The avid materialistic model of consciousness (and life in general) leaves no room, it seems, for any idea of immaterial souls or selves, which inhabit and command the body. Subsequently, one interpretation of the implications of this view is that free will/consciousness is nonexistent, as seen above in Wright's statement. Dennett aims to refute this implication.[39] Free will, for Dennett, arises from the same algorithmic progression of evolution. "Free will is a real but non pre-existing feature of our existence. . . . It is also not what tradition declares it to be: a God-like power to exempt oneself from the causal fabric of the physical world. It is an evolved creation of human activity and beliefs . . . ".[40] For Dennett, consciousness is a series of algorithmic physical processes. However, he insists that the whole can be 'freer' than the sum of its parts.[41] He postulates that freedom is introduced to algorithmic processes in greater degrees, depending on the available alternative options in decision making, which the brain has in the multiple drafts model. Dennett suggests that an environmental switch can introduce a degree of freedom, allowing for instance, a tree to 'decide' to blossom in spring:

> But even a simple switch, turned on and off by some environmental change, marks a *degree of freedom.* . . . A system has a degree of freedom when there is an ensemble of possibilities of one kind or another. . . . As arrays proliferate, forming larger switching networks, the degrees of freedom multiply dizzyingly, and the issues of control grow complex and non-linear.[42]

Over the course of evolutionary time, the complexity of the degrees of freedom multiplies exponentially. This eventuates the evolution of the brain, which maintains ascendancy over the intricate paths of information and decision making. "Any lineage equipped with such an array confronts a problem: What information ought to modulate passage through this array of forking paths in a multi-dimensional space of possibilities? That is what a brain is for".[43] In Dennett's view, the brain acts as a command centre, which allows different decisions to be made, relying on information stored in memory and sensory inputs as its guide.[44] Therefore, he is attempting to propose a model of consciousness that stems solely from within the evolutionary process. This development of the brain/consciousness became highly complex in early *Homo sapiens.*

CONSCIOUSNESS AND LANGUAGE

In a recent public discussion with Rowan Williams at Oxford University in 2012, Dawkins signified that language may be a unique evolutionary development with profound implications for human evolution. Language is also a cardinal issue for Dennett, who proposes that the evolution of the brain was essentially complete prior to the development of language.[45] However, there may be an issue with the word 'complete'; evolution is an ongoing process, though it could be suggested that the brain had developed to a degree that is virtually indistinguishable from its current state. It has been argued, notably by highly influential linguist Noam Chomsky, that the brain has been endowed genetically with the capability for language: "One component of the human mind-brain, then, is a genetically determined initial configuration, which we may call 'the initial state of the language faculty'".[46] Similarly, Dennett argues that the evolution of the brain's capacity for language is fundamental to any concept of mind, as it presupposes complexities in thought processes unparalleled in any conscious system without such a capacity; the complexities of the human mind are made possible by language.[47] Although this is speculative, given that it is difficult to quantifiably discount nonlingual consciousnesses, Dennett suggests that without the capacity for language, the current manifestations of thoughts could not be possible. Comparable to Dennett, Chomsky also acknowledges the momentous influence the development of linguistic prowess has for conscious thoughts:

> Without this capacity [for language] it might have been possible to "think thoughts" of a certain restrained character, but with the capacity in place, the same conceptual apparatus would be freed for the construction of new thoughts and operations such as inference involving them, and it would be possible to express and interchange these thoughts. At that point evolutionary pressures might have shaped the further development of the capacity . . .[48]

Dennett and Chomsky thus both explain that the brain's capacity for language has drastically improved human thought processes. With language, thought processes can become formalized to such a degree that would have previously been impossible. Dennett and Chomsky propose an almost cyclical view. The mind-brain evolves the capacity for language, which in turn allows for a far more complex mind-brain—self-consciousness. This evolved capacity for language, Dennett explains, resulted in the "most remarkable expansion of human mental powers", the advent of civilization.[49] How the mind, endowed with lingual thoughts, led to the expedient development of human civilization (in less than ten thousand years) will be the focus of the next section.

On the issue of consciousness, we noted how Dawkins points toward Dennett's philosophy. This exposition of Dennett's philosophy of consciousness was necessary for three reasons. Firstly, by adding Dennett's perspective on consciousness and its evolution onto Dawkins' view, we gain a more comprehensive picture of evolution; we can see how between Dawkins and Dennett, an evolutionary view of all facets of life inclusive of human consciousness can be postulated (though one that is not without many criticisms). Secondly, Dennett's philosophy of consciousness gives us the foundation to progress into our study of an evolutionary view on culture, which we will explore in the next section on Dawkins' concept of memetics. Dawkins himself explains that Dennett's model of consciousness is highly significant for this subject.[50] Thirdly, a gradual/materialistic view on consciousness, such as the one Dawkins espouses, will have significant implications for how we consider God's interaction with humanity in Chapter Five. In advocating his evolutionary view on consciousness, Dennett relies heavily on philosophy. Though science is densely incorporated into the explication of his view, it is a philosophical treatise. In this philosophy, the advent of human language allows for the subsequent development of human civilization. Therefore, we will now examine the evolution of human civilization in the evolutionary framework of Dawkins' perspective.

Memetics: Cultural Evolution

The controversial subject of memetics, which as we shall see, has been subject to serious criticism, stems from the term 'meme'. Coined by Dawkins in his 1976 book, *The Selfish Gene*, the word has since been included in the Oxford English Dictionary, and defined as follows: "An element of a culture that may be considered to be passed on by non-genetic means, especially imitation".[51] The premise of Dawkins' thesis holds that cultural traits can evolve in a way that is similar to genetic traits in biological evolution. The meme is the cultural equivalent to the gene; it is the unit of cultural transmission. Consistent with the theme of this chapter, we will survey Dawkins' views on nongenetic aspects of evolution, manifest in the evolution of culture or civilization. It is Dawkins' meme theory that provides a theoretical framework for such an endeavour, and will be the focus of this section.

Subsequent to Dawkins' introduction of his meme thesis, the concept has received much attention, and several scholars have contributed to the theory. Dennett, for example, has embraced the idea of memes and developed the concept from his own perspective. Dawkins also endorses British psychologist Susan Blackmore's work, declaring that she has "pushed memetic theory further than anyone".[52] We will now explore the theory of memes proposed by Dawkins et al. This task will be divided into an overview of memetics, a defense of memetics, and the implications of cultural evolution for broader evolution theory.

INTRODUCING THE MEME

Culture, for Dawkins, epitomizes in a single word the uniqueness of the human species.[53] Similar to biological life, Dawkins suggests that culture can also be described in evolutionary terms, and can be discerned in species such as classifications of birds and monkeys. However, it is in the human species that cultural evolution is prevalent in unprecedented proportions. This, according to Dennett, is due to our capacity for linguistic communicative skills, an intrinsic element of his evolutionary model of consciousness. To illustrate cultural evolution, Dawkins employs language itself as an archetypal example:

> Geoffrey Chaucer could not hold a conversation with a modern Englishman, even though they are linked to each other by an unbroken chain of some twenty generations of Englishmen, each of whom could speak to his intermediate neighbours in the chain as a son speaks to his father.[54]

Therefore, language must have undergone some form of evolution for there to be sufficient disparity between the English language of the two time periods, that would prevent a fluid conversation between Chaucer and a modern English speaker. Language is thus a salient example of cultural evolution; it is a nonbiological subject (though we did note that language does have a biological basis) that clearly changes over time—as the above reference illustrates. In addition, the rate at which language evolves is expedient compared with biological evolution.[55] The amount of change accumulated in the biological evolution of the human species since the time of Chaucer is infinitesimal, but language has mutated a great deal. Although language is one instance of nongenetic evolution, it is also evident in fashion, customs, ceremonies, art, architecture, and engineering. The catalyst for Dawkins' theoretical framework of memes is this realization that culture evolves in a way analogous to genetic evolution (though this analogy has limitations, which we will encounter later). It is the attempt to extend his view of Darwinism beyond biology: ". . . I think Darwinism is too big a theory to be confined to the narrow context of the gene. The gene will enter my thesis as an analogy, nothing more".[56]

As have we seen in Chapter Two, the process of evolution hinges upon genetic replication and transmission. If culture is subject to a form of evolution, Dawkins argues that there must be a unit of transmission for culture, a unit parallel to the gene in biological evolution. The meme is this unit; it is the focus of a theoretical framework for understanding how cultural traits evolve. He presents a synopsis of memes:

> Examples of memes are tunes, ideas, catch phrases, clothes fashions, ways of making pots or building arches . . . memes propagate themselves in the meme pool by leaping from brain to brain via a process which, in the broad sense, can be called imitation. If a scientist hears, or reads about, a good idea, he passes it on to his colleagues and students. He mentions it in his articles and his [sic] lectures. If the idea catches on, it can be said to propagate itself, spreading from brain to brain. . . . N. K. Humphrey neatly summed up an earlier draft of this chapter '. . . memes should be regarded as living structures, not just metaphorically but technically'.[57]

Memes can be described essentially as ideas, but ideas that are memorable and that can be passed on. Dennett, who is explicitly supportive of Dawkins' concept, clarifies the consideration of memes as ideas as cultural units independently subject to natural selection:

> These newfangled replicators are, roughly, ideas. Not the "simple ideas" of Locke and Hume . . . but the sort of complex ideas that form themselves into distinct memorable units. For example the ideas of: arch, wheel, wearing clothes, vendetta, right triangle, alphabet, calendar, the Odyssey, calculus, chess, perspective drawing, evolution by natural selection, impressionism, Greensleeves, "read my lips", deconstructionism. Intuitively, these are identifiable cultural units.[58]

These ideas, Dennett suggests, depend on the infrastructure of the human mind as vehicles, in the same way genes depend on the infrastructure of organisms to survive and be propagated. As seen in Chapter Two, Dawkins' perspective on biological life viewed bodies as ephemeral amalgams of genes being sifted through by natural selection. Correspondingly, Dennett views ideas in a separate sphere of evolution, in which the human mind is an ephemeral amalgamation of memes. He encapsulates his view in the following idiom: "A scholar is just a library's way of making another library".[59]

Persisting with the gene-meme analogy, Dawkins describes memes as information (genes, recall, can also be thought of as information).[60] Consistent with this description, he also postulates that memes, as information stored in the brain, could be in principle visible under a microscope.[61] Equivalently, Dennett postulated that thoughts (in this case memes) could be locatable within the brain. This illustrates that in this regard, Dawkins and Dennett's views are virtually synonymous. Memes, as information stored in the brain, can also impose significant influence over human physiology, evident in memes for various lifestyles. Memes for dieting, exercise, and health have led to a taller, healthier species and longer life expectancies. As stated above, there has been infinitesimal biological evolution in humans over the last several centuries, but physical differences can be a consequence of cultural evolution, as Dennett explains:

> What have changed dramatically are human health, diet, and living conditions; these are what have produced the dramatic change in phenotype, which is 100% due to cultural transmission: schooling, the spread of new farming practices, public health measures, and so forth.[62]

There are, however, aspects of memes that betray a stringent interpretation of the gene-meme analogy. For example, although it is evident that memes can have significant influence over humanity's physical traits, memes need not possess advantageous qualities for the host. Genes, as explained in Chapter Two, will be statistically less frequent in the gene pool if they have a negative influence on the organism's survival. Memes, however, need only be advantageous to themselves in terms of their copying proficiency. It is not necessary that they have positive effects on the person's survival to be successful in the meme-pool. Dawkins illustrates this by offering the example of a meme for celibacy: "A gene for celibacy is doomed to failure in the gene pool. . . . But still, a meme for celibacy can be successful in the meme pool".[63] Concurrent opinions are expressed by Dennett. He feels that memes need not be 'good' in the sense that 'good' is interpreted as a positive influence on organisms' survival competency. Nor do memes need to have a positive influence on their host's social, ethical, scientific, or political advancement:

> If there is one proposition that would-be memeticists agree on, it is that the flourishing of an idea—its success at replicating through a population of minds—and the value of an idea—its truth, its scientific or political or ethical excellence—are only contingently and imperfectly related. Good ideas can go extinct and bad ideas can infect whole societies.[64]

Memes for war, torture, and exploitation can spread despite negative sociological impact, whereas memes for fair-trade or gender and racial equality can struggle to be propagated. Whether or not a meme is deemed 'good' or 'bad' is not an empirical matter, but one of subjective opinion. To illustrate, I have chosen as examples uncontentious issues: fair trade and equality as 'good'; and war, torture, and exploitation as 'bad'. There are memes that, depending on the interpreter, could be held to be either 'good' or 'bad': memes for euthanasia, contraception, abortion, or capitalism. The proposal of labeling memes 'good' or 'bad' in this theoretical—and not ethical—context will be a criticism of memetics explored later. Fundamentally, Dawkins suggests that the propagation of memes is not as contingent on their positive or negative consequences as genes are.

Furthermore, memes have a greater propensity for longevity in comparison with genes. Dawkins contrasts the philosophical or artistic memes of individuals with individuals' genes: "Socrates may not have a gene or two alive in the world today as G. C. Williams has remarked, but who cares? The meme complexes of Socrates, Leonardo, Copernicus, and Marconi are still going strong".[65] As we noted in Chapter Two, only half of an individual's genes are passed on to the next generation through procreation. Therefore, as the generations go by, the particular collection of genes that make up an individual becomes scattered throughout the gene pool. After several generations, an individual's genes have been "dissolved in the common gene pool".[66] Memes, in contrast, need not be diluted as they are passed on.

FORMALIZATION AND DEFENSE OF MEMETICS

Kate Distin, expert in meme theory, makes it clear that for Dawkins' theory of memes to have credibility, memetics must work in the context of three essential elements of evolution: selection, variation, and replication.[67] She argues that genetic evolution is based upon these three premises: 1) there must be selective pressures, that is, not every gene will survive; 2) there must be variation, that is, genes must be distinguishable from one another; and 3) replication, that is, genes must be replicated and passed on. Dennett also holds these three elements (selection, variation, and replication) as essential to evolution.[68] Further corroboration of these criteria can be taken from Susan Blackmore, who in addition maintains not only must these criteria be met, but if they are, then evolution is inevitable.[69] In other words, if these premises are in place then evolution will transpire. Harvard philosopher Peter Godfrey-Smith, however, while acknowledging that these or similar criteria are often presented as succinct outlines of the evolutionary process, notes that they may be oversimplified and subject to counterexamples.[70] This echoes a recurrent criticism of Dawkins' model of evolution—that it is presented in an oversimplified manner.

Notwithstanding such criticism, to investigate whether memes fit these criteria, Distin examines them individually. Firstly, she examines whether there are selective pressures within cultural ideas; if there is evidence that some memes survive and some do not. She perceptively observes:

> If memes, like genes, are selected via their phenotypic effects, then it is at the phenotypic level that we must search for the evidence. Again, there is plenty of evidence for selection in culture: theories, tunes and methods that are popular at present; ideas that have been rejected within living memory; written records of the theories, fashions, skills and music of past generations, all demonstrate the differential survival of certain areas of culture.[71]

Distin concludes in this quotation, that there must exist some selective pressures for differential survival of certain memes. Dennett also proposes that memes are in competition for space in the human brain (given that he views the brain as the physical space in which thoughts exist), and are therefore subjected to a version of selection.[72] Examples of differential survival among memes point to the conclusion that memes are subject to selective forces. Subsequently, memes satisfy the first criterion. The second criterion, Distin asserts, is replication. For Distin, memes also exhibit replication, as it is a quality that defines memes themselves:

> It is obvious that a key feature of memetic content must be its replicability; without this property no representation could be a meme. In practice that transmission of memetic content will be facilitated by such standard cultural methods as imitation, teaching and everyday communication.[73]

Replication of memes occurs from imitation. In fact, Dawkins derived the word 'meme' from the Greek word *mimeme*, meaning that which is imitated.[74] Notwithstanding this definitional attribute of memes, Dawkins understands imitation in a broad sense, as the copying fidelity of meme imitation need not be as precise as genetic replication.[75] Blackmore offers a similar view, as she explains that a story may be imitated by retelling the "gist" of the story. This qualifies the re-telling of the story as a memetic transmission, though the exact actions and words of the original story need not be imitated perfectly.[76] The essence of an idea can be considered the meme, and not the particulars.

The third criterion of evolution, variation, is also argued by Distin to be manifest in memes. As explained in Chapter Two, variation is introduced to the gene pool through errors in the replication process. Correspondingly, variation exists in the meme pool as a result of lapses in the proficiency of meme replications. Memes may mutate and subsequently vary in their transmission.[77] This point is consistent with Dawkins/Blackmore's use of the concept of imitation in a broad sense, rather than an inexorable replication process. As memes are often transmitted imperfectly, variation becomes ubiquitous in the meme pool, as copying discrepancies mutate the original memes, and the two varying memes are propagated exponentially. It can then be concluded that, at least from the perspective of the scholars mentioned here, memes satisfy the criteria for evolution by natural selection. Therefore, through the framework of memetics, ideas and hence culture may be understood as 'Darwinian'.

To further strengthen the validity of meme theory, Blackmore addresses three possible criticisms of the concept. The first potential criticism pertains to the specification of a meme; the unit of the meme is not definitively specifiable. Whether a particular section of a musical piece is considered the meme, or whether the piece in its entirety is considered the meme, is a question that may present an impasse for explications of memetics. Blackmore, however, suggests that the nonspecifiable nature of a meme is not tantamount to a persuasive argument against the theory: "I have heard people dismiss the whole idea of memetics on the grounds that 'you can't even say what the unit of a meme is'. Well that is true, I cannot. And I do not think it is necessary. A replicator does not have to come neatly parceled up in ready-labeled units".[78] Blackmore eschews the suggestion that the study of memes can be hindered as there is no definable unit that can be empirically labeled a meme. To illustrate this, she adopts the parallel example of genetics. "This intrinsic uncertainty about just what to count as a gene has not impeded progress in genetics and biology".[79] The unclassifiable nature of genes does not lessen the significance of advances in genetics. Memetics mirrors genetics in this context; the unclassifiable nature of memes should not, from Blackmore's perspective, diminish the significance of advances in memetics.

The second prospective criticism is the heretofore illusiveness of the mechanisms that copy and store memes. In genetic evolution, the copying and storage mechanism is DNA, though in the case of memes, it is still unknown. This potential criticism is disregarded by Blackmore as irrelevant, again taking the parallel example of genetics. Though we now understand the copying and storage processes of DNA, the science of evolution progressed appreciably before its discovery in the 1950s. "In the first century of Darwinism an enormous amount was achieved in the understanding of evolution without anyone having any idea about chemical replication, the control of protein synthesis or what on earth DNA was doing".[80] Blackmore concludes, then, that the current inconclusive status of meme mechanisms does not constitute a problem for the study of memes. In addition, Dawkins theorized that memes could in principle be visible under a microscope. Dennett also suggested that thoughts could be locatable, physical events in the brain. Therefore, there is no *a priori* reason why the mechanisms of memetics will never be understood in the same way that DNA is now understood.

The third possible criticism of Dawkins' theory of memes is the potential classification of memetic evolution as 'Lamarckian'.[81] Blackmore defines Lamarckian evolution as follows: "the principle of the inheritance of acquired characteristics. That is, if you learn something or undergo some change during your lifetime, you can pass it on to your offspring".[82] In sexually reproductive biological species, Lamarckism is incongruent with the process of genetic inheritance. Blackmore insists that Lamarckism in sexual, biological evolution is "simply not true".[83] In cultural evolution, however, there are existent examples of Lamarckism. Memetic inheritance can be Lamarckian in the following case: a meme for a food recipe can become mutated if an individual adds extra salt. The meme for this recipe will then be transmitted as the mutated version with extra salt. Consequently, this memetic transmission can be seen as Lamarckian. However, Blackmore also discounts the criticism that memetic evolution is Lamarckian as irrelevant. Her rationalization for discounting the Lamarckian criticism is that it is based on an overstringent use of the gene-meme analogy. "My conclusion apropos Lamarck is that the question 'Is cultural evolution Lamarckian' is best not asked. The question only makes sense if you draw certain kinds of strict analogy between genes and memes but such analogies are not justified".[84] Blackmore therefore defends memetics against the three potential criticisms mentioned here. If one takes the defenses of memetic theory by Distin et al. as valid, then we can use the idea of memes to explain how evolution occurs beyond biology. This, Dawkins explains, was his intention behind promoting the concept: "It was always intended to be a way of dramatizing the idea that a Darwinian replicator doesn't have to be a gene. It can be a computer virus. Or a meme. The point is that a good replicator is just a replicator that spreads, regardless of its material form".[85]

THE IMPLICATIONS OF MEMETICS

Memetics is used as a way of understanding a process of cultural evolution. It is an attempt to extend an evolutionary worldview beyond biology, as opposed to a view that focuses purely on the differential survival of genes. Perhaps the most profound implications of memetics in the context of this project relates to our understanding of human behaviour. British archaeologist Stephen Shennan contributed a book to the discourse on memes, *Genes, Memes and Human History*, in which he explains how, post–World War II, many biologists attempted to extrapolate theories of behaviour from evolution theory. "This involved looking at behaviour in terms of selection; that is to say, looking at how variations in behaviour relate to variations in survival, in reproduction and in the rearing of offspring".[86] Shennan proceeds to explain that the advent of human civilization introduces two new variables that must be considered intrinsic to the study of human evolution, and subsequently, human behaviour as explained from an evolutionary standpoint. Firstly, he proposes that "Natural Selection on people's survival and reproductive success can occur through selection on their cultural traditions, not simply on their genes via their genetically inherited dispositions".[87] Cultural traits, understood in this context as memes, manipulate the survival competency of humans, thus altering the course of natural selection. Examples of this can be found in memes for medicine, which help humans live longer and increase reproductivity, therefore, influencing genetic selection. The second variable Sheenan proposes is that

> [p]rocesses of cultural selection can also operate, such that the frequencies of cultural attributes can change through time not as a result of natural selection affecting people's survival and reproductive success but as a result of conscious and unconscious decision-making based on a variety of criteria.[88]

Memetic evolution is influenced far more by conscious decision than genetic evolution. As we noted, memetic selection can also operate irrespective of reproductive successes, as we encountered earlier; memes need not possess a selective advantage. Consequently, memes can successfully populate the meme pool, influencing genetic selection negatively instead of positively. The example of a meme for celibacy given by Dawkins earlier illustrates this point sufficiently. A meme for celibacy directly influences genetic selection by removing genes from the selective process. However, as a meme, celibacy still propagates itself and becomes prevalent in the meme pool. The implications for developing this Darwinian viewpoint is that by acknowledging human cultural evolution, the evolutionary picture begins to complicate exponentially.

In other words, subsequent to memetic evolution, attempts to comprehensively understand human behaviour in terms of Darwinian natural selection of genes will be ultimately insufficient. "Their [the sociobiologists:

Dawkins et al.] achievement is to explain much of human behaviour in terms of the past selection of genes; to apply Darwin's great theory to psychology. But in concentrating on genes alone they miss out on the importance and power of the social world".[89] To establish a possibly more definitive Darwinian perspective, the coalescing theoretical processes of both memetic and genetic evolution must be considered together. This concept is dealt with by Peter Baofu, another scholar who has contributed a book-length treatise to the idea of memes. Baofu insightfully suggests that in studying human behaviour, both genes and memes need to be considered. However, human behaviour is not contingent on either genetic or memetic evolution. It is also not a consequence of both evolutionary processes operating in tandem, but it can only be understood from a case-by-case analysis: "It all depends on a given case, or a group of cases".[90] It cannot be claimed that one particular aspect of human behaviour is a result of genetic evolution, nor can it be suggested that another aspect is a result of memetic evolution. It depends on an individual and their complex memetic and genetic background. In some cases, a person's behaviour may be primarily as a result of their genetics. In others, it may be primarily as a result of their memetics. In other cases still, it may be a complex amalgamation of the two.

In conclusion to this section, it was demonstrated how Dawkins et al. attempt to expand an evolutionary framework beyond biology and into the social realm. Dawkins' theory of memes, and subsequent additions to its theoretical base from other prominent academics in various fields, aid the task of establishing an evolutionary stance, from which Dawkins seeks to understand the world. We can contest that this evolutionary worldview, though marketed as hostile to theology, could in fact offer a theologically fruitful model for discourse. Memetics is an intrinsic part of that evolutionary worldview because it suggests that the expanse of Darwinism is not confined to biological evolution in Dawkins' *weltanschauung*. Darwinian evolution, as it is presented by Dawkins, was shown in this section to permeate human culture, as cultural traits (memes) satisfy the criteria for an evolutionary process. The evolutionary view of human civilization in memetics can be added to Dawkins' evolutionary view of biological life. Therefore, this permits us to view all aspects of life through an evolutionary lens. The origin and evolution of life itself, the onset of consciousness, and subsequent development of human culture can all be now understood in terms of an evolutionary paradigm. One of the most significant implications for this evolutionary perspective is the issue of purpose in the universe, which the next section will now consider.

Evolution and a Purposeless Universe?

Heretofore, we have explored Dawkins' view of biological evolution (Chapter Two) and his commitment to an evolutionary theory of culture. We have engaged with his evolutionary view: that all facets of life—life itself, subsequent consciousness, and culture—arise from naturally evolved processes. Attempting to explain everything in terms of how it evolved from more elementary predecessors compels Dawkins to consider what implications this view may have for considering any degree of purpose in life. The theological and philosophical overtones in discussing the matter of purpose highlight an overlap between the interests of theology and Dawkins' materialism. Thus it may offer one area for dialogue. As this contentious issue is a prominent philosophical implication of Dawkins' outlook, attention to the issue must be given in this section.

The crux of Dawkins' view is the proposition that the universe is unmitigatedly devoid of purpose. The influential philosopher Bertrand Russell encapsulated his view on the issue of purpose, which can also be used to neatly summarize Dawkins' approach:

> There is no law of cosmic progress, but only an oscillation upward and downward, with a slow trend downward on the balance owing to the diffusion of energy. This, at least, is what science at present regards as most probable, and in our disillusioned generation it is easy to believe. From evolution, so far as our present knowledge shows, no ultimately optimistic philosophy can be validly inferred.[91]

Russell's words aptly summarize the purposelessness implied in Dawkins' interpretive stance on the evolutionary picture of life. From Dawkins' linear/branched perspective of evolution, he acknowledges only with a degree of acquiescence, that the issue of purpose arises. This acquiescence presupposes his subsequent dismissal of the issue. In his view, purpose is a characteristically human sentiment, commonly juxtaposed onto nature, which is inherently random. For Dawkins, this human construct should now be discarded with pride:

> We humans have purpose on the brain. We find it hard to look at anything without wondering what it is 'for', what the motive is for it, or the purpose behind it. . . . Show us almost any object or process and it is hard for us to resist the 'Why' question—the 'what is it for?'

question. . . . Today we pride ourselves on having shaken off such primitive animism.[92]

Dawkins considers purpose as a concept emanating logically from 'why' questions; humans are predisposed to engage in what he deems a futile enterprise of attributing purpose or meaning to inane randomness by asking 'why?'. The initial validity of such 'why' questions, however, is impugned by Dawkins. Questioning habitually infers the possibility of answers, and consequently, once a question is posed, the existence of an answer is presumed. Dawkins, however, discerns that these 'why' questions may be inappropriate and inapplicable: "questions can be simply inappropriate, however heartfelt their framing".[93] His philosophical approach therefore hinges on the inherent meaninglessness of nature. The unrelenting neutrality manifest in nature necessitates an unequivocal presupposition that the universe operates in a truly aimless, mechanistic manner. One example in nature that is sufficiently demonstrative of such callousness is the breeding habits of the female digger wasp.[94] The female digger wasp will perniciously sting its prey (a grasshopper, bee, or caterpillar) with such a degree of precision as to paralyze it but not kill it, thus keeping the meat fresh. The wasp then proceeds to lay her eggs inside the victim, allowing her larvae to feed on the fresh meat. It is unknown whether or not the victim is aware of being eaten alive from inside or whether the sting acts as an anesthetic, numbing the pain.[95] The draconian temperament evident in the female digger wasp's breeding method exemplifies the cruelty and indifference existent in the natural world. Based on examples such as this—though there are many others—Dawkins concludes that a benevolent creator could not have designed creatures that revel in such barbarity. However, it has been suggested, notably by Gould among others, that the interpretation of the world as a cruel place may stem from a cultural context that was "measured in terms of battles won and enemies destroyed".[96]

Moreover, Dawkins illustrates that purposelessness is evident in the conspicuous absence of a hypothetical gene for anesthetizing an antelope before it is eaten by a cheetah, or the fact that a school bus can needlessly crash, resulting in massive loss of young lives. The poignancy of such examples, Dawkins tells us, is precisely what we should expect if the world is genuinely devoid of purpose:

> [I]f the universe were just electrons and selfish genes, meaningless tragedies like the crashing of this bus are exactly what we should expect, along with equally meaningless good fortune. Such a

universe would be neither evil nor good in intention. It would manifest no intentions of any kind. In a universe of blind physical forces and genetic replication, some people are going to get lucky, and you won't find any rhyme or reason in it, nor any justice. The universe we observe has precisely the properties we should expect if there is, at bottom, no design, no purpose, no evil and no good, nothing but blind pitiless indifference.[97]

The striking feature of Dawkins' view is the futility, pervasive in the natural world—the "blind pitiless indifference". The concept of futility, however, is again viewed as a purely human sentimental construct, not representative of anything absolute or legitimate. Consideration of futility in nature is a misappropriation, an illogical error of human reasoning. "Futility? What nonsense. Sentimental, human nonsense. Natural selection is *all* futile".[98]

Dennett elaborates on this view of purpose, offering a treatise congruent with Dawkins' denunciation of meaning in nature, though Dennett's treatise is grounded in Darwinian terms. He aligns himself with the reductionist approach of Dawkins encountered in Chapter Two. Darwinian evolution, in Dennett's view, perfectly exemplifies reductionism; it is reductionism incarnate. He defines reductionism as ". . . simply the commitment to non-question begging science without any cheating by embracing mysteries or miracles at the outset".[99] This again highlights Dennett's naturalism, which we defined earlier as the belief that nothing is beyond the scope of scientific explanation. He differentiates between this "bland" reductionism, which he endorses, and another "preposterous" reductionism, which maintains that any higher-level sciences are reducible to lower-level sciences. Dennett's version of reductionism (which he labels 'good' reductionism), when applied to Darwinism, emphasizes the algorithmic nature of evolution. It is inherently causal, and consequently, it must be fallacious to insist that the world contains any purpose or intentionality.

It is suggested by Dennett that intentionality bears the mark of mind or consciousness. If we recall Dennett's view on mind, he considers intentionality to itself be a product of evolution; mind arises from the mindless: ". . . intentionality doesn't come from on high; it percolates up from below, from the initially mindless and pointless algorithmic processes that gradually acquire meaning and intelligence as they develop".[100] Intentionality itself is a construct of the human mind, subsequent to the evolution of life and origin of the universe. Consequently, to speak of intentionality innate in the universe is a misconception, an erred chronological reasoning. This view is perceptibly similar to Dawkins' perspective above, which considered purpose and futility as sentimental human constructs.

To substantiate this theme, Dennett refers to language, which we noted was viewed as a monumental development in his outline of the evolution of consciousness. Moreover, language played a key role in the development of human civilization, and was subsequent to consciousness. Therefore language, in Dennett's view, is very recent in the evolutionary picture. Bearing this in mind, Dennett highlights an interesting philosophical issue: when philosophers consider meaning, they are constricted to the use of the linguistic apparatus of words, which themselves have their own meaning and need to be considered first:

> The further working assumption, particularly among English-speaking philosophers, has been that until we get clear about how words can have meaning, we are unlikely to make much progress on the other varieties of meaning, especially such staggering issues as the meaning of life.[101]

A problem arises when it is considered that words get their meaning from us. Our meanings are therefore dependent solely on the functions that we ourselves have attributed. However, Dennett suggests that what appears to be a perpetual paradox can be solved by viewing the problem within a Darwinian framework. Meaning evolves from simpler origins, and can be considered, consequently, as being retrospectively accredited. Meaning then, in Dennett's view, is an effect of evolution, and has no causal significance:

> If meaning gets determined by the selective forces that endorse certain functional roles, then all meaning may seem, in a sense, to be only retrospectively attributed: what something means is not an *intrinsic* property it has, capable of making a difference in the world at the moment of its birth, but at best a retrospective coronation secured only by an analysis of the subsequent effects engendered.[102]

Dennett elaborates on this theme to incorporate other aspects and potential criticisms of his philosophical argument. These intricacies, however, do not bear any weight on the fundamental conclusions under examination here—that meaning is a by-product of evolutionary developments (language and consciousness). When Dennett contemplates the issue of purpose and its relevance to discourse on evolution, his conclusions are consistent with that of

Dawkins—that the universe is devoid of any meaning or purpose. To illustrate this, he employs the example of a replicating virus, similar to influenza:

> Love it or hate it, phenomena like this exhibit the heart of the power of the Darwinian idea. An impersonal, unreflective, robotic, mindless little scrap of molecular machinery is the ultimate basis for all the agency, and hence meaning, and hence consciousness, in the universe.[103]

For brevity, then, we can consider that Dennett shares Dawkins' philosophical view of absolute purposelessness in the physical operations of the universe.

Given that this approach is interpretive, corroboration should be sought for validation; Dawkins' view is not a rogue philosophy but a legitimate interpretation shared among key authoritative voices in the area. One example of such a voice is Ernst Mayr, encountered in Chapter Two as a key evolutionist who agreed with Dawkins on certain issues such as the tandem random/nonrandom operations of natural selection. Both Mayr and Dawkins considered evolution to operate due to inherently random genetic mutations followed by inherently nonrandom selection. Mayr, however, also disagreed on other aspects of evolution, such as natural selection's focus on genes. Regarding the issue of purpose, Mayr's interpretation of the evolutionary picture is consistent with Dawkins' outlook. Mayr is explicit in his castigation of any line of reasoning that projects a sense of purpose onto the evolutionary progression of life:

> The final argument of the anti-selectionists usually is: "But all these adaptations are so obviously purposive that there must be some internal purposive force!" One must object vigorously to this line of argument. An individual can have purpose but an evolutionary line cannot. There is no need whatsoever, indeed there is no excuse whatsoever, for considering adaption as evidence of purpose.[104]

It may be interpreted as evidence for purpose in evolution that species have apparently perfectly adapted to their environment. These seemingly perfect adaptations are, however, according to Mayr, the result of long periods of trial and error.[105] Therefore, Mayr refutes the interpretation that sees purpose in organisms' adaptations. The apparent progress or ideal adaptations are a proxy of natural selection; they are not guided toward progress and adaptations. Mayr succinctly summarizes his view: "If an organism is well adapted, if it shows superior fitness, this is not due to any purpose of its ancestors or of an outside agency, such as 'Nature' or 'God,' that created a superior design or plan".[106] Moreover, he says, "Natural selection is never goal orientated. It is misleading and quite inadmissible to designate such broadly generalized concepts as survival or reproductive success as definite and specified goals".[107] Mayr, then, repudiates the possibility that evidence for purpose can be found upon reflection on the evolutionary processes. The tandem random/nonrandom functionality of evolution (discussed in Chapter Two) is not purposive, goal directed, or intentional; it is a mindless, natural process.

Further corroboration to support this view can be found with another influential evolutionist, Theodosius Dobzhansky, also encountered in Chapter Two and identified as a "religious man". Consistent with Mayr's view, Dobzhansky insightfully explains that ". . . natural selection is automatic, mechanical, planless, and opportunistic"—yet Dobzhansky may accept a wider purpose not evident in biology.[108] Though Dobzhansky notes the apparent purposefulness in adaptations, he views these adaptations as unguided, unplanned products of natural selection—a view congruent with Mayr and Dawkins. "The adaptedness is neither devised nor planned by any external conscious agent; it is not guaranteed by a providential ability of living matter to act purpose-fully. Rather, it has evolved and is being maintained and often improved by natural selection".[109] Ostensibly, the four authoritative voices studied in this section maintain the principle that evolution is a nonpurposive process; that underlying the evolution of the natural world are mindless, automotive operations. For Dawkins, this is clearly indicative of a meaningless, purposeless world, and moreover, that meaning and purpose themselves as concepts are effects and not causes in the universe.

It is from this purposelessness that Dawkins derives the most significant conclusion in the context of this work: the absence of a God. The lack of meaning in the evolutionary picture leads him to his atheistic convictions. In *The God Delusion*, Dawkins professes that evolution theory acts as a consciousness raiser in considering the existence of a creator God. He argues:

> Darwinism raises our consciousness in other ways. Evolved organs, elegant and efficient as they often are, also demonstrate revealing flaws—exactly as you'd expect if they have an evolutionary history, and exactly as you would not expect if they were designed. . . . Our consciousness is also raised by the cruelty and wastefulness of natural selection. Predators seem beautifully 'designed' to catch prey animals, while the prey animals seem equally beautifully 'designed' to escape them.[110]

Though Dawkins postulates a variety of arguments for the nonexistence of God, his atheist persuasions are largely derived from the absence of directed design in nature, exposed by evolution theory. He professes that the theory of evolution made it possible to be an "intellectually fulfilled atheist".[111] We have already suggested in Chapter One that Dawkins' atheist convictions have been significantly criticized by a number of authoritative voices. However, in the above passage, Dawkins also alludes to the "cruelty and wastefulness of natural selection". It is this aspect of evolution that Dawkins suggests is difficult to square with the concept of a beneficent creator. Discussing this point will be a major theme in Chapter Five.

This section has explored a cardinal feature of Dawkins' evolutionary and atheistic worldview: the issue of purposelessness in the evolutionary view of life. It is partly this element of Dawkins' evolutionary worldview that signifies his particular perspective as hostile to theology, and as we had discussed in Chapter One, it is because of this hostility that Dawkins is taken as a dialogue partner for theology. We will demonstrate how through dialogue with such a contrary worldview, theology may be enriched by its criticisms, forcing it to re-examine traditional concepts in the context of a pluralistic intellectual marketplace. Dawkins' insistence on the purposeless/atheistic implications of evolution, explored in this section, makes him a good example of a critical 'other' to engage with. At this point, we will continue to develop Dawkins' evolutionary worldview by exploring another topic in which theology has a 'vested interest': morality. Dawkins' evolutionary perspective on morality will also have significant theological implications when we explore traditional theological understandings of evil in Chapter Five.

The Evolution of Altruism

In following Dawkins' evolutionary *weltanschauung*, which views the universe as inherently purposeless, the issue of morality becomes apparent. In an entirely causal, mindless world, what explanation could there be for morality and ethics? Would an ethical reality contradict the 'survival of the fittest' aphorism used to describe the evolutionary process?[112] To address this quandary, Dawkins provides an account of morality that is consistent with the evolutionary framework heretofore presented. Building upon the theorization of previous scholars, he outlines an account of how altruism could evolve as a consequence of natural selection. This section will outline Dawkins' presentation of how a moral system evolved, incorporating other relevant scholarly contributions to this evolutionary perspective of altruism.

An analysis of ethics from this scientific standpoint has great theological significance, and is thus consistent with the pluralistic/interdisciplinary methodology outlined in Chapter One. To illustrate, the acclaimed ethicist Jeffrey Stout, for example, discussed the importance of gaining diverse ethical perspectives, amalgamating a multidimensional, pluralistic ethical society: "Our capacity to live peaceably with each other depends upon our ability to converse intelligibly and reason coherently".[113] It is suggested in this work that an evolutionary perspective will satisfy this criterion of providing theologians with a different view of ethics, offering a new dimension for consideration. Stout also seeks to dissolve boundaries between post-Enlightenment ethical philosophy and the religious ethical dimension.[114] Engaging in dialogue with an ethical model from an evolutionary perspective will greatly contribute to this task. Moreover, it is the altruistic, ethical dimension of Jesus (though not Christianity) that Dawkins himself finds commendable. He applauds Jesus for his "genuinely original and radical ethics", and therefore, there is a discernible space for dialogue and mutual benefit between the theological and evolutionary ethical mindset.[115] For these reasons, Dawkins' evolutionary account of altruism will now be explored.

The necessity of an explanation of altruism from an evolutionary context becomes apparent if we briefly recapitulate Dawkins' thesis on genes. He views a body as an amalgamation of genes that have acquired a sense of individuality. This subjective sense of individuality arises because genes that are more cooperative than their counterparts are favored by natural selection. A further cardinal characteristic of genes in Dawkins' model is selfishness. Permitting Dawkins' anthropomorphism (which, we noted, was criticized by philosopher Mary Midgley), he describes the behaviour of genes as fundamentally selfish; the only 'concern' of genes is to become more numerous in the gene pool:

> If we allow ourselves the licence of talking about genes as if they had conscious aims, always reassuring ourselves that we could translate our sloppy language back into respectable terms if we wanted to, we could ask the question, what is a single selfish gene trying to do? It is trying to get more numerous in the gene pool.[116]

Acknowledging that the primary 'concern' of genes is becoming more numerous in the gene pool, and that this 'concern' governs their behaviour, one would expect that, subsequently, the behaviour of organisms is ubiquitously selfish. However, this is not the case, as altruistic behaviour is clearly manifest in humans and other species. Dawkins therefore offers an explanation of how inherently selfish aims result in altruistic behaviour. The crux of his thesis is as follows: "The key point . . . is that a gene might be able to assist replicas of itself which are sitting in other bodies. If so, this would appear as individual altruism but it would be brought about by gene selfishness".[117] At this point, we should stress that Dawkins' evolutionary account of altruism is one topic that we could suggest goes beyond the boundaries of science, and is significantly speculative. Later, we will again draw upon Fern Elsdon-Baker to criticize Dawkins on this point. Notwithstanding such criticism, the influential Australian philosopher Peter Singer also synopsises the seeming paradox of altruism in natural selection:

> Darwinian thinking suggests that we are not likely to be naturally altruistic. How can a self-sacrificing trait that benefits the group at the expense of the individual survive? It seems that self-sacrificing tendencies would be eliminated from the gene pool, no matter how much they help the group. But there may be selective forces that encourage behaviour that looks like altruism, and may be altruistic in its motivation, even though in specific circumstances it brings benefits to the apparently altruistic individual.[118]

This premise allows Dawkins to reconcile the 'selfish gene' concept with the reality of altruism. Dawkins achieves this reconciliation by positing an evolutionary explanation for altruistic behaviour, focusing on the genes 'behaving' altruistically toward copies of themselves, a selfish act that has the appearance of altruism. For genetic behaviour to be beneficial to replicas of genes in other bodies, Dawkins suggests that genes must utilize some method enabling them to recognize copies of themselves. He insightfully illustrates that the recognition of copies of genes can be explained by statistical probability; close relatives of individuals have a greater statistical probability of sharing genes than distant relatives. As parents and offspring share 50 percent of their genes, altruistic acts toward kin are common. Therefore, an individual could appear to be acting altruistically toward another individual, though it is the genetic selfishness of the individual that provides the underlying motives. It is in a particular gene's own selfish interest to encourage an individual to behave altruistically, if the benefactor of such altruistic behaviour shares the same gene. Renowned evolutionary biologist W. D. Hamilton, often cited by Dawkins as a major influence, encapsulates this point:

> As a simple but admittedly crude model we may imagine a pair of genes g and G such that G tends to cause some kind of altruistic

behaviour while g is null. Despite the principle of 'survival of the fittest' the ultimate criterion which determines whether G will spread is not whether the behaviour is to the benefit of the behaver but whether it is to the benefit of the gene G; and this will be the case if the average net result of the behaviour is to add to the gene pool a higher concentration than does the gene pool itself. With altruism this will happen only if the affected individual is a relative of the altruist, therefore having an increased chance of carrying the gene . . .[119]

The more distant the relatedness between the altruist and the benefactor(s), the less probable it is that they will share genes. Therefore, the justification of such altruistic behaviour, in terms of the inverted benefit to the altruists' own genes, needs to be greater. Up to this point, Dawkins has determined how altruism does not contradict an evolutionary view, by providing us with an explanation of how it evolved. This outline serves the purpose of establishing that point, though in reality, the altruistic behaviour of organisms is vastly more complex. Dawkins highlights the oversimplification of the calculations discussed so far:

> In any case the calculation is only a very preliminary first approximation to what it ideally should be. It neglects many things, including the ages of the individuals concerned. . . . There is no end to the refinements of the calculation that could be achieved in the best of all worlds. But real life is not lived in the best of all possible worlds. We cannot expect real animals to take into account in coming to an optimum decision. We shall have to discover, by observation and experiment in the wild, how closely real animals actually come to achieving an ideal cost-benefit analysis.[120]

Dawkins' materialist explanation for altruism allows us to consider how altruism may not be contrary to natural selection. Dawkins then develops this concept to include 'reciprocal altruism'. Reciprocal altruism arises when individuals act altruistically toward one another with the anticipation that the altruistic deed will be reciprocated in future instances. To convey the central premise of reciprocal altruism, Dawkins hypothesizes the behaviour of a particular bird species:

> Suppose a species of bird is parasitized by a particularly nasty kind of tick which carries a dangerous disease. . . . Normally an individual bird can pull off its own ticks when preening itself. There is one

place however—the top of the head—which it cannot reach with its own bill. . . . An individual may not be able to reach his own head, but nothing is easier than for a friend to do it for him. Later, when the friend is parasitized himself, the good deed can be paid back. Mutual grooming is in fact very common in both birds and mammals.[121]

Reciprocal altruism of this kind requires conscious foresight and the ability to recognize and remember individuals. This is necessary in order for the altruistic act to be reciprocated. As humans have a long memory and highly developed competency for individual recognition, Dawkins suggests that reciprocal altruism is amplified in our species.[122] This is an oversimplified model of altruism that offers a mechanism for an evolutionary explanation for morality. However, it will ultimately fail to fully appreciate the complexities of real behaviour and the possibilities that individuals may 'cheat', benefiting from the altruism of others though not expending energy or taking risks. Dawkins acknowledges this possibility: "There is no end to the fascinating speculation which the idea of reciprocal altruism engenders when we apply it to our own species. Tempting as it is, I am no better at such speculation than the next man, and I leave the reader to entertain himself".[123] An infinite number of determinants are existent in real interactions of humans. Notwithstanding, this model provides an evolutionary foundation for the development of altruistic behaviour. In this particular case, however, the altruistic behaviour is only explained by the ultimate benefit to the altruists themselves.

Dennett develops this point. Within the theoretical framework of evolution, altruistic behaviour would be expected to be uncommon. This eventuates in the paradox that this chapter used as a starting point, as altruistic behaviour is clearly manifest. "Aside from occasional short-lived freaks of nature, altruists seem to be ruled out by the fundamental principles of evolution. . . . It's a dog-eat-dog world, and nice guys *inevitably* finish last".[124] However, as the evolutionary system becomes more complex, elements of altruistic behaviour will eventually emerge, though this behaviour is fundamentally governed by selfish wants. Thus a pseudo-altruism emerges.[125] This is the variety of altruism recognized by Dawkins as discussed above. Dennett also perceptively notes that there are no methods, as of yet, that can distinguish between this pseudo-altruism and 'genuine' altruism, if such a thing as 'genuine' altruism can be defined.[126] Dennett quotes distinguished evolutionary biologist George C. Williams, previously encountered in Chapter Two, to portray the prevailing thoughts on the evolution of morality: "I account for morality as an accidental capability produced, in its boundless stupidity, by a biological process that is normally opposed to the expression of such a capability".[127]

Is morality, then, just a manifestation of the inherent selfish behaviour of the genetic yearning for reproduction? Authoritative voices in evolutionary science and philosophy, distinguished philosopher of biology Michael Ruse[128] and Harvard entomologist (scholar of the scientific study of insects) Edward O. Wilson, adopt such a view. Dennett cites their co-authored 'The Evolution of Ethics', published in *New Scientist* in 1985: "Morality, or more strictly our belief in morality, is merely an adaptation put in place to further our reproductive ends".[129] Ruse and Wilson thus view morality as an epiphenomenon. Ruse reiterates this concept in his own writings. "People think that there is an objective morality, even though there is not. As E. O. Wilson and I once put it: 'Ethics is a collective illusion of the genes, put in place to make us good cooperators. 'Nothing more, but also nothing less'".[130] Wilson also postulated that "[h]uman behaviour . . . is the circuitous technique by which human genetic material has been and will be kept intact. Morality has no other demonstrable function".[131] Again, we must stress that these postulations are philosophical conclusions based on particular interpretations of evolutionary theory, such as Dawkins' selfish gene concept.

The view of morality of which Ruse and Wilson—among others—are proponents is, however, not shared by Dawkins; he provides an addendum to the view that altruism exists only as a proxy of innate selfishness. He explains that we have acquired such a degree of consciousness that our genetic nature is no longer the main influence on our behaviour, even if our morality may be derived from genetic selfishness. "We, alone on earth, can rebel against the tyranny of the selfish replicators".[132] Dennett offers similar perspectives, writing that our advanced consciousness, of which language is an instrumental capacity, classifies our species as a 'new' type of moral agent.[133] We have the potential to recognize our behaviour's natural origins and understand the rationale behind them. However, this is not our conscious reasoning. Our conscious minds can differentiate new reasons for behaviour, and that factor sets us apart from other animals, leaving us with the ultimate responsibility for our own actions.[134] Moreover, Dawkins explicitly argues against the idea that genes are the sole determinants of our behaviour: "Genes have no monopoly on determinism".[135] He also suggests that memetics (the model of cultural evolution explored earlier) now has a greater influence on our behaviour than genetics.[136]

As Dawkins has offered a genetic explanation for the origin of morality, the castigation of a behavioural theory constructed in purely genetic terms may seem counterintuitive. A solution to what may seem a self-contradiction on

Dawkins' part can be found with Dennett, who provides an explanation while consistently staying within the evolutionary boundaries that have characterized Dawkins' worldview until this point. To illustrate this solution, Dennett quotes Friedrich Nietzsche: "the cause of the origin of a thing and its eventual utility, its actual employment and place in a system of purposes, lie worlds apart".[137] Dennett, incorporating Nietzsche's words, claims that though there is a genetic, evolutionary explanation for the origin of a particular system, in this case altruism, it does not logically follow that such a system will be used for the purposes that shaped its evolution in the first instance. Though altruism evolved as a proxy of gene selfishness, it is not consequential that gene selfishness governs all altruistic behaviour. Altruism can be utilized by our conscious minds, for our own ends, whatever they may be:

> It must be true that there is an evolutionary explanation of how our memes and genes interacted to create the policies of human cooperation that we enjoy in civilization—we haven't figured out all the details yet, but it must be true unless there are skyhooks[138] in the offing—but this would not show that the result was for the benefit of the genes (as principal beneficiaries).[139]

Our genetic disposition for procreation—which is the originating point of genetic selfishness—is undoubtedly a major influence on our behaviour, manifest in common acts of self-sacrifice in order to save a child, or early death as a result of lascivious behaviour. Notwithstanding, Dennett explains that genetic objectives cannot be considered our sole *raison d'être*, "But we must not turn this important fact about our biological limitations into the massively misleading idea that the *summum bonum* at the source of every chain of practical reasoning is the imperative of our genes".[140]

To summarize Dawkins' view of altruism, then, we can recall Peter Baofu's proposition noted earlier in this chapter. Human behaviour is not wholly contingent on either genetics or memetics (or any other influence). It is a complex amalgamation of various factors, depending on the situation. Altruism, the subject of deliberation here, is no exception, whatever its genetic, evolutionary origins.[141] Dawkins' emphasis on the importance of cultural (including our consciousness) influence on human morality has been misinterpreted to suggest that altruism is not biological in origin. This misinterpretation is evident in a paper by Jessica C. Flack and Frans B. M. de Waal, titled '"Any Animal Whatever": Darwinian Building Blocks of Morality in Monkeys and Apes', published in the *Journal of Consciousness Studies*.[142]

In this publication, they cite Dawkins: "Be warned that if you wish, as I do, to build a society in which individuals co-operate generously and unselfishly toward a common good, you can expect little help from biological nature. Let us try to teach generosity and altruism, because we are born selfish".[143] They interpret this as evidence of Dawkins' denial of the biological origins of altruism: ". . . as Dawkins suggests, the origins of morality . . . are not biological".[144] However, it has been demonstrated in this section that Dawkins attempts to provide a logical account, based in biology, for the origins of morality. Though as he suggests, our conscious minds and cultural influences may now be more influential in our behaviour than our genes. Although Flack and de Waal suggest morality has a biological origin, it has now been taken to a new level in the social realm. Fundamentally, Dawkins attempts to account for our altruistic behaviour from an evolutionary perspective.

This section has explored Dawkins' proposed explanation for the evolutionary origins of morality. This explanation sought to solve the paradox outlined at the beginning of the section—how morality exists in a world governed by natural selection. His model for altruistic behaviour was presented in terms of biology, but then understood as highly influenced by our evolved conscious capacities. It may or may not be contested that this particular facet of Dawkins' evolutionary worldview is inimical to theology. Theological thinkers have identified themselves on both sides of this fence. For example, Nancey Murphy and George Ellis suggest that naturalistic accounts of morality such as Dawkins' reduce the moral to the nonmoral, ". . . explaining away the phenomenon for which they intend to account".[145] On the other hand, philosophers such as Paul Thompson suggest that an evolutionary view on ethics is a promising field of study,[146] while theologian Philip Clayton suggests that an evolutionary view of ethics does not contradict religious belief.[147] For the purposes of dialogue with Dawkins, we can, in the context of this project, support the view of theologian Neil Messer. Messer interestingly suggests that although an evolutionary account of morality has its caveats, it can be incorporated into a theological worldview. While due caution is necessary regarding the speculative nature of evolutionary accounts of morality, he proposes that

> an account of human being as moral being, developed on the basis of a theological understanding that the world and humans have been created "very good" by God, is well able to assimilate the proposal that aspects of moral experience emerged as a result of the evolutionary process that gave rise to our species.[148]

CRITIQUE OF DAWKINS' EVOLUTIONARY *WELTANSCHAUUNG*

Until this point, this chapter has explored the evolutionary worldview of Dawkins. Four particular aspects of this worldview (consciousness, cultural evolution, purpose, and morality) that hold significant theological implications were considered. However, this evolutionary worldview has its weaknesses and limitations. To gain insight from a broader array of scientific and philosophical hermeneutics, we will now examine criticisms of Dawkins' *weltanschauung*. The objective of exhibiting a critique is to show that we are engaging in a dialogue with Dawkins while acknowledging that diverse discourse exists on the possibility of an evolutionary worldview, much of which is critical of Dawkins' own stance. Therefore, we need to provide a rigorous academic critique of Dawkins' evolutionary views on consciousness, memetics, purpose, and altruism respectively.

CRITIQUE OF THE EVOLUTIONARY VIEW ON CONSCIOUSNESS

In this chapter, we encountered Dawkins' evolutionary approach to the study of consciousness, which is heavily reliant on Dennett. Therefore, we must now present a critique of the evolutionary view of consciousness that advocates that consciousness is a product of the algorithmic processes underlying the evolution of life. The materialist, evolutionary perspective on consciousness understands consciousness or mind as a product of natural selection; it is the culmination of physical processes. Therefore, in the materialist view, consciousness is a late arrival on the evolutionary scene. Distinguished physicist and philosopher of science Bernard d'Espagnat offers a fundamentally different interpretation of the nature of consciousness. He states, "Instead of the existence of consciousness following from the existence of objects, the existence of objects seems somehow to follow from the prior existence of consciousness (or consciousnesses) . . . the concept of consciousness is necessarily prior to the concept of phenomena".[149] D'Espagnat proposes a view antithetical to Dawkins and Dennett's—that some form of consciousness precedes the physical world. He justifies this assessment by referring to his own field of study, quantum physics (which we briefly introduced in Chapter Two).

Although we noted in Chapter Two that quantum physics remains a contentious area in scientific discourse, we can acknowledge the prominent physicist Paul Davies' assessment that on the subatomic level (objects smaller than an atom, e.g., protons/neutrons), the behaviour of particles seems to be contingent upon an observer: "Quantum mechanics exposed the subtle way in which observer and observed are interwoven".[150] Davies here refers to the principle of uncertainty of subatomic particles, which renowned physicist Stephen Hawking summarizes as follows: "[T]he more precisely you measure speed, the less precisely you can measure position, and vice versa".[151] It is because of the relationship between the observer (mind) and the observed (matter) that d'Espagnat opposes the concept of mind emanating from matter. "Atoms are relative to our minds, but if so, then to say that mind only comes from atoms in the brain is inconsistent".[152] A concurrent view is proffered by Johnjoe McFadden, who believes that the inherent uncertainty of quantum mechanics provides us with free will—opposed to the mechanistic, pseudo-free will of Dennett.[153] If d'Espagnat's interpretation is correct, then Dawkins and Dennett's view on mind arising from matter may be inconsistent.

Further criticism of the evolutionary model of consciousness can be found in the work of the influential Oxford mathematical physicist Roger Penrose. Penrose challenges an evolutionary view of consciousness, suggesting that it offers no selective advantage that necessitates its evolution. It was, if we recall, this aspect of consciousness that Dawkins found perplexing.[154] To illustrate his view, Penrose draws upon his own field of mathematics. He postulates that the human mind's propensity for mathematics offers no advantage in terms of natural selection. Therefore, he concludes that the mind could not be a product of evolution.[155] The fact that the human mind is able to formulate conscious judgments (such as the validity of one algorithm over another) is for Penrose indicative that "external insights" or nonalgorithmic processes exist in the mind. "In order to decide whether or not an algorithm will actually *work*, one needs *insights*, not just another algorithm".[156] This is contrary to the materialist view, in which the mind is solely the result of various inputs (the multiple drafts model). Notwithstanding this point, we noted in Dawkins' views on the evolution of altruism that a capacity, such as one for mathematics, may have evolved to serve a certain purpose, but is then used for something else, that is, actually doing mathematics. Subsequently, though the capacity for doing mathematics may not be of any selective advantage, it may have evolved as a corollary of another capacity that did hold a selective advantage. Penrose himself acknowledges this point:

> It seems to me to be clear that the musings and mutterings that we indulge in, when we . . . become philosophers, are not things that are *in themselves* selected for, but are necessary 'baggage' (from the point of view of natural selection) that must be carried by beings who indeed *are* conscious, and whose consciousness has been selected by

natural selection, but for some quite different and presumably very powerful reason.[157]

However, in disavowing a materialist model of mind arising solely from algorithmic processes of natural selection, Penrose fails to supersede such a model with one of his own. Though insistent on a nonalgorithmic model of mind, he admits that his perspective is highly circumstantial—not methodical, but largely predicated upon intuition.[158] Therefore, one could conclude that Penrose's argument lacks substance. Dennett offers a counter-critique of Penrose, maintaining that Penrose's view on the nonalgorithmic nature of mind is insubstantial. "Penrose is holding out for a phenomenon that is truly noncomputable, not just impractical to compute. . . . Penrose has a hunch that someday we're going to find a skyhook. This is the hunch of a brilliant scientist, but he himself admits that it is only a hunch".[159] Notwithstanding Dennett's counter-criticism, we can acknowledge that Penrose's critique may highlight a caveat for engaging with Dawkins' view on mind: that perhaps Dawkins is attempting to explain phenomena that cannot be explained solely in his Darwinian terms.

In the evolutionist understanding, mind arose from the mindless, mental from the physical. Moreover, Dawkins and Dennett argue that this progression was itself purposeless. A contrary view on mind, however, is espoused by Paul Davies. In outlining his views on mind, Davies refers to both mind itself, and meaning in the universe. His supposition stresses that mind is indicative of a deeper meaning, not a coincidental consequence of sequential algorithmic, evolutionary processes:

> I cannot believe that our existence in this universe is a mere quirk of fate, an accident of history, an incidental blip in the great cosmic drama. Our involvement is too intimate. The physical species *Homo* may count for nothing, but the existence of mind in some organism on some planet in the universe is surely a fact of fundamental significance. Through conscious beings the universe has generated self-awareness. This can be no trivial detail, no minor by-product of mindless, purposeless forces. We are truly meant to be here.[160]

Davies offers an interpretation of the scientific picture of the world that sees mind as a significant feature of the universe, not merely a product of mindless forces, as in Dawkins' view. Davies feels that the subjective experience of purpose and the fact that the universe seems to be comprehensible suggests that there is a deeper profundity to the universe than mindless processes: "[T]he fact that science works, and works so well, points to something profoundly significant about the origin of the cosmos".[161]

Further criticisms that focus specifically on Dennett's view on consciousness are offered by Irish philosopher Joan McCarthy in her work, *Dennett and Ricoeur on the Narrative Self*. She critiques Dennett's emphasis on the importance of language in his model of consciousness. McCarthy feels Dennett's model is too heavily reliant on linguistic properties:

> To put it briefly, language use enables humans to do all kinds of weird and wonderful things, like imagining, anticipating, and evaluating: and also creating, communicating, and philosophizing. However, prioritizing linguistic ability in a hierarchy of features associated with ourselves has worrying consequences.[162]

As noted, Dennett postulated that it was with the development of language that humans were able to formalize thoughts to an unprecedented degree, and therefore to become 'fully' conscious. Dennett distinguishes between sentience and consciousness based upon linguistic prowess: in order to be considered conscious, an individual must have the capacity for language.

> In order to be conscious . . . it is necessary to have a certain sort of informational organization that endows that thing with a wide set of cognitive powers (such as the powers of reflection and re-representation). This sort of internal organization does not come automatically with so-called "sentience". It is not the birthright of mammals or warm-blooded creatures or vertebrates; it is not even the birthright of human beings. It is an organization that is swiftly achieved in one species, ours, and in no other. Other species no doubt achieve somewhat similar organizations, but the differences are so great that most of the speculative translations of imagination from our case to theirs make no sense.[163]

A complex system such as language must be in place for Dennett to consider an individual conscious as opposed to sentient. McCarthy suggests that this is too narrow a view of consciousness.[164]

Moreover, McCarthy criticizes Dennett's model as epistemologically and ontologically fragile, because she interprets it as both arbitrary (epistemologically fragile), and not 'real' in the same way a scientifically defined object is 'real' (ontologically fragile).[165] Similar criticisms are synopsised by neuroscientist Merlin Donald, when he proclaims that Dennett's *Consciousness*

Explained could have been more aptly titled *Consciousness Explained Away*.[166] Both McCarthy and Donald thus claim that Dennett's model, by explaining a methodical system, dissolves the reality of subjectively experienced consciousness. This interpretation of Dennett's model, however, could be viewed more as a neutral observation than a constructive criticism. Though Dennett does not agree that his model views the self as illusory[167] (or ontologically fragile, to utilize McCarthy's terminology), he comments that there is little fundamental difference between his model and Donald's. Consequently, Donald's critique seems to rest upon the foundations of a misinterpretation. Dennett explains:

> Donald makes it clear on page one that he conceives of it as an antidote of sorts to my books, *Consciousness Explained*, and *Darwin's Dangerous Idea*. However, the last chapter of Donald's book, *The Triumph of Consciousness*, could serve quite well as the last chapter of this book. How can this be? Because Donald, like many others, has hugely understated the bounty to be found in Darwin's "strange inversion of reasoning." He says in his Prologue: "This book proposes that the human mind is unlike any other on this planet, not because of its biology, which is not qualitatively unique, but because of its ability to generate and assimilate culture" . . . Exactly.[168]

Dennett, contrary to Donald's assessment, actually places great emphasis on the importance of the mind; as we noted throughout this chapter, he suggested that it led to the advent of culture, which in turn actually alters the genetic evolution of the human species through medicine and diet. In that sense, Dennett views the mind as anything but arbitrary.

We can find further support for our conclusion that Donald's critique is based upon a misinterpretation of the materialist view of consciousness in Donald's own work. He suggests that Dennett's position views consciousness as superfluous: "The neo-Darwinian Hardliners Dennett has embraced are a staunch band of revolutionaries. . . . They share an uncompromising belief in the irrelevance of the conscious mind and the illusory nature of free will".[169] However, as we established, Dawkins and Dennett place heavy emphasis on the role of the conscious mind, particularly in terms of morality and responsibility for one's own actions. However, Donald could be correct in suggesting that Dennett's view on the mind is ultimately superfluous, given that it arose through purposeless processes. If one were to interpret Donald in this way, then his position would echo that of Paul Davies, who uses subjective experience and the success of science as an indication that the mind has a deeper meaning.

CRITIQUE OF MEMETICS

In Chapters Two and Three of this book, we demarcated between the predominantly scientific aspects of Dawkins' evolutionary model (Chapter Two), and the predominantly philosophical/theological aspects (Chapter Three). However, pertaining to memetics, Dawkins fails to distinguish between empirical science and the speculative nature of memetics. Fern Elsdon-Baker posits such a criticism:

> He brought little evidence, beyond the anecdotal, to bear in his development of ideas. . . . The logic was persuasive and the argument fascinating, but it was basically conjectural. In his countless forays beyond the boundaries of his native ethology, Dawkins is sometimes right and sometimes wrong. His arguments are occasionally speculative and some are more or less unprovable one way or the other, at least at present. But one criticism I would make is that his speculation has no obvious boundaries, so it is always unclear what is dispassionate, clear-sighted scientific speculation and what simply represents Dawkins' own personal and political agenda. And I would argue that this does not in any way constitute objective science.[170]

Elsdon-Baker admits that Dawkins' arguments/metaphors in relation to nonempirical concepts (such as memetics) within his system may be logically coherent and often compelling. Notwithstanding, her criticism of Dawkins' failure to sufficiently differentiate between empirical and nonempirical is substantial. Memetics is one such example where Dawkins may inappropriately encompass nonscience into his scientific worldview. The philosopher Mary Midgley notes a similar point, suggesting that "[m]eme-language is not really an extension of physical science but, as so often happens, an analogy . . . ".[171]

Dawkins' meme theory has also been criticized by Distin, whose contribution to memetics was noted earlier in this chapter. She criticizes him specifically on his attitude toward religious memes. Dawkins' discernible contempt for religion severely impedes his objectivity in outlining his conceptual theory for evolutionary analysis of culture—Dawkins' memetic approach to religion will be studied in more depth in the next chapter. He conspicuously differentiates between memes that pervade the meme-pool because they have an intrinsic self-perpetuating nature, analogous to a virus (he categorizes faith as one such virus), and memes that are propagated due to their own merit (he would suggest scientific ideas as an example).[172] Distin encapsulates the point: "Dawkins contrasts such 'viruses' with 'good' memes. He says that we should be careful not to apply the viral analogy to all ideas and all aspects of human culture: some are more like 'good genes' than self-serving, 'Duplicate Me' viruses".[173] This distinction is problematic as it is inherently subjective, a matter of personal preference: ". . . Dawkins comes perilously close to labeling only those things of which he approves, as 'great' and 'nonviral'".[174] Distin suggests that the distinction in question emanates from a misinterpretation of Dawkins' own thesis. Classification of certain memes as 'good' and certain memes as 'bad' is an inappropriate, epistemic error: ". . . neither gene nor meme theory has anything to say about the intrinsic value (i.e. 'goodness') of the information that its replicators carry".[175] This criticism is particularly important in the context of a theological project given Dawkins' subjective contempt for religion, which we highlighted as a significant limitation of dialogue.

Dennett acknowledges the validity of such a criticism. He does not comment on the religion-virus analogy (which he endorses[176]), but he acknowledges the criticism in terms of viewing science as 'good'. Dennett explains that one would be correct to question Dawkins: "Where is your demonstration that these 'virtues' are *good* virtues? . . . Where, then, is the Archimedean point from which you can deliver your benediction on science? There is none. About this, I agree wholeheartedly . . . ".[177] Here we see an uncharacteristic disagreement between Dennett and Dawkins. The force of the critique thus suggests that Dawkins' subjectivity on labeling science as good and religion as a virus may undermine his objectivity. Consequently, Distin's critique is substantial.

The legitimacy of Dawkins' use of memetics as a subject itself has also been questioned. Anthropologist Robert Aunger, a contributor to meme theory, highlights areas of contention in considering memetics as a legitimate conceptual framework for discourse. He quotes seminal American mathematician Martin Gardner's disdain for memetics:

> Memetics is no more than a cumbersome terminology for saying what everybody already knows and that can be more usefully said in the dull terminology of information transfer. . . . A meme is so broadly defined by its proponents as to be a useless concept, creating more confusion than light, and I predict that the concept will soon be forgotten as a curious linguistic quirk of little value.[178]

Furthermore, Alister McGrath suggests that although at first he found the idea of the meme exciting and felt it had potential, he later concluded that the meme offered no further explanatory power than standard models of cultural studies.[179] Corroborating sentiment can be found in distinguished philosophers such as Bruce Edmonds and Holmes Rolston III. Edmonds and Rolston question the substance of memetics in terms of its potential as an explanatory, predictive framework that will offer academics new insights into phenomena such as cultural evolution.[180] The disagreement pertaining to the status of memetics is evident in the last issue of the online, peer-reviewed *Journal of Memetics: Evolutionary Models of Information Transmission*, which ceased publication in 2005 after eight years. In the journal's final issue, Edmonds himself describes memetics as a "short-lived fad" that has failed.[181] However, in the same issue, others such as British scientist Derek Gatherer remain more optimistic on the future of memetics: "[M]emetics can survive as a data-oriented branch of the social simulation field specializing in the evaluation of co-evolutionary or cultural models".[182] Moreover, through personal correspondence with Dennett, I questioned him as to whether he was still as confident as he once was regarding memetics. He responded unequivocally, "More so. And I am pleased to see that the most serious researchers are beginning to agree, though they often, for various reasons, try to avoid using the term. See my essay on the New Replicators in the *Oxford Encyclopedia of Evolution*".[183] Consequently, we can say that the legitimacy of memetics is continually being intently debated among academics, which is a significant caveat against incorporating it into a dialogue.

CRITIQUE OF A PURPOSELESS WORLD

In this chapter, we also noted that Dawkins proposes a view of the world that sees purpose only as a by-product of human consciousness—that purpose only exists as it is attributed retrospectively by humans. Michael Ruse holds a similar position:

> The design of organisms is to be understood in terms of their survival and reproduction, as Darwin insisted. And the strange causal connections come out because of Darwin. Something is of value because it leads to the end of survival and reproduction, but this survival and reproduction are in turn the reason why it exists. A leads to B, but then B in turn leads to A. There is no backward causation here, nor is there . . . some kind of intentionality. A does not have B in mind, nor does a creator have B in mind when A is made. It is rather a cyclical situation, where the first leads to the second and

then back to the first. Darwinism does not have a design built in as a premise, but the design emerges . . .[184]

Ruse suggests that purpose may not be inherent in the universe, but it has emerged through the evolutionary process. An organism's purpose is to reproduce, though the organism itself exists because of reproduction. Francisco J. Ayala espouses a similar view. We noted earlier that Ayala did not interpret the world as teleological with preconceived plans. However, he echoes Ruse by insightfully observing that purpose may exist if we conceive reproduction as a 'goal' of life:

> Natural selection can be said to be a teleological process in two ways. Firstly, natural selection is a mechanistic end-directed process which results in increased reproductive efficiency. Reproductive fitness can, then, be said to be the end result or goal of natural selection. Secondly, natural selection is teleological in the sense that it produces and maintains end-directed organs and processes, when the function or end-state served by the organ or process contributes to the reproductive fitness of the organisms.[185]

Pursuing this cyclical method of considering purpose, the issue of 'first causes' inevitably arises. Ruse does not produce a deliberation on first causes, though he acknowledges that the cyclical mode of thought on purpose is apt in considering the notion that "[w]here we are today fits very comfortably with the Western tradition of thinking about organisms and final causes".[186] Therefore, according to Ruse, the immense degree of purpose that emerges from within the evolutionary process may be consistent with considering a 'first cause'. The purpose that emerges from evolution may in fact actually point to a wider purpose, contrary to Dawkins' worldview. This conclusion has been adopted by Midgley, who insightfully explains that the world is "riddled with purpose". The innumerable instances of purpose ". . . all fit together well enough to produce the remarkable degree of order in the world which, so surprisingly, makes science possible and which gives rise to the idea of a unifying purpose".[187]

Moreover, we noted that significant scientific authorities interpret the evidence of evolution as purposive. Simon Conway Morris is one such example. As we noted, Conway Morris postulates that there are particular tendencies in the evolutionary process, which can thus be considered purposeful.[188] In addition, Conway Morris also echoes the sentiments of Paul Davies and Roger Penrose, who see the mind as indicative of a deeper purpose. The mind's comprehension of mathematics, which is reflective of an objective reality, portrays for Conway Morris an innate conscious intentionality in the evolutionary process:

> If however, the universe is actually a product of a rational Mind, and evolution is simply the search engine that in leading to sentience and consciousness allows us to discover the fundamental architecture of the universe—a point many mathematicians intuitively sense when they speak of the unreasonable effectiveness of mathematics—then things not only start to make much better sense, but they are also much more interesting. Farewell bleak nihilism; the cold assurances that all is meaningless. . . . Of course our brains are a product of evolution, but does anybody seriously believe consciousness itself is material? Well, yes . . . but their explanations seem to have made no headway. We are dealing with unfinished business. God's funeral? I don't think so. Please join me beside the coffin marked atheism. I fear, however, there will be very few mourners.[189]

Theological reflections on purpose in Chapter Five will refer to the view outlined by Dawkins in this chapter. However, at this point, we can recognize that Dawkins' perspective is not the only available option.

CRITIQUE OF EVOLUTIONARY ALTRUISM

Above, we duly acknowledged Fern Elson Baker's criticism of Dawkins, for his failure to adequately distinguish between what can be regarded as scientifically demonstrable theory, and philosophical extrapolations from science. This criticism is also pertinent with regard to Dawkins' presentation of evolutionary altruism. Although Dawkins' theories on the evolutionary origins of morality are founded upon his interpretation of evolutionary science, they are in essence more philosophical than scientific. Thus, as with his meme hypothesis, Dawkins fails to responsibly distinguish between science (which methodologically is empirical) and philosophy, which is a hermeneutical discipline. However, the presentation of an evolutionary account of altruism was also considerably reliant on Dennett, who as noted in the introduction to this chapter, emphasizes the philosophical importance of Darwinism. As a result, Dennett is perhaps less vulnerable to such criticism in this regard, despite being in alignment with Dawkins' view. Dennett presents his interpretation of evolutionary altruism as a philosophical treatise (although, through personal correspondence, Dennett has postulated that evolutionary theories of culture are, in theory, just as scientifically verifiable as any other aspects of the biosphere, but they just have not been adequately demonstrated at present—see appendix).

The substance of Dawkins' evolutionary view of morality has also been criticized, notably by Midgley. Midgley challenges what she terms the "excesses of psychological egoism" of Dawkins' Darwinian moral perspective. Midgley claims that for Dawkins, altruism exists only as a façade; that seemingly altruistic behaviour is in reality governed by selfish wants. "The victory of gene-selection is taken to establish egoism, to prove that existing forms of altruism, though present, are not what they seem, and are really only forms of self-interest".[190] More recently, she has argued that a "Dawkinsist" understanding of the evolution of morality cannot account for the nuance of conflicting behavioural motives.[191] Theologian James Mackey is equally suspicious of Dawkins' understanding of morality, as he articulates:

> Dawkins's Darwinism has a god alright; and a morality that fits its nature. The blind god is "evolution" and its ruling moral principle is: whether by enterprise or chance mutation you gain monetary advantage in the struggle of all against all for life ever more abundant, use this superior fitness entirely for yourself, for helping the weak will only hold you back.[192]

Midgley and Mackey's assessment of Dawkins' view on morality here echo that of E. O. Wilson and Ruse, who stated that morality was merely an effect of our selfishness. However, we noted that Dawkins is perhaps more cautious on the explanatory power of his view on altruism than Midgley gives him credit for. It was also considered how Dawkins acknowledges that when his understanding of the evolution of altruism is played out in reality, it becomes so complex that there is no end to possible speculation of how it operates.[193] Furthermore, Dawkins, and particularly Dennett, provide an addendum to the gene-centred view of moral behaviour. This is also recognized by Neil Messer, who suggests that Dennett provides a more sophisticated reductionist approach to morality that is incorporative of Dawkins' notion of memes.[194] Messer, however, also acknowledges that the concept of memetics has also been severely criticized. This may also damage Dawkins and Dennett's explanation of moral behaviour given its reliance on memes.[195] Therefore, Dawkins and Dennett's reliance on memes to explain morality may be criticized to the same extent that memetics itself has. This is, again, an important caveat in engaging in a theological dialogue with Dawkins on his view on the evolution of morality. As Messer suggests, it is important to acknowledge these caveats if we are to attempt to engage in dialogue, or as he puts it, "assimilate the proposal that aspects of moral experience emerged as a result of the evolutionary process that gave rise to our species" into a theological conception.[196]

CONCLUSION

This chapter has examined the philosophical outlook that arises from Dawkins' interpretation of the science of evolution. It has done so in terms of four distinct issues; consciousness, cultural evolution, purpose, and morality. This evolutionary *weltanschauung* advanced by Dawkins teems with issues of theological importance. Therefore, by developing this philosophical approach, we can provide clear routes for intellectual engagement between Dawkins and theology. It was seen that Dawkins rejects the philosophical dualism of Descartes, and stringently opposes the concept that the mind is more than matter. The theological implications of such a view, and its scientific credibility, will allow for insightful discussion in Chapter Five, pertaining to particular religious doctrines such as the relationship between humanity and God. It was also noted how Dawkins attempts, with his meme theory, to provide a satisfactory account of how Darwinian natural selection can account for the evolution of culture and civilization. This memetic account for the evolution of culture has subsequently been endorsed and developed further by Dennett, among others, though it is not without its problems. Notwithstanding such problems, a memetic framework for understanding the evolution of culture will be employed in the next chapter, to contribute to theologians' efforts at understanding the evolution of religious belief. Thus it highlights a distinct area for dialogue between theology and Dawkins' view on evolution.

A further cardinal element of Dawkins' approach is his view that the universe is devoid of purpose. The theological implications of this element of an evolutionary philosophy will be more thoroughly interpreted from within a theological context in Chapter Five. Therefore, it was important that Dawkins' view on the matter be examined in the context of seeking a dialogue. We also explored how Dawkins seeks to solve the paradox between the apparent ruthlessness of natural selection and the apparent existence of altruism, most prevalent in *Homo sapiens*. He hypothesizes how morality may be understood as evolving naturally through the evolutionary process. This view also has important theological implications that will be considered in Chapter Five. To give balance to this chapter, a variety of criticisms of this particular evolutionary philosophy were also provided. We noted that while the evolutionary worldview of Dawkins may be grounded in science, it is in fact heavily hermeneutical. Therefore, we acknowledged other interpretations/critiques of the four main points of the chapter.

Notes

1. Paul Ricoeur, *Oneself as Another*, trans. Kathleen Blamey (Chicago: University of Chicago Press, 1992), 297.

2. For example, the philosopher of evolution Fern Elsdon-Baker uses the term 'staunch ally' in *The Selfish Genius: How Richard Dawkins Rewrote Darwin's Legacy* (London: Icon Books, 2009), 126.

3. Daniel C. Dennett interview with the author, May 2012.

4. For examples, see Richard Dawkins, ed., *The Oxford Book of Modern Science Writing* (Oxford: Oxford University Press, 2008), 254; also, Richard Dawkins, *Unweaving the Rainbow: Science, Delusion and the Appetite for Wonder* (London: Penguin, 1998), 208; also, *DDI*, 12.

5. Daniel C. Dennett interview with the author, May 2012.

6. Karl Rahner, *Theological Investigations Vol. XXI: Science and Christian Faith*, trans. Hugh M. Riley (London: Darton, Longman & Todd, 1983), 150.

7. Émile Durkheim, *The Elementary Forms of the Religious Life* (Oxford: Oxford University Press, 2001), xvii.

8. *DDI*, 19.

9. *TSG*, 59.

10. Ibid., 59.

11. Ibid., 50.

12. Dennett scrutinizes Gould's opinions in *Darwin's Dangerous Idea: Evolution and the Meaning of Life* (London: Penguin, 1995), constituting the book's largest chapter. Gould in turn criticised Dennett's perspective of evolution as overly simplistic; 'Darwinian Fundamentalism', *The New York Review of Books* 44, no. 10 (June 1997).

13. Daniel C. Dennett, *Content and Consciousness* (London: Routledge, 1969), ix.

14. Ibid., ix.

15. *TGD*, 180.

16. Daniel C. Dennett, *Consciousness Explained* (London: Allen Lane, 1991), 29–30.

17. Ibid., 28.

18. Ibid., 34.

19. Daniel C. Dennett, *Brainchildren: Essays on Designing Minds* (London: Penguin, 1998), 132.

20. Dennett, *Consciousness Explained*, 35. However, Dennett does allude to the fact that dualism could avoid this apparent logical quagmire if there could be a heretofore unstudied kind of physical thing. One could contest that such a situation arose in modern physics with the discovery of 'Dark Matter'. This, however, would force a digression too far into physics and furthermore, to suggest that 'mind stuff' is in fact 'dark matter' could turn out to be a weak and nonempirical argument.

21. Dennett, *Consciousness Explained*, 33.

22. Dennett, *Brainchildren: Essays on Designing Minds*, 135.

23. In collection of short essays published in 2010 and edited by John Brockman of edge.org, 125 of the world's most prominent intellectual voices were posed the question, 'What will change everything?' In this collection, the issue of artificial intelligence, or decoding brain processes or thoughts as purely physical, is a prominent theme throughout. John Brockman, ed., *This Will Change Everything: Ideas That Will Shape the Future* (New York: HarperCollins, 2010).

24. For example, Brown University philosopher Jaegwon Kim, 'The Mind–Body Problem', Ted Honderich, ed., *The Oxford Companion to Philosophy* (Oxford: Oxford University Press, 1995), 580.

25. Endnotes to *TSG*, 278–80.

26. Dennett, *Consciousness Explained*, 111.

27. Ibid., 112.

28. Ibid., 214.

29. *DDI*, 73–83.

30. Ibid., 76.

31. Daniel C. Dennett, 'In Darwin's Wake, Where Am I?', *Proceedings and Addresses of the American Philosophical Association* 75, no. 3 (Nov. 2001): 17. Text reads, "made of cranes, made of cranes".

32. *DDI*, 371.

33. Stephen Jay Gould, 'Darwinian Fundamentalism', *The New York Review of Books* 44, no. 10 (June 1997).

34. Dennett, *Consciousness Explained*, 173–74.

35. Chapter 7 of *Consciousness Explained*, 171–227, provides an outline of the evolution of consciousness in more depth.

36. Ibid., 189.

37. Ibid., 187, though this is not to suggest that there is a direct correlation between brain size and intelligence.

38. Quoted in Daniel C. Dennett, *Freedom Evolves* (London: Allen Lane, 2003), 1.

39. Ibid., 1.

40. Ibid., 13.

41. Ibid., 106.

42. Ibid., 162. Italics in original.

43. Ibid., 162.

44. Ibid., 162.

45. Dennett, *Consciousness Explained*, 190.

46. Noam Chomsky, 'Knowledge of Language: Its Elements and Origins', *Philosophical Transactions of the Royal Society of London* 295, no. 1177 (Oct. 1981): 223–34.

47. Dennett, *Consciousness Explained*, 190.

48. Noam Chomsky, *Language and Problems of Knowledge: The Managua Lectures* (Cambridge, MA: MIT Press, 1988), 170. Though Dennett and Chomsky agree that the evolution of a capacity for language had a major influence on the development of thought, Dennett strongly critiques Chomsky on his views on the limits of scientific analysis of language and the mind. See chapter 13 of *DDI*, 370–400.

49. Dennett, *Consciousness Explained*, 190.

50. Dawkins, *Unweaving the Rainbow: Science, Delusion and the Appetite for Wonder*, 306–7.

51. "Meme," Oxford English Dictionary Online, Web, 10 May 2010.

52. *TGD*, 196.

53. *TSG*, 189.

54. Ibid., 189.

55. Ibid., 189. There are however, biological entities that evolve at an equivalent or more rapid pace, such as the AIDS virus. It cannot be upheld, then, that culture is universally evolving faster than biology. Robert Aunger, 'Introduction', in Robert Aunger, ed., *Darwinizing Culture: The Status of Memetics as a Science* (Oxford: Oxford University Press, 2000), 13.

56. *TSG*, 191.

57. Ibid., 193.

58. Daniel C. Dennett, 'Memes and the Exploitation of Imagination', *The Journal of Aesthetics and Art Criticism* 48, no. 2 (Spring 1990): 127–28.

59. Ibid., 128.

60. Richard Dawkins, *The Extended Phenotype: The Long Reach of the Gene* (Oxford: Oxford University Press, 1982), 109.

61. Ibid., 109.

62. *DDI*, 338.

63. *TSG*, 198, save to the extent that this hypothetical gene is 'turned off' or recessive.

64. Daniel C. Dennett, 'Forward' to Aunger, ed., *Darwinizing Culture: The Status of Memetics as a Science*, vii.

65. *TSG*, 199.

66. Ibid., 199.

67. Kate Distin, *The Selfish Meme* (Cambridge: Cambridge University Press, 2005), 68. Dawkins cited Distin as a scholar of memetics who has contributed a book-long work to the topic. *TGD*, 196.

68. Daniel Dennett, 'The New Replicators', in Mark Pagel, ed., *The Oxford Encyclopedia of Evolution* (Oxford: Oxford University Press, 2002), 83.

69. Susan Blackmore, 'On Memes and Temes', Lecture at TED (Feb. 2008). Blackmore differs slightly in her terminology. She uses the term 'hereditary' in place of 'replication', but in this context, both terms can be treated as mutual synonyms.

70. Peter Godfrey-Smith, 'Conditions for Evolution by Natural Selection', *The Journal of Philosophy* 104, no. 10 (Oct. 2007): 489.

71. Distin, *The Selfish Meme,* 68.

72. Daniel C. Dennett, 'Memes and the Exploitation of Imagination', *The Journal of Aesthetics and Art Criticism* 48, no. 2 (Spring 1990): 131. Blackmore further emphasizes this point in the lecture cited above.

73. Distin, *The Selfish Meme*, 69.

74. *TSG*, 192. Dawkins abbreviates '*mimeme*' to bear more resemblance to the word 'gene'.

75. Ibid., 192. Also, Susan Blackmore, *The Meme Machine* (Oxford: Oxford University Press, 1999), 6.

76. Blackmore, *The Meme Machine*, 6.

77. Distin, *The Selfish Meme*, 48–56.

78. Blackmore, *The Meme Machine*, 53.

79. Ibid., 54.

80. Ibid., 56.

81. Lamarckian evolution is named after the evolutionary theories of French naturalist Jean-Baptiste de Lamarck (1744–1829).

82. Ibid., 59.

83. Ibid., 60.

84. Ibid., 62.

85. Richard Dawkins, 'The Man Behind the Meme', interview with Jim Holt, *Slate* (1 Dec. 2004), Web, 2 May 2012.

86. Stephen Shennan, *Genes, Memes and Human History: Darwinian Archaeology and Cultural Evolution* (London: Thames & Hudson, 2002), 22. Dawkins endorses Shennan's work in *TGD*, 196.

87. Ibid., 35.

88. Ibid., 35.

89. Blackmore, *The Meme Machine*, 235.

90. Peter Baofu, *Beyond Nature and Nurture: Conceiving a Better Way to Understand Genes and Memes* (Newcastle: Cambridge Scholars Press, 2006), 138.

91. Bertrand Russell, *Religion and Science* (Oxford: Oxford University Press, 1935), 26.

92. *ROOE*, 112.

93. Ibid., 114.

94. Dawkins acknowledges that this particular example in the natural world contributed to the deterioration of Charles Darwin's faith in a benevolent creator, as it illustrates such indifferent cruelty. However, Dawkins' portrayal of Darwin as an atheist may not be completely accurate, as Alister McGrath has pointed out. We will discuss this further in Chapter Five.

95. Ibid., 111–12; also, *TGSOE*, 370.

96. Stephen Jay Gould, *Ever Since Darwin* (London: Penguin, 1977), 88.

97. Ibid., 155.

98. *TGSOE*, 392.

99. *DDI*, 82.

100. Ibid., 205.

101. Ibid., 402.

102. Ibid., 412.

103. Ibid., 203.

104. Ernst Mayr, *Evolution and the Diversity of Life: Selected Essays* (Cambridge, MA: Harvard University Press, 1976), 42.

105. Ibid., 42.

106. Ibid., 366.

107. Ibid., 388.

108. Theodosius Dobzhansky, *Mankind Evolving* (New Haven: Yale University Press, 1962), 335.

109. Theodosius Dobzhansky, *Genetics of the Evolutionary Process* (New York: Columbia University Press, 1970), 4–5.

110. *TGD*, 134.

111. Richard Dawkins, *The Blind Watchmaker: Why the Evidence of Evolution Reveals a Universe Without Design* (London: Penguin, 1986), 6.

112. The phrase 'survival of the fittest' is a common synonym for Darwin's theory of evolution by natural selection. It was coined by Herbert Spencer in 1864 after reading *The Origin of Species*. Darwin later adopted the phrase in later editions of *The Origin*. Spencer incorporated Darwinian evolution into his discourse on philosophical, political, and social matters, just as this project is considering the influence evolution has on theological theory.

113. Jeffrey Stout, *Ethics After Babel: The Languages of Morals and Their Discontents* (Cambridge: James Clarke, 1988), 3.

114. Ibid., 5.

115. Richard Dawkins, 'Atheists for Jesus' (Apr. 2006), Web, 28 Oct. 2010. To ensure the contextualization of this reference, in this article Dawkins claims the religions have largely corrupted the ethical visions of Jesus: "[H]e would be appalled at what is being done in his name". Dawkins' view, as taken from this paper, could be likened to Mahatma Gandhi's statement that "I like your Christ but not your Christians, your Christians are nothing like your Christ".

116. *TSG*, 88.

117. Ibid., 88.

118. Peter Singer, *A Darwinian Left: Politics, Evolution and Cooperation* (London: Weidenfeld & Nicolson, 1999), 55.

119. W. D. Hamilton, *Narrow Roads of Gene Land: The Collected Papers of W. D. Hamilton Volume 1: The Evolution of Social Behaviour* (New York: W. H. Freeman, 1996), 7.

120. *TSG*, 98.

121. Ibid., 183.

122. Ibid., 187.

123. Ibid., 188.

124. Dennett, *Freedom Evolves*, 196.

125. Dennett labels this variety of altruism 'Benselfishness', as he quotes Benjamin Franklin speaking to John Hancock on the signing of the U.S. Declaration of Independence, 4 July 1776: "We must indeed all hang together, or, most assuredly, we shall all hang separately". This

quotation highlights that what may appear to be altruistic actions are actually taken for the self-benefit of individuals. Therefore, the apparent altruism is governed by selfish motives.

126. Ibid., 197.

127. Ibid., 193.

128. Private email correspondence between Ruse and Dennett was apparently leaked onto the Internet by William A. Dembski, who co-edited a publication with Ruse, *Debating Design: From Darwin to DNA*. The private emails were not authorized to be leaked to the public, and consequently, the authenticity of the source cannot be verified. The full apparent correspondence, which shows a heated exchange between Ruse and Dennett on issues pertaining to evolution and anti-evolution movements in the United States, is available online.

129. *DDI*, 470.

130. Michael Ruse, 'The Evolution of Ethics, Past and Present', in Philip Clayton and Jeffery Schloss, eds., *Evolution and Ethics: Human Morality in Biological and Religious Perspective* (Cambridge and Grand Rapids, MI: Eerdmans, 2004), 27.

131. Edward O. Wilson, *On Human Nature* (London: Penguin, 1978), 161.

132. *TSG*, 201.

133. Dennett, *Freedom Evolves*, 259–60.

134. Ibid., 260–61.

135. Richard Dawkins, *A Devil's Chaplain: Selected Essays* (London: Phoenix, 2003), 127.

136. *TSG*, 3.

137. *DDI*, 470.

138. 'Skyhooks' are what Dennett uses to describe evolutionary steps that have not themselves been the product of evolution. One example of such would be a Deity. Of course, Dennett disregards any suggestion that there are any such skyhooks present in the evolution process.

139. Ibid., 470.

140. Ibid., 472.

141. Baofu, *Beyond Nature and Nurture: Conceiving a Better Way to Understand Genes and Memes*, 138.

142. Jessica C. Flack and Frans B. M. de Waal, '"Any Animal Whatever": Darwinian Building Blocks of Morality in Monkeys and Apes', *Journal of Consciousness Studies* 7, no. 1–2 (Jan.–Feb. 2000), 1–29. Also published in Leonard Katz, ed., *Evolutionary Origins of Morality: Cross-Disciplinary Perspectives* (Exeter: Imprint, 2000).

143. Ibid., 2, quoted from *TSG*, 3.

144. Ibid., 2.

145. Nancey Murphy and George F. R. Ellis, *On the Moral Nature of the Universe: Theology, Cosmology and Ethics* (Minneapolis: Fortress Press, 1996), 235.

146. Paul Thompson, 'Evolutionary Ethics: Its Origins and Contemporary Face', *Zygon* 34, no. 3 (Sept. 1999): 473–84.

147. Philip Clayton, 'Biology and Purpose: Altruism, Morality, and Human Nature in Evolutionary Perspective', in Clayton and Schloss, eds., *Evolution and Ethics: Human Morality in Biological and Religious Perspective*, 336.

148. Neil Messer, *Selfish Genes and Christian Ethics: Theological and Ethical Reflections on Evolutionary Biology* (London: SCM, 2007), 246.

149. Bernard d'Espagnat, *Reality and the Physicist* (Cambridge: Cambridge University Press, 1989), 212.

150. Paul Davies, *The Mind of God: Science and the Search for Ultimate Meaning* (London: Penguin, 1992), 32.

151. Stephen Hawking and Leonard Mlodinow, *The Grand Design: New Answers to the Ultimate Questions of Life* (London: Bantam, 2010), 71.

152. Bernard d'Espagnat, *On Physics and Philosophy* (Princeton: Princeton University Press, 2006), 268.

153. Johnjoe McFadden, *Quantum Evolution* (London: HarperCollins, 2000), 314.

154. *TSG*, 59.

155. Roger Penrose, *The Large, the Small and the Human Mind* (Cambridge: Cambridge University Press, 2000), 114.

156. Roger Penrose, *The Emperor's New Mind* (Oxford: Oxford University Press, 1989), 536, italics in original.

157. Ibid., 528, italics in original.

158. Penrose, *The Large, the Small and the Human Mind*, 171.

159. *DDI*, 446.

160. Davies, *The Mind of God: Science and the Search for Ultimate Meaning*, 232.

161. Ibid., 21.

162. Joan McCarthy, *Dennett and Ricoeur on the Narrative Self* (New York: Humanity Books, 2007), 73.

163. Daniel C. Dennett, 'Animal Consciousness: What Matters and Why', *Social Research* 62, no. 3 (Fall 1995): 703.

164. McCarthy, *Dennett and Ricoeur on the Narrative Self*, 80.

165. Ibid., 84–90.

166. Merlin Donald, *A Mind So Rare: The Evolution of Human Consciousness* (New York: W. W. Norton, 2001), 1.

167. Dennett writes, "You may find yourself strongly tempted to agree with Robert Wright [whom we encountered in Chapter Three of this book] that I am actually claiming that consciousness doesn't exist. It would be a shame if you allowed that conviction to distort you reading of the rest of this book." Dennett, *Freedom Evolves*, 22–23. However, his position may still be vulnerable to the criticism that he does in fact claim consciousness does not exist; Dennett merely saying otherwise does not subvert his critics.

168. Ibid., 309.

169. Donald, *A Mind So Rare: The Evolution of Human Consciousness*, 1.

170. Elsdon-Baker, *The Selfish Genius: How Richard Dawkins Rewrote Darwin's Legacy*, 15.

171. Mary Midgley, 'Why Memes?', in Hilary Rose and Stephen Rose, eds., *Alas, Poor Darwin: Arguments Against Evolutionary Psychology* (London: Jonathan Cape, 2000), 77–78.

172. Richard Dawkins, 'Viruses of the Mind', in Bo Dahlbom, ed., *Dennett and His Critics: Demystifying Mind* (Oxford: Blackwell, 1993), 18–26.

173. Distin, *The Selfish Meme*, 74.

174. Ibid., 74.

175. Ibid., 75.

176. *BTS*, 170.

177. Daniel C. Dennett, 'Back from the Drawing Board', in Dahlbom, ed., *Dennett and His Critics: Demystifying Mind*, 204–5. In the original passage, the questioner is humanities professor Richard Rorty, though this does not affect the point made.

178. Robert Augner, 'Introduction', in Augner, ed., *Darwinizing Culture: The Status of Memetics as a Science*, 2.

179. Alister McGrath, *Dawkins' God: Genes, Memes and the Meaning of Life* (Oxford: Blackwell, 2005), 125–34.

180. Bruce Edmonds, 'Three Challenges to Memetics', in Michael Ruse, ed., *Philosophy After Darwin: Classic and Contemporary Readings* (Princeton: Princeton University Press, 2009), 198–99; also, Holmes Rolston III, *Genes, Genesis and God: Values and Their Origins in Natural and Human History* (Cambridge: Cambridge University Press, 1999), 146.

181. Bruce Edmonds, 'The Revealed Poverty of the Gene-Meme Analogy—Why Memetics *per se* Has Failed to Produce Substantive Results', *Journal of Memetics: Evolutionary Models of Information Transmission* 9, no. 1 (2005): 1–4.

182. Derek Gatherer, 'Finding a Niche for Memetics in the 21st Century', *Journal of Memetics: Evolutionary Models of Information Transmission*, 9, no. 1 (2005): 6.

183. Daniel C. Dennett, interview with the author, May 2012.

184. Michael Ruse, *Darwin and Design: Does Evolution Have a Purpose?* (Cambridge, MA: Harvard University Press, 2003), 269.

185. Francisco J. Ayala, 'Teleological Explanations in Evolutionary Biology', *Philosophy of Science* 37, no. 1 (March 1970): 10.

186. Ruse, *Darwin and Design: Does Evolution Have a Purpose?*, 270.

187. Mary Midgley, 'Why the Idea of Purpose Won't Go Away', *Philosophy* 86, no. 338 (Oct. 2011): 554–55.

188. Simon Conway Morris, *Life's Solution: Inevitable Humans in a Lonely Universe* (Cambridge: Cambridge University Press, 2003), xii.

189. Simon Conway Morris, 'Darwin Was Right. Up to a Point', *The Guardian*, 12 Feb. 2009.

190. Mary Midgley, 'Selfish Genes and Social Darwinism', *Philosophy* 58, no. 225 (July 1983): 376.

191. Mary Midgley, *The Solitary Self: Darwin and the Selfish Gene* (Durham: Acumen, 2010), 139.

192. James Mackey, 'Dawkins's Survival of the Fittest Theory Unfit to Serve as Moral Code for Human Race', *The Irish Times* (19 July 2011).

193. *TSG*, 98 and 188.

194. Messer, *Selfish Genes and Christian Ethics: Theological and Ethical Reflections on Evolutionary Biology*, 33.

195. Ibid., 33–34.

196. Ibid., 246.

4

Religion
An Evolutionary View

INTRODUCTION

The previous two chapters provided the scientific and philosophical conceptual infrastructure of Dawkins' worldview (Chapters Two and Three respectively). This worldview understands every facet of life, from its primordial origins through to the complexities of human consciousness, behavior, and cultural interaction, in terms of evolutionary science and philosophy. In the context of an intellectual exchange between theology and Dawkins, an interesting issue becomes apparent: how the religious behavior of humans can be explained through evolution. Therefore, Dawkins' understanding of how religion evolves is an essential issue for consideration in a theological study. This is particularly important because, as Alister McGrath has suggested with characteristic insight, in modern times the meaning of theology has widened to include an "analysis of religious beliefs—even if these beliefs make reference to no god at all. . . ".[1] With this understanding of theology, then, Dawkins' efforts to study the evolution of religion can be considered a theological task. However, we should acknowledge that there is division among theologians on this issue. Tina Beattie and Nicholas Lash, for example, have suggested that Dawkins and others have adopted an elitist and petulant attitude toward this study of religious beliefs, hindering their objectives.[2] However, as we shall see, other theologians and religious philosophers, such as Nancey Murphy and Alvin Plantinga, see the evolutionary study of religion as theologically beneficial.

This chapter will thus explore an evolutionary view of religion promoted by Dawkins. In the service of a better and more rounded understanding of Dawkins' position, it must be understood that his views on the origins of religion can be placed within a wider context of theorizations in the area; Dawkins does not exist in an intellectual vacuum. Although he is a leading voice in this area, his ideas, like those of all philosophers, theologians, and scientists, are molded by his peers. Consequently, to fully understand Dawkins, we must constantly look at his wider hermeneutical circle. In doing so, we will also incorporate other scholars who also seek to interpret religious belief in terms of evolution. However, much of the secondary scholarship we will focus on follows Dawkins' evolutionary philosophy and builds upon it. This will justify our reliance on secondary scholars throughout this chapter, particularly those whose studies of religion Dawkins specifically endorses—for example, Robert Hinde, Pascal Boyer, and Scott Atran.[3]

MOTIVES, METHOD, AND LIMITATIONS

MOTIVES

In Dawkins' perspective, it is not just features of biological life that are interpreted in terms of natural selection, but also nonempirical subjects such as culture and morality. In espousing this approach, Dawkins seeks a holistic image of the developmental history of all aspects of life, from the physical to the mental realms, grounded in terms of evolutionary science. Therefore, in dialoguing with this worldview, we become obliged to account for the evolution of religion, an influential element of human life, and an indispensable topic for this theological work. Dawkins understands human culture in terms of his view of Darwinism. Therefore religion, as a prevalent feature of human culture, must also be understood in terms of natural selection. As Dawkins observes, "Knowing that we are products of Darwinian evolution, we should ask what pressure or pressures exerted by natural selection originally favored the impulse to religion".[4]

Dawkins gains support for an evolutionary account of religion from Dennett, as he suggests that the ubiquity of religious belief in human civilization necessitates an explanation:

> All human groups it seems, have practiced religion. Groups have gone without agriculture, without clothing, without laws, without money, without the wheel or without writing, but not, apparently, without religion. . . . Religion, moreover, does not seem to have been a mere passing phase in human evolution; even in the most technocratic and materialistic corners of contemporary civilization, religion has found niches in which to flourish.[5]

For Dennett, the pervasiveness of religion, both in human history and modernity, impels by its nature an evolutionary explanation. Further support for Dawkins on this matter is evident in the work of zoologist Robert A. Hinde, in his work *Why Gods Persist*. Hinde acknowledges the 'selection pressures', seen above in Dawkins' statement, and suggests that certain evolved human propensities are satisfied by religion, and it can therefore be treated as a Darwinian development:

> [I]t has been argued that a number of basic human propensities, which are probably ubiquitous in humans, though differing in degree between individuals and cultures, can be satisfied through religion. . . . To the extent that such is the case, the nature of religious beliefs must have been selected over time to satisfy human propensities, and is thus basically Darwinian.[6]

Within Dawkins' evolutionary framework presented in Chapter Three, cultural concepts were considered to evolve in an analogous fashion to biological traits—Dawkins and others considered memetics as a framework for this cultural evolutionary process. While Hinde does not employ the terminology of memetics, he is implying that religious ideas evolve within a Darwinian framework (though again, use of the term 'Darwinian' is problematic, given that much debate still ensues over the processes of natural selection). Moreover, it is also true that the human propensities alluded to here could be considered either cultural or biological. Hinde detracts from this issue: "This, of course, carries no implication about the relative importance of genetic or cultural selection".[7] At this point, we should recall the sentiment of Peter Baofu, who posited that human behavior (such as the religious behavior currently in question) cannot be understood solely in terms of genetic or memetic evolution, or of both processes functioning in tandem. Human behavior can only be understood on a case-by-case basis.[8] This is a particular caveat of viewing religion in terms of evolution, as it may fail to appreciate the complexity of the evolution of an individual's religious persuasion. (We will deal with this point in greater depth later in this chapter.) Notwithstanding this caveat, the fundamental point is that religion is understood by Dawkins as an evolutionary development.

Dawkins also postulates that when considering the economics of natural selection (that selection will eliminate wasteful acts that expend time and energy, as they detract from an organism's survival competency), religion becomes a pertinent topic for analysis in evolutionary terms, as it is strikingly wasteful in time and energy (although, perhaps the contempt that Dawkins shows for religion as explored earlier sways his opinion in this regard). In order for religion to achieve universality in human civilization, Dawkins suggests it must have equitable or greater benefit for its costs:

> The question gains urgency from standard Darwinian considerations of economy. Religion is so wasteful, so extravagant; and Darwinian selection habitually targets and eliminates waste. Nature is a miserly accountant, grudging the pennies, watching the clock, punishing the smallest extravagance. . . . Nature cannot afford frivolous *jeux d'esprit.* Ruthless utilitarianism trumps, even if it doesn't always seem that way.[9]

Again, Dennett supports Dawkins, as he is perturbed by the seemingly wasteful practices of religious belief, and subsequently, demands an evolutionary explanation:

> On the face of it, there are plenty of reasons for religion *not* to exist. As Burkert notes, gods are expensive—sometimes ruinously so. . . . Any phenomenon that apparently exceeds its functional justification cries out for explanation. The activity is, in a word, uneconomical, and as the economists are ever reminding us, there is no such thing as a free lunch. Evolutionary biologists agree: in the long run, features of the evolving world do not persist unless they pay for themselves.[10]

The uneconomical nature of religion that Dawkins emphasizes is also a catalyst for the anthropologist/psychologist Scott Atran to explore how religion could have developed. In his book *In Gods We Trust*, he insists that religion becomes an evolutionary dilemma, as it is expensive and costly in terms of time, emotional expenditure, and cognitive effort.[11]

In our current dialogue with Dawkins, we can find support for considering an evolutionary view of religion as a theological matter, thus highlighting an overlap of interests between Dawkins and theology. For example, the classicist Walter Burkert, in his acclaimed work *Creation of the Sacred*, insightfully suggests that this mode of investigation into the origin of religion follows from inquiries of natural theology (understood by McGrath as how God may be known through the natural order[12]). "The inquiry concerning 'natural theology in the widest sense,' including its historical dimension, thus turns into this question: what has been the *raison d'être* for religion in the evolution of human life and culture hitherto?"[13] Investigating the origin of religion is thus, in Burkert's view, a theological and historical matter. We can discern, then, two primary motives for providing an analysis of religion in evolutionary terms. Firstly, the ubiquity and uneconomical nature of religious beliefs beg an evolutionary explanation. Secondly, we can argue, along with Burkert, that such an analysis of religion can be considered a theological enterprise, and hence, indispensable for this work.

METHOD

In Chapter Three, we encountered the materialist system for the understanding of consciousness and how such consciousness evolved. As we noted, Dawkins is explicitly supportive of a materialist view on mind, which contrasts with the traditional philosophical dualism of Descartes. It is within this context of the materialist, evolutionary view on mind that this chapter will engage in the study of religious ideas. Therefore, in dialogue with evolutionary materialism (the task of this project as a whole), the methodological approach to religion can be summed up by referral again to Dennett: ". . . in order to explain the hold that various religious ideas and practices have on people, we need to understand the evolution of the human mind".[14] The human mind is defined here as "a system or organization within the brain that has evolved in much the same way our immune system or respiratory system or digestive system has evolved".[15] Dawkins insists that humans are intuitionally dualist. Therefore, he suggests, our minds are predisposed for religion. "Native dualism and native teleology predispose us, given the right conditions, to religion . . . ".[16] The evolution of religion will consequently be studied here by referral to theorization on the evolution of capacities of the human mind—the mind's cognitive processes. The anthropologist and authoritative voice in the study of the evolution of religion, Pascal Boyer, encapsulates this methodological approach, which we will dialogue with:

> [T]he study of cognitive processes, however incipient in current cognitive psychology, allows us to reformulate many classical problems of anthropology and to put forward more precise hypotheses about the acquisition and transmission of cultural representations.[17]

Dawkins' analysis of religion within this cognitive framework is the foundational methodology for this chapter, and also for the field of study known as the 'cognitive science of religion'. The Finnish professor of comparative religions and pioneer of this field, Ilkka Pyysiäinen, explains: "The idea that religious thought and behavior are made possible by evolved cognitive capacities which are the same for all humans . . . is the basis for a 'cognitive science of religion'".[18] To elaborate, the mechanisms that constrain the proliferation of religious[19] concepts and beliefs—the constraints of natural selection—are not arbitrarily created in minds.[20] Religious beliefs are understood in this approach, as the result of how the human mind/brain has developed. The cognitive science of religion maintains that "[t]he architecture of mind . . . shapes beliefs, thus creating cross-culturally recurrent patterns. This implies that not all concepts and beliefs have an equal potential for becoming widespread".[21] It seeks to understand how religious beliefs are successful in terms of how they have developed from the evolved cognitive capacities of the human mind. Fundamentally, religious beliefs are considered as a result of the structure of the mind/brain.

To analyze religion within an evolutionary framework, then, is to view beliefs as emerging from the natural cognitive mechanisms—as an epiphenomenon. As Dawkins explains, it is to view religion as an "accidental by-product—a misfiring of something useful . . . ".[22] Dennett and Ryan T. McKay also adopt Dawkins' approach, summarized thusly: "The currently dominant evolutionary perspective on religion remains a by-product perspective. . . . On this view, supernatural (mis)beliefs are side effects of a suite of cognitive mechanisms adapted for other purposes".[23] Dawkins is therefore implying that this evolutionary explanation of religion diminishes its 'truth value'. Again, the fact that Dawkins' atheism clearly influences his perspective on the matter makes evident the limitations of a dialogue with him. However, as we will show later, an evolutionary understanding of religion is not necessarily atheistic.

A further methodological supposition that we must clarify for this chapter is that when considering religious beliefs, we are speaking in terms of beliefs that are common among humanity. As Dawkins explains, "Religious behavior can be called a human universal . . . ".[24] Denomination-specific beliefs, such as the Christian resurrection, will not be considered as a direct result of cognitive process, but rather as an idiosyncrasy of the development of particular contextual religions, for example, Christianity. Scott Atran emphasizes this point in his treatise by explaining that differences among religions can be ascribed to differences in the content of beliefs in the supernatural, but not differences in the origin/cognitive structure of those beliefs.[25] It is the cross-cultural aspects of religious beliefs, then, that are the subject of an evolutionary study of religion, as Boyer discerns:

Although anthropology generally assumes that the systems of ideas grouped under the label "religion" are essentially diverse, a number of recurrent themes and concepts can be found in very different cultural environments. . . . I will try to show that we can reduce the apparent contingency of cross-cultural resemblance, and that of transmission, if we take into account the fact that universal cognitive processes limit the range of variation of cultural ideas.[26]

Consequently, this chapter, in dialogue with Dawkins' perspective, will focus on aspects of religious belief that are ubiquitous in human civilization, corresponding to the ubiquity of biological aspects of human consciousness. The methodology of this chapter is then two-fold. Firstly, it will analyze the evolution of religion in terms of how it correlates to Dawkins' evolutionary *weltanschauung*. Secondly, it will take a panoramic perspective of 'religion'; we will analyze the aspects of religion that are cross-culturally pervasive.

LIMITATIONS OF DAWKINS' EVOLUTIONARY VIEW OF RELIGION

As stated above, Dawkins is primarily concerned with the evolution of aspects of religious belief that have commonality within all human civilization, such as belief in God/gods. This can be taken as a limitation of Dawkins' perspective; while it provides our dialogue with a focus, it needs to be understood that religions are pluralistic in nature. Therefore, although Dawkins may attempt to account for religion in terms of its belief in deities, certain religious systems are predominantly characterized by ritual or by values. Consequently, by attempting to account for religiosity *in general* in human culture, our study is limited by not being truly representative of the diverse nature of religions. We will, however, in a dialogue with Dawkins, seek to establish a panoramic view of the evolution of religion. This difficulty in attempting to account for religion is duly noted by Hinde:

Although Christians give it primacy, belief is by no means all there is to religion. In Judaism, structural beliefs . . . are less important than historical narrative. Hinduism does not *necessarily* imply any doctrinal agreement except in so far as it influences conduct. . . . For Buddhist teachers, values and experience come first, and there is much less emphasis on belief.[27]

Subsequently, we can acknowledge that Dawkins' account of religion from an evolutionary standpoint may not be as successful at representing the true nuance and diversity of religious belief. Boyer also alludes to the complexities of religious belief when engaging not with one faith tradition, but considering religion in general, "*at all times and all the time*, innumerable variants of religious notions were and are created inside individual minds".[28] Thus religion, as Atran notes, is hardly definable.[29]

An additional limitation of Dawkins' attempt to study religion from an evolutionary perspective pertains to the nature of the evolutionary process itself. We can state, and need not defend the idea, that religion is a purely human phenomenon. Therefore, it can be assumed that religion developed at an uncertain point after the arrival of *Homo sapiens* on the evolutionary scene. Thus, as with all evolutionary developments, we are dealing with a vast and unquantifiable time-scale. Conceding to this actuality, Burkert insightfully highlights how an evolutionary approach to the study of religion can be problematic:

> Yet there is no way of testing the hypothesis, be it through 30,000 or 300,000 or 3,000,000, years . . . by scientific standards, the hypothesis loses its point. We can only vaguely reconstruct the decisive cultural conditions. While uncertainties multiply with time, the evidence evaporates.[30]

Given the incomprehensibly vast time-scales involved in the evolutionary process, constructing an accurate representation of the evolution of religion seems an unattainable goal. Consequently, our study will be more reliant on, as Burkert writes, "[p]robabilities, selective observations, and hunches"[31] than on the empiricism usually associated with scientific method. The cognitive science of religion, then, if we use this term to encompass our endeavour in this chapter, is not a verifiable science, but informed theorization that most likely, though not definitively, reflects the true evolution of religion. Therefore, hermeneutics may play an important role in how this vision of religion is presented.

To summarize, then, we can distinguish two significant limitations of Dawkins' proposed study. Firstly, to study religion within the framework we have established can be limiting, as it does not reflect the complexity, plurality, and nuance of religiosity. Secondly, the gradual nature and vast time-scales that characterize the evolutionary process make it difficult to produce a study with any degree of exactness, and we are left with what must be a hermeneutical study. Taking these limitations into account, however, we can proceed by giving greater weight to the motives, rather than limitations, of this chapter. We can propose that, in the context of a dialogue with Dawkins, there is an imperative to engage in an evolutionary view of religion. However, we must acknowledge that there are limitations to this endeavour.

COGNITIVE ORIGIN OF AGENCY

Consistent with Dawkins' attempt to use evolutionary science to understand religion, we will now explore the cognitive origin of the concept of gods; a concept paramount to religiosity. However, preparatory to outlining a cognitive perspective on the origins of god concepts, we must develop a foundational comprehension of how we view other consciousnesses, as gods are primarily conscious agents in religion and mythology. Dawkins suggests that in order to appreciate the cognitive origin of God concepts, we can refer to Dennett's philosophical perspective on how we view others' consciousness: "We may understand this hypothesis better in light of what . . . Dennett has called the 'intentional stance'".[32] Dennett coined the term 'the intentional stance' in his 1987 title of the same name. The intentional stance represents how conscious entities, such as humans, can ascribe intentions to other entities. He encapsulates the premise as follows:

> First, you decide to treat the object whose behaviour is to be predicted as a rational agent; then you figure out what beliefs the agent ought to have, given its place in the world and its purpose. Then you figure out what desires it ought to have, on the same considerations, and finally you predict that this rational agent will act to further its goals in the light of its beliefs. A little practical reasoning from the chosen set of beliefs and desires will in most instances yield a decision about what the agent ought to do; that is what you predict the agent will do.[33]

The intentional stance is a conceptual disposition that allows us to interact with other agents, by attributing to them a 'theory of mind'; fundamentally, we assume that other humans, for instance, have thoughts, beliefs, and intentions similar to our own, though they are not the same.[34] This allows us to make predictions of others' behaviour; the child *desires* the lollipop on the table, and we can therefore predict that the child will reach for that lollipop; it "gives us predictive power we can get by no other method".[35]

Dawkins endorses this theory, and illustrates how the intentional stance can have significant Darwinian survival value, which thus led to its evolution and current widespread status in life. "When you see a tiger, you had better not delay your prediction of its probable behaviour".[36] A superior intentional stance will contribute to the survival competency of an individual, as it will allow them a greater benefit in avoiding predators. Furthermore, an intentional stance can allow a predator to hypothesize on how its prey will behave, and thus become more proficient at catching them. Therefore, Dawkins suggests, the intentional stance evolved by virtue of its survival value. "It seems to me entirely plausible that the intentional stance has survival value as a brain mechanism that speeds up decision making in dangerous circumstances, and in crucial social situations".[37] As human brains are highly complex, they are capable of comprehending high orders of intentionality, not just to *believe* that the tiger *wants*. I can *believe* that the safari park attendant *wants* the lion to *want* to chase the gazelle rather than him. This is an example of third-order intentionality, though Dawkins demonstrates how we can easily comprehend fifth-order intentionality: "[T]he shaman *guessed* that the woman *realized* her man *believed* that the woman *knew* he *wanted* her".[38] So Dawkins postulates that the intentional stance—the ability to attribute intentions, wants, beliefs, and so forth to other entities—became an innate feature of consciousness through natural selection. Humans, with our complex consciousness, are remarkably proficient at comprehending others' beliefs, as the examples of higher-order intentionality illustrate.[39]

Our minds/brains have the evolved mechanisms to recognize other mind/brains. On this matter, Dawkins draws attention to the psychologist and influential proponent of the cognitive science of religion Justin Barrett,[40] who labels our ability to recognize other minds as an 'agency detection device', or ADD.[41] It is this ADD that allows humans to comprehend the orders of intentionality discussed above. Due to the selection pressures that eventuated the ADD, it is an extremely sensitive cognitive faculty. To illustrate this point, both Dennett and Barrett highlight anthropologist Stewart Guthrie's contribution to discourse on the cognitive origins of religion, his acclaimed work *Faces in the Clouds: A New Theory of Religion*.[42] Guthrie considers the evolutionary rationalization for our agency detection device's hypersensitiveness (speaking of rationalization is of course anthropomorphic language, used only as analogy, and does not suggest conscious rationalization by nature). He succinctly articulates his theory: "It is better to mistake a boulder for a bear than a bear for a boulder".[43] The costs of misrepresenting an inanimate object (a boulder) for a predator (bear) is negligible compared with the costs of misrepresenting a predator for an inanimate object, which could result in serious harm or death.

Given these circumstances in which the ADD evolved, Dawkins suggests that it can often 'misfire' or proffer a 'false positive' agency detection; it can lead us to believe there is agency where there is none.[44] He draws from Barrett, and insists that it can become 'hyperactive', which prompted Barrett to coin the acronym, HADD, 'hyperactive agency detection device'.[45] Consequently, it can be presumed that the cognitive development of a HADD causes the human brain to indiscriminately attribute agency, even when there is none. Pyysiäinen's stance on the HADD is consistent with Dawkins. He stresses that the hyperactivity of the HADD is an innate property of human cognition, and not exceptional.[46] Moreover, he elaborates on the circumstances in which humans' HADD causes us to intuitively postulate agency; he explains that the HADD is initiated automatically in instances where entities appear to move or act as if by conscious intention.[47] It is this postulation of agency, as a result of Barrett's HADD, that Dawkins suggests may lead to the development of religious concepts.[48] Boyer offers a comparable perspective: "Barrett is certainly right that our agency-detection systems are involved in the construction of religious concepts".[49] For Dawkins, the hyperactivity of our evolved penchant for recognizing other minds leads us to postulate gods and religious concepts, leading to the onset of religion. Our psychological penchant for recognizing agency identifies an agent as God.

We can perhaps see evidence of this idea in the conceptual approach adopted by William Paley in his influential elucidation of the argument from design, in which he sought to establish the rationality of considering the existence of divinity. Paley, preceding Darwin's theory of evolution, takes a watch as an analogy for anything complex, such as a living organism.[50] Paley then attributes the perplexities of complex life—which at his time were not understood through evolutionary science—to an agency, a watchmaker (God). The premise for Paley's argument, then, may be held as an example of Dawkins' argument, that humans are cognitively primed to attribute unknown causality to agency. Therefore, it could be theorized that humans began to assume intentional causality for events in the natural world, such as rain and clouds, and attribute the intentions to gods.[51] This hypothesis is substantiated by the ubiquity of archaic religious and mythological gods intrinsically associated with weather phenomena; Ra and Apollo, for example, were sun gods in Egyptian and Roman mythology respectively. Similar gods responsible for natural phenomena are prevalent in Greek, Aztec, and Celtic mythology.

Dawkins acknowledges that this theory of the origin of religious concepts is one strain of thought among others. He highlights the work of Atran and Boyer, among others, as intriguing explorations of the origins of religious belief. Moreover, Burkert among others pursues the concept of the HADD to postulate how particular aspects of religious belief were formulated.[52] Other proponents of Dawkins' evolutionary worldview, such as Susan Blackmore, have also considered other human experiences that may have contributed to religious belief, such as a psychological response to mortality.[53] Therefore, Dawkins' evolutionary perspective of religion is one element of a wider field of scholarship. However, his main focus in this area pertains to how religion can be understood through his memetic understanding of cultural evolution.

A Memetic View of Religion

Burkert notes that religion is developed in the cultural realm; it is not directly linked to our biology—we have seen throughout this chapter that religion grew out of primordial psychological propensities, and is then adapted and propagated through culture:

> The biological program develops on its own according to pre-determined patterns, which reach back far beyond the emergence of humans and have long been inscribed in the genetic code. It has never been shown that religiosity rises spontaneously in such a way; religion depends on the formative impact of cultural learning. The prospect for discovering religious genes is dim.[54]

However, this assertion could be problematic. If we again recall Peter Baofu's view, that human behavior cannot be considered as a result of genes or memes, or both acting in tandem; the reality is far more complex. Notwithstanding such a caveat, because religion can be viewed as predominantly cultural, we should, in the context of a dialogue with Dawkins, consider how his framework for cultural evolution applies to religion; we should consider a memetic view of religion. As we noted, Dawkins uses memetics as a way to understand the evolution of culture in an analogous manner to biological evolution; the meme is an analogy for the gene. Placing religion in this context, the evolutionary biologist David Sloan Wilson analogises religion as an organism, and proposes that we take seriously this analogy and view religion in light of its evolution.[55] Biblical parallels with this analogy can also be found in St. Paul, who compared the Church to the human body (1 Cor. 12:20).

In Dawkins' original elucidation of the meme, he takes the idea of God as an archetypal meme to portray the concept:

> Consider the idea of God. We do not know how it arose in the meme pool. Probably, it originated many times by independent mutation. In any case, it is very old indeed. How does it replicate itself? By spoken and written word, aided by great music and great

art. Why does it have such a high survival value? . . . The survival value of the god meme in the meme pool results from its great psychological appeal.[56]

In this passage, we can note the consistency between Dawkins' perspective and the analysis of this chapter thus far. We have already discussed in this chapter how the concept of God satisfies particular cognitive/psychological faculties such as our HADD. This, for Dawkins, contributes to the survival value of the meme for God. A cardinal aspect of Dawkins' perspective on the God meme, however, is that it does not reflect reality; God, for Dawkins, is a vacuous meme:

> The 'everlasting arms' hold out a cushion against our own inadequacies which, like a doctor's placebo, is none the less effective for being imaginary. These are some of the reasons why the idea of God is copied so readily by successive generations of individual brains. God exists, if only in the form of a meme with high survival value, or infective power, in the environment provided by human culture.[57]

On this point, we can note that Dawkins' perspective may be problematic, as his atheism and contempt for religion become evident. As we noted in our limitations, this may hinder his objectivity. As Nicholas Lash suggested, it is bad academic practice to hold subjects with the contempt that Dawkins does. This criticism will also be discussed later.

Notwithstanding this precarious aspect of extending theological dialogue to encompass hostile perspectives such as Dawkins', we can proceed and recall that memes, unlike genes, need not be particularly advantageous for their hosts. Memes need only be advantageous to themselves in terms of their copying proficiency. Dawkins thus suggests that the God meme does not need to hold truth value in order to proliferate in the meme pool (though, it should be noted that this is in no way a definitive statement that the God meme is not true). A parallel perspective is offered by Boyer, who reinforces the idea that religious memes can be merely proficient replicators:

> In this account, familiar religious concepts and associated beliefs, norms and emotions are just better-replicating memes than other types of concepts, norms, etc., in the sense that their copy-me instructions work better. . . . Human minds exposed to these concepts end up replicating them and passing them on to other

people. On the whole, this seems the right way to understand diffusion and transmission.[58]

Acknowledging this concept (that memes need not be true/beneficial to be propagated), we must now consider how Dawkins and others identify particular aspects of religious memes that enforce their proliferation of the meme pool. One example is the concept of 'hell fire', which may ensure the transmission of, and adherence to, religious ideas. As Dawkins explains:

> To take a particular example, an aspect of doctrine which has been very effective in enforcing religious observance is the threat of hell fire. Many children and even some adults believe that they will suffer ghastly torments after death if they do not obey priestly rules . . . unconscious memes have ensured their own survival by virtue of those same qualities of pseudo-ruthlessness which successful genes display. The idea of hell fire is, quite simply, *self-perpetuating*, because of its own deep psychological impact. It has become linked with the god meme because the two reinforce each other, and assist each other's survival in the meme pool.[59]

The threat of hell as punishment for nonconformity to religious memes acts as a warning to potential hosts. This warning is so psychologically dramatic that it ensures the religious memes' perpetuation. We can see the results of this perpetuating mechanism exemplified in the attitude of the French seventeenth-century philosopher/mathematician, Blaise Pascal. Pascal formulated and proposed an infamous 'wager', which states that one has little to lose, but a lot to gain (not being consigned to eternal torture in hell) by believing in God. Therefore, one should live as if one believes that God exists.[60] In Pascal's wager, we can distinguish how the salient fear of hell leads him to advocate for the perpetuation of belief in God. Consequently, Pascal's wager can perhaps be held as an example of the practical application of Dawkins' thesis—that the meme for hell perpetuates religious memes.[61]

Another potential example of memes perpetuating themselves is offered by Dawkins: the negative stigmatization of doubt and the promotion of faith. He takes as an example the apostle Thomas' doubt: "Unless I see the nail marks in his hand and put my finger where the nails were, and put my hand into his side, I refuse to believe" (John 20:25). Dawkins' interpretation of this biblical passage maintains that the author wishes to convey Thomas in a negative light, in comparison with the other apostles whose faith was stronger; the author wishes to fundamentally portray doubt or the requirement of evidence as a negative attribute. In this way, Dawkins suggests, religious memes discourage criticism and reinforce their perpetuation. "[T]he meme for blind faith secures its own perpetuation by the simple unconscious expedient of discouraging rational inquiry".[62] However, Dawkins does not seem to acknowledge the engagement of religious thinkers with hostile criticism. This point was addressed in Chapter One, as we noted with referral to Nicholas Lash, that theology is significantly self-critical. Gerard J. Hughes, for example, places emphasis on the importance of religious belief to seriously address intellectual challenges: "[I]f it [religious belief] is to appear intellectually honest, religious believers must be able to deal with any challenges in a way which respects what is best in that culture".[63] Moreover, this book itself seeks to contribute to theology encouraging inquiry by engaging with an antagonistic dialogue partner.

The crux of Dawkins' view on this matter, he reiterates, is that religious memes are ". . . to the benefit of only the religious ideas themselves, to the extent that they behave in a somewhat gene-like way, as replicators".[64] As we noted earlier, Dennett adopted and furthered Dawkins' theory of memes. In the case of religious memes, Dennett also articulates a corresponding standpoint:

> [I]f religions have survived and are so dominant in human life, it must be because they aid our survival. Maybe, maybe not. They may aid our survival, or they may survive as unshakeable habits. . . . The way to find an objective standpoint from which to investigate the hypothesis is to acknowledge that cultural items can spread whether or not they're good for us—graffiti, pornography, all sorts of dubious fashions. You don't have to suppose that they're good for us to look at them with an evolutionist's eye.[65]

We can also identify direct correlation between Dennett's perspective on religious memes, and Dawkins' view on the piety associated with faith over doubt, which he interprets from John's passage on Thomas' doubt. Dennett analogises religious memes as parasitic, serving no good purpose but their own replication, by methods such as discouraging inquiry (virtually synonymous to Dawkins' view):

> Indeed, those phenomena *may* fulfill basic functions for us, but they may also do *us* no good at all, rather earning their keep by serving as cultural parasites whose only master is their own replication. For instance, the meme declaring that *reason is an inappropriate arbiter in*

matters of faith serves the replicative interests of whatever meme it joins, automatically deflecting rational criticism.[66]

Dennett's passage here may be interpreted as contradicting his earlier statements, which proffered that there can be no way to demonstrate the subjective 'goodness' of memes, unless he is considering 'good' to contribute to biological survival. His examples of memes for 'graffiti' and 'pornography' are classified as 'dubious', but this classification is entirely subjective as they do not necessarily pertain to biological survival. Dennett himself acknowledged this point previously, by questioning, "Where is your demonstration that these 'virtues' are *good* virtues? . . . ".[67] Notwithstanding this potential criticism of Dennett, he shares Dawkins' view that religious memes can be perpetuated while having no positive effect on their hosts (though 'positive' could again be subjective, unless considered in terms of survival value).

Susan Blackmore also considers religion as an example of memetic evolution. She proposes that religion be considered a 'memeplex'; a grouping of intricately bound together memes. Considering religion as a memeplex, Blackmore maintains that various religious memes are in fact beneficial, and consequently, as these beneficial memes are inextricably linked with others, the other memes become perpetuated by proxy:

> [R]eligions serve a real function. They supply answers to all sorts of age-old human questions such as: Where do we come from? Why are we here? Where do we go when we die? Why is the world full of suffering? The religious answers may be false but at least they are answers. Religious communities may give people a sense of belonging, and have been shown to improve social integration in the elderly. . . . Religions may also incorporate useful rules for living, such as the dietary laws of Judaism or rules about cleanliness and hygiene which may once have protected people from disease. These useful functions help carry other memes along.[68]

While Dawkins considers that religious memes may have no positive effect on their hosts and still be propagated, Blackmore observes that particular religious memes may be biologically beneficial. Therefore, particular memes that are biologically beneficial (rules for hygiene, etc.) propagate other nonbiologically beneficial memes as they are bound together in the memeplex. However, this viewpoint need not work exclusively from Dawkins' view, that memes with no benefit can be propagated themselves.

Like Dawkins, Blackmore also posits that religious memes use 'tricks' (similar to the threat of hell fire, as we have seen in Dawkins' depiction, or the discouraging of inquiry, as both Dawkins and Dennett highlighted) that contribute to their proliferation in the meme pool. One such distinguishable 'trick' is the 'altruism trick':

> Many believers are truly good people. In the name of their faith they help their neighbours, give money to the poor, and try to live honest and moral lives. If they are successful then generally people come to like and admire them and so are more inclined to imitate them. In this way, not only does good and honest behaviour spread, but the religious memes that were linked to that behaviour spread too.[69]

In this view, religious memes can have an analogically symbiotic relationship with positive behavior. A similar interpretation is found in Boyer's study of religion, as he notes, "To some extent, religious concepts are *parasitic* upon moral institutions".[70] Moreover, Blackmore espouses the view that religious memes, by using this 'altruism trick', become indistinguishable from good behavior, and subsequently, cruel ideas can become perpetuated as 'good'; any behavior that is deemed 'religious' may also be deemed as 'good'. To illustrate, she highlights various Muslim teachings that, she insists, create misery, though they are perceived as 'good' because they are religious:

> Even cruelty can be redefined as good. The Koran states that it is good to give a hundred lashes to an adulteress and have no pity on her. . . . Women are routinely locked away and, if they are allowed out, must walk behind the man and be suitably covered—which in many countries means being covered head to toe in a smothering garment with just a tiny grille to look out of. Obeying such rules to the letter makes a Muslim 'good', regardless of the misery it creates.[71]

Although Islamic apologists may challenge Blackmore on these issues, we can abstain from an ethical critique of her view and consider her point as it pertains to an evolutionary account of religion—that the entanglement of religious memes with virtue may contribute to their ongoing success. For Blackmore, the intrinsic association between 'good' and 'religious' allows cruel memes to become perpetuated by their religious connotations.

Dawkins also highlights the beauty of religious music, art, and literature as influential elements of how religions become successful: "[B]eautiful music, art and scriptures are themselves self-replicating tokens of ideas".[72] Therefore, religious music and art perpetuate religious beliefs by virtue of being memorable events in a person's, or more particularly a child's mind. Thus ritual becomes a decisive factor in individuals' adoption of religious belief. Hinde offers a similar view. "If the religious building has a special atmosphere, if the religious specialists and others present speak in an unusual tone of voice, if the adults behave in a special way, the situation will be marked as special . . . ".[73] Dennett also conjectures that religious ritual overstimulates human emotions.[74] Dennett takes his cue from Boyer, who interestingly explains how music, for instance, can overstimulate the human brain:

> The equivalence between octaves and the privileged role of particular intervals like the perfect fifth and fourth are consequences of the organization of the cortex. To exaggerate a little, what you get from musical sounds are 'super-vowels' (the pure frequencies as opposed to the mixed ones that define ordinary vowels) and pure 'consonants' (produced by the rhythmic instruments and the attack of most instruments). These properties make music an intensified form of sound-experience . . .[75]

Therefore, music is so successful "because it activates some of our capacities in a particularly intense way".[76] Correspondingly, art, Boyer explains, overstimulates our visual cortex by focusing on pure colors that would not be found in our natural habitats.[77] This overstimulation of our cognitive capacities again accounts for the success of art in human cultures. Similarly, Boyer proposes that religion's success is due, at least in part, to its overstimulation of human cognitive systems, such as those that have already been discussed in this chapter (our HADD):

> The reason why religion can become much more serious and important than the artifacts described so far (music/art) is that it activates inference systems that are of vital importance to us: those that govern our most intense emotions, shape our interaction with other people, give us moral feelings and organise social groups.[78]

Consequently, Hinde discerns that as a religious ritual becomes a special/memorable event in a person/child's mind, it becomes an influential aspect in the development and perpetuation of religion. Moreover, as Boyer notes, religion becomes special given its overstimulation of cognitive faculties. Thus, from Dawkins' evolutionary perspective, it can be understood that religious ritual may be pivotal to the persistence of religions. Religion's ability to satisfy various psychological and social propensities contributes to its obtaining and maintaining prevalence in human civilization. To encapsulate this section then, we can identify how utilizing the memetic framework may contribute to our understanding, from an evolutionary mindset, of how religion continues to flourish.

CRITIQUE OF THE EVOLUTIONIST VIEW ON RELIGION

In dialogue with Dawkins' evolutionary materialism, we have now considered how religion can be understood within the framework of natural selection. At this point, we must now review/critique this perspective on religion. The major point of contention we will put forth concerns the implications of an evolutionary explanation of religion for its truth value. However, the memetic account of religion has also been the subject of criticism, which must be represented here to give a balanced approach.

We have noted that Dawkins feels an evolutionary explanation of religion diminishes its truth value—it is an "accidental by-product". Dennett (and McKay) also classified the religious beliefs that were the subject of this chapter, as 'misbeliefs'. However, this classification requires an explanation of what vindication Dawkins and Dennett have for insisting that beliefs are fallacious. In an attempt to justify this atheistic sentiment, Dennett suggests that the explanatory prowess of an evolutionary account of religion, such as we have just presented, dissolves its potential truth value; by explaining religion naturally, we can explain it away as a natural phenomenon, "Once people start 'catching on,' a system that has 'worked' for generations can implode overnight".[79] A similar perspective is found in Boyer's work, who correspondingly postulates that cognitive accounts of religious beliefs deflate them altogether.[80]

The prominent philosopher Alvin Plantinga, however, subscribes to an alternative standpoint. Plantinga proposes that although it can be shown that our religious belief systems can arise as a result of our cognitive processes, the theist can willfully maintain that these cognitive processes reflect truth.[81] To exhibit how religion arose naturally through our cognitive and societal development is to say nothing of its truth. Therefore, a cognitive science of religion is not necessarily an atheistic study. The Catholic critic of Dawkins Thomas Crean articulates this point well: "Even if Professor Dawkins were able to show that belief in God was likely to emerge from certain useful human propensities, as distinct from objective evidence, he would have done nothing at all to discredit theism".[82] Plantinga also uses the Freudian argument of 'God as wish-fulfillment' to insightfully illustrate his stance. Freud envisaged the human conceptualization of a God to emanate from the fear of being without parental, or more specifically, paternal protection:

> As we already know, the terrifying impression of helplessness in childhood aroused the need for protection—for protection through love—which was provided by the father; and the recognition that this helplessness lasts throughout life made it necessary to cling to the existence of the father, but this time, a more powerful one.[83]

However, Plantinga demonstrates how Freud's argument tells nothing of the 'truth' of God. "So, even if she [a theist] agrees with Freud that theistic belief arises from wish-fulfillment, she will think that this particular instance of wish fulfillment is truth-aimed; it is God's way of getting us to see that he is in fact present . . . ".[84]

To substantiate this premise, we can acknowledge von Balthasar's perception of God. Similar to Freud, von Balthasar understands the person–God relationship as a projection of the need for parental affection: "The first image of God, that of *myth*, could be described as the religious projection of the primordial experience of loving human fellowship . . . a grace promised in the first experience of childhood and which is unable to be fully granted by parents . . . ".[85] In von Balthasar's view, we can see Plantinga's stance exemplified; von Balthasar acknowledges the Freudian image of God, but does not take this to diminish the legitimacy of God's existence. Alister McGrath also maintains that explaining religious systems from an evolutionist perspective does not "erode the legitimacy of natural theology".[86] He appeals to Barrett, who as we have noted is a leading authority in this area and has been an instrumental scholar in this chapter. Barrett, concurring with Plantinga and McGrath, defends a theistic approach to the cognitive science of religion: ". . . I see much promise in the cognitive sciences to enrich our understanding of how humans might be 'fearfully and wonderfully made' (Ps. 139:14) to readily (though not inevitably) understand God sufficiently to enjoy a relationship with Him".[87] The prominent theologian/scientist Celia Deane-Drummond advocates a similar view, although she is explicitly skeptical and highly critical of evolutionary explanations for religious belief. Deane-Drummond notes that the evolution of a capacity for religious belief is precisely what one would have anticipated had God intended to communicate with humanity. She outlines her position as follows: "While I am not persuaded that evolutionary psychology 'explains' religion, I am more certain that the basic *capacity* for religious belief, and complex thought more generally, is grounded in an evolutionary account of brain development".[88]

Moreover, contemporary scholars such as Nancey Murphy not only encourage a naturalistic understanding of religion, but find examples of the search for such understandings in theological scholars such as early twentieth-century Irish theologian George Tyrrell. Murphy notices a correlation between Tyrrell's renowned work and the conceptual backdrop for the cognitive science of religion.[89] Tyrrell views the need to understand the nature of religious beliefs as an epoch of religious belief itself. "To find the object which shall explain this religious need and bring it to full self-consciousness is the end and purpose of the whole religious process".[90] Similarly, philosopher/psychologist William James espouses a similar mentality in his classic work, *On the Varieties of Religious Experience*. James seeks to understand religious belief from a biological and psychological perspective (comparable to the cognitive, evolutionary view we have explored in this chapter). Moreover, he is insistent that the value of religious belief does not disintegrate with such understanding:

> When I handle them biologically and psychologically as if they were mere curious facts of individual history, some of you may think it a degradation of so sublime a subject, and may even suspect me, until my purpose gets more fully expressed, of deliberately seeking to discredit the religious side of life. Such a result is of course absolutely alien to my intention . . .[91]

Therefore, the study of the nature of religious beliefs, from an evolutionary/cognitive perspective, does not, consequently, diminish the truth value of religious systems. This point constitutes our cardinal critique of the school of thought that sees the evolutionary/cognitive study of religion as detrimental to its potential truth value.

Furthermore, substantial criticisms of the memetic account of religion have been presented by scholars such as McGrath. As we noted in Chapter Three, Dawkins uses faith as an example of a meme to illustrate that it can be considered a 'virus'; it can be replicated and transmitted merely because it is a good replicator (he discussed how religion may become a good replicator by discouraging doubt and the threat of hell). However, McGrath also perceptively notes that by discussing religion in such a way, Dawkins subtly presents his memetic theory as damaging to religion. McGrath explains:

There is a verbal sleight of hand at work here, a rhetorical device apparently being presented as if it is good science. As everyone knows, viruses are *bad* things; they are contagious, parasitic entities, which exploit their hosts. The rhetorically freighted "argument" that God is a virus amounts to little more than thinly veiled insult, rather than rigorous evidence-based reasoning.[92]

In an evolutionary or memetic account of religion, the classification of the God meme as a virus or 'bad' is subjective and has no experimental evidence. These classifications are, McGrath elaborates, value judgments based on self-referentiality.[93] A memetic account of religion can offer no value judgments upon religion, as McGrath summarizes:

The general approach to the diffusion of ideas may allow some insights about how beliefs spread within a culture. But it can't tell us anything about whether this belief itself is right or wrong, good or bad. This won't stop people drawing such conclusions—but they are not valid conclusions. And they are most certainly not *scientific* conclusions.[94]

Scott Atran also offers a critique of the memetic account of religion. Although Atran supports the general edifice of the evolutionary perspective on religion, he critiques the conceptual framework of memetics based on the principle that memetic copying fidelity is low. Moreover, he perceptively observes that there are striking inconsistencies in religious beliefs among religious groups. He validates this point by referring to studies conducted on the lack of uniformity in interpretations of the Ten Commandments. "One student project . . . aimed to show that at least members of the same church have some normative notion of the Ten Commandments, that is, some minimal stability of content that could serve for memetic selection".[95] The results of this study indicate a salient dissonance within a religious group's interpretation of religious concepts, a result that Atran conjectures would be repeated in almost any other religious group. "I suspect that similar results would obtain for almost any congregation . . .".[96] Religious ideas are too varied, for Atran, to serve as memes. Therefore, he postulates that a memetic account of religion is not appropriate (although we did note that Susan Blackmore addressed a similar criticism of memetics in general by contending that meme transmission need not be as meticulous as gene transmission).

CONCLUSION

By considering an evolutionary perspective on religion, we have shown how the amalgamated scientific and philosophical aspects of the worldview we have taken Dawkins to represent may be practically useful for the gains of the theologian. We have taken a particular analysis of religious belief (which is consistent with the definition of theology proffered by Alister McGrath at the beginning of this chapter) and placed it under a microscope using the hermeneutical lens of evolutionary materialism. In doing so, we have shown how dialogue with Dawkins et al.'s understanding of evolution can place religion in the context of the evolution of all life, biological and cerebral. Through this dialogue, it may now be possible to understand how religious beliefs and thinking originated, and have subsequently been shaped through the process of natural selection in the biological and cultural realms. We also exhibited how several authoritative religious scholars, such as Plantinga, McGrath, Murphy, and others, embrace this vision of the understanding of religious belief. It can be seen as enriching our understanding as opposed to dissolving religion's truth value.

Declaring our motives and our method for this chapter, we set out our intellectual approach to the topic—how we would engage in the area and why it is intrinsic to the wider context of this project's dialogical relationship with Dawkins. In this section, we also acknowledged that there are limitations to this approach, but that these are not so limiting as to deter us from the endeavour; we proceeded with the appropriate degree of trepidation, highlighting these limitations as they became evident throughout. This chapter presented a review of Dawkins' evolutionary account of religion, relying on the conceptual framework of Chapters Two and Three. Dialoguing with an evolutionary understanding of consciousness, we were able to distinguish how aspects of religious belief satisfied evolved cognitive propensities. Therefore, we concluded that Dawkins feels religious beliefs may arise as an epiphenomenon of the development of our mind/brain. While the nuances of the reality of the formation of religious systems may admittedly be diluted through this method, it may potentially obtain a panoramic perspective, one that contributes to the understanding of religious beliefs. As Anselm defined theology, "faith seeking understanding", the perspective offered in this chapter has contributed to our understanding of faith from a biological and cognitive point of view. Dawkins' memetic framework for the study of culture was also considered, as it may potentially allow us to seriously consider (perhaps more literally than intended) St. Paul's analogy of the Church as an organism (though in this case, we extended the analogy to all religious beliefs). This chapter has essentially explored how Dawkins' views on the evolution of religion could be incorporated into theology as a part of the dialogue this work seeks to establish. This dialogue will be continued in the next chapter, where the book will reach its culmination.

Notes

1. Alister McGrath, *Christian Theology: An Introduction*, 3rd ed. (Oxford: Blackwell, 2003), 138.

2. Tina Beattie, *The New Atheists: The Twilight of Reason and the War on Religion* (London: Darton, Longman & Todd, 2007), 7; also, Nicholas Lash, 'Where Does the God Delusion Come From?', *New Blackfriars* 88, no. 1017 (Sept. 2007): 510.

3. *TGD*, 177.

4. *TGD*, 163.

5. Daniel C. Dennett, 'Appraising Grace: What Evolutionary Good Is God?', *The Sciences* (Jan./Feb. 1997): 39.

6. Robert A. Hinde, *Why Gods Persist: A Scientific Approach to Religion*, 2nd ed. (Oxon: Routledge, 1999), 99.

7. Ibid., 99.

8. Peter Baofu, *Beyond Nature and Nurture: Conceiving a Better Way to Understand Genes and Memes* (Newcastle: Cambridge Scholars Press, 2006), 138.

9. *TGD*, 163

10. Dennett, 'Appraising Grace: What Evolutionary Good Is God?', 39.

11. Scott Atran, *In Gods We Trust: The Evolutionary Landscape of Religion* (Oxford: Oxford University Press, 2002), 4.

12. McGrath, *Christian Theology: An Introduction*, 3rd ed., 208.

13. Walter Burkert, *Creation of the Sacred: Tracks of Biology in Early Religions* (Cambridge, MA: Harvard University Press, 1996), x. The term 'natural theology in the widest sense' was proffered by Lord Adam Gifford in 1886 as the theme for the Gifford Lectures, which take place yearly across four leading Scottish universities, Aberdeen, Edinburgh, Glasgow, and St. Andrews. Burkert's *Creation of the Sacred* grew out of the Gifford lectures he gave at the University of St. Andrews in 1989. Several of these lectures have been adapted into book form and become classic works of theology and philosophy, such as William James' *On the Variety of Religious Experience* (New York: Penguin, 1982), originally published in 1902.

14. *BTS*, 107.

15. Ibid., 107.

16. *TGD*, 181.

17. Pascal Boyer, *The Naturalness of Religious Ideas: A Cognitive Theory of Religion* (Berkeley: University of California Press, 1994), xi.

18. Ilkka Pyysiäinen, 'Cognition and Culture in the Construction of Religion', in Ilkka Pyysiäinen and Veikko Anttonen, eds., *Current Approaches in the Cognitive Science of Religion* (London: Continuum, 2002), 1.

19. Pyysiäinen, however, uses the term 'supernatural' where I have used the term 'religious'. I have treated these terms as synonyms here, although they are not truly synonymous. For our intentions here, however, it does not detract from the argument to treat the two terms as synonyms. We could say that 'religious' beliefs are a subset of beliefs that one would call 'supernatural'. Though theologians may take issue with this classification, I will not digress into a

semantic discussion as it bears no weight on the argument, nor do I seek to espouse this view. We will also note in Chapter Five how religious beliefs may not be supernatural.

20. Ilkka Pyysiäinen, *Supernatural Agents: Why We Believe in Souls, Gods and Buddhas* (Oxford: Oxford University Press, 2009), 3.

21. Ibid., 3–4.

22. *TGD*, 188.

23. Daniel C. Dennett and Ryan T. McKay, 'The Evolution of Misbelief', *Behavioural and Brain Sciences* 32, no. 6 (2009): 504.

24. *TGD*, 166.

25. Atran, *In Gods We Trust: The Evolutionary Landscape of Religion*, 9.

26. Boyer, *The Naturalness of Religious Ideas: A Cognitive Theory of Religion*, 4–5.

27. Hinde, *Why Gods Persist: A Scientific Approach to Religion*, 2nd ed., 5.

28. Pascal Boyer, *Religion Explained* (London: Heinemann, 2001), 37.

29. Atran, *In Gods We Trust: The Evolutionary Landscape of Religion*, 15.

30. Burkert, *Creation of the Sacred: Tracks of Biology in Early Religions*, 20.

31. Ibid., 20.

32. *TGD*, 181.

33. Daniel C. Dennett, *The Intentional Stance* (Cambridge, MA: MIT Press, 1987), 17.

34. This assumption can be challenged philosophically, in that as we cannot think others' thoughts, we cannot use Descartes' *cogito ergo sum* argument to verify the existence of other minds. As Dennett does not demarcate between the physical and the mental, however, and as we can observe the physiology of others' brains, we can safely assume that they have similar consciousnesses.

35. Dennett, *The Intentional Stance*, 23.

36. *TGD*, 182.

37. Ibid., 182–83.

38. *TGD*, 183. Italics mine.

39. Research has indicated that this propensity becomes established in humans aged between four and six years. Heinz Wimmer and Josef Perner, 'Beliefs about Beliefs: Representation and Constraining Function of Wrong Beliefs in Young Children's Understanding of Deception', *Cognition* 13, no. 1 (Jan. 1983): 103. Further research also indicates that the inability to comprehend other minds is a specific trait of autism and a significant component of autistic children's social impairment. Simon Baron Cohen, Alan M. Leslie, and Una Frith, 'Does the Autistic Child Have a Theory of Mind?', *Cognition* 21, no. 1 (Oct. 1985): 37.

40. *TGD*, 184.

41. Justin L. Barrett, 'Cognitive Science, Religion and Theology', in Jeffery Schloss and Michael Murray, eds., *The Believing Primate* (New York: Oxford University Press, 2009), 85.

42. Justin L. Barrett, *Why Would Anyone Believe in God?* (Plymouth, UK: AltaMira, 2004), 3; also, Dennett and McKay, 'The Evolution of Misbelief', 502.

43. Quoted by Dennett and McKay; 'The Evolution of Misbelief', 502.

44. *TGD*, 184.

45. Ibid., 184.

46. Pyysiäinen, *Supernatural Agents: Why We Believe in Souls, Gods and Buddhas*, 13.

47. Ibid., 13.

48. *TGD*, 188.

49. Boyer, *Religion Explained*, 167.

50. Dawkins' *The Blind Watchmaker* takes its title from this argument, which he commends as logical and well informed.

51. *BTS*, 118.

52. For example, Burkert illustrates how humanity's experience of suffering may have led to postulations of agents responsible for suffering—that suffering was punishment from gods (we will

find parallels between this view and traditional theological images of original sin in Chapter Five). Burkert, *Creation of the Sacred: Tracks of Biology in Early Religions*, 113.

53. Susan Blackmore, *Dying to Live: Science and Near Death Experience* (London: HarperCollins, 1993), 17. However, this materialist view of the human experience of mortality has been criticised by theologians such as Carol Zaleski, 'Near Death Experiences', in Jerry Wall, ed., *The Oxford Handbook of Eschatology* (Oxford: Oxford University Press, 2010), 625.

54. Burkert, *Creation of the Sacred: Tracks of Biology in Early Religions*, 13–14.

55. David Sloan Wilson, *Darwin's Cathedral: Evolution, Religion and the Nature of Society* (Chicago: University of Chicago Press, 2002), 1.

56. *TSG*, 192–93.

57. Ibid., 193.

58. Boyer, *Religion Explained*, 42–43.

59. *TSG*, 197–98.

60. Blaise Pascal, *Pensées* (London: Penguin, 1979), 149–55, originally published in 1669.

61. In *The God Delusion*, Dawkins offers a critique of Pascal's wager; however, he does not highlight it as an example of the meme for hell perpetuating itself and other religious memes.

62. *TSG*, 198.

63. Gerard J. Hughes, *Fidelity Without Fundamentalism: A Dialogue with Tradition* (London: Darton, Longman & Todd, 2010), 59.

64. *TGD*, 165.

65. Daniel C. Dennett, 'Religion's Just a Survival Meme', *Science and Theology News* (16 June 2006), Web, 12 Feb. 2011.

66. Dennett, 'Appraising Grace: What Evolutionary Good Is God?', 41–42.

67. Daniel C. Dennett, 'Back from the Drawing Board', in Bo Dahlbom, ed., *Dennett and His Critics: Demystifying Mind* (Oxford: Blackwell, 1993), 204–5.

68. Susan Blackmore, *The Meme Machine* (Oxford: Oxford University Press, 1999), 188–89.

69. Ibid., 189.

70. Boyer, *Religion Explained*, 218.

71. Blackmore, *The Meme Machine*, 190.

72. *TGD*, 200.

73. Ibid., 77.

74. *BTS*, 122–23.

75. Boyer, *Religion Explained*, 150–51.

76. Ibid., 151.

77. Boyer, *Religion Explained*, 151.

78. Ibid., 154.

79. *BTS*, 156–57.

80. Pascal Boyer, 'A Reductionistic Model of Distinct Modes of Religious Transmission', in Harvey Whitehouse and Robert McCauley, eds., *Mind and Religion: Psychological and Cognitive Foundations of Religiosity* (Walnut Creek, CA: AltaMira, 2005), 4.

81. Alvin Plantinga, 'Games Scientists Play', in Schloss and Murray, eds., *The Believing Primate*, 147.

82. Thomas Crean, O.P., *A Catholic Replies to Professor Dawkins* (Oxford: Family Publications, 2008), 68.

83. Sigmund Freud, 'Religious Ideas as Wish Fulfillments', in Chad Meister, ed., *The Philosophy of Religion Reader* (New York: Routledge, 2008), 502.

84. Plantinga, 'Games Scientists Play', 147.

85. Hans Urs von Balthasar, *The Von Balthasar Reader*, ed. Medard Kehland and Werner Loser (New York: Crossroad, 1997), 99.

86. Alister E. McGrath, *Darwinism and the Divine: Evolutionary Thought and Natural Theology* (Chichester: Wiley-Blackwell, 2011), 267.

87. Justin L. Barrett, 'Cognitive Science, Religion, and Theology', in Schloss and Murray, eds., *The Believing Primate*, 76.

88. Celia Deane-Drummond, *Christ and Evolution: Wonder and Wisdom* (London: SCM, 2009), 68.

89. Nancey Murphy, 'Cognitive Science and the Evolution of Religion: A Philosophical and Theological Appraisal', in Schloss and Murray, eds., *The Believing Primate*, 270.

90. George Tyrrell, *Through Scylla and Charybdis, or the Old Theology and the New* (London: Longman, Green & Co.), 207. However, the understanding of the religious need alluded to by Tyrrell may not necessarily be an evolutionary understanding, such as the one this chapter has engaged with.

91. James, *On the Varieties of Religious Experience: A Study in Human Nature*, 1.

92. McGrath, *Dawkins' God: Genes, Memes and the Meaning of Life*, 135–36.

93. Ibid., 136.

94. Ibid., 138.

95. Atran, *In Gods We Trust: The Evolutionary Landscape of Religion*, 249.

96. Ibid., 249.

Evil, Evolution, and God

Dawkins and Theology in Dialogue

INTRODUCTION

In Chapters Two and Three, we began our dialogue with Dawkins by exploring his worldview. These chapters enabled us to begin to explore avenues where Dawkins' scientific hermeneutic could be utilized by the theologian. In the last chapter, we took his outlook on evolution and particularly his meme theory, and examined how it can be applied it to religion. In doing so, it was argued that Dawkins' evolutionary perspective of culture could be integrated into a theological project that contributes to Anselm's classic definition of theology, '*fides quaerens intellectum*', as it seeks to understand the origins and development of religious faith as a concept. This chapter will continue to show how bringing Dawkins' worldview into consideration could be beneficial for theology. As we have seen in Chapter Three, Dawkins uses the existence of evil to pose a challenge to theistic belief. Consequently, this chapter will centre around this fulcrum, which we will term Dawkins' 'theodicy challenge'. The term 'theodicy', coined by the seventeenth-century philosopher Gottfried Leibniz, is a theological attempt to reconcile the existence of evil with an omnipotent/beneficent creator. We will first address the question of whether Dawkins could be considered a servant of theology, and then introduce Dawkins' theodicy challenge, and demonstrate how it can be used as a challenge to theism (though as we will see, Dawkins does not use it to validate atheism).

DAWKINS AS A SERVANT OF THEOLOGY?

In Chapter One, we noted that there are significant limitations when engaging in a dialogue with Dawkins. One such limitation is that Dawkins' comprehension of theology is weak at best. He has thus been rightly criticized on this point by a number of scholars. Dawkins' misinterpretations of theology and Christianity are particularly acute given that he seeks to castigate theological themes. This is one of Dawkins' most prominent weaknesses, as one can seriously question the legitimacy of his critiques if he does not demonstrate a solid comprehension of the topics he is critiquing. Therefore, one could easily adopt the position that Dawkins is not a worthy dialogue partner for theology, given that his treatment of theological themes is so devoid of substance. Gerard J. Hughes, for example, points to the fact that Dawkins fails to grasp the allegorical nature of aspects of the Bible.[1] Hughes illustrates that when texts are read out of their context, they are more vulnerable to misinterpretations: "In some future era, even our own culture could be open to much misunderstanding. Imagine a future generation which . . . did not realize that *Animal Farm* is an allegorical novel, and read it as a description of some extraordinary episode in evolutionary history".[2] Hughes continues to assert how the opening chapters of Genesis can be misinterpreted in a similar fashion, to be taken as a "factual description of the stages in which the matter in the universe was organized into the cosmos as we know it".[3] There are clear examples of such misreading, for example, in Dawkins' thoughts on the theological concept of original sin. Original sin has been the subject of much theological investigation—some of which will be discussed in this chapter—and represents interesting notions around the responsibility of humanity and the existence of suffering. Yet Dawkins highlights both his misreading of the allegorical nature of the Genesis narrative, and his ignorance of theological thinking on the issue in the following passage:

> Adam (who never existed) bequeathed his "sin" in his bodily semen (charming notion) to all of humanity. That sin, with which every newborn baby is hideously stained (another charming notion), was so terrible that it could be forgiven only through the blood sacrifice of a scapegoat. But no ordinary scapegoat would do. The sin of humanity was so great that the only adequate sacrificial victim was God himself.[4]

However, Hughes makes the very interesting assertion that Dawkins has been given encouragement to misread and misinterpret the Bible and theological tradition: "[H]e has been given considerable encouragement to do so by the way in which Christians themselves have misread the bible and in so doing have failed to see which are the truths which the biblical texts convey".[5] Many Christians have succumbed to the same misinterpretations of the Bible and theology that Dawkins has. A situation has thus arisen where Dawkins and Christian apologists have been engaged in an ongoing debate that is based upon faulty premises, as Hughes articulates. "Thus, some Christians have responded to misdirected criticisms by trying to defend creationism, or the moving star of Bethlehem, as though the bible is trying to make truth claims about cosmogony or astronomy, rather than about monotheism and Christology".[6] The prevalence of such debate was discussed earlier, as we referred to the lively polemic around the teaching of intelligent design in the United States. In this sense, a large part of the tension between Dawkins and Christianity stems from both sides of the debate misunderstanding key principles of biblical and theological scholarship.

What Hughes does suggest, though, is that it is "to a considerable extent our own fault that Christianity has been so misunderstood".[7] It is the responsibility of theologians, educators, and others, to ensure that Christianity is faithfully proclaimed and understood. This is particularly important when it comes to discussing Christian themes with those from outside the tradition, if we are to take the necessity of interfaith dialogue as an imperative. We can also advance Hughes' idea slightly, to suggest that Dawkins may be taken as a representative of those who, either from an antagonist or apologetic standpoint, have misinterpreted the Bible or theological tradition. In other words, could it be assumed that Dawkins' misunderstandings are often echoed in the public? It would appear from the previously mentioned debates around intelligent design, and Hughes' references to apologetic defenses of creationism, that this is indeed the case. Therefore, popular misinterpretations of theological concepts and traditions could arguably be considered as a failing of theology. Something that Dawkins may offer to theology is to make evident its failings in adequately conveying its own message, as Hughes explains: "To conclude, then. Dawkins does indeed provide a useful wake-up call to make the accepted conclusions of most biblical scholars and most theologians much more widely known and accepted in the Christian churches".[8]

Hughes is thus implying that theology is failing to accurately represent itself in the public sphere. If Dawkins, as a member of the nontheological public, is misreading theology, then it could be argued that theologians are ultimately to blame for this misreading. Dawkins' misinterpretations could be seen to indicate a deficit of theology in the public, which David Tracy identified as one of the three distinct audiences that theology addresses: the public, the academy, and the church.[9] Particularly in the context of modern pluralism and the accessibility of knowledge, the 'public' audience of theology is becoming increasingly important. If Dawkins understands religion to be historically a tool of oppression and terror, then it is arguably the responsibility of theology that its own rich history of commitment to social justice is not being properly conveyed. We have already indicated Dawkins' understating of the role of religious faith in the civil rights movement, but further examples of the role of religion in social justice abound in history, such as the influence of Catholic social teaching and in particular Pope John Paul II on the Polish Solidarity movement in the 1980s.[10] If the view of religion as a tool of the oppressor is a popular one, as Dawkins' popularity would suggest, then theology is failing to portray its own history and themes.

Similarly, in Dawkins' ongoing crusade against religion, he brings to the fore the troubled history of science and religion. In doing so, he highlights another of theology's weaknesses—an unsettled, often dismissive attitude toward advancements in science that may appear to have implications for how we view God and the world, as Hughes observes:

> Believers have on the whole a bad record in the way we respond to the advancement of science and the growing complexity of morality in our technologically and environmentally ever more complex world. We have tended to sound, and often to be, reluctant to accept undisputed scientific findings so that we can try to work out how they can be integrated into our overall picture of our world as God's creation. The lessons of Galileo, biblical criticism, evolutionary biology, contemporary physics, psychology and medicine forever seem to catch believers unprepared, nervous, and defensive. At his best, Dawkins calls attention to that fact.[11]

The perennial advancement of our scientific understanding has had significant theological implications. We have already indicated areas of theology where science may bear weight on our concepts of the world. For example, evolutionary science has arguably shown that we can no longer view ourselves as the pinnacle of creation, as we are merely part of an ongoing process. As Christian apologists respond to Dawkins' arguments against theism by referring to concepts of intelligent design, and search for evidence of divine intervention in the creation of life, they highlight a nervous defensiveness, to use Hughes' terms. This defensive approach, as we shall see throughout this chapter, is unnecessary, as any truth, be it scientific or theological, aids our intellectual development. It helps us to grow in our own understanding. The scientific advancements of the human race can then be easily viewed from a theological perspective, as Jesus said, "I come that you may have life and have it to the full"

(John 10:10). This sentiment is masterfully conveyed by the Second Vatican Council:

> People have always striven to develop their human life through their own effort and ingenuity, and nowadays they extend their mastery over nearly all spheres of activity through science and technology. . . . The achievements of the human race are a sign of God's greatness and the fulfillment of his mysterious design.[12]

Scientific concepts, even if they are intentionally presented in an atheistic manner, as in Dawkins' work, can be integrated into a theological conception of the world. We will see how this is to be achieved throughout this chapter.

Therefore, although Dawkins represents a hostile worldview, he can also be taken to exemplify the disparity between theology and much of the public. He calls attention to the fact that theology's integration of science is perhaps not as widely known as it should be—we will again see evidence of this in the following sections as significant theological work on incorporating scientific ideas often breaks from the mainstream, traditional beliefs, as opposed to being mainstream theology itself. In highlighting the prevalence of a nervous, defensive attitude, Dawkins' scientific criticisms are in fact of use to theology as they show how theology, in a sense, is not succeeding in the public sphere. Dawkins' criticisms could paradoxically offer food for thought for the theologian. He may then be considered an appropriate, if unwitting, dialogue partner. Moreover, this chapter will show that if Dawkins' criticisms are to be earnestly probed, taking his scientific worldview into account, then he may even end up unintentionally offering a new dimension for consideration on classical theological problems. To demonstrate how this dialogue will be useful, this chapter will now examine Dawkins' particular version of the problem of evil.

The question that was posed at the beginning of this section now needs to be addressed: whether Dawkins can be considered in some sense to be a servant of theology. We have already shown throughout this book that Dawkins fails to grasp much of theology. Another recent example demonstrates further how Dawkins fails to appreciate the complexity of the composition of the Bible, and appears ignorant of the history of biblical scholarship, as he writes, "Whatever else the Bible might be—and it really is a great work of literature—it is not a moral book and young people need to learn that important fact because they are very frequently told the opposite".[13] While Dawkins himself acknowledges that the historical contexts cannot be understated when it comes to appreciating the moral zeitgeist of a particular culture,[14] he seems to hold a double standard when it comes to the Bible; he does not take into account the historical context within which the Bible was written. Moreover, he ignores the vast amount of theological work in areas such as biblical hermeneutics, exegesis, ecumenical theology, and moral theology. However, although it can be asserted that Dawkins certainly 'needs to learn' more about theology, it could also be argued that we need to learn from him. His critiques may serve as a challenge for theology to improve upon itself, facing up to prevalent misunderstandings which, according to Hughes, we need to take responsibility for. Paradoxically then, Dawkins could be considered a servant to theology if his critiques, however misguided, can be used to help theology better itself and combat public misinterpretations. In responding to Dawkins' criticisms, theology may find itself better articulated and with more substantial thinking on particular areas, thus helping in the theological task of spreading the good news. Essentially, Dawkins challenges theology to "awake from its slumber" (Rom. 13:11) in critical areas and become a more coherent, constructive, and critical voice in the public forum.

DAWKINS' THEODICY CHALLENGE

In Dawkins' *River Out of Eden*, we encounter what can be termed a 'theodicy challenge'. He quotes Darwin on the suffering and pain of natural selection, exemplified in the seemingly callous breeding habits of the wasp *Ichneumonidae*. Dawkins suggests that such examples of pain and suffering, omnipresent in nature, led Darwin to retreat from his Christian beliefs. Darwin wrote, "I cannot persuade myself that a beneficent and omnipotent God would have designedly created the *Ichneumonidae* with the express intention of their feeding within the living bodies of Caterpillars".[15] From this passage, Dawkins uses Darwin's words to challenge traditional theism, by asserting that the pain and suffering in the natural world are exactly as we would expect "if there is, at bottom, no design, no purpose, no evil and no good, nothing but blind, pitiless indifference".[16] McGrath agrees that from Darwin's writings, we can deduce that he found "the existence of pain and suffering in the world an unbearable intellectual and moral burden".[17] That the existence of pain and suffering, among other issues, led Darwin to depart from traditional Christianity, seems unquestionable. As McGrath quotes from Darwin's autobiography, "I can hardly see how anyone ought to wish Christianity to be true . . . ".[18]

However, McGrath makes an important clarification. Darwin's departure from his traditional Christian views cannot justify what Dawkins seems to imply; that based upon the pain/suffering of natural selection, Darwin was intellectually opposed to the idea of God. Interestingly, Darwin wrote that he had never been an atheist, but 'agnostic' was the most appropriate description for his stance on the God question.[19] McGrath thus critiques Dawkins for not elaborating on the interesting subject of the entanglement of Darwin's scientific and religious beliefs: "Yet, Dawkins' discussion of the complex and fascinating interaction of Darwin's scientific and religious views is most disappointing, and fails to deal satisfactorily with the issues involved".[20]

Dawkins' main contention in what we will hereafter refer to as his theodicy challenge is that such mindless pain or suffering is entirely consistent with the Godless, mechanistic worldview he is taken to represent in this book. Correspondingly, he maintains that the idea of a purposeful universe created by a benevolent and omnipotent divinity is difficult to square with such pain and violence in the natural world.[21] Dawkins is knowingly referring to a philosophical conundrum known as the 'problem of evil'; "[T]heologians worry away at the 'problem of evil'".[22] Consequently, by engaging in a discussion with this theological issue, Dawkins is perhaps unwittingly supporting our claim that he is a valuable conversation partner for theology. The influential writer C. S. Lewis, who gained acclaim for his theological writings, neatly summarized the dilemma as follows: "If God were good, He would wish to make His creatures perfectly happy, and if God were almighty, He would be able to do what he wished. But the creatures are not happy. Therefore, God lacks either goodness, or power, or both".[23]

The problem of evil has commonly been adopted by many prolific philosophers to validate an atheistic hermeneutic. One significant example is Bertrand Russell, who stated, "Here we find in this world a great deal of injustice, and so far as that goes that is a reason for supposing that justice does not rule in the world; and therefore so far as it goes it affords a moral argument against deity and not in favor of one".[24] J. L. Mackie, another eminent modern philosopher, proposed that the problem of evil "may be presented as a formally valid disproof of the set of propositions which constitutes traditional theism, as a demonstration that this set is internally inconsistent, so that these propositions cannot all be true".[25] More recently, the scientist Victor J. Stenger incorporated the problem of evil into his work, which sought to vilify atheism from a scientific perspective: "In the language of science, the empirical fact of unnecessary suffering in the world is inconsistent with a god who is omniscient, omnipotent, and omnibenevolent. Observations of human and animal suffering look just as they can be expected to look if there is no God".[26]

The prevalence of suffering and pain can be held, according to Russell and Mackie, among others, as one argument, or one element of a wider argument, against the existence of a deity. John Haught also recognizes the problem of evil as an oft-used crutch upon which atheism leans. "Atheism also arises, of course, among those who consider it impossible logically to reconcile the idea of an all-powerful and omnibenevolent God with the fact of evil and suffering in the world".[27] Alister McGrath goes as far as to suggest it is one of the Christian faith's greatest vulnerabilities,[28] while Hans Küng discerns it as "the rock of atheism".[29]

Dawkins, however, does not rest his atheistic hermeneutic upon the problem of evil. For him, the problem of evil bears no significant weight in considering the existence of a deity: "[N]either the problem of evil nor moral considerations in general would shift me far, one way or the other, from the null hypothesis [complete uncertainty over God's existence]".[30] Dawkins points out that the problem of evil only has implications for a particular image of God, or particular characteristics associated with traditional theism (the set of propositions that J. L. Mackie used to form his 'disproof', which Mackie himself acknowledged was tentative at best). It is not a solid argument against the concept of God itself:

> 'Theodicy' (the vindication of divine providence in the face of the existence of evil) keeps theologians awake at night. The authoritative *Oxford Companion to Philosophy* gives the problem of evil as 'the most powerful objection to traditional theism'. But it is an argument only against the existence of a good God. Goodness is no part of the *definition* of the God Hypothesis, merely a desirable add-on.[31]

Although the problem of pain does not explicitly justify atheism, the seemingly paradoxical concept of a beneficent creator and a world teeming with examples of suffering has certainly challenged the concepts of benevolence and omnipotence, attributes traditionally associated with the divine, as noted by David Hume:

> God's power is infinite. Whatever he wills is executed. But neither man [*sic*], nor any other animal, is happy. Therefore he does not will their happiness. . . . Is God willing to prevent evil, but unable? Then is he impotent. Is he able, but not willing? Then is he malevolent. Is he both able and willing? Whence then is evil?[32]

The academics mentioned above are significant examples, among others such as William Rowe[33] and Richard Swinburne,[34] who recognize that suffering in the world poses a problem to belief in a benevolent/omnipotent creator. Dawkins, while not arguing for atheism from this perspective, does show how such suffering is consistent with, though not wholly indicative of, his atheistic worldview. It can be seen, therefore, as a challenge to develop a theology, or more specifically at this point, a theodicy, encompassing the problem of evil, that can dialogue with the mechanistic stance of Dawkins. Opening a dialogical relationship with Dawkins is the wider goal of this project itself, and consequently, considering a theodicy that can successfully account for the problem of evil in a mechanistic world can be a vital element of such dialogue. This will be attempted by discussing models of God's relationship with creation later. But it must be asked at this point what Dawkins himself brings to this dialogue, because as we have seen, he is neither unique nor original in posing the problem of evil as a challenge to theology.

In fact, the concept has been a prominent and multifaceted theological motif for many centuries. Theological scholar Michael L. Peterson, in his volume *The Problem of Evil: Selected Writings*, among others, suggests that the Book of Job is a literary exploration of the theodicy paradox, challenging whether we live in a moral universe—an underlying theme of the Old Testament writings:[35]

> How then can I dispute with him? How can I find words to argue with him? Though I were innocent, I could not answer him; I could only plead with my Judge for mercy. Even if I summoned him and
>
> he responded, I do not believe he would give me a hearing. He would crush me with a storm and multiply my wounds for no reason. He would not let me catch my breath but would overwhelm me with misery. If it is a matter of strength, he is mighty! And if it is a matter of justice, who can challenge him? Even if I were innocent, my mouth would condemn me; if I were blameless, it would pronounce me guilty. (Job 9:14-19)

Thus it can be argued that the issue played a role in early religious texts. Moreover, significant attempts to intellectually resolve the problem of evil have also been proffered by church fathers Irenaeus and Augustine, among others, such as Thomas Aquinas. Although Aquinas did not offer a comprehensive, stand-alone deliberation on the problem of evil, he does address it on several occasions that are scattered throughout his writings.[36] Both Irenaeus and

Augustine explain evil as a result of human sin (the fall); however, there are differences in their approaches. For example, the Augustinian tradition views evil as a direct consequence of an intentional disobedience, while Irenaeus mitigated the maliciousness of sin, and viewed evil as a challenge for humankind's development toward perfection. Theologian John Hick, in his popular work *Evil and the God of Love*, offers a succinct and useful summary of the differences between the two classical theodicies:

> Instead of the fall of Adam being presented, as in the Augustinian tradition, as an utterly malignant and catastrophic event, completely disrupting God's plan, Irenaeus pictures it as something that occurred in the childhood of the race, an understandable lapse due to weakness and immaturity rather than an adult crime full of malice and pregnant with perpetual guilt. And instead of the Augustinian view of life's trials as a divine punishment for Adam's sin, Irenaeus sees our world of mingled good and evil as a divinely appointed environment for man's [*sic*] development towards the perfection that represents the fulfillment of God's good purpose for him.[37]

So Dawkins' use of theodicy as a challenge to theism cannot be considered especially revolutionary. It is, however, an illuminating issue that points toward Dawkins' evolutionary metanarrative or *weltanschauung*, which we encountered in Chapter Three. To show how theology may benefit from considering Dawkins' theodicy challenge, we must contextualise it against the backdrop of how the problem of evil has traditionally been dealt with.

DAWKINS' THEODICY CHALLENGE CONTEXTUALISED

Dawkins' Darwin-inspired theodicy challenge takes a central place in his view on the purposelessness of the world. As we discussed in Chapter Three, this view (in his opinion) grows organically from his hermeneutical depiction of how life came to be, through a series of random events (genetic mutations) followed by nonrandom natural selection. Thus the question arises, whether the scientific basis of Dawkins' worldview (which was unbeknownst to those church fathers/theologians who originally tackled the issue) will provide a new dimension of the problem of evil for theology to explore. Is it conceivable that current developments in the scientific understanding of evolution may have insightful implications for discourse on the theodicy problem? Distinguished Swedish theologian Ulf Gorman, in his contribution to the Macmillan *Encyclopedia of Science and Religion*, answers this question in the positive.[38]

Alister McGrath, similarly, suggests that Darwin's approach (of which Dawkins is a modern proponent) moves theodicy into new territory.[39] This sentiment is echoed by many established theologians engaged in dialogue between theology and science, for example Christopher Southgate[40] and Neil Messer, who suggests that Darwinian evolution raises a particular form of the problem of evil: "[T]he kind of world disclosed to us by evolutionary biology appears very different from the kind of world depicted in key biblical sources of the doctrine of creation".[41] The fact that theologians of the stature of McGrath, Southgate, and Messer insist that evolution brings with it new considerations for the theodicy problem, acts as a catalyst for us to investigate Dawkins' particular theodicy challenge. In order to probe Dawkins' challenge, we will now deliberate on how 'traditional' thought on theodicy can form the background against which Dawkins' theodicy challenge can be contextualised.

If we refer to the influential theodicies of Irenaeus and Augustine, we can notice a distinct trend in their thinking, namely, that the focus of their explanations is on the human experience of suffering, and explanations are given in human terms; they see evil as the result of human sin. More recent contributions to the theological problem of evil are akin to the church fathers in their human-centred approach. Alvin Plantinga's influential 'Free Will Defense', which broadly cites human free will as an explanation for the existence of evil, can be held as an example: "To create creatures capable of *moral good*, therefore, He must create creatures capable of moral evil".[42] Although there are notable exceptions to this tendency,[43] John Haught insists that anthropocentric theodicies bound up in language of sin and guilt have dominated Western thinking on the issue.[44] This is apparent from Paul Ricoeur's assertion that for him, one of the most striking aspects of the religious vision of God is the dualistic concept of accusation and consolation.[45] In this view, God becomes an "organizing power in a world that operates in terms of the law of retribution".[46] In Ricoeur's 'ethical vision', pain and suffering become understood predominantly as penalties for human sin. Ricoeur does acknowledge that within the Adamic myth (with which, according to Haught, Ricoeur associates his ethical vision), nonhuman evil did exist as a concept in the form of the serpent; the serpent, "at the very heart of the Adam myth, stands for evil's other face . . . pregiven evil, evil that attracts and seduces man".[47] Yet Ricoeur maintains that the theology behind the Adamic myth is portrayed in the human picture of sin and subsequent punishment: "the basic spectacle of the tragic hero, innocent and guilty".[48]

Similar to Ricoeur, influential scientist/theologian Pierre Teilhard de Chardin asserts that original sin (a vivacious theological concept itself, of which

Teilhard himself was undoubtedly apprehensive) was proposed as a solution of sorts to the problem of evil.[49] The doctrine of original sin was subject to intensive criticism by Enlightenment thinkers such as Voltaire and Jean-Jacques Rousseau.[50] However, the point relevant to our current discussion that Teilhard (similar to Ricoeur) makes, is that evil (pain and suffering) has been ingrained into Western Christian thought to represent a consequence of human sin: ". . . Christianity has developed under the overriding impression that all the evil around us was born from an initial transgression".[51] More specifically, John Hick suggests that it is the Augustinian interpretation of the initial transgression that has become the dominant model: "[T]he doctrine of a fearful and calamitous fall of man long ago in the 'dark backward and abysm of time', and of a subsequent participation by all men in the deadly entail of sin, is, as we have seen, deeply entrenched".[52] Ian G. Barbour agrees that the most influential Christian position on original sin has been Augustinian.[53] Fundamentally, the predominant approach taken to theodicies is that evil is viewed as retribution. In essence, evil was interpreted in human terms.

Moreover, this 'traditional' representation of evil assumes an original state of perfection. If evil is retribution for sin, then the mere existence of evil presupposes an "initial transgression", as Teilhard de Chardin writes.[54] This is to say that if evil is understood in this traditional way, it follows that an initial state absent of sin and evil became undone through an original sin. In the Christian tradition, this original sin is presented symbolically in Genesis as Adam and Eve's disobedience to God (Gen. 3:1-21). It could be noted that with regard to the doctrine of original sin, much theological debate has ensued regarding atonement for sin. Christological theories have been proffered by church fathers such as Anselm, which see the crucifixion of Christ as a reconciliatory event, in which humans sins are atoned for.[55] Discourse in this area is ongoing, evident in the work of Jürgen Moltmann[56] and Neil Messer, among others. Messer, for example, suggests that approaches to the problem of evil are "more satisfactory from the perspective of a Christian tradition . . . ". While Christological responses to the theodicy problem may be an insightful area of discourse, they are perhaps too Christ-centred in the pluralistic context of this study. Therefore, while acknowledging that other theologizing exists regarding the 'reconciliation' between God and humanity in the Christ event, theodicies have predominantly explained evil, pain, and suffering as a result of a human transgression. That is to say that evil has traditionally been intrinsically linked with humanity, who spoiled the initial paradise.

This is the context in which we can view Dawkins' theodicy challenge. In suggesting that Dawkins' theodicy challenge may offer new dimensions to theology, it must be asked if he brings anything unique to an age-old theological dilemma. If theology extends its reach beyond traditional subject matter to be inclusive of hostile positions such as Dawkins', what can the theologian gain? To illustrate how the dialogue between theology and Dawkins can be fruitful, we can discern two particular aspects of Dawkins' theodicy challenge that offer insights for the theologian to consider. Firstly, Dawkins' stringent emphasis on the gradualness of evolution challenges any anthropocentric vision of theodicy. Secondly, in the evolutionary model that Dawkins promotes, humans are very late arrivals on the evolutionary scene, which raises doubts over the legitimacy of a fall from paradise. These issues, which will be addressed in the next section, may not be exhaustive, but they will substantiate the argument that dialogue with Dawkins is a worthwhile enterprise.

How Dawkins' View Challenges Traditional Theodicy

Anthropocentricism

As we noted, traditional theodicies could be deemed anthropocentric given their focus on humanity. In dialogue with Dawkins, as a representative of evolutionary materialism, such an anthropocentric comprehension of the problem of evil could, in the context, be highly insufficient. We can gain support for this assertion by referring to McGrath, who acknowledges how evolution, within which Dawkins' worldview is grounded, becomes an obstacle for anthropocentric theodicies. McGrath suggests that the ontological distance between humans and the animal kingdom is contracted as a result of Darwin's theory of evolution, and consequently, the problem of pain and suffering is no longer limited to humans.[57] In an evolutionary worldview, there is ontologically little that distinguishes humans from the rest of life. This was argued interestingly by Gould, who pointed out that this fact may have important theological implications, despite the fact he argues for the disentanglement of science and religion. Moreover, from Dawkins' representation of evolution, as opposed to Gould's, greater emphasis is placed on the gradualness of evolution.[58] In Dawkins' view, therefore, it is even more difficult, philosophically, to discuss humanity as distinct from other life, given that all of life is the product of a gradual, ongoing process. This is not to say, however, that humans are not unique in several respects. The extent to which humanity employs language and culture, among other traits, is overwhelmingly greater than other animals, as noted in Chapters Three and Four. However, given our kinship with animals, made known through our understanding of evolution, it becomes extremely difficult, if not impossible, to consider suffering in purely human terms, which has historically been the predominant view.

McGrath also dutifully points out that the extent to which suffering is prevalent through the course of evolution far exceeds the capabilities of traditional theodicies. He asserts that evolution envisages the emergence of animals "involving suffering and apparent wastage that go far beyond the concerns of traditional theodicy".[59] This is due to the evolutionary process containing an incomprehensible degree of nonhuman suffering, exemplified in Darwin's example of the *Ichneumonidae*, which Dawkins uses as the foundation to launch his theodicy challenge. However, there is a problem with this argument, which we had mentioned in Chapter Three; Irish theologian Cathriona Russell, following from Gould, suggests that the interpretation of the callous world teeming with suffering may in fact stem from a cultural context.[60] Notwithstanding this caveat, in the following passage, Dawkins himself attempts to portray the level of nonhuman suffering to which McGrath alludes:

> The total amount of suffering per year in the natural world is beyond all decent contemplation. During the minute that it takes me to compose this sentence, thousands of animals are being eaten alive, many others are running for their lives, whimpering with fear, others are slowly being devoured from within by rasping parasites, thousands of all kinds are dying of starvation, thirst, and disease.[61]

Consequently, in McGrath's view, the understanding of evil in the traditional, anthropocentric framework of sin and retribution fails to account for the vast amount of nonhuman suffering. Haught provides a complementary opinion upon his reflection on evolution. He perceptively notes that the continuity of evolution (a theme prevalent in Dawkins' thought) significantly weakens any theology of suffering that is limited to humans. "In view of the evolutionary continuity and kinship that we now know to exist between ourselves and all other kinds of life, it would be unjustifiably arbitrary to overlook God's sharing in the wider-than-human story of life's suffering".[62] Theologians Christopher Southgate and Andrew Robinson make a similar point, as they assert that "a somewhat neglected element in the problem of evil is the issue of the suffering of *nonhuman* creatures".[63]

The concept of nonhuman (and human) suffering viewed within Dawkins' atheistic *weltanschauung* poses no intellectual difficulty. In a universe comprised of electrons and genes, with no mindful creator, meaningless suffering such as is ubiquitous in the natural world is exactly as we would expect. Dawkins' ontology is devoid of any sense of good and bad. Although good and bad arise within the process of evolution, they do not exist as *a priori* concepts, as he clarifies:

> The universe has no mind, no feelings, no personality, so it doesn't do things in order to hurt or please you. Bad things happen because *things* happen. Whether they are bad or good from our point of view doesn't influence how likely it is that they will happen. Some people find it hard to accept this. They'd prefer to think that sinners get their comeuppance, that virtue is rewarded. Unfortunately, the universe doesn't care what people prefer.[64]

Notwithstanding this philosophical outlook, Dawkins does differentiate between the mindless universe and the living world. Although the mechanisms of the universe's causal chain can lead to suffering as a result of natural disasters, this suffering is not inflicted deliberately. However, in the case of the living world, the concept of deliberateness must be reconsidered:

> Although it is definitely not true that the weather, or an earthquake, is out to get you (for they don't care about you one way or the other) things are a bit different when we turn to the living world. If you are a rabbit, a fox is out to get you. If you are a minnow, a pike is out to get you.[65]

He articulates then, that suffering can, in the living world, be deliberate. So while his views on the meaninglessness of the universe can account for suffering as a result of causal processes such as natural disasters, it cannot account for suffering as a result of deliberate actions. In order to account for forms of suffering that could be interpreted as deliberate or mindful, Dawkins appeals to natural selection. "Natural selection, the struggle for existence as Darwin called it, means that every living creature has enemies that are working hard for its downfall".[66] For Dawkins, then, suffering can also become prevalent given that living organisms predominantly behave in such a way as to advance their own ends, namely, survival and propagation of their own genes. In Chapter Three, we discovered how Dawkins uses this point (that living things behave in such a way as to propagate their genes) to even explain self-sacrificial behaviour and the origins of altruism—although humans, he suggests, have the capacity to transcend these genetic dispositions. Acknowledging these crevices in Dawkins' view, he suggests that the violent struggle for existence introduces suffering not just as a result of the mindless, mechanistic universe at work, but also as a consequence of living creatures deliberately inflicting suffering on others in their fight for survival.

However, Dawkins needs to be challenged on this point as to what constitutes deliberateness. As we noted, the philosopher Mary Midgley criticized Dawkins for ascribing conscious intentions to unconscious genes. Similarly, discussing life as deliberately acting to struggle for survival may not be fully appropriate. This brings up again the recurrent critique of Dawkins for oversimplifying evolution, and stretching language too far, therefore diluting the true nature of the process. However, McGrath and Dawkins agree that such criticism is based upon a misrepresentation of Dawkins' position; he uses such language to convey how genes and living things behave. Similarly, pertaining to the discussion on animals causing suffering in the fight for survival, Dawkins also speaks of 'deliberateness' to illustrate how animals behave: "If you are a rabbit, a fox is out to get you. If you are a minnow, a pike is out to get you. I don't mean that the fox or pike *thinks* about it, although it may. I'd be equally happy to say that a virus is out to get you, and nobody believes viruses *think* about anything".[67] Actions of living organisms may not be mindful in the literal sense, but intentionality is ascribed to unconscious agents to convey how living things such as viruses behave. A virus may not consciously inflict suffering upon an animal, yet its quest for survival has it behave in such a way. This distinguishes suffering as a result of mechanistic events such as earthquakes from suffering as a result of actions taken by living organisms, as Dawkins illustrates:

> [E]volution by natural selection has seen to it that viruses, and foxes, and pikes, behave in ways that are actively bad for their victims—behave as though deliberately out to get them—in ways that you couldn't say of earthquakes or hurricanes or avalanches. Earthquakes and hurricanes are bad for their victims, but they don't take active steps to do bad things . . . they just happen.[68]

In Dawkins' atheistic worldview, the existence of evil can thus be understood either in terms of creatures' struggle for survival, or as the result of the mechanistic causal processes of the natural world. In this sense, Dawkins' outlook is challenged more by the existence of altruism than of suffering. Evil, in a worldview predicated upon the 'survival of the fittest', would appear to be consistent.

In a theological view, however, the problem of the immense amount of suffering becomes salient. Reflecting upon natural selection, the philosopher of biology David Hull poses the theological dilemma: "The God of the Galápagos is careless, wasteful, indifferent, almost diabolical. He is certainly not the sort of God to whom anyone would be inclined to pray".[69] In light of Darwinian evolution, a theological worldview will not only have to account for evil in the human experience, à la church fathers, but now also the immense history of suffering over the course of several billion years of evolution. Pain and suffering are not only understood to be far more prevalent in light of evolution, but they are also prerequisites for evolutionary change and progress.[70] If we recall the generational sieve in Dawkins' view on evolution discussed in Chapter Two, we can appreciate the significance of death in the evolutionary process itself. Without death, it would not be possible for natural selection to eliminate those genes that are detrimental to survival from the gene pool. In essence, without the suffering of death, evolution could not function. The presence of suffering, then, is not only exponentially greater in our perception of the world post-Darwin, but it is an intrinsic part of the coming to being of life itself. Therefore, considering Dawkins' theodicy challenge, which stems from evolution, may force theology to reengage with the issue in the context of considering the immense degree of nonhuman suffering in the evolutionary process.

To substantiate this point, we can turn to the theological substance gained from extending the human-centred view on suffering outwards in light of evolution. The eminent feminist eco-theologian Sallie McFague, for example, likens an anthropocentric vision of nature to a male-centred or Western-centred vision of the world: "Women, nature and the poor are viewed in the same way—the male gaze, the anthropocentric gaze, and the colonial gaze are similar".[71] McFague contends that anthropocentrism leads to the objectification of nature (of which animals are a part), and seeks to establish a relational model between humanity and creation that is more 'courteous' and less 'arrogant' than an anthropocentric perception; extending the anthropocentric vision provides a more holistic and tolerant theology.[72] The suffering of nature, in McFague's view, should thus be incorporated into a theological hermeneutic. The challenging of anthropocentrism, which Dawkins' worldview encourages by exhibiting the extensive suffering and continuity in the biosphere, has also resulted in theological discussion among other notable scholars. Rosemary Radford Ruether, Anne Primavesi, and Thomas Berry, for examples, all engage with topics such as a reinterpretation of the notion of human dominion which, it can be argued, was set forth in Genesis[73]. Thus the human-centred approach in theology has been undoubtedly shaken as a consequence of scientific understanding of human kinship with other life.

Ruether, for example, calls for the human-centred outlook, such as has been the case in traditional theodicies, to be revised. "Women must also criticize humanocentrism, that is, making humans the norm and crown of creation in a way that diminishes the other beings in the community of creation".[74] Dawkins himself would agree, as he writes that prioritizing human suffering could be considered as 'speciesist', and that such thinking is remarkably 'un-evolutionary'.[75] Celia Deanne-Drummond also insightfully illustrates that Darwinian science has led to a paradigm in theological discourse where the interrelatedness among species and balance of nature are dominant themes.[76] Here, we can find a source of mutual agreement between Dawkins and theology, which may serve to further strengthen the theological motif of moving beyond anthropocentrism. If a dialogue between Dawkins and theology is established, then theology can refer to Dawkins in order to promote the concept of reconsidering the anthropocentric mindset.

In summary, we can assert that Dawkins' theodicy challenge can be utilized for theological discourse in terms of how his worldview calls into question an anthropocentric mindset, particularly with regard to the problem of evil; in other words, theology can rely on Dawkins for support on this matter, despite the fact that he generally holds a hostile position. Our aim here is not to fully extrapolate on the possible avenues discourse could take when Dawkins' theodicy challenge and evolutionary worldview are taken into account. What we wish to establish as a result of this project is that such avenues exist where future research could prove to be insightful. We can take from Dawkins' theodicy challenge that the traditional purview of theological explanations of evil fail to account for the level and necessity of suffering in the evolutionary process. Moreover, they fail to account for the kinship between humans and other animals that evolutionary science has dramatically unveiled. In this sense, Dawkins can be said to be a contributory dialogue partner for theology—even if this dialogue is one-sided given his contempt for the subject. Given that the presuppositions of Dawkins and theology regarding the existence of God are so polarized, the dialogue between the two is particularly complex and abounds with caveats. While we can note the difficulties and intricacies of a dialogue with Dawkins, we can assert here that his theodicy challenge may be used to substantiate the theological ambition of moving beyond anthropocentrism, specifically in relation to the problem of evil.

THE FALL

As we have seen, the traditional understanding of sin, evident in what Ricoeur calls the 'Adamic myth', represents a 'turning away' from perfection toward sin. This 'turning away' or 'fall' is held as a solution of sorts to the problem of evil, accounting for its existence, particularly in the Augustinian theodicy. This theological motif, which lies behind the Genesis mythology, views suffering as a result of sin or a rejection of God after the creation event. The world was created in a state of perfection or goodness—"God saw all that he made, and it was very good" (Gen. 1:31)—and subsequently corrupted. In the words of Haught, the ethical vision that according to Ricoeur and Teilhard de Chardin has permeated Western Christian thought so thoroughly, "assures a created perfection that went awry".[77] Ricoeur interestingly challenges the basis of this interpretation of Genesis, as he insightfully explains:

> All the speculations on the supernatural perfection of Adam before the fall are adventitious contrivances which profoundly alter the original naive, brute meaning; they tend to make Adam superior and hence a stranger to our condition, at the same time they reduce the Adamic myth to a genesis of man from a primordial superhumanity.[78]

Correspondingly, Ian G. Barbour asserts that the Augustinian tradition's biblical foundations are ambiguous. He contends that the Augustinian tradition emphasizes too strongly humanity's fundamental evilness, whereas the Bible "sees humanity as ambivalent, capable of both good and evil, rather than as fundamentally evil. 'Thou has made him little less than God, and dost crown him with glory and honor' (Ps. 8:5)".[79]

Notwithstanding, sin, and the subsequent evil-as-retribution, has predominantly been associated with a human rebellion (an original sin); a culprit has always been sought.[80] Haught articulates the background thinking from which this theology develops: "If creation had been originally a fully accomplished affair, we would understandably want to identify whoever or whatever it was that messed things up so badly for us".[81] For Haught, this has led to a perennial 'witch hunt', seeking to place blame on someone or something for the tragedies encountered in human life:

> The assumption that a price in suffering must always be paid for the defilement of human freedom of a primordial purity of creation has underwritten the entrenched habit of looking for victims. It has legitimated a history of scapegoating that has only exacerbated violence and misery.[82]

Dawkins himself does not explicitly refer to the implications evolutionary theory may have for the concept of original sin, though he strongly (and perhaps unfairly) criticizes the concept on moral grounds. Dawkins describes original sin as perhaps the "nastiest" aspect of Christianity. He writes, "[M]ore shameful than the death itself [Christ's crucifixion] is the Christian theory that it was necessary. It was necessary because all humans are born in sin. Every tiny baby, too young to have a deed or thought, is riddled with sin: original sin".[83] Dawkins could, however, be criticized for misrepresenting the Christian understanding of original sin. As we noted, the concept of original sin had already been strongly criticized at least since the Enlightenment, and has been the subject of much deliberation from thinkers such as Ricoeur and Teilhard de Chardin. Yet in Dawkins' denunciation of the doctrine, he focuses on its depiction in the writings of Aquinas, which long precede developments in theology, ethics, and even science. Dawkins' lack of theological substance, evident here, substantiates the criticisms and limitations we noted in Chapter One. But despite Dawkins' misrepresentation of theology, in the context of his stance on evolution, the concept of original sin as traditionally understood must be challenged.

As we have mentioned, it is altruism as opposed to evil that requires special explanation in Dawkins' worldview. One of Dawkins' most significant contributions to evolutionary thought, though not without its predecessors, was his outline of an evolutionary view of altruism. In Dawkins' depiction of natural selection, we noted that the 'survival of the fittest' schema under which selection operates, on the surface runs contrary to our experience of altruism in humans and even in other species. Evolution, as Dawkins presents it, would expectedly produce a biosphere that is completely and thoroughly selfish. The existence of altruism poses a paradox for this view. However, he offers a persuasive if often misinterpreted view on how to solve this paradox.[84] Fundamentally, behaviour that appears to be altruistic at the individual level could in fact be born of genetic selfishness (this was discussed in more detail in Chapter Three).

The image of evolution Dawkins presents is inherently devoid of altruism, until it eventually evolves, as a proxy of gene selfishness. Dawkins' view, then, presents a picture of the evolution of life that teems with suffering from the very beginning; living things are engaged in an uncompromising fight for survival until altruism evolves. Moreover, as we noted, suffering and death play an important role in allowing evolution to transpire. Recalling philosopher David Hull, the process can be described as incredibly 'wasteful', even 'diabolical'.[85] However, in the context of how evolution 'creates' life, suffering itself can be simultaneously said to be 'creative'; it is through death that evolution brings about new life. John Polkinghorne, an important figure in the science-religion dialogue, describes death as a "prerequisite of new life".[86] This view is diametrically opposed to a dominant trend in theological thought, which views suffering primarily as a result of sin. From Dawkins' standpoint, suffering cannot be seen as the result of a rebellion against a perfect creation, as suffering is a linchpin in the process of evolution itself. From a plainly chronological point of view, the traditional theological understanding of suffering is inconsistent with the scientific picture of the world, because as Teilhard de Chardin clarifies, ". . . long before man death existed on earth. And in the depths of the heavens, far from any moral influence of the earth, death also exists".[87] Consequently, by challenging theology to develop a theodicy that accounts for what can be deemed the 'creative suffering' inherent in natural selection, Dawkins' theodicy challenge brings to the fore a theological/scientific paradox—that classical theology predominantly views evil as a result of sin after the creation of life and a paradisiacal state, while science shows suffering to be an integral element in the creation of life itself.

From a dialogue with Dawkins, we can note that suffering has been present throughout life's history and long precedes altruism. Therefore, it is difficult to envisage how suffering can be considered only as a result of human sin. It is for these reasons, Polkinghorne confesses, that the Christian notion of the fall is the most difficult to reconcile with scientific thought.[88] Similarly, Philip Clayton highlights his own inclinations that our evolutionary understanding precludes the theological idea of an initial paradise.[89] Polkinghorne also contends that it is difficult to envisage suffering as "having arisen subsequent to an unfallen state, with the associated notion that a radical change occurred as the consequence of some disastrous ancestral act".[90] Further support for this position can be found from Haught, who explains that a previous state of perfection would be opposite to the evolutionary character of nature.[91] He emphasizes the innocence of the victims of suffering in the evolutionary process, which for him undermines the traditional view of suffering as punishment for original sin: "Where there is no guilt, there is no need for retribution".[92] In light of evolution, the expiatory (atonement) understanding of evil becomes for Haught too narrow a view.[93] The traditional understanding of suffering as a result of the fall becomes precarious in light of how we understand suffering to be integral to the evolutionary process. Polkinghorne insightfully illustrates this point by contrasting the image of sin in the writings of St. Paul with the scientific picture of evolution:

> Paul speaks of the way that 'sin came into the world through one man and death through sin, and so death spread to all men because all men sinned' (Romans 5.22). How does this square with our knowledge that *homo sapiens* evolved from more primitive hominids, which themselves evolved from preceding animal life, and ultimately from the inanimate shallow seas of early Earth, and that death was always present in the animal world. We detect no sign of a sharp discontinuity in the course of earthly or cosmic history, no indication of a golden age from which our present plight descends by degeneration.[94]

Acknowledging evolution, and in particular Dawkins' emphasis on its gradualness and the suffering of life, we can understand how the concept of the fall requires theological revision. The image of a created perfection gone awry stands in contrast to the progressive and painful nature of the evolution of the world, as we understand it from Dawkins. In the views of Clayton, Polkinghorne, and Haught, among others, it has become unfeasible to persist in understanding suffering in the context of a fall from a created perfection as it has been traditionally understood. If this realization comes about through a dialogue with Dawkins' evolutionary worldview, then he could be considered as a substantial theological resource.

Theological revision of the fall has been attempted by theologians such as Teilhard de Chardin. Teilhard sought to decisively reinterpret original sin by discarding the notion that it was a conscious human turning away. He seeks to widen the understanding of the fall to encompass not just humanity but all of being; he gives sin a cosmic dimension: "[O]riginal sin, taken in its widest sense, is not a malady specific to the Earth, nor is it bound up with human generation. It simply symbolizes the inevitable chance of evil which accompanies the existence of all participated being".[95] For Teilhard, the responsibility for the 'fault' is not rested on the shoulders of humanity, but spread across the entire universe. "The *whole* world has been corrupted by the fall . . . ".[96] From his paleontological background and understanding of evolutionary science, he appreciates the wider-than-human nature of evil, and the chronological discrepancy that occurs when considering evil as a result of human sin. Therefore, he opts for a more panoramic perspective than the traditional view that sees the fall stand as a theodicy. The highly influential German systematic theologian Paul Tillich, similarly, "universalizes the primordial fault", thereby moving away from considering human sin as the cause of suffering and the corruption of the world.[97] Comparable to Teilhard de

Chardin, Tillich dialectically identifies 'being' with evil.[98] He sees creation and the fall as coinciding; that there was no original state of perfection. "Creation and the Fall coincide in so far as there is no point in time and space in which created goodness was actualized and had existence".[99]

Haught goes further, by suggesting that Tillich has not sufficiently taken the idea of evolution into account in his theology.[100] While Tillich persists with the fall as an element of man's [*sic*] tragic destiny (that sin was an unavoidable), Haught legitimately questions the expiatory view of suffering altogether. Disillusioned with the traditional 'scapegoating' of culprits in original sin, he seeks a theology focused on future hope; perfection was not created and lost, but rather, the world is a part of a creative process moving toward perfection:

> [I]t is not necessary to picture the perfection to which our hearts aspire as though it were something that once existed and has now been lost. It may be more appropriate instead to picture perfection as a state that has never yet been actualized but that we may hope will come into being in the future in accordance with God's vision of what is good, true, and beautiful. One of the important implications of evolution for theodicy is that it allows for the transpositioning of the ideal of perfection from an imagined past to a possible future.[101]

For Haught, evolution presents great difficulties for the notion of an original state of perfection. "Evolution, to repeat our theme, means that the world is unfinished. But if it is unfinished, then we cannot justifiably expect it to be perfect".[102] Rather than attempt to redefine the fall (which Tillich himself admits becomes quite complex[103]), Haught shifts his theological focus in an eschatological direction: "The Bible's eschatological orientation arouses hope for an unprecedented future, even as it deflects our pining for a paradisiacal past".[104] A comparable shift is also endorsed by Moltmann, who states, "The revision of the doctrine of creation which is, in my view, necessary today . . . is a changeover to *an eschatological understanding of creation*".[105]

Dialoguing with evolution has led to multifarious analyses and reinterpretations of the fall. For example, philosopher/theologian Patricia Williams, in her fascinating work *Doing Without Adam and Eve*, calls for a more pliable hermeneutic of the Genesis narrative of the fall. She suggests this narrative can no longer be held as a viable theological account of evil, as Adam and Eve can be seen as "irrelevant symbolic figures in an imaginary garden rather than the cause of all our woe".[106] Jack Mahoney S.J. also notes that persisting with the traditional image of the fall and the crucifixion of Christ as an expiatory event "serves only to strain the belief of believers . . . ".[107] Haught's position is comparable, though he focuses more on promoting a new eschatological vision, therefore only (perhaps) diminishing the legitimacy of Adam and Eve by proxy. Ian G. Barbour also promotes skepticism with regard to a fall from paradise in light of evolution: "I have suggested, however, that neither a primeval state of perfection nor a historical fall are credible today".[108]

An alternative view has been adopted by prominent theologians such as R. J. Berry, who has persisted to an extent with the historicity of Adam and the fall, even within an evolutionary context. Berry, for example, holds that evolution does not deny the historical Adam or the fall, but seeks to change the interpretation of Adam as the first *biological* human:

> [T]here is nothing in theistic evolution as such that denies the existence of a historic Adam and a historic fall . . . it is entirely possible to suggest that Adam actually existed in time and that God's image conferred upon him extended outwards to his contemporaries as well as to his offspring . . .[109]

In Berry's view, Adam can be interpreted as a representative of humanity; he becomes the species' "spiritual founder".[110] In a different, but not contrary interpretation, scholars such as Polkinghorne have proposed that the fall be understood as a symbolic "turning away from God into the self that occurred with the dawning of hominid self-consciousness . . . ".[111] Thus the historicity of Adam is somewhat retained, yet a new hermeneutic for understanding the meaning of the Genesis account of the fall can be developed. In stark contrast to these interesting theological proposals, writers in N. C. Nevin's edited volume *Should Christians Embrace Evolution?* insist, in a way similar to Williams, that evolution shatters the Adamic myth. However, these writers give authoritative primacy to scripture and deny evolution altogether:

> What is at stake? A lot: the truthfulness of the three foundational chapters of the entire Bible (Genesis 1–3), belief in the unity of the human race, belief in the ontological uniqueness of human beings among all God's creatures, belief in the special creation of Adam and Eve in the image of God . . . belief that suffering and death today are the result of sin and not part of God's original creation, and belief that natural disasters today are the result of the fall and not part of God's original creation . . . belief in evolution erodes these foundations . . . We have to choose one or the other.[112]

Again, our task here is not to fully explore these fascinating avenues of theology, but to demonstrate that such avenues stem from a serious engagement with evolution. However, Dawkins' stance on evolution would be particularly difficult to reconcile with the theological concept of the fall. As we noted, he views evolution as inherently selfish, with altruism originally only becoming manifest as a result of selfishness. Moreover, with Dawkins' views on the serendipitous nature of evolution, and hence even the existence of humanity, the concept of a perfectly 'good' state preceding sin is difficult to intellectually accept. Therefore, through a dialogue with Dawkins, theology could be strongly encouraged to make a substantial transition away from the idea of the fall (noting of course that such a transition has to some extent already begun).

A SCIENTIFIC ACCOUNT OF EVIL

Given that Dawkins' representation of the world sees suffering as the result of inherently mindless and purposeless processes (the causal chain of the universe and natural selection), it can be stated that he accounts for evil by reference to science; evil is the result of mindless processes understood by physics, chemistry, and biology. Although Dawkins' view is atheistic, this interpretation of evil can also be adopted within a theistic framework. This conclusion has been adopted by theologians such as Arthur Peacocke, a leading voice on the interaction between science and theology. He proposes, similar to Dawkins, that the chance events leading to the existence of life are also the events that led to evil. Consequently, he maintains that science aids a defensible theodicy.[113] The religious scientist Francisco J. Ayala also allows natural selection to account for evil, thereby mitigating God's responsibility: "The irony that the theory of evolution, which at first had seemed to remove the need for God in the world, now has convincingly removed the need to explain the world's imperfections as failed outcomes of God's design".[114] Professor of religion Chris Doran elaborates on Ayala's position: "In other words, believers no longer are burdened with trying to prove the goodness and love of God in light of natural evil because evolutionary processes are responsible for bad design, not God".[115]

These views are consistent with Dawkins' explanation of evil. However, within a theological worldview, such a perception can still become problematic, as Alister McGrath perceptively illustrates. "Yet Christian theology believes that there is a problem here, even if it is one of its own making. The Christian affirmation of the goodness of God seems to be called into question by the existence of pain and suffering within a supposedly good creation".[116] Even if evolution as Dawkins presents it can account for evil, this leaves open an important theological question: What is God's relationship to the world, and why does it allow for such suffering?

To briefly summarize, it has been demonstrated in this chapter how a serious engagement with Dawkins' theodicy challenge can develop and enrich dialogue between theology and science. From dialogue with Dawkins, as a representative of a particular school of thought on evolution, we noted the weaknesses in aspects of traditional theodicies when viewed in an evolutionary context. We discussed how discourse in these areas has led to insightful hermeneutical revisions of theological motifs such as original sin and the fall. It was also shown that, if Dawkins' ontological picture was acknowledged, then the concept of the fall as a theodicy itself would eventually collapse. Subsequently, Haught seeks to shift the theological focus in an eschatological direction. But this shift is one aspect of a broader problem that stems from our analysis of Dawkins' influence on theodicy. This problem asks how divine beneficence can be squared with the scientific image of the world. How, in light of evolutionary science, can divine providence be related to the "venerable cosmography of modern science"?[117]

This is a cardinal issue that stems from our dialogical methodology of engaging with other worldviews, which, we have argued throughout, is a positive step for theology. Furthermore, in the context of this project, we are placing particular emphasis on Dawkins' scientific hermeneutic. In doing so we are suggesting, comparably to Gerard J. Hughes, that Christians may have something to learn from Dawkins' criticisms.[118] Our task here will be to discuss a relational model between God and creation that also serves as an answer to Dawkins' theodicy challenge—how beneficence can be reconciled with the scientific picture. This effort corresponds to the assertion from Southgate and Robinson, that a fully articulated theodicy must give an account of a relationship between God and creation.[119] Moreover, consistent with the task of this work as a whole, we will consider what impact Dawkins himself will have on such a discussion. To achieve this goal, we will demonstrate the conceptual difficulties in considering both naturalism and supernaturalism as theological frameworks in the context of dialogue with science.

PROBLEMS WITH NATURALISM AND SUPERNATURALISM

As we have seen, a number of significant theological and scientific authorities—Arthur Peacocke and Franciso J. Ayala are examples—hold a comparable view to Dawkins' naturalistic stance on suffering; that the mechanisms of the natural world account for evil. In this interpretation, suffering experienced by living creatures is the result of natural processes, such as the Darwinian fight for survival. But there is a prominent difference in that Dawkins' atheistic view does not need to account for a relationship between God and the world. Viewing naturalism through a theological lens, the salient issue becomes how God is to fit into the picture painted by science. This highlights, again, the distance between the conceptual backgrounds of Dawkins and the theologian. As we have discussed, this makes the dialogue we seek more difficult and complex than engaging with philosophies more amenable to theology. Yet it was argued in Chapter One that such an engagement will gain more headway for theology than a dialogue between more consistent viewpoints.

The God-shaped void left by naturalism leads the eminent philosopher of religion David Ray Griffin to identify a naturalistic viewpoint as a common source of conflict between science and religion. He articulates the view that "as long as science is associated with this form of naturalism, science will be regarded as antithetical to any significantly religious outlook".[120] Similarly, prominent historian of science William Provine points to a hermeneutically naturalistic view of Darwinism (that would be consistent with Dawkins' portrayal) as illustrative of an atheistic view:

> [M]odern evolutionary biology tells us, that nature has no detectable purposive forces of any kind. . . . Modern science directly implies that the world is organised strictly in accordance with deterministic principles or chance. . . . There are no purposive principles whatsoever in nature. There are no gods and no designing forces that are rationally detectable.[121]

Furthermore, Griffin acknowledges that Dawkins' emphasis on the gradualism in evolution is particularly naturalistic.[122] For Dawkins, the gradualism in evolution leads him to disqualify any divine influence in the process, as he outlines:

> In Darwin's view, the whole point of the theory of evolution by natural selection was that it provided a non-miraculous account of the existence of complex adaptations. For Darwin, any evolution that had to be helped over the jumps by God was not evolution at all. . . . In light of this, it is easy to see why Darwin constantly reiterated the *gradualness* of evolution.[123]

The gradualness removes the need for divine involvement—it leaves no causal gaps in which God can work. However, Alister and Joanna McGrath perceptively illustrate that Dawkins is using naturalism to attack a 'God of the Gaps' argument. The 'God of the Gaps' phrase, coined by Methodist preacher and chemist Charles A. Coulson, refers to the argument that God is required as explanation for the gaps in scientific understanding.[124] The McGraths explain that this line of argumentation is "foolish" and has been abandoned in the twentieth century—the explanatory power of Christian faith is now stressed as a whole, rather than a retreat into "ever diminishing gaps".[125] Therefore, consistent with our current attempt to demonstrate how Dawkins may be of benefit to theology, the McGraths suggest that "we must thank him for helping us kill off this outdated false turn in the history of Christian apologetics. It is a good example of how dialogue between science and Christian theology can lead to some useful outcomes".[126]

To further critique Dawkins' atheistic outlook on naturalism (which received a more thorough exploration in Chapter Three), it could be compared to the Christian theologian Charles Hardwick's outline of naturalism. Hardwick indicates four premises, each of which can be contrasted with a mirror premise of supernaturalism:

> (1) That only the world of nature is real; (2) that nature is necessary in the sense of requiring no sufficient reason beyond itself to account either for its origin or ontological ground; (3) that nature as a whole may be understood without appeal to any kind of intelligence or purposive agency; and (4) that all causes are natural causes so that every natural event is itself a product of other natural events.[127]

Arthur Peacocke, however, illustrates that only premises (2) and (3) are anti-theistic in that they preclude the belief in an independent creator God.[128] Moreover, these two premises, (2) and (3), are philosophically fragile. He insightfully explains: "Both (2) and (3) are in fact, metaphysical assumptions made by Hardwick and are therefore not deducible from the content of the sciences as such".[129] Propositions (2) and (3) are philosophical assumptions, not deducible by recourse to science. Therefore, we can, along with Peacocke, criticize attempts by Dawkins to imply atheism from naturalism. Naturalism is not synonymous with atheism. Griffin proposes a similar critique of Dawkins (and Darwin) in this regard. He suggests that the philosophical commitment to naturalism predicates their emphasis on the gradualness of evolution.[130] Similarly, we suggested in Chapter Two, Dawkins' and Gould's scientific disagreements were in fact predicated upon philosophical outlooks. This again makes visible the blurring of the boundaries between science and philosophy in

Dawkins' work. Dawkins' scientific outlook could be argued to have developed from a philosophical predisposition, substantiating Paul Ricoeur's concept of the detour of interpretation of all knowledge.[131] Moreover, philosophical naturalism has itself been criticized by prominent philosophers such as Karl Popper,[132] who wrote:

> I reject the naturalistic view: It is uncritical. Its upholders fail to notice that whenever they believe to have discovered a fact, they have only proposed a convention. Hence the convention is liable to turn into a dogma. This criticism of the naturalistic view applies not only to its criterion of meaning, but also to its idea of science, and consequently to its idea of empirical method.[133]

Notwithstanding these critiques, from Dawkins and others, we can see a source of tension, in that naturalism and theism appear to be irreconcilable. This is because if a God were postulated, it would be vulnerable to a criticism of being obsolete. Dawkins eschews the notion that a creator God may exist outside of a naturalistic understanding. For example, a God that initiated the naturalistic process made known through the sciences would be, for Dawkins, completely irrelevant, and nothing like the God of the Bible or other religious texts.[134] In his understanding, such a deist God may be compatible with the naturalistic image portrayed by science, but such a God would become conceptually redundant. Therefore, David Ray Griffin suggests, religion seems to require supernaturalism.[135]

However, if supernaturalism is supposed, then the theological problem of evil reemerges. Griffin posits that if God possesses the capability to intervene in the physical world, then nonintervention becomes a divine decision.[136] Therefore, Griffin logically concludes, "[P]eople can still justifiably ask why God does not intervene to prevent particularly horrible events".[137] This potential criticism forms the basis for Dawkins' theodicy challenge, as explored earlier in this chapter. A possible answer to this question was postulated by the early twentieth-century Lutheran theologian Rudolf Otto, to whom Griffin turns. Otto sought to establish the view that the world was created in a supernatural event, but thereafter was bound by naturalistic laws.[138] Otto also contends that events that appear to be evil were planned in such a way as to eventually reveal providence and meaning.[139] The reality of pain and suffering is not a deterrent to the belief that the world has meaning, albeit hidden from the scope of human comprehension. Haught also recognizes that this is a common interpretation, as he explains:

One response is that of blind, unconditional trust in God in spite of apparent absurdity. Accordingly, not being able to make theological sense of the Darwinian recipe should not prevent the devout from still trusting that there may be a hidden meaning in evolution, one that it would be presumptuous to try to access. . . . If we take this posture of pure trust, we might conjecture that what appears to be absurd contingency from a human perspective could be the tangled underside of a tapestry which, from God's vantage point on the other side, is a tightly woven pattern. As for the struggle, cruelty, waste and pain in evolution—evidence, at least to many, of a universe beyond the pale of providence—Darwin's recipe has absolutely nothing qualitatively new to add to the perennial challenges to faith. . . . Many deeply religious people, including some scientists and neo-orthodox theologians, are quite content to take this approach to evolution.[140]

Griffin, though, points out that in response to scientific scrutiny, this position becomes tentative. "A position that can be advocated only on this basis has little chance of being regarded by the scientific community as more rational than its present worldview [predominantly atheistic naturalism]".[141] It opens a philosophical problem: whether it is more rational to consider the world as planned to include evil as part of a grand scheme, or whether it is more rational to adopt atheism. Otto himself also acknowledges that the position is riddled with weakness and requires a "courageous will to believe".[142] Pertaining to our current discussion, the problem raised by this view is how could a divine plan or supernatural intervention incorporate or allow such suffering as is made evident through evolution. Griffin perceptively highlights this: "[T]he old question, however, is whether, given the enormous evils of the evolutionary process and human history, this view of the universe is even remotely credible".[143] Correspondingly, Peacocke astutely recognizes that both the problem of evil and the scientific picture of the world appear to be inconsistent with considering a supernaturalistic vision:

[S]etting aside the immense moral issues about why God does not intervene to prevent rampant evil, this could give rise, more fundamentally, to an incoherence in our understanding of God's nature. It suggests an arbitrary and magic-making Agent far removed from the concept of the One who created and is creating the world as science reveals. That world now appears convincingly closed to external causal interventions of the kind that classical philosophical theism postulated . . .[144]

To summarize then, a naturalistic viewpoint can be seen as theologically conflicted, as on the surface it appears to lead to atheism or deism. God, in this view, according to James Mackey, ". . . squats outside the world, in the form of a mind containing from eternity the final plan for the universe, and therefore the fully formulated truth of all that ever was, is, or will be. A total travesty of the reality, as we know it to be".[145] This image of God would be highly vulnerable to Dawkins' criticism of indifference—that God has no role in the world. Conversely, if supernaturalism is adopted as a conceptual framework, even if it only views the world as having a supernatural origin, then the suffering of life in natural selection becomes a salient issue. In deciding whether to opt for naturalism or supernaturalism, we are led to a theological conundrum; a naturalistic view will satisfy the problem of evil, but relegate God to obsoleteness, while a supernaturalistic view begs the question as to why God would create a world of suffering and not intervene to prevent it. The dilemma is appropriately encapsulated by Peacocke: "So the problem is: how can one conceive of the God who is the Creator of this world affecting events in it without abrogating the very laws and regularities to which God has given existence and continuously sustains in existence?"[146] A relational model of God and creation must be provided in which a) God is not redundant and b) the natural laws are regimental to the point where God is excluded from involvement in evil. If this can be achieved, we can overcome two of Dawkins' substantial criticisms of theism: irrelevance and sadism.[147] By attempting to overcome these criticisms, we will, by proxy, revise or strengthen theological themes that can be incorporated into future dialogical settings. This will contribute to our task of exhibiting how dialogue with Dawkins' work can be beneficial to theology. In order to address these issues (provide a theological model that satisfies a) and b) above), we will now explore four distinct theological themes; the autonomy of creation, panentheistic relational models, futurity, and *kenosis*.

AUTONOMY OF CREATION

Arthur Peacocke illustrates that opting for supernaturalism poses intellectual difficulties as it appears inconsistent with the scientific worldview, and also forces "immense moral issues", namely, the problem of evil.[148] Therefore, it has been attested, a naturalistic worldview can be adopted to both acknowledge scientific understanding and allow natural mechanisms to account for evil (as with Haught, Ayala, Peacocke, and others). But as we indicated, a theological worldview will also need to account for the role of God to prevent this naturalistic stance from merging into deism, or even atheism. In order to pose such a theological explanation, we will now examine how a naturalistic world can be held within the scope of a theological vision; we will consider the theological reasoning behind envisioning an autonomous creation.

As opposed to being indicative of atheism or deism, the consideration of an autonomous world is for Haught and others a theological necessity. "Contingency, for instance, may be troubling to those fixated on the need for design in nature, but an openness to accidents seems essential for creation's autonomy and eventual aliveness".[149] The contingency of the natural world, strongly emphasized by Dawkins, conveys creation's independence. This independence is, Haught argues, of great importance; in order for God to have a relationship with creation, they must be distinct.[150] He draws upon the ideas of Teilhard de Chardin, who posits that "differentiation is an effect of, not a deterrent to, true union",[151] and juxtaposes a Trinitarian relational model with the God–world relationship:

> The principle . . . "true union differentiates" applies both to the internal life of the Trinity and also to the God-world relationship. True union is not homogeneity or uniformity, but a relationship that paradoxically allows the conjoined entities to realize a deeper freedom and distinctiveness than they could find in isolation.[152]

What is emphasized by Teilhard de Chardin and Haught is the distinctiveness between God and creation. According to theologian Maureen Junker-Kenny, such distinctiveness, particularly between creator and creature, is also evident in the biblical cosmogony. "Decisive in the biblical account is the distinction between creator and creature which . . . sets the creature free from her originator".[153] This will also be a decisive factor in discussion on relational models between God and creation later. Contrary to Dawkins' criticism on the redundancy of God in a naturalistic framework, Haught et al. propose that the autonomy of the world is not only theologically palatable, but is in fact a substantial element of our understanding of the God–world relationship. Without this distinction, there can be no true relationship.

Furthermore, in order for the world to be considered truly autonomous, Haught maintains that there must be an accession to randomness.[154] The concept of a strict teleology in nature, which Dawkins so staunchly rejects, is as unpalatable to Haught as it is to Dawkins (though as we shall see, a broader teleology is permitted). A world that is planned (which Otto, among others, tentatively promotes) becomes for Haught a pointless puppet.[155] Thus the apparent absence of a rigid teleology in the scientific worldview, for Haught, only further strengthens his convictions that creation is autonomous. This autonomy subsequently allows for a dialectical relationship between God and creation. For Haught, Teilhard, and Moltmann, among others, an interventionist relational model, or a preordained plan in creation would deny a true relationship. This view is also more consistent with the scientific picture of the world, particularly as Dawkins presents it, with his emphasis on contingency. Moreover, Haught explains, this position is not merely an attempt to refigure a theological view to accommodate science,[156] but it can be discerned as a theological motif in traditional theologians such as Aquinas. Aquinas also felt that a world with no degree of chance would "be contrary to the nature of providence and to the perfection of the world . . .".[157] Moreover, according to Brian Davies, Aquinas believes God to be somehow causally constrained; the world is made full of autonomously interacting 'things'.[158]

John Polkinghorne echoes Aquinas' sentiment, by insisting that 'chance and necessity'[159] are "fully consonant with Christian theology".[160] Furthermore, Polkinghorne posits that a world operating through chance and necessity proves that God is "no cosmic tyrant, holding all in tight control".[161] A God who holds a tyrannical ascendency over creation is viewed unfavorably by Polkinghorne. Peacocke also endorses this view, as he posits, contrary to Einstein's infamous statement, that God does play dice.[162] In other words, God allows the world freedom. The prominent Irish theologian Diarmud O'Murchu also offers a consistent interpretation: "Chance and necessity are not about blind, mindless forces, but can be understood as the dynamics of freedom and possibility that characterize an essentially creative universe".[163] Haught summarizes the view neatly as follows: "Catholic theology may plausibly suppose that the random, experimental character of evolution is consistent with a divine love that longs for the world to make something of itself instead of being constantly tinkered with or pulled like a puppet".[164]

Consequently, Haught et al. promote a relational model of God and creation that is compatible with Dawkins' emphasis on randomness in natural selection. Again, it becomes apparent how opening dialogue with Dawkins can enrich and provide substance to a theological view; randomness is a prerequisite for a theological vision, as it ensures the distinctiveness necessary for true relationship. Despite coming from a vastly different conceptual standpoint with relation to the 'God question', Dawkins' emphasis on randomness in the scientific picture may bring interdisciplinary merit to a theological vision of an autonomous world. A vision of the world's autonomy allows theology to view evil in a comparable context to Dawkins—as a result of natural processes, and not of divine sadism, as in Dawkins' theodicy challenge. This is another example of how Dawkins' critiques can add substance to theology. Yet viewing the world as autonomous does not make clear the relevance of a creator. Moreover, there is ambiguity in how Haught and others can hold an eschatological vision while also denying a strict teleology. The question becomes, as Peacocke asserts:

> In a world that consists of the nexus of causes and whole-part influences that is explicated by the sciences, how might God be conceived as influencing particular events, or patterns of events, in the world without interrupting the regularities observed at various levels studied by the sciences?[165]

Subsequently, we must now consider how Dawkins (as the representative of an intellectual other) may influence how potential divine relevance is theologically appropriated—how God is considered relevant in a relationship with an autonomous world. This leads us to consider panentheistic relational models.

PANENTHEISM

In order to construct a theological vision that maintains God's relevance in creation while also acknowledging the autonomy of the world, we can turn to particular elements of panentheism. Drawing from Ph.D. research, scholar Michael W. Brierley outlines a comprehensive, though not exhaustive, review of theologians who either identify themselves as panentheists or have been identified as such by others.[166] The extensiveness to which panentheism has been adopted (he lists in excess of fifty prominent proponents) leads Brierley to suggest that panentheism has become a "doctrinal revolution".[167] It is weakly defined as "the belief that the Being of God includes and penetrates the whole universe, so that every part of it exists in Him".[168] The adverb 'weakly' is used here, along with Brierley, to acknowledge that ambiguity permeates discourse on panentheism; it is highly subject to hermeneutical investigation, as Brierley astutely clarifies. "The essays in this volume [Philip Clayton and Arthur Peacocke, eds., *In Whom We Live and Move and Have Our Being*] demonstrate that 'panentheism' covers a multitude of descriptions of the relationship between God and cosmos".[169] This ambiguity will become apparent as we engage further with the topic, particularly as we highlight differences between Philip Clayton and Arthur Peacocke's panentheistic visions. Currently, though, we can assert that panentheism is pertinent to our current theme for three reasons.

Firstly, it is an attempt to view God's relationship with the world that may bridge the theological gap left by posing a completely autonomous world. Secondly, as Brierley suggests, panentheism is in part a response to science. "Insofar as idealism represented theology's assimilation of evolutionary values, it is possible to see panentheism as the theological response to science and the Enlightenment".[170] Panentheism partially owes its development as a reaction to advances in our scientific understanding—from which Dawkins also develops his worldview. This shows how a theological movement such as panentheism, and Dawkins' atheism, while arriving at polemical destinations through hermeneutical routes, can arguably be traced to a similar source: the advancement in our understanding through science. This is an example of common ground from which to engage in a dialogical relationship with Dawkins, despite the epistemic differences. Thirdly, Brierley also posits humanity's experience of suffering in the twentieth century as a historical pressure that partly led to the adoption of panentheism.[171] The twentieth-century world wars, and particularly the holocaust, led to an experience of evil so grand that it forced theological revision on the issue. Among others,[172] the acclaimed twentieth-century Jewish philosopher Hans Jonas[173] has also stressed the need to reevaluate theological ideals based on the experience of suffering on such a grand scale as at Auschwitz.[174] Comparably, as it was argued in this chapter, the encounter with great suffering through the study of evolution can also force theological revision. Consequently, panentheism is also relevant to our current subject as it is in part a response to the encounter with great evil/suffering; panentheism may offer a response to the theodicy problem. It is for these reasons that we will now attend to the subject of panentheism.

According to Philip Clayton, a key proponent, panentheism understands the world as within God, and at the same time, God transcends the world.[175] Arthur Peacocke, also an authority in panentheistic discourse, proposes a comparable definition to the one that we, along with Brierley, deemed weak: "Panentheism is the belief that the Being of God includes and penetrates all-that-is, so that every part of it exists in God and (as against pantheism) that God's Being is more than it and is not exhausted by it".[176] In a panentheistic model, the world is 'in' God, yet God is also more than the world. As stated above, these definitions of panentheism contain ambiguity that necessitates clarification. It must be asked, along with Brierley, in what sense can the world be considered "in" God?[177] There needs to be a more definitive view on the relationship between God and the world than the "in" of these definitions.

Brierley highlights a clarification in this regard by theologian Jay McDaniel, whom Brierley identifies as a "key panentheist".[178] McDaniel discerns two distinct panentheistic relational models: emanationist and relational. Emanationist panentheism, McDaniel insightfully explains, views the cosmos as a direct expression of God's being:

> To look at the God–Universe relation in this way, is to believe . . . that the "stuff" of which the world consists is an expression of the very "stuff" that constitutes detail, is directly expressive of the will or purposes of God. . . . Emanationist panentheists view nature's creativity as God's creativity.[179]

Relational panentheism, alternatively, allows the world a greater degree of independence. "Relational panentheism . . . sees the world as having *some* degree of creative independence from God".[180] We need not deliberate too intently on the differences between these two 'panentheisms'. The point we seek to establish is that the distinction between panentheisms, as emphasised by McDaniel, highlights the ambiguity that permeates discussion on the topic. This ambiguity has been acknowledged by several of its key proponents.[181] It is partly due to this ambiguity that John Polkinghorne is cautious toward the idea of panentheism itself. Consequently, he declines to use the term to describe his own position.[182] As a result, the term 'panentheism' is not definitive enough to describe a useful relational model between God and creation. However, panentheistic themes may provide substance for our current dialogue with Dawkins on his critiques of theology.

PANENTHEISTIC RELATIONAL MODELS

As we have stated, we are turning to panentheism to consider a relational model that allows the world independence yet does not relegate God into retirement. Clayton suggests, consistent with our appraisal of naturalism, that a "sharp distinction between God and the world has led in the modern period to deism and to the apparent impossibility of divine action".[183] Therefore, referring to McDaniel's definitions of the two panentheisms, a more quantifiable understanding of the degree of independence between God and the world needs to be established—as opposed to McDaniel's "some". For Clayton, giving the world too much independence results in a deistic model. Yet, we have also expressed that there are significant theological problems with an interventionist model of God. Clayton thus proposes a dialectical view of God's relationship with the world, which he admits cannot be grasped by unequivocal language.[184] In his variety of panentheism, "The world is neither indistinguishable from God nor (fully) ontologically separate from God".[185] To clarify his position, Clayton outlines what he calls the 'panentheistic analogy'. Among other significant authorities,[186] he proposes that the God–world relationship is analogous to the mind–body relationship:

> The body is to mind as the body/mind combination—that is human persons—is to the divine. The world is in some sense analogous to the body of God; God is analogous to the mind which indwells the body, though God is also more than the natural world taken as a whole . . . the power of this analogy lies in the fact that mental causation, as every human agent knows it, is more than physical causation and yet still a part of the natural world.[187]

This particular description of the panentheistic analogy, however, poses two problems in our current discussion. Firstly, it describes God's relationship with the world in terms of his relationship with human persons. This necessitates a more definitive conception of what constitutes a human person, as opposed to a human being. This contentious issue is the subject of much theological, philosophical, and even scientific debate.[188] By not clearly defining the human person, Clayton may risk inadvertently excluding individuals from a relationship with God. Secondly, Clayton asserts here, and elsewhere, that God can engage in the natural world by interaction with the realm of human mentality.[189] In his view, God can influence the world through human thought, in an analogous fashion to how minds influence bodies. Subsequently, in order for Clayton to view God as acting in this way, while maintaining a scientifically acceptable viewpoint, he breaks from a purely materialist view on the issue of consciousness.[190] In the context of a dialogue with Dawkins' materialism, this highlights a contrast, as Dawkins supports Dennett's evolutionary view on consciousness, which we elaborated upon in Chapter Three. In the materialist view of Dawkins, there is nothing that separates the mental from the physical. Any divine action at this level would then be an interruption of physical causality. Therefore, the insistence on the physical nature of mind becomes antagonistic to Clayton's stance. Furthermore, Clayton's view here may also conflict with the gradualness of evolution in Dawkins' picture. It raises the question of when was the 'first' human interaction with God? If the mental gradually evolved along with humanity, there is no definitive point where God could suddenly began to interact with the world, unless Clayton posed that this interaction was gradual also.

Furthermore, God's interactions with the world would be incredibly recent in evolutionary history (approximately one hundred thousand years out of four billion). This view on divine interaction would then be quite limited when viewed in the context of the vastness of evolutionary history.

However, Clayton perceptively points out that an alternative to Dawkins' materialist picture of evolution (specifically at this point, the evolution of mind) can be sustainable. He argues for 'supervenience': "In the most general terms, supervenience means that one level of phenomena or type of property (in this case, the mental) is dependent upon another level (in this case, the biological or neuro-physiological), while at the same time not being reducible to it".[191] Clayton echoes the view of emergence (prominent in the writings of Stephen Jay Gould) in evolution, which was held as an alternative to Dawkins' reductionism. Clayton is suggesting that 'the whole can be more than the sum of its parts'. Moreover, if Gould's 'punctuated equilibrium' view of evolution were endorsed over Dawkins' emphasis on gradualness, it would add weight to Clayton's argument. With the view of punctuated equilibrium, mentality could have been a very rapid development (in fact, as we noted, even Dennett himself acknowledges that consciousness was quite rapid in evolutionary terms, though he strongly critiques punctuated equilibrium). This stance also echoes the theological proposals regarding the historicity of Adam as the species' 'spiritual founder'. This proposal, as we discussed, considers a distinctive 'first' human—though this was not a genetically distinct person, but spiritual. There could be, in this view, a point in history where God initiated a relationship with humanity, by interacting with the spiritual founder of the species—an 'Adam'. However, this proposition diverges so far from Dawkins' model that it may present an impasse for dialogue. The question of whether God began an interaction with a spiritual founder of the species (a historical Adam) should be left open at this point for future theological investigation.

Apart from these fascinating theological issues that arise from Clayton's panentheism, we can acknowledge, relevant to our current discussion, that he presents a panentheistic model that allows God to influence the world, albeit by distinguishing the mental from the physical. Moreover, if Clayton is correct that the mental cannot be reduced to the physical (against Dawkins), then this view of God's interaction with the world could be considered naturalistic. If mind evolved through natural selection, though was itself not reducible to physical matter, this would still be a naturalistic view. Thus God's actions in influencing the mental realm would not be intervening in physical causation; it would not be supernatural. Clayton's panentheism could then, perhaps, solve the problem of God's relevance in a naturalistic world. Consequently, as David Ray Griffin articulates, panentheism (though we have seen that that this term is far from definitive) is a version of natural theism.[192]

There are, however, two significant problems from a theological perspective with Clayton's 'panentheistic analogy' as a relational model. The first is a criticism proposed by Peacocke. Peacocke opposes the divine embodiment analogy, as for him it places God and the world in the same ontological order. "The total network of regular, natural events, in this perspective, is viewed as in itself the creative and sustaining action of God. Of course, this network of events in not identical with God and is *not God's body*, for it is not in a sense a 'part' of God as such".[193] He reiterates a similar sentiment later in the same book: "Let me make it clear from the outset that I am not postulating that the world is 'God's body', for, although the world may best be regarded as 'in' God (panentheism), God's Being is distinct from all created beings in a way that we are not distinct from our bodies".[194] Peacocke is explicit then, as he distinguishes that although the world is *in* God, the world is not *part* of God. The criticism put forth is that the mind/body analogy does not sufficiently distinguish God from the world. This point again highlights the difficulty in panentheism, as to what constitutes 'some independence' in Jay McDaniel's definition. Peacocke asserts that the mind/body analogy does not allow sufficient distinction. This distinction, as we ascertained, holds significant theological importance, apparent in our encounter with the theme of the autonomy of creation.

The second problem with Clayton's panentheistic analogy is particularly significant in our current discussion as it pertains to theodicy. If, as in this model, God can influence human thought, then the problem of evil becomes apparent. Brierley perceptively notes how this problem becomes evident in Clayton's panentheism: "[O]n this type of reading, panentheism offers no assistance with theodicy, since God remains ultimately responsible for evil, as in classical theism; it does not ease the problem of evil, but neither does it make it worse".[195] Clayton himself accedes to this problem. "[I]f God has this sort of power and regularly intervenes in the world in this way, working miracles for the encouragement of believers, then God is responsible for unspeakable evils".[196] Consequently, while Clayton (and those who accept his panentheism) may have a model that allows for God's relevance in a naturalistic worldview, it does have two significant theological problems; it may not allow for sufficient distinction between God and creation, and it may fail to exonerate God from the responsibility of evil. These theological problems are also distinct from the supplementary scientific and philosophical problems that would arise in a dialogical relationship with Dawkins' more extreme materialist view, such as the physicality of mind.

Notwithstanding, it is, according to Haught, these "troublesome features" of evolution that a theology in conversation with science must address today".[197] Moreover, as theologian David F. Ford and others maintain, modern theology must engage with contrary viewpoints: "But today believers are unavoidably in encounter with worldviews and individuals whose whole ethos and conception of reality questions and contradicts theirs".[198] It is not adequate to perennially relate theology to worldviews that are accommodative of our own; we must engage with 'the other'. The task of this work, in contributing to this ongoing encounter with 'the other', is asking what contribution Dawkins can make to theology as the embodiment of a particular 'other'. This task is also necessary, given how atheistic naturalism is, according to Keith Ward and others, so prominent in academia.

To summarize thus far, Clayton's panentheism, as understood through the mind/body analogy, may be a substantive theological model, given that it has authoritative supporters and allows God to influence the world in a naturalistic way. However, in dialogue with a proponent of a more extreme naturalistic model, such as Dawkins, it becomes problematic. This is particularly true, given that it offers little to mitigate Dawkins' theodicy challenge. We must then ask, is it possible to allow God to influence the world without being accountable for evil? As opposed to God influencing the world through interaction with humanity, Peacocke postulates that God creates the world *through* the natural processes made known to us through the sciences. "The processes revealed by the sciences are in themselves God acting as creator, and God is not to be found as some kind of additional influence or factor added on to the processes of the world God is creating".[199] The laws themselves that govern the world can be viewed as God acting. Yet, Peacocke is explicit in maintaining a distinction between God and creation, by noting that the natural processes are God's *actions*, not God himself.[200] This distinguishes Peacocke's view from considering God as merely a pseudonym for the laws of nature (this view has been proffered by scientists such as Stephen Hawking, and is essentially atheistic).[201]

From Peacocke's perspective, God interacts with the world by affecting the whole world-system. God's intentions then become manifest in the world from whole-system interactions through a "trickle down effect":

Any such interaction of God with the world-System would be initially with it as a whole. One would expect this initial interaction to be followed by a kind of 'trickle-down' effect as each level affected by the particular divine intention then has an influence on lower levels and so on down the hierarchy of complexity to the level at which God intends to effect a particular purpose.[202]

However, in a later publication, Peacocke revises this position somewhat. He explains that the whole-system interaction lacks the personal character of the profound human experience of God.[203] He provides a supplementary note to his view, by postulating that the two forms of divine interaction with the world—1) on the level of the human person, akin to Clayton, discussed above, and 2) on the level of the whole, as in his own work—are not mutually exclusive.[204] He proceeds to clarify how these two particular outlooks on divine interaction may be considered in unison: "I am inclined to postulate a divine whole–part influence at all levels, but with an increasing intensity and manifestation of divine intention from the lowest physical levels up to the personal level, where it could be at its most concentrated and focused".[205] Peacocke subsequently endorses a hybrid view of the whole–part influence he originally put forth, and Clayton's image of the divine–person interaction.

Yet this view is still vulnerable to Dawkins' theodicy challenge; as Peacocke himself acknowledges, "This renders the problem of evil particularly acute".[206] To account for this, Peacocke appeals to passibility (the doctrine that God suffers).[207] Peacocke uses God's sharing in the suffering to mitigate the theodicy problem:

> Hence when faced with this ubiquity of pain, suffering and death in the evolution of the living world . . . we were impelled to infer that God, to be anything like the God who is Love in Christian belief, must be understood to be suffering in the creative process of the world. Creation is costly to God. Now, when the natural world, with all its suffering, is panentheistically conceived of as 'in God', it follows that the evils of pain, suffering and death in the world are internal to God's own self.[208]

Peacocke's model thus allows for God to be relevant in the world, yet also attempts to comprehend evil, by allowing God to share the burden (passibilism)—a view shared by others.[209] However, we should make the important clarification, along with Brierley, between this mode of passibilism and 'theopaschism'. "The hallmark of passibilism is that God suffers in God's own nature, or that God suffers outside of the Son, Jesus. Doctrines in which God suffers only insofar as God the son suffers, are expressions only of theopaschism . . . ".[210] This point distinguishes Peacocke's view on God's suffering from a purely Christological response, evident in scholars such as Moltmann,[211] Christopher Southgate, and Neil Messer among others (such Christological theodicies may hold significant theological merit, but in dialogue with non-Christian worldviews such as atheism, they could be seen as beyond the scope of this project). Consequently, given that Peacocke's panentheistic model attempts to account for theodicy, it may be considered to be in a better position to dialogue with the worldview of Dawkins than that of Clayton. Moreover, Peacocke stresses the role of chance/randomness in the natural world.[212] He suggests that God may allow the universe to unfold and explore its own potentialities through random events (presumably, aside from the whole-system interactions we have already discussed).[213] This facet of his model may also allow for less-problematic dialogue between theology and Dawkins, despite the epistemic divergence on the issue of God. In this sense, Dawkins could be considered a useful resource as his philosophy can influence whether we adopt Peacock's model over Clayton's to allow a more fluid dialogue to occur.

To introduce two further theological themes that will contribute to the task of ascertaining how Dawkins may influence theology, we can turn our attention to Haught. The themes of futurity and *kenosis* will be presented in terms of Haught's theology of evolution, though we will also exhibit where he can gain support from other distinguished theologians. We will ultimately argue that these two themes, which are not mutually exclusive, a) place the theologian in a better position to dialogue with Dawkins than interventionist visions of God, and b) will be more favorable than the panentheistic relational models discussed thus far, if Dawkins is considered as a legitimate dialogue partner for theology.

JOHN HAUGHT'S THEOLOGY OF EVOLUTION

In order to preserve a theological worldview and simultaneously acknowledge the explanatory power of scientific naturalism, in which Dawkins grounds his atheism, Haught relies on "explanatory pluralism". This position, defended by philosophers such as Robert N. McCauley, suggests that multiple explanations for phenomena can be given that are not solely reliant on lower levels, as with the reductionism that Dawkins defends.[214] To portray the concept of explanatory pluralism, Haught proffers the following example:

> Suppose there is a pot of water boiling on your stove. A friend comes
> by and asks you why it is boiling. You may answer your friend's

question by saying that it's boiling because the molecules of water are escaping as the pot heats up. This is a perfectly good explanation, but it does not rule out others. You may also tell your friend that the pot is boiling because you turned the stove on, also a perfectly good explanation, but one that allows for even deeper explanation. You may also respond, third, that the pot is boiling because you want to brew some tea. Each of the three explanations may be offered without any one of them competing with or ruling out the others.[215]

The important point, which is insightfully illustrated here by Haught, is that a variety of explanations can be given for the same phenomena, without being in competition. As it pertains to our study on theology and science, it can be used to show that although scientific naturalism can theoretically account for all physical processes of the world (as with Dawkins), this does not rule out a theological explanation. Here we find a substantial weakness in Dawkins' view, as he offers no justification for ruling out multiple explanations. Haught uses the origin of life as an example to clarify this point:

> [N]o matter how brilliant or convincing a scientific theory of life's origin may be, I am not obliged to conclude, as materialist scientists and philosophers do, that life came about on our planet because of a specifiable concentration of physical events *rather than* because of divine goodness and generosity. There are multiple levels of explanation.[216]

As a result, it can be asserted that the emphasis on contingency in Dawkins' worldview does not conceptually preclude divine intentionality. The mechanisms of the world may be explicable through reductionism, and also through divine intention; one does not rule out the other. John Polkinghorne also offers a congruent interpretation. He distinguishes between questions of 'how' and 'why', which can give two varying explanations of the same phenomena, yet not be in competition.[217] We have already encountered Dawkins' dismissal of 'why' questions, which further substantiates the point that this becomes a significant weakness in his worldview. Explanatory pluralism then, may circumvent dialogical problems by offering room for both worldviews to exist, as Polkinghorne wrote, "giving a two-eyed perspective on the one reality".[218] As it pertains to our current discussion on a relational model between God and creation, explanatory pluralism offers a way of dialoguing with materialism without precluding God's relevance. Materialism and divine intention become two distinct but related layers of explanation.

FUTURITY

With explanatory pluralism, the theological problem of how God influences the world, or how divine intentions become manifest, is still in need of deliberation. In this regard, Haught draws upon the theological notion of futurity. We had alluded to the fact that Haught sought an eschatological vision of reality, as opposed to the classical traditions of the fall. We must now provide further detail of this eschatological vision as it pertains to providing a relational model between God and creation.

In this regard, Haught draws heavily from Teilhard de Chardin, who sought to make a dramatic shift in how God is conceived. Teilhard makes a decisive departure from the Aristotelian notion of a prime mover,[219] which has been a predominant concept in Western intellectual history. "[E]ver since Aristotle there have been almost continual attempts to construct 'models' of God on the lines of an outside Prime Mover, acting *a retro* [starting from the beginning]".[220] In light of evolution, Teilhard confesses that he has grown suspicious of the idea of an 'instantaneous creation', and suggests that there may be an "ontological contradiction latent in the association of the two words".[221] In contrast to the Aristotelian prime mover or 'first cause', Teilhard calls for an eschatological vision of God: "In future only a God who is functionally and totally 'Omega' can satisfy us".[222] Although, as we have stated, this vision of God does represent a decisive departure from the predominant view of God as prime mover, there are biblical foundations for viewing God as both the beginning (in keeping with the Aristotelian tradition) and also the end (akin to what Teilhard seeks): "I am the alpha and the omega, the beginning and the end" (Rev. 1:8).

Haught labels Teilhard de Chardin's quest for this image of God a 'metaphysics of the future'.[223] This metaphysics could be considered an image of reality extraneous to scientific thinking—consistent with explanatory pluralism. The aim of Teilhard's metaphysics is, according to Haught, to convey that any explanation of the universe requires "a transcendent force of attraction to explain the *overarching* tendency of matter to evolve toward life, mind and spirit".[224] As we have established, the materialist evolutionary worldview that Dawkins espouses writes off experiences such as 'mind' and 'spirit' to the workings of the brain. Yet for Haught, this perspective fails to appreciate the reality of subjective experience.[225] The evolution of an "inner sense", which in the materialist program can be equated to illusion, is for Haught indicative of a fundamental force of evolution; there is a sense of the "coming of the future".[226] There is a teleological dimension to this hermeneutic of evolution, though this teleology could be considered more characteristically metaphysical than the teleology of, for example, Simon Conway Morris and his views on evolutionary convergence. It is a conception of reality "in which all things are drawn perpetually toward deeper coherence by an ultimate force of attraction, abstractly identified as Omega, and conceived of as an essentially *future* reality".[227] Haught then, following from Teilhard de Chardin, identifies the 'future' as God. "The term 'God' in this revised metaphysics must once again mean for us, as it did for many of our biblical forebears, the transcendent future horizon that draws an entire universe, and not just human history, toward an unfathomable fulfilment yet to be realised".[228]

This view can be supported for two distinct reasons. Firstly, as American theologian Gloria L. Schaab posits, it appreciates the dynamic of *becoming* that evolution exemplifies.[229] The evolving nature of life runs contrary to a static vision of reality. Secondly, it takes into consideration the promissory aspect of biblical faith.[230] Haught demonstrates that God reveals God's self in the Bible in the form of a promise, by citing two highly significant instances that exemplify this theme: God's call to Abraham (Genesis 12), and Jesus' post-Easter appearances.[231] Haught suggests that these promissory events are cornerstones in the development of the Christian community. Therefore, an image of God such as the one he presents in terms of futurity is consistent with the foundations of biblical faith:

> Promissory events are what brought Israel into being, and it is the intensely promissory events surrounding the appearances of Jesus to his disciples that give rise to the Christian community and its reborn hope. . . . In other words, the whole universe may now be thought of as anticipatory, that is, of being already grasped by the futurity of the divine mystery that comes to awareness in biblical traditions.[232]

In the context of our current endeavour (dialogue with Dawkins) these biblical aspects of Haught's theology may be too narrowly Christian—though they may substantiate his view when examined from a theological perspective, which could be a question for further research. However, Haught's image of God-as-future does benefit our task, as it a) stems from the same foundation as Dawkins (evolutionary science) and b) does not conflict with the scientific picture of naturalism (as it is metaphysical).

Furthermore, Haught can find support for an Omega image of God in the writings of major theologians such as Rahner. Haught's emphasis on the 'coming of the future' as a key theme in Christian theology is strikingly reminiscent of Rahner, who explained that, "Christianity is a religion of the future. It can indeed be understood only in light of the future which it conceives as absolute future gradually approaching the individual and humanity as a whole".[233] In addition, Rahner also conceived God as "absolute future", which could be equated to Haught's conception of God as a "future horizon".[234] Similarly, Wolfhart Pannenberg proposes that the "glory of Yahweh" will become manifest at the end of history.[235] John Polkinghorne is another influential voice who proposes a similar eschatological perspective. "I do . . . acknowledge that the *ultimate* destiny . . . will indeed be a state in which God is 'all in all' (1 Cor. 15:28)".[236]

The metaphysical perspective that Haught proposes views the seemingly meaningless universe as meaningful in light of future hope:

> [O]ften the inference is made that the whole evolutionary process is . . . inherently meaningless. Viewed theologically, however, such events—even the most painful and tragic—may be consistent with the unfinished character of a universe that can become fully intelligible only when it opens itself completely to the coming of the future.[237]

Interestingly, in this passage, Haught refers again to the theodicy problem: "events—even the most painful and tragic". In a sense, Haught treads very close to the view of Rudolf Otto, by postulating that evil is the result of a divine plan in which providence will eventually be revealed. But Haught makes an important clarification in his metaphysics of the future: he considers the world as incomplete. The incompleteness of creation, for Haught, offers a bilateral way to make theologically palatable the evolutionary character of the world and the existence of evil. Firstly, drawing from Rahner, he suggests that the notion of revelation presupposes an evolving cosmos.[238] He reasons that the "fullness of divine infinity cannot be received instantaneously by a finite cosmos. Such a reception could only take place gradually".[239] This gradual reception, he explains, ". . . might appear to science as cosmic and biological evolution".[240] To validate this argument, Haught proposes that a world created in a state of perfection would have neither autonomy nor true relationship with a creator (which we considered as a theological necessity earlier):

[A]ny creation that is all light from the outset, completely unblemished by any shortcomings, would be already finished. And such a creation could really never become distinct from its maker. If it were perfect from the start the world would have no autonomy, no narrative self-identity and no 'otherness' vis-à-vis its maker. In other words, it would not be a world at all but a simple appendage to deity.[241]

This leads us into the second aspect of the bilateral explanatory prowess of an incomplete creation. Haught accounts for evil by appealing to the (necessary) incompleteness of creation, as he insightfully explains: "[S]uch evils are the dark side of an unfinished universe. An incomplete cosmos by definition is one that has not yet been brought to perfection, and it is in the *inevitable* darkness of its present incompleteness that excessive suffering, physical evil, and sin too, can gain a foothold".[242] Haught's eschatology then comes into play, as he incorporates the idea of hope into the vision of God as future. "[T]he appropriate religious response to suffering and evil is not to make legitimate room for these in the world by way of a theodicy based on guilt and punishment, or even pedagogy, but to hope for a future of new creation in which God will decisively conquer them".[243] Haught's eschatological vision hopes for the eventual defeat of evil by the goodness of God.

This vision of God can be consistent with the materialist view of Dawkins because it is metaphysical, and not strictly scientific. "[T]he sense of being grasped by the power of the future is palpable to religious experience, but it cannot be translated without remainder into scientifically specifiable concepts . . .".[244] Theology offers an *ultimate* explanation, one that can co-exist with the naturalistic image of natural selection. Nature appears to be, Haught concedes, autonomously *self*-creative (which is, he suggests, a catalyst for Dawkins' atheism). In this autopoietic (autonomously creative) view, there does not appear to be any provision for divine involvement in nature.[245] As we have stressed, part of the aim of this chapter is to account for the presence of evil without recourse to deism; to envisage a relevant God, but yet one that is not ultimately responsible for evil. In this sense, Haught's theology is well placed for dialogue with the naturalistic stance of Dawkins. His account of evil and view on naturalistic creation may provide the theologian with the intellectual tools to engage with Dawkins' theodicy challenge and his views on contingency. In Haught's metaphysics of the future, God is more relevant than that of deism, as creation is ongoing and eschatological. However, contrary to Clayton and Peacocke et al. who seek to understand how God acts, Haught provides a substantial theological explanation for why God does not act directly in the world. This leads us into another facet of theology that Haught and other significant theological authorities espouse (though as we shall see, to different degrees): divine *kenosis*.

KENOSIS

Kenosis, or divine self-emptying, is a powerful Christological theme represented in the divine Word becoming flesh (John 1:14).[246] According to Moltmann, following from St. Paul, ". . . Christ's history was understood as *kenosis* for the sake of the redemption of God-forsaken men and women".[247] Both Moltmann and Polkinghorne highlight Philippians (2:5-11) as the quintessential kenotic text in the New Testament:

> Have this mind among yourselves, which is also in Christ Jesus; who, though he was in the form of God, did not count equality with God a thing to be grasped, but *emptied himself*, taking the form of a servant, being born like another. And being in human form he humbled himself and became obedient unto death, even death on the cross. Therefore God has highly exalted him . . .[248]

In Christ, God emptied himself of divine form, becoming the servant of humanity. Moltmann calls this God's 'self-humiliation'.[249] This theme of humility is prominent in the Gospels, particularly in John (13:14-17). In this passage, Jesus washes the feet of the disciples to portray a powerful message of equality among persons: "no servant is greater than his master, nor is a messenger greater than the one who sent him" (John 13:16). Christ surrenders himself into the role of the servant. Comparably, God surrenders himself in a 'self-giving', by becoming human and mortal in Christ, which is, according to the kenotic view, an act of humility itself. The Christological theme of *kenosis* is then extended to make sense of God's relationship with creation. "In the twentieth century, the application of kenotic ideas has been extended beyond a strictly Christological focus to include other aspects of God's relationship with creation".[250] In other words, God's creation becomes a kenotic event. (Though there are distinctions between views of *kenosis*, this is the cardinal theme.)[251]

As it has been argued, a theism that is to dialogue with the scientific worldview of Dawkins must be naturalistic, as a supernaturalistic view is highly vulnerable to Dawkins' theodicy challenge and the explanatory power of contingency in science. It is partly for these two reasons[252] that Ian G. Barbour suggests many contemporary theologians[253] are led to speak of God's voluntary self-limitation (*kenosis*) in creating a world.[254] Barbour incisively writes:

> With the rise of modern science nature was increasingly seen as a self-sufficient mechanism in which God could act only by intervention from outside in violation of the laws of nature . . . the long and wasteful history of evolution suggests that God does not intervene frequently or coercively.[255]

This assessment would be congruent with Dawkins' evolutionary *weltanschauung* explored in Chapter Three. Dawkins views every facet of the world as explicable in terms of its lower levels, that is, that every phenomenon including mind is explicable in terms of physics and chemistry. On this point, Dawkins would go further than Barbour, and suggest not that God does not intervene frequently, but rather, not at all (given, in his view, God's nonexistence). Yet there are parallels between Barbour and Dawkins, in that they both accept that science appears to portray nature as a self-contained process. Consequently, God appears to be either powerless, or disinterested (the theodicy conundrum discussed earlier).

Kenosis, however, for Haught and others, provides a theologically substantive explanation for the autonomy of the workings of nature. In the kenotic view, God "lovingly renounces any claim to domineering omnipotence".[256] It is out of love that God relinquishes his omnipotence in order to create a free world. (As we have already discussed, a perfect world bound under constant divine manipulation would not be autonomous and therefore not distinct from God; it would not be a creation at all but a "divine appendage", as Haught wrote.) Moltmann elaborates on this concept:

> From the creation . . . God's self-humiliation and self-emptying deepen and unfold. Why? Because the creation proceeds from God's love, and this love respects the particular existence of all things, and the freedom of the human beings who have been created. A love that gives the beloved space, allows them time . . . freedom is the power of lovers who can withdraw in order to allow the beloved to grow and to come. Consequently, it is not just self-giving that belongs to creative love; it is self-limitation too; not only affection, but respect for the unique nature of the others as well. If we apply this perception to the Creator's relation to those he has created, what follows is a

restriction of God's omnipotence, omnipresence and omniscience for
the sake of conceding room to live to those he has created.[257]

In this passage, Moltmann neatly summarizes the theme of a kenotic
hermeneutic of creation; God limited his own omnipotence to grant freedom
to the world. In order for the world to have independence, and thus the
possibility of a true relationship, God gives to the world its own "autonomous
principles of operation".[258] In this sense, God is, according to Peacocke, "taking
a risk".[259] Evil is then understood as a consequence of the loving act of 'letting
creation be', as opposed to divine sadism as in Dawkins' criticism. Haught
and Moltmann have proceeded to suggest that it is through *kenosis* that God
paradoxically becomes powerful; God's self-limitation in creation is, in itself,
an act of omnipotence. Therefore, Moltmann explains, "We might put it
epigrammatically and say that God never appears mightier than in the act of
his self-limitation, and never greater than in the act of his self-humiliation".[260]
Then, if evil is the result of contingency or naturalism, and if contingency is a
result of God's own self-limitation in *kenosis*, then *kenosis* can be considered as
a theological framework in which to view the naturalistic vision of evolution.
The seemingly purposeless and random mechanistic operations of the world can
be hermeneutically understood as a kenotic creation, as opposed to inherently
atheistic. Consequently, the emphasis on contingency exemplified in Dawkins'
scheme can be used to reinforce a kenotic vision of creation. In this sense,
Dawkins can be a valuable partner for theological dialogue, despite holding a
different epistemic view. To illustrate this, we can turn again to Haught:

> [S]uch an expression of divine "power" is not only consonant with,
> but ultimately explanatory of, the curious world that evolutionary
> science now presents to us. The randomness, struggle and seemingly
> aimless meandering that the evolutionary story of life discloses as
> the underside of its marvellous creativity is consistent with the idea
> that the universe is the consequence of an infinite love. The key to
> such an interpretation lies in faith's staggering discovery that a truly
> effective power takes the form of self-emptying compassion.[261]

We have ascertained now that a kenotic image of God will appreciate both the
degree of contingency and evil in the natural world, which Dawkins holds as
an argument against theism. However, it needs to be clarified to what degree
God is self-limited. Barbour, for instance, illustrates that key proponents of
kenosis (including himself) allow for God to intervene (albeit subtly) in the

world.[262] Similarly, other theologies, such as the particular panentheistic models we have discussed, also allow for certain modes of divine interaction.[263] This is where a considerable difference will become evident in a dialogue between theology and Dawkins. The proposal that God intervenes in creation, however infrequently or subtly, will not harmonize with Dawkins' view of a completely self-sustained system (though, our task here is not to marry Dawkins' view with theology, but merely show where theology may benefit from dialogue). Moreover, the provision for direct divine interaction with the world once again highlights the theodicy problem. This issue is not as problematic in the theology of Haught as it is with Peacocke, Barbour, Clayton, or Polkinghorne et al., as Haught's view on divine involvement is more metaphysical; it is a longing of creation into the future, as opposed to direct intervention. Moreover, he strongly emphasizes the autonomy of the world, in which paradoxically, God becomes more present. "[T]his 'absent' God is 'present' to and deeply united with the evolving world precisely by virtue of selflessly allowing it to achieve deeper autonomy . . . ".[264]

The influential Jewish philosopher Hans Jonas pursues a comparable route. Jonas' theology was heavily influenced by his experience of the holocaust.[265] Theologian Christian Wiese writes that Jonas' "cosmogonic speculation" was an intellectual struggle to reconcile God as creator with the phenomenon of evil, exemplified in the holocaust.[266] For Jonas, the only God that could allow such suffering as experienced in the holocaust is one who has "renounced his being, divesting his deity".[267] The immensity of evil in the world exemplified in the holocaust implies for Jonas that God cannot act in the world. The experience of evil in the holocaust leads theologian David Jenkins to the same conclusion: "God is not an arbitrary meddler nor an occasional fixer. This is morally intolerable. . . . However he interacts or transacts he cannot intervene as an additional and inserted and occasional historical cause".[268] These views on God and evil could be compared with our discussion on reenvisioning God's relationship with the world based on the experience of evil in natural selection (the basis of Dawkins' theodicy challenge). Dissatisfaction with the notion that evil on such a scale as the holocaust can take place without intervention from God leads Jonas and Jenkins to the conclusion that God is unable to intervene (consistent with God relinquishing his power in a kenotic creation).

Jonas disavows both a teleological dimension to evolution and direct interaction from the divine.[269] In this sense, Haught suggests that Jonas' view on evolution is concurrent with Stephen Jay Gould (and presumably, Dawkins) on the inherent randomness in the world.[270] Therefore, Jonas' perspective on the planless nature of the world, coupled with the world's complete self-autonomy, make it amenable to the materialist position of Dawkins. Moreover, as it has been stated, Jonas' worldview is predicated upon his experience of great evil in World War II. The experience of great evil (in our understanding of natural selection) is also, as we have seen, a catalyst for Dawkins' theodicy challenge. Thus Jonas' theology satisfies the two distinct aspects of Dawkins' worldview this chapter has engaged with: evil and randomness.

Consequently, if we are to engage in dialogue with Dawkins, and consider what substance the worldview he promotes will offer to theology, we will be swayed further toward a model similar to Jonas or Haught, than toward an interventionist model. Allowing for complete autonomy of the world without divine intervention in the physical realm powerfully mitigates the strength of Dawkins' theodicy challenge, while simultaneously appreciating the self-contained contingency in the naturalistic worldview. Jonas' worldview, in this regard, is the most consistent with Dawkins'. However, as Christian Wiese explains, his image of the powerless God, though absolved from involvement in evil, can be interpreted as the utter forsakenness of humanity, leading to nihilism.[271] Haught offers a comparable critique, by positing that "what Jonas' speculation leaves out unnecessarily is an adequate basis for religious hope in cosmic and human redemption".[272] Haught's promissory vision is not as vulnerable to the critique of nihilism, as it based on future hope.

In addition, Haught's promissory vision of God is metaphysical to the point that it also satisfies the emphasis on contingency in naturalism. A definitive alignment with Jonas, Haught, or any other model of God need not be produced at this point. What seeks to be demonstrated is that engaging with viewpoints such as Dawkins offers us conceptual material that needs to be considered in theological discourse. If we allow Dawkins to have input into theological discussion, we can see how one can find justification to be swayed away from interventionist models of God and toward a more metaphysical model such as the concept of futurity (Haught et al.), or perhaps even as far as a completely powerless God (Jonas). Adopting a dialogue that includes the materialist position of Dawkins, therefore, bears weight upon the ongoing debate over whether or not God can intervene in the world.[273]

CONCLUDING REMARKS

Given Dawkins' strident hostility toward religion and theology, the predominant approach to his work has been confrontational; distinguished theological scholars such as Keith Ward and Alister McGrath set out to refute Dawkins' arguments for atheism and the socially/morally destructive nature of religion. They systematically challenge Dawkins on the logical or philosophical basis for his arguments against religious belief, most pronounced in *The God Delusion*. While acknowledging these polemics, this work sought to offer a fresh approach by proposing an earnest dialogue between theology and Dawkins' scientific and ideological position, which can be identified as atheistic evolutionary naturalism/materialism. This is a complex task, given the polarized presuppositions of Dawkins and theology particularly with regard to the God question. There are many caveats of such a dialogue, for example Dawkins' contempt for the very subject of theology. However, it is also a necessary task in the contemporary context. The worldviews, values, and intellectual endeavours of multifarious cultures and disciplines are being thrust together in unprecedented ways through technological revolutions. Theology needs to establish itself not just as a discipline in its own right, but in the midst of this new intellectually diverse paradigm. Theology must engage itself with a plurality of positions, and we have taken a dialogue with Dawkins to exemplify this necessity.

The perennial recycling of traditional theological subject matter will not suffice in this modern context. The boundaries of theological investigation need to be broadened, which, this book argued, will provide new dimensions for future theological study. The pressing need for a pluralistic, interdisciplinary theology is exponentially greater in the current intellectual climate where information and ideas are so freely shared though technological innovations. In our global village, dialoguing with Dawkins will contribute to this aim by stretching theology to the most hostile corners of the intellectual marketplace. Moreover, by considering a view as critical of theology as Dawkins', we also show the extent to which theology is self-critical, giving it a more robust, multidisciplinary character. In this sense, this book is in part a response to criticism put forth by Dawkins himself and by others—that religious belief discourages rational inquiry. As stated, engaging theology with Dawkins is significantly problematic given the epistemic differences between the two; however, it is precisely because of such differences that Dawkins is a good candidate for dialogue. The fact that theology will seriously consider dialoguing with such an antithetical voice and vehement critic gives it strength.

This chapter has demonstrated how an investigation of Dawkins' evolutionary *weltanschauung* can offer new dimensions to theological debate. Acknowledging the evolutionary character of Dawkins' perception of the world can sway opinion on important theological motifs. To illustrate, we have shown how considering the scientific naturalism Dawkins espouses would favor a move away from traditional anthropocentric visions of theodicy and the fall. Dawkins' emphasis on the interrelatedness of all life, and the gradualness of evolution, may preclude theological hermeneutics that fail to recognize the wider-than-human narrative of life. In fact, given the insignificance of humanity in terms of the vastness of biological time and diversity of living systems, any anthropocentric notions seem intellectually problematic. The traditional interpretations of suffering as a result of a human transgression (a fall) appear too narrow in light of the grand narrative of evolution.

Furthermore, in a dialogical relationship with Dawkins, we have acknowledged his emphasis on causal explanations of suffering in terms of the mechanisms of the natural world and of the fight for survival of natural selection. In light of this view, one would be encouraged away from interventionist models of God's interaction with the world, and toward a theological vision that stresses the necessity of the world's autonomy (such as the theme of *kenosis*). The nature of scientific understanding as Dawkins presents it restricts theological perceptions that do not adequately appreciate the role of chance and necessity in the mechanistic workings of the universe.

Yet this is not an exhaustive list of theological motifs that will be influenced by an engagement with a hostile worldview such as Dawkins'. By demonstrating how Dawkins can be of benefit as a conversation partner for theology, particularly in the modern context, we may open doors for future research of other contrary positions, or perhaps further exploration of Dawkins. In this sense, we do not seek to have the last word. Moreover, strictly speaking, this is not the first instance where theology has dialogued with hostile worldviews; for example, the influential movement of liberation theology championed by theologians such as Gustavo Gutiérrez can be seen to draw heavily from Marxism.[274] Taking the emphasis on pluralism and dialogue in contemporary theology seriously, this work can contend that true pluralism will not exclusively focus on dialogue with worldviews and values easily amenable to theology. In the context of this project, we have noted that significant interpretations of evolution are far more amenable to a theological worldview, and we could have exclusively opened dialogue with these views. However, such exclusivity will make no legitimate headway. On the other hand, engaging with Dawkins, who from a theological point of view can be taken as the archetypal contrarian, will test the limits of pluralism: How far out of the theological comfort zone are we willing to go?

As a final thought on Dawkins and Darwinism, he is in part a good conversation partner because he transcends academic disciplines. He advocates the expansion of Darwinism beyond his native field of biology to encompass explanations of moral behaviour, culture, and pertinently for a theological project, religious belief. However, attempting to view human civilization in a

Darwinian framework can be viewed with much suspicion. This is in part due to the historical application of the Darwinian 'survival of the fittest' mindset to social policy. There have been attempts to justify some of the darkest points in human history, such as Nazism and eugenics, by referral to Darwinism. Such atrocities have undoubtedly left a permanent scar on the face of human history, and represent periods of history that no moral person would wish to revisit. Therefore, it is understandable how apprehension toward using Darwinism to explain human behaviour may arise. We can see evidence of this suspicion in the influential theologian Henri de Lubac. Writing when the holocaust was still fresh in memory, he suggests that an atheistic philosophy of science leads to tyranny and dictatorship.[275] However, we have noted that Dawkins stresses how humans have evolved beyond genetically determined behaviour; we can rebel against our Darwinian nature. In other words, a Darwinian worldview, even one as materialist as Dawkins', does not preclude moral behaviour.

The overall conclusion of this book is that the Darwinian worldview Dawkins promotes, though not without many criticisms, may in fact shed light on theological conundrums, such as evil and God's relevance in a causal world. Furthermore, there is a necessity to engage in dialogue with the materialist worldview in the context of the modern pluralistic setting. A dialogue with Dawkins' scientifically based worldview can thus enrich a theological vision, giving us, to repeat Polkinghorne's phrase, "a two-eyed perspective on the one reality".[276] Here is where Dawkins does fail to account for explanatory pluralism—that different explanations for phenomena may be layered and not in conflict. In this sense, we can assert that science may comprehend the workings of the universe, but theology through dialogue with science, can interpret it in a wider context of the creation of God; to use Stephen Hawking's phrase, science may one day know the mind of God,[277] but theology can also appreciate its majesty. A Darwinian worldview, even one presented in such a materialist fashion, is not necessarily in conflict with theology. Quite the contrary; it can offer a new dimension for consideration. As Jack Mahoney writes:

> Because our common human experience is being faced with a major advance in our scientific understanding of human origins, intellectual integrity invites us to place that experience alongside our past and present religious beliefs, and in the process to hope to cast light on both. . . . The dialectical activity of submitting experience to the bar of belief and of submitting belief to the bar of experience is today a requirement of every believer on pain of leaving their experience unanchored and their belief unsubstantiated.[278]

I can finish this chapter, then, by recalling the sentiment of the individual who is most responsible for the origin of the spectrum of scientific and philosophical ideas that abound in the pages of this work: Charles Darwin. The following passage from *On the Origin of Species* offers a sentiment that I hope this work portrays:

> There is grandeur in this view of life, with its several powers, having been originally breathed into a few forms or into one; and that, while this planet has gone cycling on according to the fixed law of gravity, from so simple a beginning endless forms most beautiful and most wonderful have been, and are being, evolved.[279]

Notes

1. Gerard J. Hughes, 'Dawkins: What He, and We, Need to Learn', *Thinking Faith—The Online Journal of the British Jesuits* (18 Jan. 2008), Web, 20 Dec., 2011.

2. Ibid.

3. Ibid.

4. Richard Dawkins, 'A Shameful Thought for the Day: Pope Benedict XVI Presides over a Church That Continues to Promote the Repugnant Idea of Original Sin', *The Guardian* (24Dec. 2010).

5. Hughes, 'Dawkins: What He, and We, Need to Learn'.

6. Ibid.

7. Ibid.

8. Ibid.

9. David Tracy, *The Analogical Imagination: Christian Theology and the Culture of Pluralism* (London: SCM, 1981), 1–6.

10. At the risk of oversimplification, Solidarity was an anti-Soviet social movement that eventually formed a political wing and were elected to lead the Polish government in 1989.

11. Hughes, 'Dawkins: What He, and We, Need to Learn'.

12. 'The Church in the Modern Word', in Austin Flannery, ed., *Vatican II—The Conciliar and Post Conciliar Documents* (Dublin: Dominican Publications, 1981), 33–34.

13. Richard Dawkins, 'Why I Want All Our Children to Read the King James Bible', *The Guardian* (19May 2012).

14. *TGD*, 262–72.

15. *ROOE*, 111.

16. Ibid., 155.

17. Alister McGrath, *Dawkins' God: Genes, Memes and the Meaning of Life* (Oxford: Blackwell, 2005), 74. Darwin's personal experiences with pain and suffering undoubtedly contextualise his beliefs on the matter. His own illnesses and the death of his daughter are well-documented examples of such personal trauma.

18. Ibid., 75.

19. Ibid., 76.

20. Ibid., 72.

21. *ROOE*, 111–55. This chapter was adapted from Dawkins' 'God's Utility Function,' in *Scientific American* 1195, no. 90 (Nov. 1995): 80–85.

22. Ibid., 154.

23. C. S. Lewis, *The Problem of Pain* (London: Whitefriars, 1940), 14.

24. Bertrand Russell, *Why I'm Not a Christian* (London: Routledge, 1957), 20.

25. J. L. Mackie, *The Miracle of Theism: Arguments for and Against the Existence of God* (Oxford: Oxford University Press, 1982), 4. Mackie however, upon investigation, concludes that "[w]e cannot, indeed, take the problem of evil as a conclusive disproof of traditional theism, because, as we have seen, there is some flexibility in its doctrines . . . " (176). The doctrines/ propositions to which Mackie alludes are omnipotence and benevolence, consistent with C. S. Lewis' depiction of the problem of evil.

26. Victor J. Stenger, *God the Failed Hypothesis: How Science Shows That God Does Not Exist* (New York: Prometheus, 2008), 224. Text reads "god".

27. John Haught, 'Atheism', in J. Wentzel Vrede van Huyssteen, ed., *Encyclopedia of Science and Religion*, vol. 1 (Farmington Hills, MI: Macmillan, 2003), 39.

28. Alister McGrath, *The Twilight of Atheism: The Rise and Fall of Disbelief in the Modern World* (London: Rider, 2004), 32.

29. Quoted by Michael L. Peterson, *The Problem of Evil: Selected Readings* (Notre Dame: University of Notre Dame Press, 1992), 1.

30. *TGD*, 106.

31. Ibid., 106.

32. David Hume, *Dialogues and Natural History of Religion* (Oxford: Oxford University Press, 1998), 100, originally published in 1779.

33. William Rowe, 'The Problem of Evil and Some Varieties of Atheism', *American Philosophical Quarterly* 16, no. 4 (Oct. 1979).

34. Richard Swinburne, *Providence and the Problem of Evil* (Oxford: Clarendon, 1998).

35. Michael L. Peterson, *The Problem of Evil: Selected Readings*, 23.

36. Brian Davies, *Thomas Aquinas on God and Evil* (Oxford: Oxford University Press, 2011), 6.

37. John Hick, *Evil and the God of Love* (Chippenham: Macmillan, 1966), 214–15.

38. Ulf Gorman, 'Theodicy', in *Encyclopedia of Science and Religion*, vol. 2, van Huyssteen, ed., 881.

39. Alister McGrath, *Darwinism and the Divine: Evolutionary Thought and Natural Theology* (Chichester: Wiley-Blackwell, 2011), 202.

40. Christopher Southgate, 'God and Evolutionary Evil: Theodicy in Light of Darwinism', *Zygon* 37, no. 4 (Dec. 2002): 803–24.

41. Neil Messer, 'Natural Evil After Darwin', in Michael S. Northcott and R. J. Berry, eds., *Theology After Darwin* (Milton Keynes: Paternoster, 2009), 141.

42. Alvin Plantinga, *God, Freedom and Evil* (London: Allen & Unwin, 1974), 30.

43. Notable Swiss Reformed theologian Karl Barth, for example, sought to revise the traditional notion of God's complete omnipotence, thus eliminating the theological paradox encapsulated by David Hume and C. S. Lewis cited earlier. Karl Barth, *Dogmatics in Outline* (London: SCM, 2001), 38.

44. John Haught, *Is Nature Enough? Meaning and Truth in the Age of Science* (Cambridge: Cambridge University Press, 2006), 181.

45. Paul Ricoeur, *The Conflict of Interpretations: Essays in Hermeneutics*, Don Hide, ed. (London: Athlone, 1989), 455.

46. Ibid., 455.

47. Ibid., 295–96.

48. Ibid., 296.

49. Teilhard de Chardin describes the concept of original sin as an "intellectual and emotional straightjacket", and a bar to the natural development of "our religion". Pierre Teilhard de Chardin, *Christianity and Evolution,* trans. René Hague (London: Collins, 1971), 79–80.

50. Alister E. McGrath, *Christian Theology: An Introduction*, 3rd ed., 94.

51. Teilhard de Chardin, *Christianity and Evolution,* 81.

52. Hick, *Evil and the God of Love*, 201.

53. Ian G. Barbour, *Religion and Science: Historical and Contemporary Issues* (New York: HarperCollins, 1997) 301.

54. Teilhard de Chardin, *Christianity and Evolution*, 81.

55. Oliver D. Crisp, 'Original Sin and Atonement', in Thomas Flint and Michael C. Rea, eds., *The Oxford Handbook of Philosophical Theology* (Oxford: Oxford University Press, 2009), 430–51.

56. See Richard Bauckham, 'Theodicy from Ivan Karamazov to Moltmann', *Modern Theology* 4, no. 1 (1987): 83–97.

57. McGrath, *Darwinism and the Divine: Evolutionary Thought and Natural Theology*, 202.

58. Though Dawkins places emphasis on the gradualness of evolution, one cannot rule out the possibility of significant and rapid development within the evolutionary process, consistent with the 'punctuated equilibrium' hypothesis of Gould. Furthermore, Dawkins himself suggests that there may be rare—perhaps even unique—instances where evolution is rapid. At the previously mentioned discussion between Dawkins and Rowan Williams at Oxford University, Dawkins suggested that the evolution of language may be one such example.

59. McGrath, *Darwinism and the Divine: Evolutionary Thought and Natural Theology*, 202.

60. Cathriona Russell, 'The Irish Elk and the Concept of Contingency', *Search* 31, no. 3 (Winter 2008): 171.

61. *ROOE*, 154.

62. John Haught, *Christianity and Science: Toward a Theology of Nature* (New York: Orbis, 2007), 101.

63. Christopher Southgate and Andrew Robinson, 'Varieties of Theodicy: An Exploration of Responses to the Problem of Evil Based on a Typology of Good-Harm Analyses', in Nancey Murphy, Robert John Russell, and William R. Stoeger, eds., *Physics and Cosmology: Scientific Perspectives on the Problem of Natural Evil* (Vatican City: Vatican Observatory, 2007), 67.

64. Richard Dawkins, *The Magic of Reality: How We Know What's Really True* (London: Bantam, 2011), 238.

65. Ibid., 238.

66. Ibid., 238.

67. Ibid., 238. Emphasis mine.

68. Ibid., 238.

69. David Hull, 'The God of the Galápagos', *Nature*, 352, no. 6335 (Aug. 1991): 486.

70. McGrath, *Darwinism and the Divine: Evolutionary Thought and Natural Theology*, 203.

71. Sallie McFague, 'The Loving Eye vs. the Arrogant Eye: Christian Critique of the Western Gaze on Nature and the Third World', *Ecumenical Review* 49, no. 2 (Apr. 1997): 185.

72. Ibid., 186.

73. See Rosemary Radford Ruether, *Sexism and God-Talk: Toward a Feminist Theology* (Boston: Beacon, 1983); also, Anne Primavesi, *Gaia's Gift: Earth, Ourselves and God After Copernicus* (London: Routledge, 2003); also, Thomas Berry, *The Sacred Universe: Earth, Spirituality, and Religion in the Twenty-First Century* (New York: Columbia University Press, 2009).

74. Ruether, *Sexism and God-Talk: Toward a Feminist Theology*, 20.

75. Richard Dawkins, 'Gaps in the Mind', in Paola Cavalieri and Peter Singer, eds., *The Great Ape Project* (New York: St. Martin's Griffin, 1993), 81.

76. Celia Deanne-Drummond, 'Theology, Ecology and Values', in Philip Clayton and Zachary Simpson, eds., *The Oxford Handbook of Religion and Science* (Oxford: Oxford University Press, 2006), 893.

77. Haught, *Christianity and Science: Toward a Theology of Nature*, 104.

78. Paul Ricoeur, *The Symbolism of Evil* (Boston: Beacon, 1969), 233.

79. Barbour, *Religion and Science: Historical and Contemporary Issues*, 269.

80. Haught, *Christianity and Science: Toward a Theology of Nature*, 102. It is interesting to note here that the seeking of a culprit for evil is not unique of theology's quest for a theodicy.

81. John Haught, *Deeper Than Darwin: The Prospect for Religion in theAge of Evolution* (Boulder, CO: Westview, 2003), 168.

82. Haught, *Christianity and Science: Toward a Theology of Nature*, 102.

83. Richard Dawkins, 'A Shameful Thought for the Day: Pope Benedict XVI Presides over a Church That Continues to Promote the Repugnant Idea of Original Sin', *The Guardian* (24Dec. 2010).

84. Misinterpretations of the Dawkins' view on altruism were shown in the writings of Michael Ruse, E. O. Wilson, and Mary Midgley in Chapter Three.

85. Hull, 'The God of the Galápagos', 486.

86. John Polkinghorne, *Reason and Reality: The Relationship Between Science and Theology* (London: SPCK, 1991), 99.

87. Pierre Teilhard de Chardin, *Christianity and Evolution*, trans. René Hague (London: Collins, 1971), 40.

88. Ibid., 99.

89. Philip D. Clayton, *God and Contemporary Science* (Edinburgh: Edinburgh University Press, 1997), 39.

90. Polkinghorne, *Reason and Reality: The Relationship Between Science and Theology*, 99.

91. Haught, *Christianity and Science: Toward a Theology of Nature*, 104.

92. Ibid., 102.

93. Ibid., 102.

94. Polkinghorne, *Reason and Reality: The Relationship Between Science and Theology*, 100.

95. Teilhard de Chardin, *Christianity and Evolution*, 40, also quoted in Haught, *Deeper Than Darwin: The Prospect for Religion in theAge of Evolution*, 166–67.

96. Ibid., 39.

97. Haught, *Deeper Than Darwin: The Prospect for Religion in theAge of Evolution*, 167.

98. Peter Slater, 'Tillich on the Fall and the Temptation of Goodness', *The Journal of Religion* 65, no. 3 (Apr. 1985): 200.

99. Paul Tillich, *Systematic Theology Vol. 2 Existence and the Christ* (London: SCM, 1957), 44.

100. Haught, *Deeper Than Darwin: The Prospect for Religion in theAge of Evolution*, 168.

101. Haught, *Christianity and Science: Toward a Theology of Nature*, 106.

102. Haught, *Deeper Than Darwin: The Prospect for Religion in theAge of Evolution*, 169.

103. Tillich, *Systematic Theology Vol. 2 Existence and the Christ*, 41.

104. Haught, *Christianity and Science: Toward a Theology of Nature*, 106.

105. Jürgen Moltmann, *The Future of Creation* (London: SCM, 1979), 116. Italics in original.

106. Patricia A. Williams, *Doing Without Adam and Eve: Sociobiology and Original Sin* (Minneapolis: Fortress, 2001), ix.

107. Jack Mahoney, *Christianity in Evolution: An Exploration* (Washington, DC: Georgetown University Press, 2011), xii.

108. Barbour, *Religion and Science: Historical and Contemporary Issues*, 269.

109. R. J. Berry, 'Review of Norman C. Nevin, ed., *Should Christians Embrace Evolution? Biblical and Scientific Responses*', *Science and Christian Belief* 22, no. 2 (Oct. 2010): 208.

110. John Bimson, 'Doctrines of the Fall and Sin After Darwin', in Northcott and Berry, eds., *Theology After Darwin*, 114.

111. John Polkinghorne, *Exploring Reality: The Intertwining of Science and Religion* (New Haven: Yale University Press, 2005), 139.

112. N. C. Nevin, ed., *Should Christians Embrace Evolution?: Biblical and Scientific Responses* (Phillipsburg, NJ: P. & R., 2009), 10.

113. Arthur Peacocke, *Theology for a Scientific Age: Being and Becoming—Natural and Divine* (Oxford: Blackwell, 1990), 125–26.

114. Francisco J. Ayala, *Darwin's Gift to Science and Religion* (Washington, DC: Joseph Henry, 2007), 174.

115. Chris Doran, 'From Atheism, to Theodicy to Intelligent Design: Responding to Work of Francisco J. Ayala', *Theology and Science* 7, no. 4 (Nov. 2009): 339.

116. McGrath, *Darwinism and the Divine: Evolutionary Thought and Natural Theology*, 204.

117. Haught, *Christianity and Modern Science: Toward a Theology of Nature,* 83.

118. Hughes, 'Dawkins: What He, and We, Need to Learn'.

119. Southgate and Robinson, 'Varieties of Theodicy: An Exploration of Responses to the Problem of Evil Based on a Typology of Good-Harm Analyses', in Murphy, Russell, and Stoeger, eds., *Physics and Cosmology: Scientific Perspectives on the Problem of Natural Evil*, 68.

120. David Ray Griffin, *Reenchantment Without Supernaturalism: A Process Philosophy of Religion* (Ithaca, NY: Cornell University Press, 2001), 24.

121. William Provine, quoted in ibid., 23.

122. Griffin, *Reenchantment Without Supernaturalism: A Process Philosophy of Religion*, 206.

123. Richard Dawkins, *The Blind Watchmaker: Why the Evidence of Evolution Reveals a Universe Without Design* (London: Penguin, 1986), 249.

124. Alister McGrath and Joanna Collicutt McGrath, *The Dawkins Delusion: Atheist Fundamentalism and Denial of the Divine* (London: SPCK, 2007), 10–11.

125. Ibid., 10–11.

126. Ibid., 11.

127. Charles Hardwick, quoted in Arthur Peacocke, *All That Is: A Naturalistic Faith for the Twenty-First Century*, Philip Clayton, ed. (Minneapolis: Fortress Press, 2007), 6.

128. Ibid., 7.

129. Ibid., 7.

130. Griffin, *Reenchantment Without Supernaturalism: A Process Philosophy of Religion*, 206.

131. Paul Ricoeur, *Oneself as Another*, 297.

132. For example, Alvin Plantinga, 'The Evolutionary Argument Against Naturalism', in James Beilby, ed., *Naturalism Defeated? Essays on Plantinga's Evolutionary Argument Against Naturalism* (Ithaca, NY: Cornell University Press, 2002), 1–15.

133. Karl Popper, *The Logic of Scientific Discovery* (New York: Routledge, 1959), 52–53.

134. Richard Dawkins, Lecture from 'The Nullifidian' (Dec. 1994), Web, 20May 2012.

135. Griffin, *Reenchantment Without Supernaturalism: A Process Philosophy of Religion*, 28.

136. Ibid., 28.

137. Ibid., 28.

138. Rudolf Otto, *Naturalism and Religion* (New York: Williams & Norgate, 1907), 129–37.

139. Ibid., 37.

140. John Haught, 'The Boyle Lecture 2003: Darwin, Design and the Promise of Nature', *Science and Christian Belief* 17, no. 1 (Apr. 2005): 9–10.

141. Griffin, *Reenchantment Without Supernaturalism: A Process Philosophy of Religion*, 28. Griffin claims that an atheistic naturalism is the predominant view within the academic community on page 24 of the same publication.

142. Rudolf Otto, *Naturalism and Religion*, 15.

143. Griffin, *Reenchantment Without Supernaturalism: A Process Philosophy of Religion*, 28.

144. Arthur Peacocke, *Paths from Science Towards God: The End of All Our Exploring* (Oxford: Oneworld, 2001), 56.

145. James Mackey, *Christianity and Creation: The Essence of Christian Faith and Its Future Among Religions: A Systematic Theology* (New York: Continuum, 2006), 62.

146. Peacocke, *Paths from Science Towards God: The End of All Our Exploring*, 57.

147. *TGD*, 18 and *ROOE*, 123.

148. Peacocke, *Paths from Science Towards God: The End of All Our Exploring*, 56.

149. Haught, *Christianity and Science: Toward a Theology of Nature*, 94.

150. Ibid., 92.

151. Quoted in ibid., 94.

152. Ibid., 94.

153. Maureen Junker-Kenny, *Habermas and Theology* (London: T. & T. Clark, 2011), 133.

154. Haught, *Christianity and Science: Toward a Theology of Nature*, 94.

155. Ibid., 94.

156. Haught suggests that Albert Einstein moulded his vision of God to make it scientifically palatable, *God After Darwin: A Theology of Evolution* (Oxford: Westview, 2000), 109.

157. Thomas Aquinas quoted in ibid., 40. Pertaining to the issue of chance, however, Aquinas does suggest that chance events may exist, but God does maintain a general or ultimate governance over the world, "And though chance events escape the influence of particular causes, in relation to God's universal plan, nothing happens by chance. . . . So things can resist a particular cause that is implementing God's government, but they cannot resist God's governance in general". Thomas Aquinas, *Summa Theologiae: A Concise Translation*, Timothy McDermott, ed. (Allen, TX: Christian Classics, 1989), 153–54.

158. Davies, *Thomas Aquinas on God and Evil*, 67–68.

159. Polkinghorne takes this phrase from the title of the influential book *Chance and Necessity* by French philosopher Jacques Monod. Interestingly, Monod's work is cited as a prominent influence on Dawkins.

160. John Polkinghorne, *Reason and Reality: The Relationship Between Science and Theology*, 83.

161. Ibid., 83.

162. Arthur Peacocke, *Creation and the World of Science* (Oxford: Oxford University Press, 1979), 95.

163. Diarmud O'Murchu, *Evolutionary Faith: Rediscovering God in Our Great Story* (Maryknoll, NY: Orbis, 2002), 198.

164. John Haught, 'Darwin and the Cardinal', *Commonweal* 132, no. 14 (Aug. 2005): 39.

165. Peacocke, *All That Is: A Naturalistic Faith for the Twenty-First Century*, 45.

166. Michael W. Brierley, 'Naming a Quiet Revolution: The Panentheistic Turn in Modern Theology', in Philip Clayton and Arthur Peacocke, eds., *In Whom We Live and Move and Have Our Being* (Cambridge and Grand Rapids, MI: Eerdmans, 2004), 2–5.

167. Ibid., 4.

168. Ibid., 5.

169. Ibid., 5.

170. Ibid., 13.

171. Ibid., 13.

172. For example, David Jenkins, *God, Miracle and the Church of England* (London: SCM, 1987), 63–64.

173. John Cobb Jr. identifies Jonas broadly as a process theist (a particular subset of panentheism). John B. Cobb Jr., 'Hans Jonas as a Process Theologian', in Sandra B. Lubarsky and David Ray Griffin, eds., *Jewish Theology and Process Thought* (Albany: State University of New York Press, 1996), 159–62. Cobb does acknowledge that subtle differences exist, which prevent one from identifying Jonas as a legitimate process theologian.

174. Hans Jonas, *Mortality and Morality: A Search for God after Auschwitz*, Lawernce Vogal, ed. (Evanston, IL: Northwestern University Press, 1996), 133.

175. Philip Clayton, *The Problem of God in Modern Thought* (Cambridge and Grand Rapids, MI: Eerdmans, 2000), 149.

176. Peacocke, *Paths from Science Towards God: The End of All Our Exploring*, 57.

177. Brierley, 'Naming a Quiet Revolution: The Panentheistic Turn in Modern Theology', 5.

178. Ibid., 5.

179. Jay B. McDaniel, *Of Gods and Pelicans: A Theology of Reverence for Life* (Louisville: John Knox, 1989), 26–27.

180. Ibid., 27, emphasis mine.

181. For examples, see Arthur Peacocke, 'Introduction', Brierley, 'Naming a Quiet Revolution: The Panentheistic Turn in Modern Theology' and Philip Clayton, 'Panentheism Today: A Constructive Systematic Evaluation', in Clayton and Peacocke, eds., *In Whom We Live and Move and Have Our Being*.

182. John Polkinghorne, *Faith, Science and Understanding* (London: SPCK, 2000), 90–92.

183. Philip Clayton, 'Panentheism in Metaphysical and Scientific Perspective', in Clayton and Peacocke, eds., *In Whom We Live and Move and Have Our Being*, 82.

184. Ibid., 82.

185. Ibid., 82.

186. For example, David Ray Griffin, Jay McDaniel, and Sallie McFague. Michael W. Brierley, 'Naming a Quiet Revolution: The Panentheistic Turn in Modern Theology', 7 (n).

187. Clayton, 'Panentheism in Metaphysical and Scientific Perspective', 83.

188. This issue becomes particularly prominent in debates on abortion and bioethics. Seminal scholars who have engaged with this point include Karol Wojtyla (Pope John Paul II), *Love and Responsibility* (London: Collins, 1960), 21–24, and Peter Singer, *Rethinking Life and Death: The Collapse of Our Traditional Ethics* (Oxford: Oxford University Press, 1995).

189. Philip Clayton, 'The Emergence of Spirit', *CTNS Bulletin* 20, no. 4 (Fall 2000).

190. Ibid.

191. Ibid., 6.

192. David Ray Griffin, 'Panentheism: A Postmodern Revelation', in Clayton and Peacocke, eds., *In Whom We Live and Move and Have Our Being*, 82.

193. Peacocke, *Paths from Science Towards God: The End of All Our Exploring*, 58, emphasis mine; also, Brierley, 'Naming a Quiet Revolution: The Panentheistic Turn in Modern Theology', 7.

194. Ibid., 109.

195. Brierley, 'Naming a Quiet Revolution: The Panentheistic Turn in Modern Theology', 7.

196. Philip Clayton, 'The Panentheistic Turn in Christian Theology', *Dialog* 38, no. 2 (Summer 1999): 3.

197. Haught, *God After Darwin: A Theology of Evolution*, 15.

198. David F. Ford, *The Future of Christian Theology* (Chichester: Wiley-Blackwell, 2011), 51.

199. Arthur Peacocke, 'Articulating God's Presence in and to the World Unveiled by the Sciences', in Clayton and Peacocke, eds., *In Whom We Live and Move and Have Our Being*, 144.

200. Ibid., 144.

201. Stephen Hawking, Interview with John Humphrys, *In God We Doubt: Confessions of a Failed Atheist* (London: Hodder & Stoughton, 2007), 54.

202. Peacocke, *Paths from Science Towards God: The End of All Our Exploring*, 110.

203. Peacocke, *All That Is: A Naturalistic Faith for the Twenty-First Century*, 47.

204. Ibid., 46.

205. Ibid., 46-47. See also Ian G. Barbour, 'John Polkinghorne on Three Scientists', *Theology and Science* 8, no. 3 (Aug. 2010).

206. Peacocke, *Paths from Science Towards God: The End of All Our Exploring*, 141.

207. Peacocke perceptively notes that the suffering of God is a theme that is becoming more widely recognized in contemporary Christian theology, and that this theme is in contrast to the classical doctrines of *impassibility*. *All That Is: A Naturalistic Faith for the Twenty-First Century*, 54.

208. Ibid., 142.

209. For example, Elizabeth Johnson, *Quest for the Living God: Mapping Frontiers in the Theology of God* (London: Continuum, 2007); also, John Haught and Brian Davies, 'The Suffering of God: Evolution and Theodicy', *Commonweal* 138, no. 11 (June 2011).

210. Michael W. Brierley, 'Introducing the Early British Passibilists', *Zeitschrift für Neuere Theologiegeschichte/Journal for the History of Modern Theology* 8, no. 2 (Jan. 2001): 218.

211. Bauckham, 'Theodicy from Ivan Karamazov to Moltmann', 83–97.

212. Peacocke, *Theology for a Scientific Age: Being and Becoming—Natural and Divine*, 64–65.

213. Peacocke, *Creation and the World of Science: The Re-Shaping of Belief*, 95.

214. Robert N. McCauley, 'Explanatory Pluralism and the Co-evolution of Theories in Science', in Robert N. McCauley, ed., *The Churchlands and Their Critics* (Oxford: Blackwell, 1996), 29.

215. Haught, *Christianity and Science: Toward a Theology of Nature*, 142.

216. Ibid., 142. Italics in original.

217. John Polkinghorne, *Quarks, Chaos and Christianity: Questions to Science and Religion* (London: Triangle, 1994), 15. It is from this work that Haught drew the 'boiling of water' analogy.

218. John Polkinghorne, 'Does Science and Religion Matter?', in Fraser Watts and Kevin Dutton, eds., *Why the Science and Religion Dialogue Matters* (Philadelphia: Templeton Foundation, 2006), 32.

219. Bertrand Russell provides a succinct account of this Aristotelian concept, "The main argument for God is the First Cause: there must be something which originates motion, and this something must itself be unmoved, and must be eternal, substance and actuality". *The History of Western Philosophy* (London: Routledge, 1946), 164.

220. Teilhard de Chardin, *Christianity and Evolution*, 240.

221. Ibid., 239, though he does not elaborate on his reasons for this assertion.

222. Ibid., 240.

223. Haught, *God After Darwin: A Theology of Evolution*, 83.

224. Ibid., 83.

225. Ibid., 88.

226. Ibid., 83.

227. Ibid., 84. Italics in original.

228. Ibid., 84.

229. Gloria L. Schaab, 'An Evolving Vision of God: The Theology of John Haught', *Zygon* 45, no. 5 (Dec. 2010): 901.

230. Haught, *Christianity and Science: Toward a Theology of Nature*, 45.

231. Ibid., 45.

232. Ibid., 45–46.

233. Karl Rahner, *Theological Investigations, Vol. VI: Concerning Vatican Council II*, trans. Karl H. and Boniface Kruger (London: Darton, Longman & Todd, 1969), 60.

234. Ibid., 62.

235. Wolfhart Pannenberg, *Faith and Reality* (London: Search, 1977), 57.

236. Polkinghorne, *Faith, Science and Understanding*, 90–91.

237. Haught, *God After Darwin: A Theology of Evolution*, 101.

238. Ibid., 39.

239. Ibid., 39.

240. Ibid., 39.

241. Haught, 'The Boyle Lecture 2003: Darwin, Design and the Promise of Nature', 9.

242. Ibid., 9.

243. Ibid., 9.

244. Haught, *God After Darwin: A Theology of Evolution*, 90.

245. Ibid., 53.

246. This theme is prominent in Pope John Paul's *Fides et Ratio*, section 93.

247. Jürgen Moltmann, 'God's *Kenosis* in the Creation and Consummation of the World', in John Polkinghorne, ed., *The Work of Love: Creation as Kenosis* (Cambridge and Grand Rapids, MI: Eerdmans, 2001), 138.

248. Emphasis in Moltmann, ibid., 138; also, John Polkinghorne, 'Kenotic Creation and Divine Action', in Polkinghorne, ed., *The Work of Love: Creation as Kenosis*, 92.

249. Moltmann, 'God's *Kenosis* in the Creation and Consummation of the World', in Polkinghorne, ed., *The Work of Love: Creation as Kenosis*, 138.

250. Polkinghorne, 'Kenotic Creation and Divine Action', in Polkinghorne, ed., *The Work of Love: Creation as Kenosis*, 92.

251. Nancey Murphy, 'Suffering as a By-Product', in Murphy, Russell, and Stoeger, eds., *Physics and Cosmology: Scientific Perspectives on the Problem of Natural Evil.*

252. Barbour actually offers five reasons. The first two are concurrent with our own engagement with Dawkins: 1) the integrity of nature in science and theology, and 2) the problem of evil and suffering. Barbour continues to propose that theology also considers God's self-limitation because of 3) the reality of human freedom, 4) the Christian understanding of the cross, and 5) feminist critiques of patriarchal models of God. These other three reasons could be used to offer further theological substance to the idea of *kenosis*; however, they would take us too far from our dialogue with Dawkins to be considered in this context. Ian G. Barbour, 'God's Power: A Process View', in John Polkinghorne, ed., *The Work of Love: Creation as Kenosis*, 1.

253. For examples, see John Polkinghorne, Jürgen Moltmann, Keith Ward, among others, in Polkinghorne, ed., *The Work of Love: Creation as Kenosis*; also Haught, *God After Darwin: A Theology of Evolution*, 49.

254. Barbour, 'God's Power: A Process View', in Polkinghorne, ed., *The Work of Love: Creation as Kenosis*, 1.

255. Ibid., 2.

256. Haught, *God After Darwin: A Theology of Evolution*, 50.

257. Moltmann, 'God's *Kenosis* in the Creation and Consummation of the World', in Polkinghorne, ed., *The Work of Love: Creation as Kenosis*, 147.

258. Haught, *God After Darwin: A Theology of Evolution*, 50.

259. Arthur Peacocke, 'The Cost of Life', in John Polkinghorne, ed., *The Work of Love: Creation as Kenosis*, 147.

260. Moltmann, 'God's *Kenosis* in the Creation and Consummation of the World', in Polkinghorne, ed., *The Work of Love: Creation as Kenosis*, 148; also, Haught, *God After Darwin: A Theology of Evolution*, 113.

261. Haught, *God After Darwin: A Theology of Evolution*, 113.

262. The examples Barbour gives are himself, Polkinghorne, Peacocke, and George Ellis. Barbour, 'God's Power: A Process View', in Polkinghorne, ed., *The Work of Love: Creation as Kenosis*, 2–3; see also Ian G. Barbour, 'John Polkinghorne on Three Scientists', *Theology and Science* 8, no. 3 (Aug. 2010).

263. For example, Philip Clayton et al. For examples of how divine interaction with the world can be understood in a variety of forms, see Barbour, 'John Polkinghorne on Three Scientists'.

264. Haught, *God After Darwin: A Theology of Evolution*, 114.

265. Jonas fought for the British army toward the end of World War II, and his mother was killed at the Auschwitz concentration camp.

266. Christian Wiese, *The Life and Thought of Hans Jonas: Jewish Dimensions* (Waltham, MA: Brandeis University Press, 2007), 120.

267. Jonas, *Mortality and Morality: A Search for God after Auschwitz'*, Lawrence Vogal, ed., 133.

268. Jenkins, *God, Miracle and the Church of England*, 63–64.

269. Jonas, *Mortality and Morality: A Search for God after Auschwitz'*, 190.

270. Haught, *God After Darwin: A Theology of Evolution*, 173.

271. Wiese, *The Life and Thought of Hans Jonas: Jewish Dimensions*, 143.

272. Haught, *God After Darwin: A Theology of Evolution*, 184.

273. An interesting summary of such debate can be found in R. J. Berry, 'Divine Action: Expected and Unexpected', *Zygon* 37, no. 3 (Sept. 2002): 717–28.

274. Christian Smith, '*Las Casas* as Theological Counteroffensive: An Interpretation of Gustavo Gutiérrez's *Las Casas: In Search of the Poor of Jesus Christ*', *Journal for the Scientific Study of Religion* 41, no. 1 (Mar. 2002): 69–73.

275. Henri de Lubac, *The Drama of Atheistic Humanism* (London: Sheed & Ward, 1949), 156.

276. Polkinghorne, 'Does Science and Religion Matter?', 32.

277. Stephen Hawking, *A Brief History of Time: From the Big Bang to Black Holes* (London: Bantam, 1988), 175.

278. Mahoney, *Christianity in Evolution: An Exploration*, xiii.

279. Charles Darwin, *On the Origin of Species* (New York: Prometheus, 1991), 408. Originally published in 1859.

Conclusion

The intention of this book is to advocate a paradigm of theological dialogue that seeks to respond to theology's most virulent critics. Without engaging in a cheap search for reference, it was argued that the current context of multiculturalism and the public character of religious antagonists force theology to address and explore the perspectives of its intellectual opposition. This book has presented such a dialogue by taking Dawkins as a representative of a worldview hostile to theology, namely atheistic or scientific materialism, and investigating whether the consideration of such a worldview may be of benefit to a theological project. The results of this endeavour will now be explained.

Dawkins espouses a worldview, grounded in evolutionary science, that seeks to explain naturalistically every facet of life, including human behavior. Dawkins' view is of particular interest to the theologian because certain aspects of human behavior that he seeks to explain have decidedly theological connotations—for example, ethics, humanity's search for purpose, and religious belief systems. Dawkins proposes an evolutionary *weltanschauung* that understands these elements of the human experience purely as products of natural selection. Moreover, this evolutionary worldview is presented by Dawkins as particularly atheistic and anti-religious; he feels the evolutionary explanation of life undermines, or in cases dissolves, a religious outlook. Throughout a dialogue with Dawkins, this project has identified significant areas of theological and religious studies that may benefit from a consideration of his materialist vision. We particularly signified how an understanding of religious belief may be enriched from a cognitive, evolutionary perspective, and how we understand humanity's place in the grand narrative of creation. We have shown how Dawkins' evolutionary materialism may also offer substance to ongoing theological debates pertaining to anthropocentricism, the fall, evil, and God's relationship with creation. Therefore, because considering the materialist position may significantly sway opinion in theological debate, we can argue that opting to take Dawkins as a conversation partner for theology is a worthwhile endeavour. Consequently, it is advocated that theology should seek a relationship with its critics, even those as hostile as Dawkins, as we may find new areas of substance rarely considered, or new possible areas of exploration.

Dawkins' atheistic picture can also be limiting as it may be deliberately presented with the goal of excluding God. Moreover, his contempt for the subject of theology and his lack of theological understanding make it difficult to engage in a rigorous academic discussion. As a result, major caveats have presented themselves as we progressed through the dialogue. Therefore, an argument could be made that the polarized positions of Dawkins and theology on key issues such as the existence of God may become insurmountable obstructions to a successful dialogue. Yet the current character of the intellectual marketplace, with the free access of information, forces theology to engage with its critics. In doing so, theology can demonstrate that it is willing to be self-critical and fight for its place as a discipline against those such as Dawkins, who see theology as irrelevant in the modern world.

In the past, the predominant attitude toward Dawkins from theology has been confrontational. Conversely, this project has sought an earnest consideration of his philosophy. However, considering the philosophy of such a contrary other may become more complex than a dialogue with thinkers of a persuasion more agreeable to theology (for example, Hegel, Ricoeur, or in terms of a dialogue with science, Francis Collins), given that we may need to search harder to find common ground. Yet through the Anselmian pilgrimage of faith seeking understanding, it is not satisfactory to consistently follow the path of least resistance. By looking for insight in less obvious places, we can find new avenues for classical theological debates to explore. We can enable theology to more fully participate in a public exchange, acknowledging the advancements in other areas of academia and what possible implications these advancements may have for theological motifs.

The methodological framework within which this work was developed was systematically outlined in the first chapter. In this section of the book, we acknowledged the strong emphasis on pluralism and interdisciplinary dialogue in contemporary theology. It was argued that the modern setting of academia requires an openness to conversation with a multitude of belief systems and intellectual disciplines. Moreover, the public character of strident critics of theology forces theology to engage in debate. Therefore, it was proposed that theology should engage in an earnest dialogue with a contrary worldview. It was then shown how Dawkins can be considered as a suitable conversation partner. In addition, we signified the conceptual approach of the project to science, religion, and Dawkins himself. Particular limitations of conversing with Dawkins were also probed in this chapter.

As Dawkins interprets every facet of human behavior in terms of evolution, Chapter Two established his interpretation of evolutionary science. This endeavour is a prerequisite for an earnest engagement with Dawkins as he grounds his worldview on science. In order to fully appreciate the scientific picture of evolution, we also indicated areas of Dawkins' scientific picture where he can gain support from influential authorities in the field. However, we also indicated significant areas of Dawkins' interpretation of evolution where he can be substantially criticized. Furthermore, it was also shown how the scientific polemic between Dawkins and Gould may be predicated upon philosophical differences, which highlight the importance of hermeneutics in science. In this chapter, we also acknowledged alternative interpretations of evolution that would appear to be more agreeable to a theological position. However, these interpretations were also criticized, which further substantiates the decision to engage with Dawkins' view.

Having established that Dawkins' scientific worldview is heavily interpretive (evident in the Dawkins–Gould polemic), Chapter Three then outlined Dawkins' philosophical *weltanschauung*. Dennett's evolutionary explanation of consciousness was also incorporated as a part of the materialist worldview that Dawkins promotes. This chapter explained how Dawkins seeks to expand the explanatory prowess of evolution beyond biology to encompass aspects of human behavior with strikingly theological connotations: ethics, culture, and humanity's understanding of purpose. We also contextualized Dawkins' worldview by presenting a rigorous critique of this position.

Chapter Four then applied Dawkins' evolutionary framework for understanding culture to the area of religious belief. In opting to interpret human behavior in terms of natural selection, theologians are presented with a new way in which to understand religious belief. Although Dawkins and many of his supporters present this methodology as a way of undermining the legitimacy of belief, we noted that there is no *a priori* reason to suggest it does. It is for this reason that several key authorities in contemporary theology have embraced the advancements in an evolutionary understanding of religion. To proffer an analogy, we could outline an evolutionary perspective on how the concepts of Euclidean geometry have been highly successful as a complex of ideas (or memes, to persist with Dawkins' terminology); yet this understanding will in no way diminish the legitimacy of geometry. Rather, it may provide a fascinating anthropological study. The same could be said of an evolutionary perspective on religion.

In Chapter Five, a direct dialogue was sought between Dawkins and theology in order to determine whether his worldview may offer substance for theological themes. Following from Alister McGrath, to cite one of the most prominent examples, we decided to take Dawkins as a serious critic of theological ideas in order to investigate whether or not we can learn from him. This chapter centred on Dawkins' theodicy challenge, which was a renewed version of the classical theological problem of evil, explicated in terms of his understanding of evolution. If Dawkins' materialist interpretation is considered, then we argued that it can sway one away from particular understandings of God, such as an interventionist image, and toward other theological models such as a kenotic creation—a God paradoxically powerful in the relinquishing of his power. It was shown how through a dialogue with Dawkins, one may favor a theological outlook that can incorporate the materialist image, which Dawkins suggests comes from our current scientific understanding.

The cardinal argument of this book is that theology should foster a more amicable relationship with its critics, given that these critics may represent particular ideologies or worldviews that in the modern context are ever more accessible with phenomena such as the Internet, online encyclopedias, and social networks. Humanity has pooled its knowledge through technological advancements in unprecedented ways, forming what the influential computer scientist W. Daniel Hillis calls "the world's collective mind".[1] In this setting, it is, as the theologian Francis Clooney S.J. suggests, "nearly impossible to justify not studying other traditions and taking their theologies into account . . . ".[2] Taking this imperative seriously, this project has held Dawkins as a representative of a 'tradition'—some, such as Michael Poole, have gone as far as to say that Dawkins' view is a 'theology'[3]—with which to formulate a dialogue, despite the fact that he is such a staunch critic of theological ideas.

Paul Tillich argued that "every religion which cannot stand ultimately the radical question that is asked by the intellectual critic, is superstition".[4] In order for theology to maintain its legitimacy, it cannot ignore its critics. It needs to assert itself in the pluralistic world that sees theology and the anti-theology of Dawkins in closer proximity than ever before. Particularly in the case of Dawkins, as he is a contemporary critic, there is a pressing need for an ongoing dialogue that must be continued after this book, given that he maintains a public profile. Moreover, he is representative of science in general, which is perennially advancing; as recently as July 2012, the discovery of the Higgs Boson may represent an important milestone in physics' understanding of the universe, which in turn may have implications for the wider dialogue between science and theology. So by engaging with Dawkins, we are advocating for a way in which we approach theology; insisting on an ongoing dialogue with its critics, alternative ideologies, and other disciplines. Although other conversation partners may be more beneficial in terms of substance, such as writers or philosophers with a view more sympathetic to theology, the hostile perspectives cannot be ignored. In other words, theology cannot become too cautious; it must venture out of its comfort zone and take on the task of honestly engaging with its critics, despite the fact that such a dialogue may be complex and wrought with difficulties. Theology must continue to explore the intellectual world, which may lead it down unlikely roads. But it is perhaps down these not oft-travelled roads that theology may find nuggets of wisdom and assert itself as committed to the Anselmian endeavour of faith seeking understanding. As the poet Robert Frost wrote in 'The Road Not Taken',

> *I shall be telling this with a sigh*
> *Somewhere ages and ages hence:*
> *Two roads diverged in a wood, and I –*
> *I took the one less travelled by, and that has made all the difference.*

Over the course of this book, we have opted to tread the theological road less travelled by taking Dawkins as an exemplar of the type of conversation partner theology must bravely open its windows of wonder to. In an academically rigorous way, theology must search for greater insight through dialogues with unlikely sources. This type of dialogue may not be easy, and may be uncomfortable. Yet, there are potential rewards of some measure, such as a greater understanding and enlarged perspective. If theology does not have the courage to explore its others in this way, we are failing Anselm's understanding of the very nature of our discipline.

Notes

1. W. Daniel Hillis, 'A Forebrain for the World Mind', in John Brockman, ed., *This Will Change Everything: Ideas That Will Shape the Future* (New York: HarperCollins, 2010), 32–36. In the article, Hillis is referring specifically to the online encyclopaedia 'Wikipedia'.

2. Francis X. Clooney S.J., 'Comparative Theology', in John Webster et al., eds., *The Oxford Handbook of Systematic Theology*, 653.

3. Michael Poole, 'A Critique of Aspects of the Philosophy and Theology of Richard Dawkins', *Science and Christian Belief* 6, no. 1 (Apr. 1994).

4. Paul Tillich, 'Religion and Its Intellectual Critics', *Christianity and Crisis* (Mar. 1995), Web, 1 July 2012.

Appendix

Interview with Daniel C. Dennett, conducted via e-mail in May 2012

Q) You have been identified as a materialist; the view that all that exists is matter, and even conscious thoughts can potentially be understood in terms of physics and chemistry. Would this be an accurate description of your position?

A) Yes.

Q) You have been critiqued for 'over-simplifying' evolutionary theory by writers such as Stephen Jay Gould. Do you think that it is appropriate to speak of evolution in terms of 'tendencies' as opposed to 'laws' as we do in physics, and do you think this has a significant impact on our appreciation of the process?

A) Gould's critique was disingenuous; he mainly objected to my defense of adaptationism and my exposure of his own misleading oversimplifications. The fact that his last long rant about evolutionary theory has been ignored by just about everybody in biology since it was published tends to support my criticisms. "Laws" do play a very different role in evolutionary theory; first, the basic laws of physics and chemistry by themselves provide most of the constraints. (Consider: there are no laws of automotive engineering or aeronautical engineering, but that doesn't make these research fields any less scientific.)

Q) How do you respond to criticism that you do not adequately separate those features of evolution you discuss which are more philosophical (the evolution of altruism or culture for example) with those which are scientifically verifiable?

A) First, theories about the evolution of altruism and culture are just as scientifically verifiable and falsifiable as the theories of other aspects of the biosphere. It just hasn't been done well yet. But since DDI was published there has been a wealth of excellent work on cultural evolution, most of it consonant with, and even in some instances building on, the analyses I offered.

Q) Are there any points of Richard Dawkins' view on evolution that you disagree with? Would it be fair to say that you both share a very similar (perhaps even identical?) interpretation of evolution?

A) On some technical details I don't feel qualified to disagree publicly even when I have my doubts. We discuss these issues, as yet unresolved. I haven't seen anything beyond a few rash overstatements to disavow in his work.

Q) Do you still feel as confident about the meme concept as you always have?

A) More so. And I am pleased to see that the most serious researchers are beginning to agree, though they often, for various reasons, try to avoid using the term. See my essay on the New Replicators in the *Oxford Encyclopedia of Evolution*.

Q) You have questioned the legitimacy of theology on several occasions. Yet you have also mentioned the importance of religion in cultural and philosophical (and sociological, mythological etc.) history and that therefore, it needs to be studied and understood. Would this not constitute the need for theology (even if it were re-framed as the study of religion as opposed to the study of God) as the theological ideas behind religion need to be understood, as well as the more objective elements, eg. the mythology of religion, the cultural influence of religion etc. (which theology also deals with).

A) I am sure that theology can be studied objectively as a complex and fascinating set of intellectual systems, but I don't think that inquiry would count as theology, since it would be 100% uncommitted to any of the doctrines. It would be a kind of anthropology, or like the sociology of science (an intermittently useful field plagued by lots of silly misunderstanding), or like literary criticism, I suppose. Dickens experts have a scholarly love of all his fictional characters, and a Christianity expert should have the same informed (and respectful) acquaintance with the many characters, saints, stories, liturgies, . . . of the denominations. That is not theology, methinks, but it is what theology could become, if divorced from apologetics and sectarian loyalties.

Bibliography

PUBLICATIONS BY RICHARD DAWKINS

Dawkins, Richard. *The Selfish Gene.* Oxford: Oxford University Press, 1976.

———. 'In Defense of Selfish Genes', *Philosophy* 56, no. 218 (Oct. 1981).

———. *The Extended Phenotype: The Long Reach of the Gene.* Oxford: Oxford University Press, 1982.

———. *The Blind Watchmaker: Why the Evidence of Evolution Reveals a Universe Without Design.* London: Penguin, 1986.

———. 'Viruses of the Mind', in Bo Dahlbom, ed., *Dennett and His Critics: Demystifying Mind.* Oxford: Blackwell, 1993.

———. Lecture from 'The Nullifidian' (Dec. 1994). Web. 20May 2012.

———. 'Reply to Michael Pool', *Science and Christian Belief* 7, no. 1 (Apr. 1995).

———. 'God's Utility Function', *Scientific American* 1195, no. 90 (Nov. 1995).

———. *River Out of Eden: A Darwinian View of Life.* London: Orion, 1996.

———. 'Obscurantism to the Rescue', *The Quarterly Review of Biology* 72, no. 4 (Dec. 1997).

———. 'The Emptiness of Theology', *Free Inquiry* 18, no. 2 (Spring 1998).

———. *Unweaving the Rainbow: Science, Delusion and the Appetite for Wonder.* London: Penguin, 1998.

———. 'An Atheist's Call to Arms', Lecture at TED (Feb. 2002).

———. *A Devil's Chaplain: Selected Essays.* London: Phoenix, 2003.

———. 'Gaps in the Mind', in Paola Cavalieri and Peter Singer, eds., *The Great Ape Project.* New York: St. Martin's Griffin, 1993.

———. *The Ancestor's Tale: A Pilgrimage to the Dawn of Life.* London: Weidenfeld & Nicolson, 2004.

———. 'The Man Behind the Meme', interview with Jim Holt, *Slate* (1 Dec. 2004). Web. 2 May 2012.

———. 'Atheists for Jesus' (Apr. 2006). Web. 28 Oct. 2010.

———. *The God Delusion.* Kent: Bantam, 2006.

———. 'Inferior Design', *The New York Times* (1 July 2007).

———. 'Do You Have to Read Up on Leprechology before Disbelieving in Them?', *The Independent* (UK) (17 Sept. 2007).

————, ed. *The Oxford Book of Modern Science Writing.* Oxford: Oxford University Press, 2008.

————. *The Greatest Show on Earth: The Evidence for Evolution.* London: Bantam, 2009.

————. 'A Shameful Thought for the Day: Pope Benedict XVI Presides over a Church That Continues to Promote the Repugnant Idea of Original Sin', *The Guardian* (24Dec. 2010).

————. 'Afterword' to Lawrence Krauss, *A Universe from Nothing.* New York: Free Press, 2012.

————. 'Why I Want All Our Children to Read the King James Bible', *The Guardian* (19May 2012).

Publications on Richard Dawkins

Betzig, Laura. 'Review: Untitled', *The Quarterly Review of Biology* 72, no. 4 (Dec. 1997).

Blanchard, John. *Dealing with Dawkins.* North Darlington: E. P. Books, 2010.

Cornwall, John. *Darwin's Angel: A Seraphic Response to The God Delusion.* London: Profile Books, 2007.

Crean, Thomas. O.P. *A Catholic Replies to Professor Dawkins.* Oxford: Family Publications, 2008.

Dennett, Daniel C. 'The Selfish Gene as a Philosophical Essay', in Alan Grafen and Mark Ridley, eds., *Richard Dawkins: How a Scientist Changed the Way We Think.* Oxford: Oxford University Press, 2006.

Eagleton, Terry. 'Lunging, Flailing, Mispunching', *The London Review of Books* (19 Oct. 2006).

————. *Reason, Faith and Revolution: Reflections on the God Debate.* London and New Haven: Yale University Press, 2007.

Elsdon-Baker, Fern. *The Selfish Genius: How Richard Dawkins Re-Wrote Darwin's Legacy.* London: Icon Books, 2009.

————. 'The Dawkins Dogma', *New Scientist,* 203, no. 2717 (July 2009).

Fallon, R. J. *Is Richard Dawkins the New Messiah? A Layman's Critique of the God Delusion.* Hull: Eka Books, 2008.

Giberson, Karl, and Mariano Artigas. *Oracles of Science: Celebrity Scientists Versus God and Religion.* Oxford: Oxford University Press, 2007.

Goodenough, Ursula. 'Review: Walking Back Through Evolutionary Time', *BioScience* 55, no. 10 (Sept. 2005).

Grigg, Richard. *Beyond the God Delusion: How Radical Theology Harmonizes Science and Religion.* Minneapolis: Fortress Press, 2008.

Haught, John. *God and the New Atheism: A Critical Response to Dawkins, Harris and Hitchens.* Louisville: Westminster John Knox, 2008.

Hughes, Gerard. 'Dawkins: What He, and We, Need to Learn', *Thinking Faith—The Online Journal of the British Jesuits* (18 Jan. 2008). Web. 20 Dec. 2011.

Hull, David. 'A Quartet of Volumes on Genetics and Evolution', *The Quarterly Review of Biology* 62, no. 3 (Sept. 1987).

Jones, Kathleen. *Challenging Richard Dawkins: Why Richard Dawkins Is Wrong about God.* London: Canterbury, 2007.

Lash, Nicholas. 'Where Does the God Delusion Come From?', *New Blackfriars* 88, no. 1017 (Sept. 2007).

Leonard, Janet L. 'Review: Untitled', *The Quarterly Review of Biology* 70, no. 3 (Sept. 1995).

Markham, Ian S. *Against Atheism: Why Dawkins, Hitchens, and Harris Are Fundamentally Wrong.* Chichester: Wiley-Blackwell, 2010.

McGrath, Alister. *Dawkins' God: Genes, Memes and the Meaning of Life.* Oxford: Blackwell, 2005.

———. 'Has Science Eliminated God?—Richard Dawkins and the Meaning of Life', *Science and Christian Belief* 17, no. 2. (Oct. 2005).

———. *The Dawkins Delusion: Atheist Fundamentalism and Denial of the Divine.* London: SPCK, 2007.

———. 'Evolutionary Biology in Recent Atheist Apologetics', in Denis R. Alexander and Ronald L. Numbers, eds., *Biology and Ideology: From Descartes to Dawkins.* Chicago: University of Chicago Press, 2010.

Midgley, Mary. 'Gene Juggling', *Philosophy* 54, no. 210 (Oct. 1979).

Muscott, Keith. 'Review of: The Selfish Genius: How Richard Dawkins Rewrote Darwin's Legacy', *Biologist* 57, no. 1 (Feb. 2010).

Orr, H. Allen. 'A Mission to Convert', *The New York Review of Books* 54, no. 1 (Jan. 2007).

Poole, Michael. 'A Critique of Aspects of the Philosophy and Theology of Richard Dawkins', *Science and Christian Belief* 6, no. 1 (Apr. 1994).

Robertson, David. *The Dawkins Letters: Challenging Atheist Myths.* Fearn, Ross-shire: Christian Focus, 2007.

Sexton, Ed. 'Dawkins and the Selfish Gene', in Richard Appignanesi, ed., *Postmodernism and Big Science: Einstein Dawkins Kuhn Hawking Darwin.* Cambridge: Icon Books, 2002.

Slane, Rob. *The God Reality: A Critique of Richard Dawkins' The God Delusion.* Eastnor Castle, Herefordshire: Day One, 2008.

Starkey, Mike. *Whose Delusion? Responding to The God Delusion by Richard Dawkins.* Kent: Church Army, 2007.

Sterelny, Kim. 'Never Apologise, Always Explain', *Bioscience* 54, no. 5 (May 2004).

———. *Dawkins vs. Gould: Survival of the Fittest.* Cambridge: Icon Books, 2007.

Ward, Keith. *Why There Almost Certainly Is a God: Doubting Dawkins.* Oxford: Lion, 2008.

Secondary Literature

Aquinas, Thomas. *Summa Theologiae: A Concise Translation*, Timothy McDermott, ed. Allen, TX: Christian Classics, 1989.

Armstrong, David M. 'Naturalism, Materialism and First Philosophy', *Philosophia* 8, no. 2–3 (1978).

Atran, Scott. *In Gods We Trust: The Evolutionary Landscape of Religion.* Oxford: Oxford University Press, 2002.

Augustine. *On the Literal Meaning of Genesis vol. 1.* Translated by John Hammond Taylor S.J. Mahwah, NJ: Paulist, 1982.

Aunger, Robert. 'Introduction', in Robert Aunger, ed., *Darwinizing Culture: The Status of Memetics as a Science.* Oxford: Oxford University Press, 2000.

Ayala, Francisco J. 'Teleological Explanations in Evolutionary Biology', *Philosophy of Science* 37, no. 1 (Mar. 1970).

———. 'Theodosius Dobzhansky: The Man and the Scientist', *Annual Review of Genetics* 10 (1976).

———. *Darwin and Intelligent Design.* Minneapolis: Fortress Press, 2006.

———. *Darwin's Gift to Science and Religion.* Washington, DC: Joseph Henry, 2007.

———. 'Darwin's Greatest Discovery: Design Without Designer', *Proceedings of the National Academy of Science of the United States of America* 104 (May 2007).

———. Statement at Templeton Prize News Conference (25 March 2010).

Bakker, Robert T. *The Dinosaur Heresies: A Revolutionary View of Dinosaurs.* Essex: Longman, 1986.

Baofu, Peter. *Beyond Nature and Nurture: Conceiving a Better Way to Understand Genes and Memes.* Newcastle: Cambridge Scholars Press, 2006.

Barbour, Ian G. *Religion and Science: Historical and Contemporary Issues.* New York: HarperCollins, 1997.

———. *When Science Meets Religion: Enemies, Strangers or Partners.* New York: HarperCollins, 2000.

———. 'God's Power: A Process View', in John Polkinghorne, ed., *The Work of Love: Creation as Kenosis.* Cambridge and Grand Rapids, MI: Eerdmans, 2001.

———. 'John Polkinghorne on Three Scientists', *Theology and Science* 8, no. 3 (Aug. 2010).

Baron Cohen, Simon, Alan M. Leslie, and Una Frith. 'Does the Autistic Child Have a Theory of Mind?', *Cognition* 21, no. 1 (Oct. 1985).

Barrett, Justin L. *Why Would Anyone Believe in God?* Plymouth, UK: AltaMira, 2004.

———. 'Cognitive Science, Religion and Theology', in Jeffery Schloss and Michael Murray, eds., *The Believing Primate.* New York: Oxford University Press, 2009.

Barrett, Justin L., and Rebekah A. Richert. 'Anthropomorphism of Preparedness? Exploring Children's God Concepts', *Review of Religious Research* 44, no. 3 (Mar. 2003).

Barth, Karl. *Dogmatics in Outline.* London: SCM, 2001.

Bauckham, Richard. 'Theodicy from Ivan Karamazov to Moltmann', *Modern Theology* 4, no. 1 (Oct. 1987).

Beattie, Tina. *The New Atheists: The Twilight of Reason and the War on Religion.* London: Darton, Longman & Todd, 2007.

Beatty, John H. 'The Evolutionary Contingency Thesis', in Elliott Sober, ed., *Conceptual Issues in Evolutionary Biology*, 3rd ed. Cambridge, MA: MIT Press, 2006.

Behe, Michael J. *Darwin's Black Box: The Biochemical Challenge to Evolution.* New York: Free Press, 1996.

———. 'A Catholic Scientist Looks at Darwinism', in William A. Dembski, ed., *Uncommon Dissent: Intellectuals Who Find Darwinism Unconvincing.* Wilmington, DE: ISI Books, 2004.

———. 'Irreducible Complexity: Obstacle to Darwinian Evolution', in William A. Dembski and Michael Ruse, eds., *Debating Design: From Darwin to DNA.* Cambridge: Cambridge University Press, 2004.

———. *The Edge of Evolution: The Search for the Limits of Darwinism.* New York: Free Press, 2007.

Berry, R. J. 'Divine Action: Expected and Unexpected', *Zygon* 37, no. 3 (Sept. 2002).

———. 'Review of Norman C. Nevin, ed., *Should Christians Embrace Evolution? Biblical and Scientific Responses*', *Science and Christian Belief* 22, no. 2 (Oct. 2010).

Berry, Thomas. *The Sacred Universe: Earth, Spirituality, and Religion in the Twenty-First Century.* New York: Columbia University Press, 2009.

Bimson, John. 'Doctrines of the Fall and Sin After Darwin', in Michael S. Northcott and R. J. Berry, eds., *Theology After Darwin.* Milton Keynes: Paternoster, 2009.

Blackburn, Simon. 'Naturalism', in Simon Blackburn, ed., *The Oxford Dictionary of Philosophy.* Oxford: Oxford University Press, 2008.

Blackmore, Susan. *Dying to Live: Science and Near Death Experience.* London: HarperCollins, 1993.

———. *The Meme Machine.* Oxford: Oxford University Press, 1999.

———. 'On Memes and Temes', Lecture at TED (Feb. 2008).

Boff, Leonardo. 'Is Cosmic Christ Greater Than Jesus of Nazareth?', *Concilium* (2007): 1

Borgman, Erik, and Felix Wilfred. 'Introduction', *Concilium* (2006): 2

Boyer, Pascal. *The Naturalness of Religious Ideas: A Cognitive Theory of Religion.* Berkeley: University of California Press, 1994.

———. *Religion Explained.* London: Heinemann, 2001.

———. 'A Reductionistic Model of Distinct Modes of Religious Transmission', in Harvey Whitehouse and Robert McCauley, eds., *Mind and Religion: Psychological and Cognitive Foundations of Religiosity.* Walnut Creek, CA: AltaMira, 2005.

Bremner, James. *The Power of Then: How the Sages of the Past Can Help Us in Our Everyday Lives.* London: Hay House, 2012.

Brierley, Michael W. 'Naming a Quiet Revolution: The Panentheistic Turn in Modern Theology', in Philip Clayton and Arthur Peacocke, eds., *In Whom We Live and Move and Have Our Being.* Cambridge and Grand Rapids, MI: Eerdmans, 2004.

———. 'Introducing the Early British Passibilists', *Zeitschrift für Neuere Theologiegeschichte/Journal for the History of Modern Theology* 8, no. 2 (Jan. 2001).

Brockman, John, ed. *This Will Change Everything: Ideas That Will Shape the Future.* New York: HarperCollins, 2010.

Burkert, Walter. *Creation of the Sacred: Tracks of Biology in Early Religions.* Cambridge, MA: Harvard University Press, 1996.

Byrne, Máire. *The Names of God in Judaism, Christianity and Islam: A Basis for Interfaith Dialogue.* Dublin: Continuum, 2011.

Chomsky, Noam. 'Knowledge of Language: Its Elements and Origins', *Philosophical Transactions of the Royal Society of London* 295, no. 1177 (Oct. 1981).

———. *Language and Problems of Knowledge: The Managua Lectures.* Cambridge, MA: MIT Press, 1988.

Clayton, Philip. *God and Contemporary Science.* Edinburgh: Edinburgh University Press, 1997.

———. 'The Panentheistic Turn in Christian Theology', *Dialog* 38, no. 2 (Summer 1999).

——. *The Problem of God in Modern Thought.* Cambridge and Grand Rapids, MI: Eerdmans, 2000.

———. The Emergence of Spirit', *CTNS Bulletin* 20, no. 4 (Fall 2000).

———. 'Panentheism Today: A Constructive Systematic Evaluation', in Philip Clayton and Arthur Peacocke, eds., *In Whom We Live and Move and Have Our Being.* Cambridge and Grand Rapids, MI: Eerdmans, 2004.

———. 'Panentheism in Metaphysical and Scientific Perspective', in Philip Clayton and Arthur Peacocke, eds., *In Whom We Live and Move and Have Our Being.* Cambridge and Grand Rapids, MI: Eerdmans, 2004.

———. 'Biology and Purpose: Altruism, Morality, and Human Nature in Evolutionary Perspective', in Philip Clayton and Jeffery Schloss, eds., *Evolution and Ethics: Human Morality in Biological and Religious Perspective.* Cambridge and Grand Rapids, MI: Eerdmans, 2004.

Clayton, Philip, and Zachary Simpson, eds. *The Oxford Handbook of Religion and Science.* Oxford: Oxford University Press, 2006.

Clooney, Francis X. 'Comparative Theology', in John Webster et al., eds., *The Oxford Handbook of Systematic Theology.* New York: Oxford University Press, 2007.

Cobb, John. 'Response to Johann Baptist Metz and Langdon Gilkey', in Hans Küng and David Tracy, eds., *Paradigm Change in Theology: A Symposium for the Future.* Worcester: Billings & Sons, 1989.

————. Jonas as a Process Theologian', in Sandra B. Lubarsky and David Ray Griffin, eds., *Jewish Theology and Process Thought*. Albany: State University of New York Press, 1996.

Collins, Francis. *The Language of God: A Scientist Presents Evidence for Belief.* New York: Basic Books, 2006.

————. 'Interview', *Newsweek* (27 Dec. 2010).

Cone, James. 'Jesus Christ in Black Theology', in Curt Cadorette et al., eds., *Liberation Theology: An Introductory Reader*. Maryknoll, NY: Orbis, 1997.

Conway Morris, Simon. *The Crucible of Creation: The Burgess Shale and the Rise of Animals*. Oxford: Oxford University Press, 1998.

————. *Life's Solution: Inevitable Humans in a Lonely Universe*. Cambridge: Cambridge University Press, 2003.

————. 'A Response to Richard Sturch', *Science and Christian Belief* 19, no. 7 (Apr. 2007).

————. 'Evolution and Convergence', in Simon Conway Morris, ed., *The Deep Structure of Biology: Is Convergence Sufficiently Ubiquitous to Give a Directional Signal?* Philadelphia: Templeton Foundation, 2008.

————. 'Darwin Was Right. Up to a Point', *The Guardian* (12 Feb. 2009).

Coyne, George V., and Alessandro Omizzolo. *Wayfarers in the Cosmos: The Human Quest for Meaning*. New York: Crossroad, 2002.

Coyne, Jerry, and H. Allen Orr. *Speciation*. Sunderland, MA: Sinauer Associates, 2004.

Crawford, Robert. *Is God a Scientist? A Dialogue Between Science and Religion*. New York: Palgrave Macmillan, 2004.

Crisp, Oliver D. 'Original Sin and Atonement', in Thomas P. Flint and Michael C. Rea, eds., *The Oxford Handbook of Philosophical Theology*. Oxford: Oxford University Press, 2009.

Daniel-Hughes, Carly. *The Salvation of the Flesh in Tertullian of Carthage: Dressing for the Resurrection*. New York: Palgrave Macmillan, 2011.

Darwin, Charles. *On the Origin of Species*. New York: Prometheus, 1991. Originally published in 1859.

Davies, Brian, ed. *Aquinas' Summa Theologiae: Critical Essays*. Oxford: Rowman & Littlefield, 2006.

————. *Thomas Aquinas on God and Evil*. Oxford: Oxford University Press, 2011.

Davies, Paul. *The Mind of God: Science and the Search for Ultimate Meaning*. London: Penguin, 1992.

————. 'The Quantum Life', *Physicsworld* 22, no. 7 (July 2009).

———. *The Eerie Silence: Are We Alone in the Universe?* London: Penguin, 2010.

———. 'Stephen Hawking's Big Bang Gaps', *The Guardian* (4 Sept. 2010).

Dean, Cornelia. 'Scientist at Work: Francisco J. Ayala', *The New York Times* (29 Apr. 2008).

Deane-Drummond, Celia. 'Theology, Ecology and Values', in Philip Clayton and Zachary Simpson, eds., *The Oxford Handbook of Religion and Science.* Oxford: Oxford University Press, 2006.

———. *Christ and Evolution: Wonder and Wisdom.* London: SCM, 2009.

De Lubac, Henri. *Le Surnaturel.* Paris: Aubier, 1946.

———. *The Drama of Atheistic Humanism.* London: Sheed & Ward, 1949.

Dembski, William A. 'The Logical Underpinnings of Intelligent Design', in William A. Dembski and Michael Ruse, eds., *Debating Design: From Darwin to DNA.* Cambridge: Cambridge University Press, 2004.

Dembski, William A., and Michael Ruse, 'General Introduction', in William A. Dembski and Michael Ruse, eds., *Debating Design: From Darwin to DNA.* Cambridge: Cambridge University Press, 2004.

Dennett, Daniel C. *Content and Consciousness.* London: Routledge, 1969.

———. *The Intentional Stance.* Cambridge, MA: MIT Press, 1987.

———. 'Memes and the Exploitation of Imagination', *The Journal of Aesthetics and Art Criticism* 48, no. 2 (Spring 1990).

———. *Consciousness Explained.* London: Allen Lane, 1991.

———. 'Back from the Drawing Board', in Bo Dahlbom, ed., *Dennett and His Critics: Demystifying Mind.* Oxford: Blackwell, 1993.

———. 'Animal Consciousness: What Matters and Why', *Social Research* 62, no. 3 (Fall 1995).

———. *Darwin's Dangerous Idea: Evolution and the Meaning of Life.* London: Penguin, 1995.

———. 'Appraising Grace: What Evolutionary Good Is God?', *The Sciences* (Jan./Feb. 1997).

———. *Brainchildren: Essays on Designing Minds.* London: Penguin, 1998.

———. 'Forward', in Robert Aunger, ed., *Darwinizing Culture: The Status of Memetics as a Science.* Oxford: Oxford University Press, 2000.

———. 'In Darwin's Wake, Where Am I?', *Proceedings and Addresses of the American Philosophical Association* 75, no. 3 (Nov. 2001).

———. 'The New Replicators', in Mark Pagel, ed., *The Oxford Encyclopedia of Evolution.* Oxford: Oxford University Press, 2002.

———. *Freedom Evolves.* London: Allen Lane, 2003.

————. *Breaking the Spell: Religion as Natural Phenomenon.* London: Penguin, 2006.

————. 'Religion's Just a Survival Meme', *Science and Theology News* (June 2006). Web. 12 Feb. 2011.

Dennett, Daniel C., and Alvin Plantinga. *Science and Religion: Are They Compatible?* New York: Oxford University Press, 2011.

Dennett, Daniel C., and Ryan T. McKay. 'The Evolution of Misbelief', *Behavioural and Brain Sciences* 32, no. 6 (2009).

De Panafieu, Jean-Baptiste. *Evolution [In Action].* London: Thames & Hudson, 2007.

Devlin, Hannah. 'Hawking: God Did Not Create the Universe', *The Times* (UK) (2 Sept. 2010).

Dieckmann, Ulf, et al., eds. *Adaptive Selection.* Cambridge: Cambridge University Press, 2004.

Distin, Kate. *The Selfish Meme.* Cambridge: Cambridge University Press, 2005.

Dobzhansky, Theodosius. *Mankind Evolving.* New Haven: Yale University Press, 1962.

————. *Genetics of the Evolutionary Process.* New York: Columbia University Press, 1970.

Donald, Merlin. *A Mind So Rare: The Evolution of Human Consciousness.* New York: W. W. Norton, 2001.

Doran, Chris. 'From Atheism to Theodicy to Intelligent Design: Responding to the Work of Francisco J. Ayala', *Theology and Science* 7, no. 4 (Nov. 2009).

Durkheim, Émile. *The Elementary Forms of the Religious Life.* Oxford: Oxford University Press, 2001.

d'Espagnat, Bernard. *Reality and the Physicist.* Cambridge: Cambridge University Press, 1989.

————. *On Physics and Philosophy.* New Jersey: Princeton University Press, 2006.

Edmonds, Bruce. 'The Revealed Poverty of the Gene-Meme Analogy—Why Memetics *per se* Has Failed to Produce Substantive Results', *Journal of Memetics: Evolutionary Models of Information Transmission* 9, no. 1 (2005).

————. 'Three Challenges to Memetics', in Michael Ruse, ed. *Philosophy After Darwin: Classic and Contemporary Readings.* Princeton: Princeton University Press, 2009.

Fisher, R. A. *The Genetical Theory of Natural Selection.* Oxford: Oxford University Press, 1958.

Flack, Jessica C., and Frans B. M. de Waal.'"Any Animal Whatever": Darwinian Building Blocks of Morality in Monkeys and Apes', *Journal of Consciousness Studies* 7, no. 1–2 (2000).

Ford, David F. 'Epilogue: Christian Theology at the Turn of the Millennium', in David F. Ford, ed., *The Modern Theologians: An Introduction to Christian Theology in the Twentieth Century*. Malden, MA: Blackwell, 1997.

———. *The Future of Christian Theology*. Chichester: Wiley-Blackwell, 2011.

Fortey, Richard. *Life: An Unauthorised Biography, A Natural History of the First Four Thousand Million Years of Life on Earth*. London: HarperCollins, 1997.

———. 'Religious Ideas as Wish Fulfillments', in Chad Meister, ed., *The Philosophy of Religion Reader*. New York: Routledge, 2008.

Gallagher, Michael Paul. *What Are They Saying about Unbelief?* Mahwah, NJ: Paulist, 1995.

Gatherer, Derek. 'Finding a Niche for Memetics in the 21st Century', *Journal of Memetics: Evolutionary Models of Information Transmission* 9, no. 1 (2005).

Giberson, Karl W., and Francis S. Collins. *The Language of Science and Faith: Straight Answers to Genuine Questions*. Downers Grove, IL: IVP, 2011.

Gibson, Daniel G., et al. 'Creation of a Bacterial Cell Controlled by a Chemically Synthesized Genome', *Science* 329, no. 5987 (July 2010).

Godfrey-Smith, Peter. 'Conditions for Evolution by Natural Selection', *The Journal of Philosophy* 104, no. 10 (Oct. 2007).

Gorman, Ulf. 'Theodicy', in J. Wentzel van Huyssteen, ed, *Encyclopedia of Science and Religion*, vol. 1. Farmington Hills, MI: Macmillan, 2003.

Gould, Stephen Jay. *Ever Since Darwin*. London: Penguin, 1977.

———. *The Panda's Thumb*. New York: Penguin, 1980.

———. 'Darwinism and the Expansion of Evolutionary Theory', *Science* 216, no. 4544 (Apr. 1982).

———. *Wonderful Life: The Burgess Shale and the Nature of History*. London: Vintage, 1990.

———. 'Nonoverlapping Magisteria', *Natural History* 106, no. 2 (Mar. 1997).

———. 'Darwinian Fundamentalism', *The New York Review of Books* 44, no. 10 (June 1997).

———. *Leonardo's Mountain of Claims and the Diet of Worms: Essays on Natural History*. New York: Random House, 1998.

———. *Rocks of Ages: Science and Religion in the Fullness of Life*. London: Jonathan Cape, 1999.

———. *The Structure of Evolutionary Theory*. Cambridge, MA: Harvard University Press, 2002.

———. *The Richness of Life: The Essential Stephen Jay Gould*. Edited by Paul McGarr and Steven Rose,. London: Jonathan Cape, 2006.

Gould, Stephen Jay, and Niles Eldridge. 'Punctuated Equilibria: The Tempo and Mode of Evolution Reconsidered', *Paleobiology* 3, no. 2 (Spring 1977).

Gould, Stephen Jay, and Elisabeth A. Lloyd. 'Individuality and Adaption across Levels of Selection: How Shall We Name and Generalize the Unit of Darwinism?', *Proceedings if the Natural Academy of Sciences of the United States of America* 96, no. 21 (Oct. 1999).

Griffin, David Ray. *Reenchantment Without Supernaturalism: A Process Philosophy of Religion*. Ithaca, NY: Cornell University Press, 2001.

———. 'Panentheism: A Postmodern Revelation', in Philip Clayton and Arthur Peacocke, eds., *In Whom We Live and Move and Have Our Being*. Cambridge and Grand Rapids, MI: Eerdmans, 2004.

Hamilton, W. D. *Narrow Roads of Gene Land: The Collected Papers of W. D. Hamilton Volume 1: The Evolution of Social Behaviour*. New York: W. H. Freeman, 1996.

Harris, Sam. *The End of Faith: Religion, Terror and the Future of Reason*. London: W. W. Norton, 2004.

Haught, John. *God After Darwin: A Theology of Evolution*. Oxford: Westview, 2000.

———. *Deeper Than Darwin: The Prospect for Religion in theAge of Evolution*. Boulder, CO: Westview, 2003.

———. 'Atheism', in J. Wentzel Vrede van Huyssteen, ed., *Encyclopedia of Science and Religion*, vol. 1. Farmington Hills, MI: Macmillan, 2003.

———. 'The Boyle Lecture 2003: Darwin, Design and the Promise of Nature', *Science and Christian Belief* 17, no. 1 (Apr. 2005).

———. 'Darwin and the Cardinal', *Commonweal* 132, no. 14 (Aug. 2005).

———. *Is Nature Enough? Meaning and Truth in the Age of Science*. Cambridge: Cambridge University Press, 2006.

———. *Christianity and Science: Toward a Theology of Nature*. Maryknoll, NY: Orbis, 2007.

Haught, John, and Brian Davies. 'The Suffering of God: Evolution and Theodicy', *Commonweal* 138, no. 11 (June 2011).

Hawking, Stephen. *A Brief History of Time: From the Big Bang to Black Holes*. London: Bantam, 1988.

———. Interview with John Humphrys, *In God We Doubt: Confessions of a Failed Atheist*. London: Hodder & Stoughton, 2007.

Hawking, Stephen, and Leonard Mlodinow. *The Grand Design: New Answers to the Ultimate Questions of Life*. London: Bantam, 2010.

Hick, John. *Evil and the God of Love*. Chippenham: Macmillan, 1966.

Hillis, W. Daniel. 'A Forebrain for the World Mind', in John Brockman, ed., *This Will Change Everything: Ideas That Will Shape the Future*. New York: HarperCollins, 2010.

Hinde, Robert A. *Why Gods Persist: A Scientific Approach to Religion*, 2nd ed. Oxon: Routledge, 1999.

Hitchens, Christopher. *God Is Not Great: How Religion Poisons Everything*. London: Atlantic, 2007.

Hughes, Gerard J. *Fidelity Without Fundamentalism: A Dialogue with Tradition*. London: Darton, Longman & Todd, 2010.

Hull, David. 'The God of the Galápagos', *Nature* 352, no. 6335 (Aug. 1991).

Hume, David. *Dialogues and Natural History of Religion*. Oxford: Oxford University Press, 1998. Originally published in 1779.

———. *A Treatise on Human Nature*. New York: Dover, 2003. Originally published in 1739.

James, William. *On the Varieties of Religious Experience: A Study in Human Nature*. New York: Penguin, 1982. Originally published in 1902.

Jenkins, David E. *God, Miracle and the Church of England*. London: SCM, 1987.

———. *God, Jesus and Life in the Spirit*. London: SCM, 1988.

Johnson, Elizabeth. *Quest for the Living God: Mapping Frontiers in the Theology of God*. London: Continuum, 2007.

Jonas, Hans. *Mortality and Morality: A Search for God after Auschwitz*. Edited by Lawrence Vogal. Evanston, IL: Northwestern University Press, 1996.

Junker-Kenny, Maureen. *Habermas and Theology*. London: T. & T. Clark, 2011.

Katz, Leonard, ed. *Evolutionary Origins of Morality: Cross-Disciplinary Perspectives*. Exeter: Imprint, 2000.

Keogh, Gary. 'How Can the Church Survive? Reflections of a Celtic Tiger Cub', *The Furrow* 62, no. 4 (Apr. 2011).

———. A New Generation of Family Values', *The Furrow* 63, no. 3 (Mar. 2012).

———. 'An Irish Church Reform Movement?', *The Furrow* 63, no. 7/8 (July/Aug. 2012).

Kerr, Fergus. *After Aquinas: Versions of Thomism*. Oxford: Blackwell, 2002.

———, ed. *Contemplating Aquinas: On the Varieties of Interpretation*. London: SCM, 2003.

Kilby, Karen. *Karl Rahner: Theology and Philosophy*. London: Routledge, 2004.

———. 'Karl Rahner's Ecclesiology', *New Blackfriars* 90, no. 1026 (Mar. 2009).

Kim, Jaegwon. 'The Mind–Body Problem', in Ted Honderich, ed., *The Oxford Companion to Philosophy*. Oxford: Oxford University Press, 1995.

King Jr., Martin Luther. 'I Have a Dream Speech', 28 Aug. 1963, Web, 10 Aug. 2012.

Kiwiet, John. *Hans Küng.* Waco, TX: Word, 1985.

Klien, Jan, and Naoyuki Takahata. *Where Do We Come From? The Molecular Evidence for Human Descent.* Berlin: Springer, 2002.

Kuhn, Thomas. *The Structure of Scientific Revolutions*, 3rd ed. Chicago: University of Chicago Press, 1962.

Küng, Hans. *Does God Exist?* London: Collins, 1978.

———. *Infallible? An Inquiry.* New York: Doubleday, 1983.

———. 'A New Basic Model for Theology: Divergencies and Convergencies', in Hans Küng and David Tracy, eds., *Paradigm Change in Theology: A Symposium for the Future.* Worcester: Billings & Sons, 1989.

———. *Theology for the Third Millennium: An Ecumenical View.* London: HarperCollins, 1991.

———. *The Beginning of All Thing: Science and Religion.* Grand Rapids, MI: Eerdmans, 2007.

Lane, Dermot A. 'Faith and Culture: The Challenge of Inculturation', in Dermot A. Lane, ed., *Religion and Culture in Dialogue: A Challenge for the Next Millennium.* Dublin: Columba, 1993.

Lawton, Graham. 'Axing Darwin's Tree', *New Scientist* 201, no. 2692 (Jan. 2009).

Lewis, C. S. *The Problem of Pain.* London: Whitefriars, 1940.

Lonergan, Bernard. *Method in Theology.* London: Darton, Longman & Todd, 1972.

Losch, Andreas. 'On the Origins of Critical Realism', *Theology and Science* 7, no. 1 (Feb. 2009).

———. 'Critical Realism—A Sustainable Bridge Between Science and Religion?', *Theology and Science* 8, no. 4 (Nov. 2010).

Lovejoy, Arthur O. *The Great Chain of Being: A Study of the History of an Idea.* Cambridge, MA: Harvard University Press, 1998. Originally published in 1936.

Mackey, James P. *Christianity and Creation: The Essence of Christian Faith and Its Future among Religions.* New York: Continuum, 2006.

———. *The Scientist and the Theologian: On the Origins & Ends of Creation.* Dublin: Columba, 2007.

———. 'Dawkins's Survival of the Fittest Theory Unfit to Serve as Moral Code for Human Race', *The Irish Times* (19 July 2011).

Mackie, J. L. *The Miracle of Theism: Arguments for and Against the Existence of God.* Oxford: Oxford University Press, 1982.

Mahoney, Jack. *Christianity in Evolution: An Exploration.* Washington, DC: Georgetown University Press, 2011.

Mayne-Kienzle, Beverly. *Hildegard of Bingen and Her Gospel Homilies: Speaking New Mysteries.* Turnhout, Belgium: Brepols, 2009.

Mayr, Ernst. *Evolution and the Diversity of Life: Selected Essays.* Cambridge, MA: Harvard University Press, 1976.

———. *One Long Argument: Charles Darwin and the Genesis of Modern Evolutionary Thought.* London: Penguin, 1992.

———. *Systematics and the Origin of Species from the Viewpoint of a Zoologist.* Cambridge, MA: Harvard University Press, 1999.

———. *What Evolution Is.* London: Phoenix, 2001.

McCarthy, Joan. *Dennett and Ricoeur on the Narrative Self.* New York: Humanity Books, 2007.

McCauley, Robert N. 'Explanatory Pluralism and the Co-evolution of Theories in Science', in Robert N. McCauley, ed., *The Churchlands and Their Critics.* Oxford: Blackwell, 1996.

McDaniel, Jay B. *Of Gods and Pelicans: A Theology of Reverence for Life.* Louisville: John Knox Press, 1989.

McDonagh, Enda. 'Beyond Pure Theology', *The Furrow* 50, no. 11 (Nov. 2009).

McFadden, Johnjoe. *Quantum Evolution.* London: HarperCollins, 2000.

McFague, Sallie. 'The Loving Eye vs. the Arrogant Eye: Christian Critique of the Western Gaze on Nature and the Third World', *Ecumenical Review* 49, no. 2 (Apr. 1997).

McGrath, Alister E. *The Foundations of Dialogue in Science and Religion.* Oxford: Blackwell, 1998.

———. *Christian Theology: An Introduction*, 3rd ed. Oxford: Blackwell, 2003.

———. *The Twilight of Atheism: The Rise and Fall of Disbelief in the Modern World.* London: Rider, 2004.

———. *A Fine-Tuned Universe: The Quest for God in Science and Theology.* Louisville: Westminster John Knox, 2009.

———. *Darwinism and the Divine: Evolutionary Thought and Natural Theology.* Chichester: Wiley-Blackwell, 2011.

Messer, Neil. *Selfish Genes and Christian Ethics: Theological and Ethical Reflections on Evolutionary Biology.* London: SCM, 2007.

———. 'Natural Evil After Darwin', in Michael S. Northcott and R. J. Berry, eds., *Theology After Darwin.* Milton Keynes: Paternoster, 2009.

Midgley, Mary. 'Selfish Genes and Social Darwinism', *Philosophy* 58, no. 225 (July 1983).

———. 'Why Memes?', in Hilary Rose and Stephen Rose, eds., *Alas, Poor Darwin: Arguments Against Evolutionary Psychology.* London: Jonathan Cape, 2000.

———. *The Solitary Self: Darwin and the Selfish Gene.* Durham: Acumen, 2010.

———. 'Why the Idea of Purpose Won't Go Away', *Philosophy* 86, no. 338 (Oct. 2011).

Miller, Kenneth. *Finding Darwin's God: A Scientist's Search for the Common Ground Between God and Evolution.* New York: HarperCollins, 1999.

———. 'The Flagellum Unspun: The Collapse of "Irreducible Complexity"', in William A. Dembski and Michael Ruse, eds., *Debating Design: From Darwin to DNA.* Cambridge: Cambridge University Press, 2004.

———. 'Answering the Biochemical Argument from Design', in Mary Kathleen Cunningham, ed., *God and Evolution: A Reader.* London: Routledge, 2007.

———. 'Falling over the Edge', *Nature* 447, no. 28 (June 2007).

———. 'Faulty Design', *Commonweal* 134, no. 17 (Oct. 2007).

———. 'Letting God Off the Hook? Reviewer Replies', *Commonweal,* 134, no. 20 (Nov. 2007).

———. *Only a Theory: Evolution and the Battle for America's Soul.* New York: Penguin, 2008.

———. 'Darwin, God and Dover', in Harold W. Attridge, ed., *The Religion and Science Debate: Why Does It Continue?* New Haven: Yale University Press, 2009.

———. 'Of Darwin, Dover and (un)Intelligent Design', *Church and State* 62, no. 2 (Feb. 2009).

Moltmann, Jürgen. *The Future of Creation.* London: SCM, 1979.

———. 'God's *Kenosis* in the Creation and Consummation of the World', in John Polkinghorne, ed., *The Work of Love: Creation as Kenosis.* Cambridge and Grand Rapids, MI: Eerdmans, 2001.

———. *Science and Wisdom.* Translated by Margaret Kohl. London: SCM, 2003.

Morris, Henry. *The Remarkable Birth of Planet Earth.* San Diego: Creation Life, 1972.

———. *Scientific Creationism.* San Diego: Creation Life, 1972.

Murphy, Nancey, and George F. R. Ellis. *On the Moral Nature of the Universe: Theology, Cosmology and Ethics.* Minneapolis: Fortress Press, 1996.

Murphy, Nancey. 'Suffering as a By-Product', in Nancey Murphy, Robert John Russell, and William R. Stoeger, eds., *Physics and Cosmology: Scientific Perspectives on the Problem of Natural Evil.* Vatican City: Vatican Observatory, 2007.

———. 'Cognitive Science and the Evolution of Religion: A Philosophical and Theological Appraisal', in Jeffery Schloss and Michael Murray, eds., *The Believing Primate.* New York: Oxford University Press, 2009.

Nevin, N. C., ed. *Should Christians Embrace Evolution?: Biblical and Scientific Responses.* Phillipsburg, NJ: P. & R., 2009.

O'Leary, Don. *Roman Catholicism and Modern Science: A History.* New York: Continuum, 2007.

O'Murchu, Diarmud. *Evolutionary Faith: Rediscovering God in Our Great Story.* New York: Orbis, 2002.

Otto, Rudolf. *Naturalism and Religion.* New York: Williams & Norgate, 1907.

Paley, William. *Natural Theology.* Oxford: Oxford University Press, 2006. Originally published in 1802.

Pannenberg, Wolfhart. *Basic Questions in Theology vol. II.* London: SCM, 1971.

———. *Faith and Reality.* London: Search, 1977.

Pascal, Blaise. *Pensées.* London: Penguin, 1979. Originally published in 1669.

Peacocke, Arthur. *Creation and the World of Science.* Oxford: Oxford University Press, 1979.

———. *Theology for a Scientific Age: Being and Becoming—Natural and Divine.* Oxford: Blackwell, 1990.

———. *Paths from Science Towards God: The End of All Our Exploring.* Oxford: Oneworld, 2001.

———. 'The Cost of Life', in John Polkinghorne, ed., *The Work of Love: Creation as Kenosis.* Cambridge and Grand Rapids, MI: Eerdmans, 2001.

———. 'Introduction', in Philip Clayton and Arthur Peacocke, eds., *In Whom We Live and Move and Have Our Being.* Cambridge and Grand Rapids, MI: Eerdmans, 2004.

———. 'Articulating God's Presence in and to the World Unveiled by the Sciences', in Philip Clayton and Arthur Peacocke, eds., *In Whom We Live and Move and Have Our Being.* Cambridge and Grand Rapids, MI: Eerdmans, 2004.

———. *All That Is: A Naturalistic Faith for the Twenty-First Century.* Edited by Philip Clayton Minneapolis: Fortress Press, 2007.

Penrose, Roger. *The Emperor's New Mind*. Oxford: Oxford University Press, 1989.

———. *The Large, the Small and the Human Mind*. Cambridge: Cambridge University Press, 2000.

Peterson, Michael L. *The Problem of Evil: Selected Readings*. Notre Dame: University of Notre Dame Press, 1992.

Plantinga, Alvin. *God, Freedom and Evil*. London: Allen & Unwin, 1974.

———. 'The Evolutionary Argument Against Naturalism', in James Beilby, ed., *Naturalism Defeated? Essays on Plantinga's Evolutionary Argument Against Naturalism*. New York: Cornell University Press, 2002.

———. 'Games Scientists Play', in Jeffery Schloss and Michael Murray, eds., *The Believing Primate*. New York: Oxford University Press, 2009.

Polkinghorne, John. *The Quantum World*. London: Longman, 1984.

———. *One World: The Interaction of Science and Theology*. London: Templeton Foundation, 1986.

———. *Reason and Reality: The Relationship Between Science and Theology*. London: SPCK, 1991.

———. *Quarks, Chaos and Christianity: Questions to Science and Religion*. London: Triangle, 1994.

———. *Faith, Science and Understanding*. London: SPCK, 2000.

———. 'Kenotic Creation and Divine Action', in John Polkinghorne, ed., *The Work of Love: Creation as Kenosis*. Cambridge and Grand Rapids, MI: Eerdmans, 2001.

———. *Exploring Reality: The Intertwining of Science and Religion*. New Haven: Yale University Press, 2005.

———. 'Does Science and Religion Matter?', in Fraser Watts and Kevin Dutton, eds., *Why the Science and Religion Dialogue Matters*. Philadelphia: Templeton Foundation, 2006.

———. 'Rich Reality: A Response to the Boyle Lecture by Simon Conway Morris', *Science and Christian Belief* 18, no. 1 (Apr. 2006).

Pope John Paul II (Wojtyla, Karol). *Love and Responsibility*. London: Collins, 1960.

———. 'The Moral Dimension of Study and Research' (1 Apr. 1980). Web. 6 June 2010.

———. 'Truth Cannot Contradict Truth', Papal Address, Rome, 1996.

———. *Fides et Ratio*, Rome, 1998.

Pope Pius XII. *Humani Generis*, Rome, 1939.

Popper, Karl. *The Logic of Scientific Discovery*. New York: Routledge, 1959.

Primavesi, Anne. *Gaia's Gift: Earth, Ourselves and God After Copernicus*. London: Routledge 2003.

Pyysiäinen, Ilkka. 'Cognition and Culture in the Construction of Religion', in Ilkka Pyysiäinen, and Veikko Anttonen, eds., *Current Approaches in the Cognitive Science of Religion*. London: Continuum, 2002.

———. *Supernatural Agents: Why We Believe in Souls, Gods and Buddhas*. Oxford: Oxford University Press, 2009.

Rae, Alastair. *Quantum Physics: Illusion or Reality?* Cambridge: Cambridge University Press, 1986.

Rahner, Karl. *Theological Investigations, Vol. VI: Concerning Vatican Council II*. Translated by Karl H. and Boniface Kruger. London: Darton, Longman & Todd, 1969.

———. *Theological Investigations, Vol. XXI: Science and Christian Faith*. Translated by Hugh M. Riley. London: Darton, Longman & Todd, 1983.

Ruether, Rosemary Radford. *Sexism and God Talk: Towards a Feminist Theology*. London: SCM, 1983.

Ricoeur, Paul. *The Symbolism of Evil*. Boston: Beacon, 1969.

———. *The Conflict of Interpretations*. Edited by Don Hide. Evanston, IL: Northwestern University Press, 1974.

———. *Oneself as Another*. Translated by Kathleen Blamey. Chicago: University of Chicago Press, 1991.

Ridley, Mark, *The Problems of Evolution*. Oxford: Oxford University Press, 1985.

———. *Genome: The Autobiography of a Species in 23 Chapters*. London: Fourth Estate, 1999.

Rolston III, Holmes. *Genes, Genesis and God: Values and Their Origins in Natural and Human History*. Cambridge: Cambridge University Press, 1999.

Rose, Hilary, and Stephen Rose, eds. *Alas, Poor Darwin: Arguments Against Evolutionary Psychology*. London: Jonathan Cape, 2000.

Ross, W. D., ed. *The Works of Aristotle Translated into English*, vol. 2. Chicago: Great Books, 1923.

Ruse, Michael. *Darwin and Design: Does Evolution Have a Purpose?* Cambridge, MA: Harvard University Press, 2003.

———. 'The Evolution of Ethics, Past and Present', in Philip Clayton and Jeffery Schloss, eds., *Evolution and Ethics: Human Morality in Biological and Religious Perspective*. Cambridge and Grand Rapids, MI: Eerdmans, 2004.

———. *Charles Darwin*. Oxford: Blackwell, 2008.

Russell, Bertrand. *Religion and Science*. Oxford: Oxford University Press, 1935.

———. *The History of Western Philosophy*. London: Routledge, 1946.

———. *Why I'm Not a Christian.* London: Routledge, 1957.

Russell, Cathriona. 'The Irish Elk and the Concept of Contingency', *Search* 31, no. 3 (Winter 2008).

Rowe, William. 'The Problem of Evil and Some Varieties of Atheism', *American Philosophical Quarterly* 16, no. 4 (Oct. 1979).

Scally, John. *To Speed on Angel's Wings: The Story of the Sisters of St. John of God.* Dublin: Columba, 1995.

———. 'A Woman for Our Time: The Enduring Legacy of Catherine of Siena', *Religious Life Review 50*, no. 267 (Mar.–Apr. 2011).

Schaab, Gloria L. 'An Evolving Vision of God: The Theology of John Haught', *Zygon* 45, no. 5 (Dec. 2010).

Schüssler Fiorenza, Francis. 'Systematic Theology: Tasks and Methods', in Francis Schüssler Fiorenza and John P. Galvin, eds., *Systematic Theology: Roman Catholic Perspectives.* Dublin: Gill & Macmillan, 1992.

Shennan, Stephen. *Genes, Memes and Human History: Darwinian Archaeology and Cultural Evolution.* London: Thames & Hudson, 2002.

Singer, Peter. *Rethinking Life and Death: The Collapse of Our Traditional Ethics.* Oxford: Oxford University Press, 1995.

———. *A Darwinian Left: Politics, Evolution and Cooperation.* London: Weidenfeld & Nicolson, 1999.

Slater, Peter. 'Tillich on the Fall and the Temptation of Goodness', *The Journal of Religion* 65, no. 3 (Apr. 1985).

Slone, David Jason. *Theological Incorrectness: Why Religious People Believe What They Shouldn't.* Oxford: Oxford University Press, 2004.

Smith, Christian. '*Las Casas* as Theological Counteroffensive: An Interpretation of Gustavo Gutiérrez's *Las Casas: In Search of the Poor of Jesus Christ*', *Journal for the Scientific Study of Religion* 41, no. 1 (Mar. 2002).

Smith, John Maynard. *On Evolution.* Edinburgh: Edinburgh University Press, 1972.

———. *Evolution Now: A Century After Darwin.* London: Macmillan, 1982.

———. *Evolutionary Genetics.* Oxford: Oxford University Press, 1989.

Sober, Elliott. 'Two Outbreaks of Lawlessness in Recent Philosophy of Biology', in Elliott Sober, ed., *Conceptual Issues in Evolutionary Biology*, 3rd ed. Cambridge, MA: MIT Press, 2006.

Southgate, Christopher. 'God and Evolutionary Evil: Theodicy in Light of Darwinism', *Zygon* 37, no. 4 (Dec. 2002).

Southgate, Christopher, and Andrew Robinson. 'Varieties of Theodicy: An Exploration of Responses to the Problem of Evil Based on a Typology of Good-Harm Analyses', in Nancey Murphy, Robert John Russell, and William R. Stoeger, eds., *Physics and Cosmology: Scientific Perspectives on the Problem of Natural Evil.* Vatican City: Vatican Observatory, 2007.

Stenger, Victor J. *God the Failed Hypothesis: How Science Shows That God Does Not Exist.* New York: Prometheus, 2008.

Stewart, Ian. *Does God Play Dice? The New Mathematics of Chaos.* London: Penguin, 1989.

Stout, Jeffrey. *Ethics After Babel: The Languages of Morals and Their Discontents.* Cambridge: James Clarke & Co., 1988.

Swinburne, Richard. *Providence and the Problem of Evil.* Oxford: Clarendon, 1998.

Teilhard de Chardin, Pierre. *Christianity and Evolution.* Translated by René Hague. London: Collins, 1971.

Thomas, Owen C. 'The Atheist Surge: Faith in Science, Secularism, and Atheism', *Theology and Science* 8, no. 2 (May 2010).

Thompson, Paul. 'Evolutionary Ethics: Its Origins and Contemporary Face', *Zygon* 34, no. 3 (Sept. 1999).

Tillich, Paul. *Systematic Theology vol. 2 Existence and the Christ.* London: SCM, 1957.

———. 'Religion and Its Intellectual Critics', *Christianity and Crisis* (Mar. 1995). Web. 1 July 2012.

Tracy, David. *The Analogical Imagination: Christian Theology and the Culture of Pluralism.* London: SCM, 1981.

———. *Dialogue with the Other: The Inter-Religious Dialogue.* Leuven: Peeters, 1990.

Tracy, David, and John B. Cobb. *Talking About God: Doing Theology in the Context of Modern Pluralism.* New York: Seabury, 1983.

Tyrrell, George. *Through Scylla and Charybdis, or the Old Theology and the New.* London: Longman, Green & Co.

Van Brema, David. 'Reconciling God and Science', *Time* (10 July 2006).

Von Balthasar, Hans Urs. *Science, Religion and Christianity.* London: Burns & Oates, 1958.

———. *The Von Balthasar Reader.* Edited by Medard Kehland and Werner Loser. New York: Crossroad, 1997.

Wallis, Claudia. 'The Evolution Wars', *Time* (2 Aug. 2005).

Ward, Keith. *God, Chance and Necessity.* Oxford: Oneworld, 1996.

———. *Is Religion Dangerous?* Oxford: Lion, 2006.

————. *Big Questions in Science and Religion.* Philadelphia: Templeton Foundation, 2008.

Watson, James. *DNA: The Secret of Life.* London: Heinemann, 2003.

Webster, John. *Barth.* London: Continuum, 2004.

Weiss, Kenneth M., and Anne V. Buchanan. *Genetics and the Logic of Evolution.* Hoboken, NJ: John Wiley & Sons, 2004.

Wiese, Christian. *The Life and Thought of Hans Jonas: Jewish Dimensions.* Waltham, MA: Brandeis University Press, 2007.

Williams, George C. *Adaption and Natural Selection: A Critique of Some Current Evolutionary Thought.* Princeton: Princeton University Press, 1966.

Williams, Patricia A. *Doing Without Adam and Eve: Sociobiology and Original Sin.* Minneapolis: Fortress Press, 2001.

Williams, Rowan. *Teresa of Avila.* London: Continuum, 1991.

Wilson, David Sloan. *Darwin's Cathedral: Evolution, Religion and the Nature of Society.* Chicago: University of Chicago Press, 2002.

Wilson, Edward O. *On Human Nature.* London: Penguin, 1978.

Wimmer, Heinz, and Josef Perner. 'Beliefs about Beliefs: Representation and Constraining Function of Wrong Beliefs in Young Children's Understanding of Deception', *Cognition* 13, no. 1 (Jan. 1983).

Zaleski, Carol. 'Near Death Experiences', in Jerry L. Walls, ed., *The Oxford Handbook of Eschatology.* Oxford: Oxford University Press, 2010.

Index

269